C000004145

Robert Louis Stevenson (13 November 1850 – 3 December 1894) was a Scottish novelist and travel writer, most noted for Treasure Island, Kidnapped, Strange Case of Dr Jekyll and Mr Hyde, and A Child's Garden of Verses. Born and educated in Edinburgh, Stevenson suffered from serious bronchial trouble for much of his life, but continued to write prolifically and travel widely, in defiance of his poor health. As a young man, he mixed in London literary circles, receiving encouragement from Andrew Lang, Edmund Gosse, Leslie Stephen and W. E. Henley, the last of whom may have provided the model for Long John Silver in Treasure Island. His travels took him to France, America and Australia, before he finally settled in Samoa, where he died. A celebrity in his lifetime, Stevenson attracted a more negative critical response for much of the 20th century, though his reputation has been largely restored. He is currently ranked as the 26th most translated author in the world.(Source: Wikipedia)

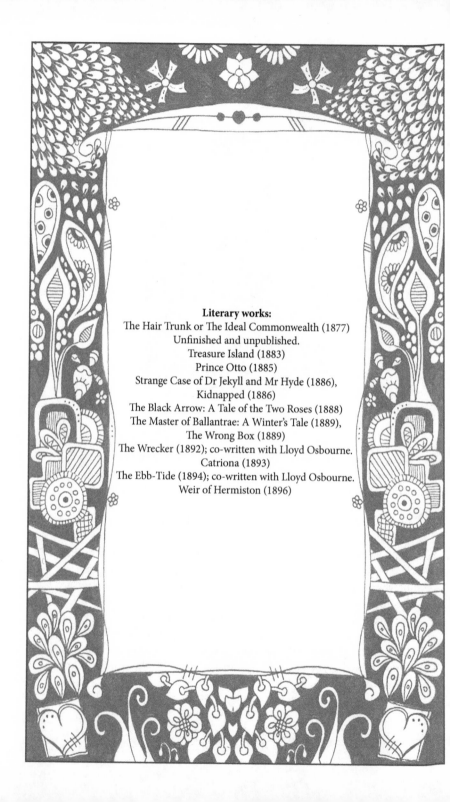

Literary works:
The Hair Trunk or The Ideal Commonwealth (1877)
Unfinished and unpublished.
Treasure Island (1883)
Prince Otto (1885)
Strange Case of Dr Jekyll and Mr Hyde (1886),
Kidnapped (1886)
The Black Arrow: A Tale of the Two Roses (1888)
The Master of Ballantrae: A Winter's Tale (1889),
The Wrong Box (1889)
The Wrecker (1892); co-written with Lloyd Osbourne.
Catriona (1893)
The Ebb-Tide (1894); co-written with Lloyd Osbourne.
Weir of Hermiston (1896)

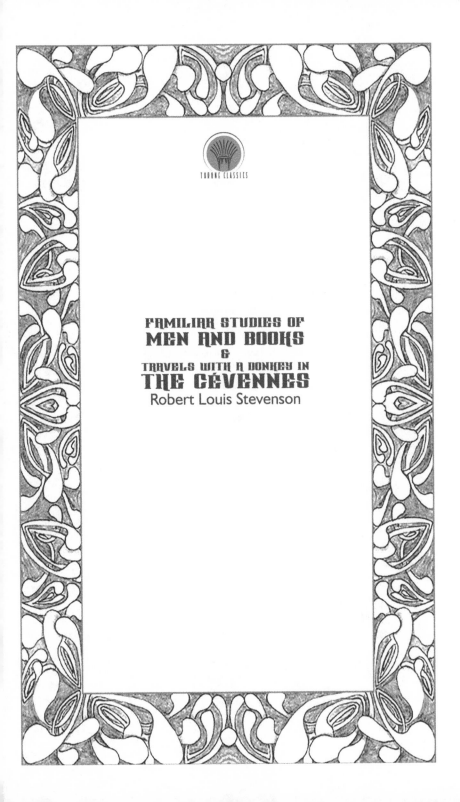

THRONE CLASSICS

FAMILIAR STUDIES OF
MEN AND BOOKS
&
TRAVELS WITH A DONKEY IN
THE CÉVENNES
Robert Louis Stevenson

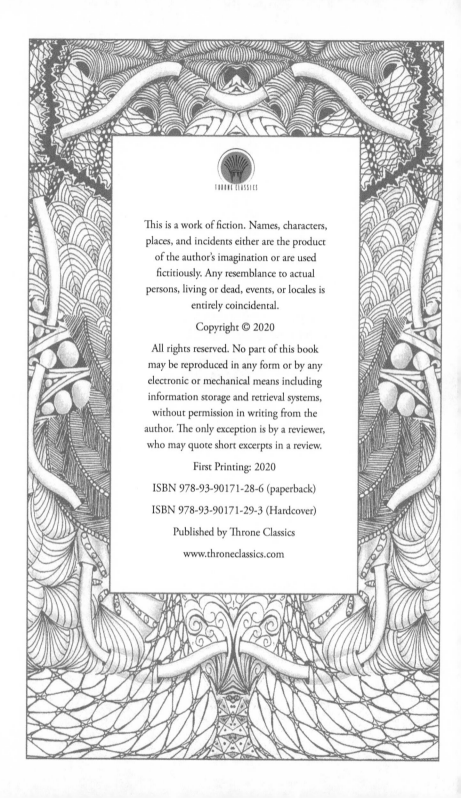

First Printing: 2020

ISBN 978-93-90171-28-6 (paperback)

ISBN 978-93-90171-29-3 (Hardcover)

Published by Throne Classics

www.throneclassics.com

Contents

FAMILIAR STUDIES OF
MEN AND BOOKS
&
TRAVELS WITH A DONKEY IN
THE CÉVENNES

FAMILIAR STUDIES OF MEN AND BOOKS

PREFACE
BY WAY OF CRITICISM.

THESE studies are collected from the monthly press. One appeared in the New Quarterly, one in Macmillan's, and the rest in the Cornhill Magazine. To the Cornhill I owe a double debt of thanks; first, that I was received there in the very best society, and under the eye of the very best of editors; and second, that the proprietors have allowed me to republish so considerable an amount of copy.

These nine worthies have been brought together from many different ages and countries. Not the most erudite of men could be perfectly prepared to deal with so many and such various sides of human life and manners. To pass a true judgment upon Knox and Burns implies a grasp upon the very deepest strain of thought in Scotland,—a country far more essentially different from England than many parts of America; for, in a sense, the first of these men re-created Scotland, and the second is its most essentially national production. To treat fitly of Hugo and Villon would involve yet wider knowledge, not only of a country foreign to the author by race, history, and religion, but of the growth and liberties of art. Of the two Americans, Whitman and Thoreau, each is the type of something not so much realised as widely sought after among the late generations of their countrymen; and to see them clearly in a nice relation to the society that brought them forth, an author would require a large habit of life among modern Americans. As for Yoshida, I have already disclaimed responsibility; it was but my hand that held the pen.

In truth, these are but the readings of a literary vagrant. One book led to another, one study to another. The first was published with trepidation. Since no bones were broken, the second was launched with greater confidence.

So, by insensible degrees, a young man of our generation acquires, in his own eyes, a kind of roving judicial commission through the ages; and, having once escaped the perils of the Freemans and the Furnivalls, sets himself up to right the wrongs of universal history and criticism. Now, it is one thing to write with enjoyment on a subject while the story is hot in your mind from recent reading, coloured with recent prejudice; and it is quite another business to put these writings coldly forth again in a bound volume. We are most of us attached to our opinions; that is one of the "natural affections" of which we hear so much in youth; but few of us are altogether free from paralysing doubts and scruples. For my part, I have a small idea of the degree of accuracy possible to man, and I feel sure these studies teem with error. One and all were written with genuine interest in the subject; many, however, have been conceived and finished with imperfect knowledge; and all have lain, from beginning to end, under the disadvantages inherent in this style of writing.

Of these disadvantages a word must here be said. The writer of short studies, having to condense in a few pages the events of a whole lifetime, and the effect on his own mind of many various volumes, is bound, above all things, to make that condensation logical and striking. For the only justification of his writing at all is that he shall present a brief, reasoned, and memorable view. By the necessity of the case, all the more neutral circumstances are omitted from his narrative; and that of itself, by the negative exaggeration of which I have spoken in the text, lends to the matter in hand a certain false and specious glitter. By the necessity of the case, again, he is forced to view his subject throughout in a particular illumination, like a studio artifice. Like Hales with Pepys, he must nearly break his sitter's neck to get the proper shadows on the portrait. It is from one side only that he has time to represent his subject. The side selected will either be the one most striking to himself, or the one most obscured by controversy; and in both cases that will be the one most liable to strained and sophisticated reading. In a biography, this and that is displayed; the hero is seen at home, playing the flute; the different tendencies of his work come, one after another, into notice; and thus something like a true, general impression of the subject may at last be struck. But in the short study, the writer, having seized his "point of view," must keep his eye steadily to that. He seeks, perhaps, rather to differentiate than truly to characterise. The proportions of the sitter must be sacrificed to the proportions of the portrait;

the lights are heightened, the shadows overcharged; the chosen expression, continually forced, may degenerate at length into a grimace; and we have at best something of a caricature, at worst a calumny. Hence, if they be readable at all, and hang together by their own ends, the peculiar convincing force of these brief representations. They take so little a while to read, and yet in that little while the subject is so repeatedly introduced in the same light and with the same expression, that, by sheer force of repetition, that view is imposed upon the reader. The two English masters of the style, Macaulay and Carlyle, largely exemplify its dangers. Carlyle, indeed, had so much more depth and knowledge of the heart, his portraits of mankind are felt and rendered with so much more poetic comprehension, and he, like his favourite Ram Dass, had a fire in his belly so much more hotly burning than the patent reading lamp by which Macaulay studied, that it seems at first sight hardly fair to bracket them together. But the "point of view" was imposed by Carlyle on the men he judged of in his writings with an austerity not only cruel but almost stupid. They are too often broken outright on the Procrustean bed; they are probably always disfigured. The rhetorical artifice of Macaulay is easily spied; it will take longer to appreciate the moral bias of Carlyle. So with all writers who insist on forcing some significance from all that comes before them; and the writer of short studies is bound, by the necessity of the case, to write entirely in that spirit. What he cannot vivify he should omit.

Had it been possible to rewrite some of these papers, I hope I should have had the courage to attempt it. But it is not possible. Short studies are, or should be, things woven like a carpet, from which it is impossible to detach a strand. What is perverted has its place there for ever, as a part of the technical means by which what is right has been presented. It is only possible to write another study, and then, with a new "point of view," would follow new perversions and perhaps a fresh caricature. Hence, it will be, at least, honest to offer a few grains of salt to be taken with the text; and as some words of apology, addition, correction, or amplification fall to be said on almost every study in the volume, it will be most simple to run them over in their order. But this must not be taken as a propitiatory offering to the gods of shipwreck; I trust my cargo unreservedly to the chances of the sea; and do not, by criticising myself, seek to disarm the wrath of other and less partial critics.

Hugo's Romances.—This is an instance of the "point of view." The five romances studied with a different purpose might have given different results, even with a critic so warmly interested in their favour. The great contemporary master of wordmanship, and indeed of all literary arts and technicalities, had not unnaturally dazzled a beginner. But it is best to dwell on merits, for it is these that are most often overlooked.

Burns.—I have left the introductory sentences on Principal Shairp, partly to explain my own paper, which was merely supplemental to his amiable but imperfect book, partly because that book appears to me truly misleading both as to the character and the genius of Burns. This seems ungracious, but Mr. Shairp has himself to blame; so good a Wordsworthian was out of character upon that stage.

This half apology apart, nothing more falls to be said except upon a remark called forth by my study in the columns of a literary Review. The exact terms in which that sheet disposed of Burns I cannot now recall; but they were to this effect—that Burns was a bad man, the impure vehicle of fine verses; and that this was the view to which all criticism tended. Now I knew, for my own part, that it was with the profoundest pity, but with a growing esteem, that I studied the man's desperate efforts to do right; and the more I reflected, the stranger it appeared to me that any thinking being should feel otherwise. The complete letters shed, indeed, a light on the depths to which Burns had sunk in his character of Don Juan, but they enhance in the same proportion the hopeless nobility of his marrying Jean. That I ought to have stated this more noisily I now see; but that any one should fail to see it for himself, is to me a thing both incomprehensible and worthy of open scorn. If Burns, on the facts dealt with in this study, is to be called a bad man, I question very much whether either I or the writer in the Review have ever encountered what it would be fair to call a good one. All have some fault. The fault of each grinds down the hearts of those about him, and—let us not blink the truth—hurries both him and them into the grave. And when we find a man persevering indeed, in his fault, as all of us do, and openly overtaken, as not all of us are, by its consequences, to gloss the matter over, with too polite biographers, is to do the work of the wrecker disfiguring beacons on a perilous seaboard; but to call him bad, with a self-righteous chuckle, is to be talking in one's sleep with Heedless and Too-bold in the arbour.

Yet it is undeniable that much anger and distress is raised in many quarters by the least attempt to state plainly, what every one well knows, of Burns's profligacy, and of the fatal consequences of his marriage. And for this there are perhaps two subsidiary reasons. For, first, there is, in our drunken land, a certain privilege extended to drunkenness. In Scotland, in particular, it is almost respectable, above all when compared with any "irregularity between the sexes." The selfishness of the one, so much more gross in essence, is so much less immediately conspicuous in its results that our demiurgeous Mrs. Grundy smiles apologetically on its victims. It is often said—I have heard it with these ears—that drunkenness "may lead to vice." Now I did not think it at all proved that Burns was what is called a drunkard; and I was obliged to dwell very plainly on the irregularity and the too frequent vanity and meanness of his relations to women. Hence, in the eyes of many, my study was a step towards the demonstration of Burns's radical badness.

But second, there is a certain class, professors of that low morality so greatly more distressing than the better sort of vice, to whom you must never represent an act that was virtuous in itself, as attended by any other consequences than a large family and fortune. To hint that Burns's marriage had an evil influence is, with this class, to deny the moral law. Yet such is the fact. It was bravely done; but he had presumed too far on his strength. One after another the lights of his life went out, and he fell from circle to circle to the dishonoured sickbed of the end. And surely for any one that has a thing to call a soul he shines out tenfold more nobly in the failure of that frantic effort to do right, than if he had turned on his heel with Worldly Wiseman, married a congenial spouse, and lived orderly and died reputably an old man. It is his chief title that he refrained from "the wrong that amendeth wrong." But the common, trashy mind of our generation is still aghast, like the Jews of old, at any word of an unsuccessful virtue. Job has been written and read; the tower of Siloam fell nineteen hundred years ago; yet we have still to desire a little Christianity, or, failing that, a little even of that rude, old, Norse nobility of soul, which saw virtue and vice alike go unrewarded, and was yet not shaken in its faith.

Walt Whitman.—This is a case of a second difficulty which lies continually before the writer of critical studies: that he has to mediate between the author whom he loves and the public who are certainly indifferent and frequently averse. Many articles had been written on this notable man. One after another had leaned, in my eyes, either to praise or blame unduly. In the last case, they helped to blindfold our fastidious public to an inspiring writer; in the other, by an excess of unadulterated praise, they moved the more candid to revolt. I was here on the horns of a dilemma; and between these horns I squeezed myself with perhaps some loss to the substance of the paper. Seeing so much in Whitman that was merely ridiculous, as well as so much more that was unsurpassed in force and fitness,—seeing the true prophet doubled, as I thought, in places with the Bull in a China Shop,—it appeared best to steer a middle course, and to laugh with the scorners when I thought they had any excuse, while I made haste to rejoice with the rejoicers over what is imperishably good, lovely, human, or divine, in his extraordinary poems. That was perhaps the right road; yet I cannot help feeling that in this attempt to trim my sails between an author whom I love and honour and a public too averse to recognise his merit, I have been led into a tone unbecoming from one of my stature to one of Whitman's. But the good and the great man will go on his way not vexed with my little shafts of merriment. He, first of any one, will understand how, in the attempt to explain him credibly to Mrs. Grundy, I have been led into certain airs of the man of the world, which are merely ridiculous in me, and were not intentionally discourteous to himself. But there is a worse side to the question; for in my eagerness to be all things to all men, I am afraid I may have sinned against proportion. It will be enough to say here that Whitman's faults are few and unimportant when they are set beside his surprising merits. I had written another paper full of gratitude for the help that had been given me in my life, full of enthusiasm for the intrinsic merit of the poems, and conceived in the noisiest extreme of youthful eloquence. The present study was a rifacimento. From it, with the design already mentioned, and in a fit of horror at my old excess, the big words and emphatic passages were ruthlessly excised. But this sort of prudence is frequently its own punishment; along with the exaggeration, some of the truth is sacrificed; and the result is cold, constrained, and grudging. In short,

I might almost everywhere have spoken more strongly than I did.

Thoreau.—Here is an admirable instance of the "point of view" forced throughout, and of too earnest reflection on imperfect facts. Upon me this pure, narrow, sunnily-ascetic Thoreau had exercised a great charm. I have scarce written ten sentences since I was introduced to him, but his influence might be somewhere detected by a close observer. Still it was as a writer that I had made his acquaintance; I took him on his own explicit terms; and when I learned details of his life, they were, by the nature of the case and my own parti-pris, read even with a certain violence in terms of his writings. There could scarce be a perversion more justifiable than that; yet it was still a perversion. The study indeed, raised so much ire in the breast of Dr. Japp (H. A. Page), Thoreau's sincere and learned disciple, that had either of us been men, I please myself with thinking, of less temper and justice, the difference might have made us enemies instead of making us friends. To him who knew the man from the inside, many of my statements sounded like inversions made on purpose; and yet when we came to talk of them together, and he had understood how I was looking at the man through the books, while he had long since learned to read the books through the man, I believe he understood the spirit in which I had been led astray.

On two most important points, Dr. Japp added to my knowledge, and with the same blow fairly demolished that part of my criticism. First, if Thoreau were content to dwell by Walden Pond, it was not merely with designs of self-improvement, but to serve mankind in the highest sense. Hither came the fleeing slave; thence was he despatched along the road to freedom. That shanty in the woods was a station in the great Underground Railroad; that adroit and philosophic solitary was an ardent worker, soul and body, in that so much more than honourable movement, which, if atonement were possible for nations, should have gone far to wipe away the guilt of slavery. But in history sin always meets with condign punishment; the generation passes, the offence remains, and the innocent must suffer. No underground railroad could atone for slavery, even as no bills in Parliament can redeem the ancient wrongs of Ireland. But here at least is a new light shed on the Walden episode.

15

Second, it appears, and the point is capital, that Thoreau was once fairly and manfully in love, and, with perhaps too much aping of the angel, relinquished the woman to his brother. Even though the brother were like to die of it, we have not yet heard the last opinion of the woman. But be that as it may, we have here the explanation of the "rarefied and freezing air" in which I complained that he had taught himself to breathe. Reading the man through the books, I took his professions in good faith. He made a dupe of me, even as he was seeking to make a dupe of himself, wresting philosophy to the needs of his own sorrow. But in the light of this new fact, those pages, seemingly so cold, are seen to be alive with feeling. What appeared to be a lack of interest in the philosopher turns out to have been a touching insincerity of the man to his own heart; and that fine-spun airy theory of friendship, so devoid, as I complained, of any quality of flesh and blood, a mere anodyne to lull his pains. The most temperate of living critics once marked a passage of my own with a cross and the words, "This seems nonsense." It not only seemed; it was so. It was a private bravado of my own, which I had so often repeated to keep up my spirits, that I had grown at last wholly to believe it, and had ended by setting it down as a contribution to the theory of life. So with the more icy parts of this philosophy of Thoreau's. He was affecting the Spartanism he had not; and the old sentimental wound still bled afresh, while he deceived himself with reasons.

Thoreau's theory, in short, was one thing and himself another: of the first, the reader will find what I believe to be a pretty faithful statement and a fairly just criticism in the study; of the second he will find but a contorted shadow. So much of the man as fitted nicely with his doctrines, in the photographer's phrase, came out. But that large part which lay outside and beyond, for which he had found or sought no formula, on which perhaps his philosophy even looked askance, is wanting in my study, as it was wanting in the guide I followed. In some ways a less serious writer, in all ways a nobler man, the true Thoreau still remains to be depicted.

Villon.—I am tempted to regret that I ever wrote on this subject, not merely because the paper strikes me as too picturesque by half, but because I regarded Villon as a bad fellow. Others still think well of him, and can find beautiful and human traits where I saw nothing but artistic evil; and by the principle of the art, those should have written of the man, and not I. Where you see no good, silence is the best. Though this penitence comes too late, it may be well, at least, to give it expression.

The spirit of Villon is still living in the literature of France. Fat Peg is oddly of a piece with the work of Zola, the Goncourts, and the infinitely greater Flaubert; and, while similar in ugliness, still surpasses them in native power. The old author, breaking with an éclat de voix, out of his tongue-tied century, has not yet been touched on his own ground, and still gives us the most vivid and shocking impression of reality. Even if that were not worth doing at all, it would be worth doing as well as he has done it; for the pleasure we take in the author's skill repays us, or at least reconciles us to the baseness of his attitude. Fat Peg (La Grosse Margot) is typical of much; it is a piece of experience that has nowhere else been rendered into literature; and a kind of gratitude for the author's plainness mingles, as we read, with the nausea proper to the business. I shall quote here a verse of an old students' song, worth laying side by side with Villon's startling ballade. This singer, also, had an unworthy mistress, but he did not choose to share the wages of dishonour; and it is thus, with both wit and pathos, that he laments her fall:—

> Nunc plango florem
>
> Ætatis teneræ
>
> Nitidiorem
>
> Veneris sidere:
>
> Tunc columbinam
>
> Mentis dulcedinem,
>
> Nunc serpentinam
>
> Amaritudinem.
>
> Verbo rogantes
>
> Removes ostio,

Munera dantes

Foves cubiculo,

Illos abire præcipis

A quibus nihil accipis,

Cæcos claudosque recipis,

Viros illustres decipis

Cum melle venenosa. [0]

But our illustrious writer of ballades it was unnecessary to deceive; it was the flight of beauty alone, not that of honesty or honour, that he lamented in his song; and the nameless mediæval vagabond has the best of the comparison.

There is now a Villon Society in England; and Mr. John Payne has translated him entirely into English, a task of unusual difficulty. I regret to find that Mr. Payne and I are not always at one as to the author's meaning; in such cases I am bound to suppose that he is in the right, although the weakness of the flesh withholds me from anything beyond a formal submission. He is now upon a larger venture, promising us at last that complete Arabian Nights to which we have all so long looked forward.

Charles of Orleans.—Perhaps I have done scanty justice to the charm of the old Duke's verses, and certainly he is too much treated as a fool. The period is not sufficiently remembered. What that period was, to what a blank of imbecility the human mind had fallen, can only be known to those who have waded in the chronicles. Excepting Comines and La Salle and Villon, I have read no author who did not appal me by his torpor; and even the trial of Joan of Arc, conducted as it was by chosen clerks, bears witness to a dreary, sterile folly,—a twilight of the mind peopled with childish phantoms. In relation to his contemporaries, Charles seems quite a lively character.

It remains for me to acknowledge the kindness of Mr. Henry Pyne, who, immediately on the appearance of the study, sent me his edition of the Debate between the Heralds: a courtesy from the expert to the amateur only too uncommon in these days.

Knox.—Knox, the second in order of interest among the reformers, lies dead and buried in the works of the learned and unreadable M'Crie. It remains for some one to break the tomb and bring him forth, alive again and breathing, in a human book. With the best intentions in the world, I have only added two more flagstones, ponderous like their predecessors, to the mass of obstruction that buries the reformer from the world; I have touched him in my turn with that "mace of death," which Carlyle has attributed to Dryasdust; and my two dull papers are, in the matter of dulness, worthy additions to the labours of M'Crie. Yet I believe they are worth reprinting in the interest of the next biographer of Knox. I trust his book may be a masterpiece; and I indulge the hope that my two studies may lend him a hint or perhaps spare him a delay in its composition.

Of the Pepys I can say nothing; for it has been too recently through my hands; and I still retain some of the heat of composition. Yet it may serve as a text for the last remark I have to offer. To Pepys I think I have been amply just; to the others, to Burns, Thoreau, Whitman, Charles of Orleans, even Villon, I have found myself in the retrospect ever too grudging of praise, ever too disrespectful in manner. It is not easy to see why I should have been most liberal to the man of least pretensions. Perhaps some cowardice withheld me from the proper warmth of tone; perhaps it is easier to be just to those nearer us in rank of mind. Such at least is the fact, which other critics may explain. For these were all men whom, for one reason or another, I loved; or when I did not love the men, my love was the greater to their books. I had read them and lived with them; for months they were continually in my thoughts; I seemed to rejoice in their joys and to sorrow with them in their griefs; and behold, when I came to write of them, my tone was sometimes hardly courteous and seldom wholly just.

R. L. S.

VICTOR HUGO'S ROMANCES.

Après le roman pittoresque mais prosaïque de Walter Scott il restera un autre roman à créer, plus beau et plus complet encore selon nous. C'est le roman, à la fois drame et épopée, pittoresque mais poétique, réel mais idéal, vrai mais grand, qui enchâssera Walter Scott dans Homère.— Victor Hugo on Quentin Durward.

VICTOR HUGO'S romances occupy an important position in the history of literature; many innovations, timidly made elsewhere, have in them been carried boldly out to their last consequences; much that was indefinite in literary tendencies has attained to definite maturity; many things have come to a point and been distinguished one from the other; and it is only in the last romance of all, Quatre Vingt Treize, that this culmination is most perfect. This is in the nature of things. Men who are in any way typical of a stage of progress may be compared more justly to the hand upon the dial of the clock, which continues to advance as it indicates, than to the stationary milestone, which is only the measure of what is past. The movement is not arrested. That significant something by which the work of such a man differs from that of his predecessors, goes on disengaging itself and becoming more and more articulate and cognisable. The same principle of growth that carried his first book beyond the books of previous writers, carries his last book beyond his first. And just as the most imbecile production of any literary age gives us sometimes the very clue to comprehension we have sought long and vainly in contemporary masterpieces, so it may be the very weakest of an author's books that, coming in the sequel of many others, enables us at last to get hold of what underlies the whole of them—of that spinal marrow of significance that unites the work of his life into something organic and rational. This is what has been done by Quatre Vingt Treize for the earlier romances of Victor Hugo, and, through them, for a whole division of modern literature. We have here the legitimate continuation of a long and living literary tradition; and hence, so far, its explanation. When many lines diverge from each other in direction so slightly as to confuse the eye, we know that we have only to produce them to make the chaos plain: this is continually so in literary history; and we shall best understand the importance of Victor Hugo's romances if we think of them as some such prolongation of one of the main lines of literary tendency.

When we compare the novels of Walter Scott with those of the man of genius who preceded him, and whom he delighted to honour as a master in the art—I mean Henry Fielding—we shall be somewhat puzzled, at the first moment, to state the difference that there is between these two. Fielding has as much human science; has a far firmer hold upon the tiller of his story; has a keen sense of character, which he draws (and Scott often does so too) in a rather abstract and academical manner; and finally, is quite as humorous and quite as good-humoured as the great Scotchman. With all these points of resemblance between the men, it is astonishing that their work should be so different. The fact is, that the English novel was looking one way and seeking one set of effects in the hands of Fielding; and in the hands of Scott it was looking eagerly in all ways and searching for all the effects that by any possibility it could utilise. The difference between these two men marks a great enfranchisement. With Scott the Romantic movement, the movement of an extended curiosity and an enfranchised imagination, has begun. This is a trite thing to say; but trite things are often very indefinitely comprehended: and this enfranchisement, in as far as it regards the technical change that came over modern prose romance, has never perhaps been explained with any clearness.

To do so, it will be necessary roughly to compare the two sets of conventions upon which plays and romances are respectively based. The purposes of these two arts are so much alike, and they deal so much with the same passions and interests, that we are apt to forget the fundamental opposition of their methods. And yet such a fundamental opposition exists. In the drama the action is developed in great measure by means of things that remain outside of the art; by means of real things, that is, and not artistic conventions for things. This is a sort of realism that is not to be confounded with that realism in painting of which we hear so much. The realism in painting is a thing of purposes; this, that we have to indicate in the drama, is an affair of method. We have heard a story, indeed, of a painter in France who, when he wanted to paint a sea-beach, carried realism from his ends to his means, and plastered real sand upon his canvas; and that is precisely what is done in the drama. The dramatic author has to paint his beaches with real sand: real live men and women move about the stage; we hear real voices; what is feigned merely puts a sense upon what is; we do actually see a woman go behind a screen as Lady Teazle, and, after a certain interval, we do actually see her very shamefully produced again. Now all these things, that remain as they were in life, and are not transmuted into any artistic convention, are terribly stubborn and difficult to deal with; and hence there are for the dramatist many resultant limitations in time and space. These limitations in some sort approximate towards those of painting: the dramatic author is tied down, not indeed to a moment, but to the duration of each scene or act; he is confined to the stage, almost as the painter is confined within his frame. But the great restriction is this, that a dramatic author must deal with his actors, and with his actors alone. Certain moments of suspense, certain significant dispositions of personages, a certain logical growth of emotion, these are the only means at the disposal of the playwright. It is true that, with the assistance of the scene-painter, the costumier and the conductor of the orchestra, he may add to this something of pageant, something of sound and fury; but these are, for the dramatic writer, beside the mark, and do not come under the vivifying touch of his genius. When we turn to romance, we find this no longer. Here nothing is reproduced to our senses directly. Not only the main conception of the work, but the scenery, the appliances, the mechanism by which this conception is brought home to us, have been put through the crucible of another man's mind, and come out again, one and all, in the form of written words. With the loss of every degree of such realism as we have described, there is for art a clear gain of liberty and largeness of competence. Thus, painting, in which the round outlines of things are thrown on to a flat board, is far more free than sculpture, in which their solidity is preserved. It is by giving up these identities that art gains true strength. And so in the case of novels as compared with the stage. Continuous narration is the flat board on to which the novelist throws everything. And from this there results for him

23

a great loss of vividness, but a great compensating gain in his power over the subject; so that he can now subordinate one thing to another in importance, and introduce all manner of very subtle detail, to a degree that was before impossible. He can render just as easily the flourish of trumpets before a victorious emperor and the gossip of country market women, the gradual decay of forty years of a man's life and the gesture of a passionate moment. He finds himself equally unable, if he looks at it from one point of view—equally able, if he looks at it from another point of view—to reproduce a colour, a sound, an outline, a logical argument, a physical action. He can show his readers, behind and around the personages that for the moment occupy the foreground of his story, the continual suggestion of the landscape; the turn of the weather that will turn with it men's lives and fortunes, dimly foreshadowed on the horizon; the fatality of distant events, the stream of national tendency, the salient framework of causation. And all this thrown upon the flat board—all this entering, naturally and smoothly, into the texture of continuous intelligent narration.

This touches the difference between Fielding and Scott. In the work of the latter, true to his character of a modern and a romantic, we become suddenly conscious of the background. Fielding, on the other hand, although he had recognised that the novel was nothing else than an epic in prose, wrote in the spirit not of the epic, but of the drama. This is not, of course, to say that the drama was in any way incapable of a regeneration similar in kind to that of which I am now speaking with regard to the novel. The notorious contrary fact is sufficient to guard the reader against such a misconstruction. All that is meant is, that Fielding remained ignorant of certain capabilities which the novel possesses over the drama; or, at least, neglected and did not develop them. To the end he continued to see things as a playwright sees them. The world with which he dealt, the world he had realised for himself and sought to realise and set before his readers, was a world of exclusively human interest. As for landscape, he was content to underline stage directions, as it might be done in a play-book: Tom and Molly retire into a practicable wood. As for nationality and public sentiment, it is curious enough to think that Tom Jones is laid in the year forty-five, and that the only use he makes of the rebellion is to throw a troop of soldiers into his hero's way. It is most really important, however, to remark the change which has been introduced into the conception of character by the beginning of the romantic movement and the consequent introduction into fiction of a vast amount of new material. Fielding tells us as much as he thought necessary to account for the actions of his creatures; he thought that each of these actions could be decomposed on the spot into a few simple personal elements, as we decompose a force in a question of abstract dynamics. The larger motives are all unknown to him; he had not understood that the nature of the landscape or the spirit of the times could be for anything in a story; and so, naturally and rightly, he said nothing about them. But Scott's instinct, the instinct of the man of an age profoundly different, taught him otherwise; and, in his work, the individual characters begin to occupy a comparatively small proportion of that canvas on which armies manœuvre, and great hills pile themselves upon each other's shoulders. Fielding's characters were always great to the full stature of a perfectly arbitrary will. Already in Scott we begin to have a sense of the subtle influences that moderate and qualify a man's personality; that personality is no longer thrown out in unnatural isolation, but is resumed into its place in the constitution of things.

It is this change in the manner of regarding men and their actions first exhibited in romance, that has since renewed and vivified history. For art precedes philosophy and even science. People must have noticed things and interested themselves in them before they begin to debate upon their causes or influence. And it is in this way that art is the pioneer of knowledge; those predilections of the artist he knows not why, those irrational acceptations and recognitions, reclaim, out of the world that we have not yet realised, ever another and another corner; and after the facts have been thus vividly brought before us and have had time to settle and arrange themselves in our minds, some day there will be found the man of science to stand up and give the explanation. Scott took an interest in many things in which Fielding took none; and for this reason, and no other, he introduced them into his romances. If he had been told what would be the nature of the movement that he was so lightly initiating, he would have been very incredulous and not a little scandalised. At the time when he wrote, the real drift of this new manner of pleasing people in fiction was not yet apparent; and, even now, it is only by looking at the romances of Victor Hugo that we are enabled to form any proper judgment in the matter. These books are not only descended by ordinary generation from the Waverley novels, but it is in them chiefly that we shall find the revolutionary tradition of Scott carried farther that we shall find Scott himself, in so far as regards his conception of prose fiction and its purposes, surpassed in his own spirit, instead of tamely followed. We have here, as I said before, a line of literary tendency produced, and by this production definitely separated from others. When we come to Hugo, we see that the deviation, which seemed slight enough and not very serious between Scott and Fielding, is indeed such a great gulph in thought and sentiment as only successive generations can pass over: and it is but natural that one of the chief advances that Hugo has made upon Scott is an advance in self-consciousness. Both men follow the same road; but where the one went blindly and carelessly, the other advances with all deliberation and forethought. There never was artist much more unconscious than Scott; and there have been not many more conscious than Hugo. The passage at the head of these pages shows how organically he had understood the nature of his own changes. He has, underlying each of the five great romances (which alone I purpose here to examine), two deliberate designs: one artistic, the other consciously ethical and intellectual. This is a man living in a different world from Scott, who professes sturdily (in one of his introductions) that he does not believe in novels having any moral influence at all; but still Hugo is too much of an artist to let himself be hampered by his dogmas; and the truth is that the artistic result seems, in at least one great instance, to have very little connection with the other, or directly ethical result.

The artistic result of a romance, what is left upon the memory by any really powerful and artistic novel, is something so complicated and refined that it is difficult to put a name upon it and yet something as simple as nature. These two propositions may seem mutually destructive, but they are so only in appearance. The fact is that art is working far ahead of language as well as of science, realising for us, by all manner of suggestions and exaggerations, effects for which as yet we have no direct name; nay, for which we may never perhaps have a direct name, for the reason that these effects do not enter very largely into the necessities of life. Hence alone is that suspicion of vagueness that often hangs about the purpose of a romance: it is clear enough to us in thought; but we are not used to consider anything clear until we are able to formulate it in words, and analytical language has not been sufficiently shaped to that end. We all know this difficulty in the case of a picture, simple and strong as may be the impression that it has left with us; and it is only because language is the medium of romance, that we are prevented from seeing that the two cases are the same. It is not that there is anything blurred or indefinite in the impression left with us, it is just because the impression is so very definite after its own kind, that we find it hard to fit it exactly with the expressions of our philosophical speech.

It is this idea which underlies and issues from a romance, this something which it is the function of that form of art to create, this epical value, that I propose chiefly to seek and, as far as may be, to throw into relief, in the present study. It is thus, I believe, that we shall see most clearly the great stride that Hugo has taken beyond his predecessors, and how, no longer content with expressing more or less abstract relations of man to man, he has set before himself the task of realising, in the language of romance, much of the involution of our complicated lives.

This epical value is not to be found, let it be understood, in every so-called novel. The great majority are not works of art in anything but a very secondary signification. One might almost number on one's fingers the works in which such a supreme artistic intention has been in any way superior to the other and lesser aims, themselves more or less artistic, that generally go hand in hand with it in the conception of prose romance. The purely critical spirit is, in most novels, paramount. At the present moment we can recall one man only, for whose works it would have been equally possible to accomplish our present design: and that man is Hawthorne. There is a unity, an unwavering creative purpose, about some at least of Hawthorne's romances, that impresses itself on the most indifferent reader; and the very restrictions and weaknesses of the man served perhaps to strengthen the vivid and single impression of his works. There is nothing of this kind in Hugo: unity, if he attains to it, is indeed unity out of multitude; and it is the wonderful power of subordination and synthesis thus displayed, that gives us the measure of his talent. No amount of mere discussion and statement, such as this, could give a just conception of the greatness of this power. It must be felt in the books themselves, and all that can be done in the present essay is to recall to the reader the more general features of each of the five great romances, hurriedly and imperfectly, as space will permit, and rather as a suggestion than anything more complete.

The moral end that the author had before him in the conception of Notre Dame de Paris was (he tells us) to "denounce" the external fatality that hangs over men in the form of foolish and inflexible superstition. To speak plainly, this moral purpose seems to have mighty little to do with the artistic conception; moreover it is very questionably handled, while the artistic conception is developed with the most consummate success. Old Paris lives for us with newness of life: we have ever before our eyes the city cut into three by the two arms of the river, the boat-shaped island "moored" by five bridges to the different shores, and the two unequal towns on either hand. We forget all that enumeration of palaces and churches and convents which occupies so many pages of admirable description, and the thoughtless reader might be inclined to conclude from this, that they were pages thrown away; but this is not so: we forget, indeed, the details, as we forget or do not see the different layers of paint on a completed picture; but the thing desired has been accomplished, and we carry away with us a sense of the "Gothic profile" of the city, of the "surprising forest of pinnacles and towers and belfries," and we know not what of rich and intricate and quaint. And throughout, Notre Dame has been held up over Paris by a height far greater than that of its twin towers: the Cathedral is present to us from the first page to the last; the title has given us the clue, and already in the Palace of Justice the story begins to attach itself to that central building by character after character. It is purely an effect of mirage; Notre Dame does not, in reality, thus dominate and stand out above the city; and any one who should visit it, in the spirit of the Scott-tourists to Edinburgh or the Trossachs, would be almost offended at finding nothing more than this old church thrust away into a corner. It is purely an effect of mirage, as we say; but it is an effect that permeates and possesses the whole book with astonishing consistency and strength. And then, Hugo has peopled this Gothic city, and, above all, this Gothic church, with a race of men even more distinctly Gothic than their surroundings. We know this generation already: we have seen them clustered about the worn capitals of pillars, or craning forth over the church-leads with the open mouths of gargoyles. About them all there is that sort of stiff quaint unreality, that conjunction of the grotesque, and even of a certain bourgeois snugness, with passionate contortion and horror, that is so characteristic of Gothic art. Esmeralda is somewhat an exception; she and the goat traverse the story like two children who have wandered in a dream. The finest moment of the book is when these two share with the two other leading characters, Dom Claude and Quasimodo, the chill shelter of the old cathedral. It is here that we touch most intimately the generative artistic idea of the romance: are they not all four taken out of some quaint moulding, illustrative of the Beatitudes, or the Ten Commandments, or the seven deadly sins? What is Quasimodo but an animated gargoyle? What is the whole book but the reanimation of Gothic art?

It is curious that in this, the earliest of the five great romances, there should be so little of that extravagance that latterly we have come almost to identify with the author's manner. Yet even here we are distressed by words, thoughts, and incidents that defy belief and alienate the sympathies. The scene of the in pace, for example, in spite of its strength, verges dangerously on the province of the penny novelist. I do not believe that Quasimodo rode upon the bell; I should as soon imagine that he swung by the clapper. And again the following two sentences, out of an otherwise admirable chapter, surely surpass what it has ever entered into the heart of any other man to imagine (vol. ii. p. 180): "Il souffrait tant que par instants il s'arrachait des poignées de cheveux, pour voir s'ils ne blanchissaient pas." And, p. 181: "Ses pensées étaient si insupportables qu'il prenait sa tête à deux mains et tâchait de l'arracher de ses épaules pour la briser sur le pavé."

One other fault, before we pass on. In spite of the horror and misery that pervade all of his later work, there is in it much less of actual melodrama than here, and rarely, I should say never, that sort of brutality, that useless insufferable violence to the feelings, which is the last distinction between melodrama and true tragedy. Now, in Notre Dame, the whole story of Esmeralda's passion for the worthless archer is unpleasant enough; but when she betrays herself in her last hiding-place, herself and her wretched mother, by calling out to this sordid hero who has long since forgotten her—well, that is just one of those things that readers will not forgive; they do not like it, and they are quite right; life is hard enough for poor mortals, without having it indefinitely embittered for them by bad art.

We look in vain for any similar blemish in Les Misérables. Here, on the other hand, there is perhaps the nearest approach to literary restraint that Hugo has ever made: there is here certainly the ripest and most easy development of his powers. It is the moral intention of this great novel to awaken us a little, if it may be—for such awakenings are unpleasant—to the great cost of this society that we enjoy and profit by, to the labour and sweat of those who support the litter, civilisation, in which we ourselves are so smoothly carried forward. People are all glad to shut their eyes; and it gives them a very simple pleasure when they can forget that our laws commit a million individual injustices, to be once roughly just in the general; that the bread that we eat, and the quiet of the family, and all that embellishes life and makes it worth having, have to be purchased by death—by the deaths of animals, and the deaths of men wearied out with labour, and the deaths of those criminals called tyrants and revolutionaries, and the deaths of those revolutionaries called criminals. It is to something of all this that Victor Hugo wishes to open men's eyes in Les Misérables; and this moral lesson is worked out in masterly coincidence with the artistic effect. The deadly weight of civilisation to those who are below presses sensibly on our shoulders as we read. A sort of mocking indignation grows upon us as we find Society rejecting, again and again, the services of the most serviceable; setting Jean Valjean to pick oakum, casting Galileo into prison, even crucifying Christ. There is a haunting and horrible sense of insecurity about the book. The terror we thus feel is a terror for the machinery of law, that we can hear tearing, in the dark, good and bad between its formidable wheels with the iron stolidity of all machinery, human or divine. This terror incarnates itself sometimes and leaps horribly out upon us; as when the crouching mendicant looks up, and Jean Valjean, in the light of the street lamp, recognises the face of the detective; as when the lantern of the patrol flashes suddenly through the darkness of the sewer; or as when the fugitive comes forth at last at evening, by the quiet riverside, and finds the police there also, waiting stolidly for vice and stolidly satisfied to take virtue instead. The whole book is full of oppression, and full of prejudice, which is the great cause of oppression. We have the prejudices of M. Gillenormand, the prejudices of Marius, the prejudices in revolt that defend the barricade, and the throned prejudices that carry it by storm. And then we have the admirable but ill-written character of Javert, the man who had made a religion of the police, and would not survive the moment when he learned that there was another truth outside the truth of laws; a just creation, over which the reader will do well to ponder.

With so gloomy a design this great work is still full of life and light and love. The portrait of the good Bishop is one of the most agreeable things in modern literature. The whole scene at Montfermeil is full of the charm that Hugo knows so well how to throw about children. Who can forget the passage where Cosette, sent out at night to draw water, stands in admiration before the illuminated booth, and the huckster behind "lui faisait un peu l'effet d'être le Père éternel?" The pathos of the forlorn sabot laid trustingly by the chimney in expectation of the Santa Claus that was not, takes us fairly by the throat; there is nothing in Shakespeare that touches the heart more nearly. The loves of Cosette and Marius are very pure and pleasant, and we cannot refuse our affection to Gavroche, although we may make a mental reservation of our profound disbelief in his existence. Take it for all in all, there are few books in the world that can be compared with it. There is as much calm and serenity as Hugo has ever attained to; the melodramatic coarsenesses that disfigured Notre Dame are no longer present. There is certainly much that is painfully improbable; and again, the story itself is a little too well constructed; it produces on us the effect of a puzzle, and we grow incredulous as we find that every character fits again and again into the plot, and is, like the child's cube, serviceable on six faces; things are not so well arranged in life as all that comes to. Some of the digressions, also, seem out of place, and do nothing

31

but interrupt and irritate. But when all is said, the book remains of masterly conception and of masterly development, full of pathos, full of truth, full of a high eloquence.

Superstition and social exigency having been thus dealt with in the first two members of the series, it remained for Les Travailleurs de la Mer to show man hand to hand with the elements, the last form of external force that is brought against him. And here once more the artistic effect and the moral lesson are worked out together, and are, indeed, one. Gilliat, alone upon the reef at his herculean task, offers a type of human industry in the midst of the vague "diffusion of forces into the illimitable," and the visionary development of "wasted labour" in the sea, and the winds, and the clouds. No character was ever thrown into such strange relief as Gilliat. The great circle of sea-birds that come wanderingly around him on the night of his arrival, strikes at once the note of his pre-eminence and isolation. He fills the whole reef with his indefatigable toil; this solitary spot in the ocean rings with the clamour of his anvil; we see him as he comes and goes, thrown out sharply against the clear background of the sea. And yet his isolation is not to be compared with the isolation of Robinson Crusoe, for example; indeed, no two books could be more instructive to set side by side than Les Travailleurs and this other of the old days before art had learnt to occupy itself with what lies outside of human will. Crusoe was one sole centre of interest in the midst of a nature utterly dead and utterly unrealised by the artist; but this is not how we feel with Gilliat; we feel that he is opposed by a "dark coalition of forces," that an "immense animosity" surrounds him; we are the witnesses of the terrible warfare that he wages with "the silent inclemency of phenomena going their own way, and the great general law, implacable and passive:" "a conspiracy of the indifferency of things" is against him. There is not one interest on the reef, but two. Just as we recognise Gilliat for the hero, we recognise, as implied by this indifferency of things, this direction of forces to some purpose outside our purposes, yet another character who may almost take rank as the villain of the novel, and the two face up to one another blow for blow, feint for feint, until, in the storm, they fight it epically out, and Gilliat remains the victor;—a victor, however, who has still to encounter the octopus. I need say nothing of the gruesome, repulsive excellence of that famous scene; it will be enough to remind the reader that Gilliat is in pursuit of a crab when he is himself assaulted by the devil fish, and that this, in its way, is the last touch to the inner significance of the book; here, indeed, is the true position of man in the universe.

But in Les Travailleurs, with all its strength, with all its eloquence, with all the beauty and fitness of its main situations, we cannot conceal from ourselves that there is a thread of something that will not bear calm scrutiny. There is much that is disquieting about the storm, admirably as it begins. I am very doubtful whether it would be possible to keep the boat from foundering in such circumstances, by any amount of breakwater and broken rock. I do not understand the way in which the waves are spoken of, and prefer just to take it as a loose way of speaking, and pass on. And lastly, how does it happen that the sea was quite calm next day? Is this great hurricane a piece of scene-painting after all? And when we have forgiven Gilliat's prodigies of strength (although, in soberness, he reminds us more of Porthos in the Vicomte de Bragelonne than is quite desirable), what is to be said to his suicide, and how are we to condemn in adequate terms that unprincipled avidity after effect, which tells us that the sloop disappeared over the horizon, and the head under the water, at one and the same moment? Monsieur Hugo may say what he will, but we know better; we know very well that they did not; a thing like that raises up a despairing spirit of opposition in a man's readers; they give him the lie fiercely, as they read. Lastly, we have here already some beginning of that curious series of English blunders, that makes us wonder if there are neither proof-sheets nor judicious friends in the whole of France, and affects us sometimes with a sickening uneasiness as to what may be our own exploits when we touch upon foreign countries and foreign tongues. It is here that we shall find the famous "first of the fourth," and many English words that may be comprehensible perhaps in Paris. It is here that we learn that "laird" in Scotland is the same title as "lord" in England. Here, also, is an account of a Highland soldier's equipment, which we recommend to the lovers of genuine fun.

In L'Homme qui Rit, it was Hugo's object to 'denounce' (as he would say himself) the aristocratic principle as it was exhibited in England; and this purpose, somewhat more unmitigatedly satiric than that of the two last, must answer for much that is unpleasant in the book. The repulsiveness of the scheme of the story, and the manner in which it is bound up with impossibilities and absurdities, discourage the reader at the outset, and it needs an effort to take it as seriously as it deserves. And yet when we judge it deliberately, it will be seen that, here again, the story is admirably adapted to the moral. The constructive ingenuity exhibited throughout is almost morbid. Nothing could be more happily imagined, as a reductio ad absurdum of the aristocratic principle, than the adventures of Gwynplaine, the itinerant mountebank, snatched suddenly out of his little way of life, and installed without preparation as one of the hereditary legislators of a great country. It is with a very bitter irony that the paper, on which all this depends, is left to float for years at the will of wind and tide. What, again, can be finer in conception than that voice from the people heard suddenly in the House of Lords, in solemn arraignment of the pleasures and privileges of its splendid occupants? The horrible laughter, stamped for ever "by order of the king" upon the face of this strange spokesman of democracy, adds yet another feature of justice to the scene; in all time, travesty has been the argument of oppression; and, in all time, the oppressed might have made this answer: "If I am vile, is it not your system that has made me so?" This ghastly laughter gives occasion, moreover, for the one strain of tenderness running through the web of this unpleasant story: the love of the blind girl Dea, for the monster. It is a most benignant providence that thus harmoniously brings together these two misfortunes; it is one of those compensations, one of those afterthoughts of a relenting destiny, that reconcile us from time to time to the evil that is in the world; the atmosphere of the book is purified by the presence of this pathetic love; it seems to be above the story somehow, and not of it, as the full moon over the night of some foul and feverish city.

There is here a quality in the narration more intimate and particular than is general with Hugo; but it must be owned, on the other hand, that the book is wordy, and even, now and then, a little wearisome. Ursus and his wolf are pleasant enough companions; but the former is nearly as much an abstract type as the latter. There is a beginning, also, of an abuse of conventional conversation, such as may be quite pardonable in the drama where needs must, but is without excuse in the romance. Lastly, I suppose one must say a word or two about the weak points of this not immaculate novel; and if so, it will be best to distinguish at once. The large family of English blunders, to which we have alluded already in speaking of Les Travailleurs, are of a sort that is really indifferent in art. If Shakespeare makes his ships cast anchor by some seaport of Bohemia, if Hugo imagines Tom-Tim-Jack to be a likely nickname for an English sailor, or if either Shakespeare, or Hugo, or Scott, for that matter, be guilty of "figments enough to confuse the march of a whole history—anachronisms enough to overset all, chronology," [27] the life of their creations, the artistic truth and accuracy of their work, is not so much as compromised. But when we come upon a passage like the sinking of the "Ourque" in this romance, we can do nothing but cover our face with our hands: the conscientious reader feels a sort of disgrace in the very reading. For such artistic falsehoods, springing from what I have called already an unprincipled avidity after effect, no amount of blame can be exaggerated; and above all, when the criminal is such a man as Victor Hugo. We cannot forgive in him what we might have passed over in a third-rate sensation novelist. Little as he seems to know of the sea and nautical affairs, he must have known very well that vessels do not go down as he makes the "Ourque" go down; he must have known that such a liberty with fact was against the laws of the game, and incompatible with all appearance of sincerity in conception or workmanship.

In each of these books, one after another, there has been some departure from the traditional canons of romance; but taking each separately, one would have feared to make too much of these departures, or to found any theory upon what was perhaps purely accidental. The appearance of Quatre Vingt Treize has put us out of the region of such doubt. Like a doctor who has long been hesitating how to classify an epidemic malady, we have come at last upon a case so well marked that our uncertainty is at an end. It is a novel built upon "a sort of enigma," which was at that date laid before revolutionary France, and which is presented by Hugo to Tellmarch, to Lantenac, to Gauvain, and very terribly to Cimourdain, each of whom gives his own solution of the question, clement or stern, according to the temper of his spirit. That enigma was this: "Can a good action be a bad action? Does not he who spares the wolf kill the sheep?" This question, as I say, meets with one answer after another during the course of the book, and yet seems to remain undecided to the end. And something in the same way, although one character, or one set of characters, after another comes to the front and occupies our attention for the moment, we never identify our interest with any of these temporary heroes nor regret them after they are withdrawn. We soon come to regard them somewhat as special cases of a general law; what we really care for is something that they only imply and body forth to us. We know how history continues through century after century; how this king or that patriot disappears from its pages with his whole generation, and yet we do not cease to read, nor do we even feel as if we had reached any legitimate conclusion, because our interest is not in the men, but in the country that they loved or hated, benefited or injured. And so it is here: Gauvain and Cimourdain pass away, and we regard them no more than the lost armies of which we find the cold statistics in military annals; what we regard is what remains behind; it is the principle that put these men where they were, that filled them for a while with heroic inspiration, and has the power, now that they are fallen, to inspire others with the same courage. The interest of the novel centres about revolutionary France: just as the plot is an abstract judicial difficulty, the hero is an abstract historical force. And this has been done, not, as it would have been before, by the cold and cumbersome machinery of allegory, but with bold, straightforward realism, dealing only with the objective materials of art, and dealing with them so masterfully that the palest abstractions of thought come before us, and move our hopes and fears, as if they were the young men and maidens of customary romance.

The episode of the mother and children in Quatre Vingt Treize is equal to anything that Hugo has ever written. There is one chapter in the second volume, for instance, called "Sein guéri, cœur saignant," that is full of the very stuff of true tragedy, and nothing could be more delightful than the humours of the three children on the day before the assault. The passage on La Vendée is really great, and the scenes in Paris have much of the same broad merit. The book is full, as usual, of pregnant and splendid sayings. But when thus much is conceded by way of praise, we come to the other scale of the balance, and find this, also, somewhat heavy. There is here a yet greater over-employment of conventional dialogue than in L'Homme qui Rit; and much that should have been said by the author himself, if it were to be said at all, he has most unwarrantably put into the mouths of one or other of his characters. We should like to know what becomes of the main body of the troop in the wood of La Saudraie during the thirty pages or so in which the foreguard lays aside all discipline, and stops to gossip over a woman and some children. We have an unpleasant idea forced upon us at one place, in spite of all the good-natured incredulity that we can summon up to resist it. Is it possible that Monsieur Hugo thinks they ceased to steer the corvette while the gun was loose? Of the chapter in which Lantenac and Halmalho are alone together in the boat, the less said the better; of course, if there were nothing else, they would have been swamped thirty times over during the course of Lantenac's harangue. Again, after Lantenac has landed, we have scenes of almost inimitable workmanship that suggest the epithet "statuesque" by their clear and trenchant outline; but the tocsin scene will not do, and the tocsin unfortunately pervades the whole passage, ringing continually in our ears with a taunting accusation of falsehood. And then, when we come to the place where Lantenac meets the royalists, under the idea that he is going to meet the republicans, it seems as if there were a hitch in the stage mechanism. I have tried it over in every way, and I cannot conceive any disposition that would make the scene possible as narrated.

Such then, with their faults and their signal excellences, are the five great novels.

Romance is a language in which many persons learn to speak with a certain appearance of fluency; but there are few who can ever bend it to any practical need, few who can ever be said to express themselves in it. It has become abundantly plain in the foregoing examination that Victor Hugo occupies a high place among those few. He has always a perfect command over his stories; and we see that they are constructed with a high regard to some ulterior purpose, and that every situation is informed with moral significance and grandeur. Of no other man can the same thing be said in the same degree. His romances are not to be confused with "the novel with a purpose" as familiar to the English reader: this is generally the model of incompetence; and we see the moral clumsily forced into every hole and corner of the story, or thrown externally over it like a carpet over a railing. Now the moral significance, with Hugo, is of the essence of the romance; it is the organising principle. If you could somehow despoil Les Misérables or Les Travailleurs of their distinctive lesson, you would find that the story had lost its interest and the book was dead.

Having thus learned to subordinate his story to an idea, to make his art speak, he went on to teach it to say things heretofore unaccustomed. If you look back at the five books of which we have now so hastily spoken, you will be astonished at the freedom with which the original purposes of story-telling have been laid aside and passed by. Where are now the two lovers who descended the main watershed of all the Waverley novels, and all the novels that have tried to follow in their wake? Sometimes they are almost lost sight of before the solemn isolation of a man against the sea and sky, as in Les Travailleurs; sometimes, as in Les Misérables, they merely figure for awhile, as a beautiful episode in the epic of oppression; sometimes they are entirely absent, as in Quatre Vingt Treize. There is no hero in Notre Dame: in Les Misérables it is an old man: in L'Homme qui Rit it is a monster: in Quatre Vingt Treize it is the Revolution. Those elements that only began to show themselves timidly, as adjuncts, in the novels of Walter Scott, have usurped ever more and more of the canvas; until we find the whole interest of one of Hugo's romances centring around matter that Fielding would have banished from his altogether, as being out of the field of fiction. So we have elemental forces occupying nearly as large a place, playing (so to speak) nearly as important a rôle, as the man, Gilliat, who opposes and overcomes them. So we find the fortunes of a nation put upon the stage with as much vividness as ever before the fortunes of a village maiden or a lost heir; and the forces that oppose and corrupt a principle holding the attention quite as strongly as the wicked barons or dishonest attorneys of the past. Hence those individual interests that were supreme in Fielding, and even in Scott, stood out over everything else and formed as it were the spine of the story, figure here only as one set of interests among many sets, one force among many forces, one thing to be treated out of a whole world of things equally vivid and important. So that, for Hugo, man is no longer an isolated spirit without antecedent or relation here below, but a being involved in the action and reaction of natural forces, himself a centre of such action and reaction or an unit in a great multitude, chased hither and thither by epidemic terrors and aspirations, and, in all seriousness, blown about by every wind of doctrine. This is a long way that we have travelled: between such work and the work of Fielding is there not, indeed, a great gulph in thought and sentiment?

Art, thus conceived, realises for men a larger portion of life, and that portion one that it is more difficult for them to realise unaided; and, besides helping them to feel more intensely those restricted personal interests which are patent to all, it awakes in them some consciousness of those more general relations that are so strangely invisible to the average man in ordinary moods. It helps to keep man in his place in nature, and, above all, it helps him to understand more intelligently the responsibilities of his place in society. And in all this generalisation of interest, we never miss those small humanities that are at the opposite pole of excellence in art; and while we admire the intellect that could see life thus largely, we are touched with another sentiment for the tender heart that slipped the piece of gold into Cosette's sabot, that was virginally troubled at the fluttering of her dress in the spring wind, or put the blind girl beside the deformity of the laughing man. This, then, is the last praise that we can award to these romances. The author has shown a power of just subordination hitherto unequalled; and as, in reaching forward to one class of effects, he has not been forgetful or careless of the other, his work is more nearly complete work, and his art, with all its imperfections, deals more comprehensively with the materials of life than that of any of his otherwise more sure and masterly predecessors.

These five books would have made a very great fame for any writer, and yet they are but one façade of the monument that Victor Hugo has erected to his genius. Everywhere we find somewhat the same greatness, somewhat the same infirmities. In his poems and plays there are the same unaccountable protervities that have already astonished us in the romances. There, too, is the same feverish strength, welding the fiery iron of his idea under forge-hammer repetitions—an emphasis that is somehow akin to weaknesses—strength that is a little epileptic. He stands so far above all his contemporaries, and so incomparably excels them in richness, breadth, variety, and moral earnestness, that we almost feel as if he had a sort of right to fall oftener and more heavily than others; but this does not reconcile us to seeing him profit by the privilege so freely. We like to have, in our great men, something that is above question; we like to place an implicit faith in them, and see them always on the platform of their greatness; and this, unhappily, cannot be with Hugo. As Heine said long ago, his is a genius somewhat deformed; but, deformed as it is, we accept it gladly; we shall have the wisdom to see where his foot slips, but we shall have the justice also to recognise in him one of the greatest artists of our generation, and, in many ways, one of the greatest artists of time. If we look back, yet once, upon these five romances, we see blemishes such as we can lay to the charge of no other man in the number of the famous; but to what other man can we attribute such sweeping innovations, such a new and significant presentment of the life of man, such an amount, if we merely think of the amount, of equally consummate performance?

SOME ASPECTS OF ROBERT BURNS

To write with authority about another man, we must have fellow-feeling and some common ground of experience with our subject. We may praise or blame according as we find him related to us by the best or worst in ourselves; but it is only in virtue of some relationship that we can be his judges, even to condemn. Feelings which we share and understand enter for us into the tissue of the man's character; those to which we are strangers in our own experience we are inclined to regard as blots, exceptions, inconsistencies, and excursions of the diabolic; we conceive them with repugnance, explain them with difficulty, and raise our hands to heaven in wonder when we find them in conjunction with talents that we respect or virtues that we admire. David, king of Israel, would pass a sounder judgment on a man than either Nathaniel or David Hume. Now, Principal Shairp's recent volume, although I believe no one will read it without respect and interest, has this one capital defect— that there is imperfect sympathy between the author and the subject, between the critic and the personality under criticism. Hence an inorganic, if not an incoherent, presentation of both the poems and the man. Of Holy Willie's Prayer, Principal Shairp remarks that "those who have loved most what was best in Burns's poetry must have regretted that it was ever written." To the Jolly Beggars, so far as my memory serves me, he refers but once; and then only to remark on the "strange, not to say painful," circumstance that the same hand which wrote the Cotter's Saturday Night should have stooped to write the Jolly Beggars. The Saturday Night may or may not be an admirable poem; but its significance is trebled, and the power and range of the poet first appears, when it is set beside the Jolly Beggars. To take a man's work piecemeal, except with the design of elegant extracts, is the way to avoid, and not to perform, the critic's duty. The same defect is displayed in the treatment of Burns as a man, which is broken, apologetical, and confused. The man here presented to us is not that Burns, teres atque rotundus—a burly figure in literature, as, from our present vantage of time, we have begun to see him. This, on the other hand, is Burns as he may have appeared to a contemporary clergyman, whom we shall conceive to have been a kind and indulgent but orderly and orthodox person, anxious to be pleased, but too often hurt and disappointed by the behaviour of his red-hot protégé, and solacing himself with the explanation that the poet was "the most inconsistent of men." If you are so sensibly pained by the misconduct of your subject, and so paternally delighted with his virtues, you will always be an excellent gentleman, but a somewhat questionable biographer. Indeed, we can only be sorry and surprised that Principal Shairp should have chosen a theme so uncongenial. When we find a man writing on Burns, who likes neither Holy Willie, nor the Beggars, nor the Ordination, nothing is adequate to the situation but the old cry of Géronte: "Que diable allait-il faire dans cette galère?" And every merit we find in the book, which is sober and candid in a degree unusual with biographies of Burns, only leads us to regret more heartily that good work should be so greatly thrown away.

It is far from my intention to tell over again a story that has been so often told; but there are certainly some points in the character of Burns that will bear to be brought out, and some chapters in his life that demand a brief rehearsal. The unity of the man's nature, for all its richness, has fallen somewhat out of sight in the pressure of new information and the apologetical ceremony of biographers. Mr. Carlyle made an inimitable bust of the poet's head of gold; may I not be forgiven if my business should have more to do with the feet, which were of clay?

Youth.

Any view of Burns would be misleading which passed over in silence the influences of his home and his father. That father, William Burnes, after having been for many years a gardener, took a farm, married, and, like an emigrant in a new country, built himself a house with his own hands. Poverty of the most distressing sort, with sometimes the near prospect of a gaol, embittered the remainder of his life. Chill, backward, and austere with strangers, grave and imperious in his family, he was yet a man of very unusual parts and of an affectionate nature. On his way through life he had remarked much upon other men, with more result in theory than practice; and he had reflected upon many subjects as he delved the garden. His great delight was in solid conversation; he would leave his work to talk with the schoolmaster Murdoch; and Robert, when he came home late at night, not only turned aside rebuke but kept his father two hours beside the fire by the charm of his merry and vigorous talk. Nothing is more characteristic of the class in general, and William Burnes in particular, than the pains he took to get proper schooling for his boys, and, when that was no longer possible, the sense and resolution with which he set himself to supply the deficiency by his own influence. For many years he was their chief companion; he spoke with them seriously on all subjects as if they had been grown men; at night, when work was over, he taught them arithmetic; he borrowed books for them on history, science, and theology; and he felt it his duty to supplement this last—the trait is laughably Scottish—by a dialogue of his own composition, where his own private shade of orthodoxy was exactly represented. He would go to his daughter as she stayed afield herding cattle, to teach her the names of grasses and wild flowers, or to sit by her side when it thundered. Distance to strangers, deep family tenderness, love of knowledge, a narrow, precise, and formal reading of theology—everything we learn of him hangs well together, and builds up a popular Scotch type. If I mention the name of Andrew Fairservice, it is only as I might couple for an instant Dugald Dalgetty with old Marshal Loudon, to help out the reader's comprehension by a popular but unworthy instance of a class. Such was the influence of this good and wise man that his household became a school to itself, and neighbours who came into the farm at meal-time would find the whole family, father, brothers, and sisters, helping themselves with one hand, and holding a book in the other. We are surprised at the prose style of Robert; that of Gilbert need surprise us no less; even William writes a remarkable letter for a young man of such slender opportunities. One anecdote marks the taste of the family. Murdoch brought Titus Andronicus, and, with such dominie elocution as we may suppose, began to read it aloud before this rustic audience; but when he had reached the passage where Tamora insults Lavinia, with one voice and "in an agony of distress" they refused to hear it to an end. In such a father and with such a home, Robert had already the making of an excellent education; and what Murdoch added, although it may not have been much in amount, was in character the very essence of a literary training. Schools and colleges, for one great man whom they complete, perhaps unmake a dozen; the strong spirit can do well upon more scanty fare.

Robert steps before us, almost from the first, in his complete character—a proud, headstrong, impetuous lad, greedy of pleasure, greedy of notice; in his own phrase "panting after distinction," and in his brother's "cherishing a particular jealousy of people who were richer or of more consequence than himself:" with all this, he was emphatically of the artist nature. Already he made a conspicuous figure in Tarbolton church, with the only tied hair in the parish, "and his plaid, which was of a particular colour, wrapped in a particular manner round his shoulders." Ten years later, when a married man, the father of a family, a farmer, and an officer of Excise, we shall find him out fishing in masquerade, with fox-skin cap, belted great-coat, and great Highland broadsword. He liked dressing up, in fact, for its own sake. This is the spirit which leads to the extravagant array of Latin Quarter students, and the proverbial velveteen of the English landscape-painter; and, though the pleasure derived is in itself merely personal, it shows a man who is, to say the least of it, not pained by general attention and remark. His father wrote the family name Burnes; Robert early adopted the orthography Burness from his cousin in the Mearns; and in his twenty-eighth year changed it once more to Burns. It is plain that the last transformation was not made without some qualm; for in addressing his cousin he adheres, in at least one more letter, to spelling number two. And this, again, shows a man preoccupied about the manner of his appearance even down to the name, and little willing to follow custom. Again, he was proud, and justly proud, of his powers in conversation. To no other man's have we the same conclusive testimony from different sources and from every rank of life. It is almost a commonplace that the best of his works was what he said in talk. Robertson the historian "scarcely ever met any man whose conversation displayed greater vigour;" the Duchess of Gordon declared that he "carried her off her feet;" and, when he came late to an inn, the servants would get out of bed to hear him talk. But, in these early days at least, he was determined to shine by any means. He made himself feared in the village for his tongue. He would crush weaker men to their faces, or even perhaps—for the statement of Sillar is not absolute—say cutting things of his acquaintances behind their back. At the church door, between sermons, he would parade his religious views amid hisses. These details stamp the man. He had no genteel timidities in the conduct of his life. He loved to force his personality upon the world. He would please himself, and shine. Had he lived in the Paris of 1830, and joined his lot with the Romantics, we can conceive him writing Jehan for Jean, swaggering in Gautier's red waistcoat, and horrifying Bourgeois in a public café with paradox and gasconnade.

A leading trait throughout his whole career was his desire to be in love. Ne fait pas ce tour qui veut. His affections were often enough touched, but perhaps never engaged. He was all his life on a voyage of discovery, but it does not appear conclusively that he ever touched the happy isle. A man brings to love a deal of ready-made sentiment, and even from childhood obscurely prognosticates the symptoms of this vital malady. Burns was formed for love; he had passion, tenderness, and a singular bent in the direction; he could foresee, with the intuition of an artist, what love ought to be; and he could not conceive a worthy life without it. But he had ill-fortune, and was besides so greedy after every shadow of the true divinity, and so much the slave of a strong temperament, that perhaps his nerve was relaxed and his heart had lost the power of self-devotion before an opportunity occurred. The circumstances of his youth doubtless counted for something in the result. For the lads of Ayrshire, as soon as the day's work was over and the beasts were stabled, would take the road, it might be in a winter tempest, and travel perhaps miles by moss and moorland to spend an hour or two in courtship. Rule 10 of the Bachelors' Club at Tarbolton provides that "every man proper for a member of this Society must be a professed lover of one or more of the female sex." The rich, as Burns himself points out, may have a choice of pleasurable occupations, but these lads had nothing but their "cannie hour at e'en." It was upon love and flirtation that this rustic society was built; gallantry was the essence of life among the Ayrshire hills as well as in the Court of Versailles; and the days were distinguished from each other by love-letters, meetings, tiffs, reconciliations, and expansions to the chosen confidant, as in a comedy of Marivaux. Here was a field for a man of Burns's indiscriminate personal ambition, where he might pursue his voyage of discovery in quest of true love, and enjoy temporary triumphs by the way. He was "constantly the victim of some fair enslaver"—at least, when it was not the other way about; and there were often underplots and secondary fair enslavers in the background. Many—or may we not say most?—of these affairs were entirely artificial. One, he tells us, he began out of "a vanity of showing his parts in courtship," for he piqued himself on his ability at a love-letter. But, however they began, these flames of his were fanned into a passion ere the end; and he stands unsurpassed in his power of self-deception, and positively without a competitor in the art, to use his own words, of "battering himself into a warm affection,"—a debilitating and futile exercise. Once he had worked himself into the vein, "the agitations of his mind and body" were an astonishment to all who knew him. Such a course as this, however pleasant to a thirsty vanity, was lowering to his nature. He sank more and more towards the professional Don Juan. With a leer of what the French call fatuity, he bids the belles of Mauchline beware of his seductions; and the same cheap self-satisfaction finds a yet uglier vent when he plumes himself on the scandal at the birth of his first bastard. We can well believe what we hear of his facility in striking up an acquaintance with women: he would have conquering manners; he would bear down upon his rustic game with the grace that comes of absolute assurance—the Richelieu of Lochlea or Mossgiel. In yet another manner did these quaint ways of courtship help him into fame. If he were great as principal, he was unrivalled as confidant. He could enter into a passion; he could counsel wary moves, being, in his own phrase, so old a hawk; nay, he could turn a letter for some unlucky swain, or even string a few lines of verse that should clinch the business and fetch the hesitating fair one to the ground. Nor, perhaps, was it only his "curiosity, zeal, and intrepid dexterity" that recommended him for a second in such affairs; it must have been a distinction to have the assistance and advice of Rab the Ranter; and one who was in no way formidable by himself might grow dangerous and attractive through the fame of his associate.

I think we can conceive him, in these early years, in that rough moorland country, poor among the poor with his seven pounds a year, looked upon with doubt by respectable elders, but for all that the best talker, the best letter-writer, the most famous lover and confidant, the laureate poet, and the only man who wore his hair tied in the parish. He says he had then as high a notion of himself as ever after; and I can well believe it. Among the youth he walked facile princeps, an apparent god; and even if, from time to time, the Reverend Mr. Auld should swoop upon him with the thunders of the Church, and, in company with seven others, Rab the Ranter must figure some fine Sunday on the stool of repentance, would there not be a sort of glory, an infernal apotheosis, in so conspicuous a shame? Was not Richelieu in disgrace more idolised than ever by the dames of Paris? and when was the highwayman most acclaimed but on his way to Tyburn? Or, to take a simile from nearer home, and still more exactly to the point, what could even corporal punishment avail, administered by a cold, abstract, unearthly school-master, against the influence and fame of the school's hero?

And now we come to the culminating point of Burns's early period. He began to be received into the unknown upper world. His fame soon spread from among his fellow-rebels on the benches, and began to reach the ushers and monitors of this great Ayrshire academy. This arose in part from his lax views about religion; for at this time that old war of the creeds and confessors, which is always grumbling from end to end of our poor Scotland, brisked up in these parts into a hot and virulent skirmish; and Burns found himself identified with the opposition party,—a clique of roaring lawyers and half-heretical divines, with wit enough to appreciate the value of the poet's help, and not sufficient taste to moderate his grossness and personality. We may judge of their surprise when Holy Willie was put into their hand; like the amorous lads of Tarbolton, they recognised in him the best of seconds. His satires began to go the round in manuscript; Mr. Aiken, one of the lawyers, "read him into fame;" he himself was soon welcome in many houses of a better sort, where his admirable talk, and his manners, which he had direct from his Maker, except for a brush he gave them at a country dancing school, completed what his poems had begun. We have a sight of him at his first visit to Adamhill, in his ploughman's shoes, coasting around the carpet as though that were sacred ground. But he soon grew used to carpets and their owners; and he was still the superior of all whom he encountered, and ruled the roost in conversation. Such was the impression made, that a young clergyman, himself a man of ability, trembled and became confused when he saw Robert enter the church in which he was to preach. It is not surprising that the poet determined to publish: he had now stood the test of some publicity, and under this hopeful impulse he composed in six winter months the bulk of his more important poems. Here was a young man who, from a very humble place, was mounting rapidly; from the cynosure of a parish, he had become the talk of a county; once the bard of rural courtships, he was now about to appear as a bound and printed poet in the world's bookshops.

A few more intimate strokes are necessary to complete the sketch. This strong young plough-man, who feared no competitor with the flail, suffered like a fine lady from sleeplessness and vapours; he would fall into the blackest melancholies, and be filled with remorse for the past and terror for the future. He was still not perhaps devoted to religion, but haunted by it; and at a touch of sickness prostrated himself before God in what I can only call unmanly penitence. As he had aspirations beyond his place in the world, so he had tastes, thoughts, and weaknesses to match. He loved to walk under a wood to the sound of a winter tempest; he had a singular tenderness for animals; he carried a book with him in his pocket when he went abroad, and wore out in this service two copies of the Man of Feeling. With young people in the field at work he was very long-suffering; and when his brother Gilbert spoke sharply to them—"O man, ye are no for young folk," he would say, and give the defaulter a helping hand and a smile. In the hearts of the men whom he met, he read as in a book; and, what is yet more rare, his knowledge of himself equalled his knowledge of others. There are no truer things said of Burns than what is to be found in his own letters. Country Don Juan as he was, he had none of that blind vanity which values itself on what it is not; he knew his own strength and weakness to a hair: he took himself boldly for what he was, and, except in moments of hypochondria, declared himself content.

The Love Stories.

On the night of Mauchline races, 1785, the young men and women of the place joined in a penny ball, according to their custom. In the same set danced Jean Armour, the master-mason's daughter, and our dark-eyed Don Juan. His dog (not the immortal Luath, but a successor unknown to fame, caret quia vate sacro), apparently sensible of some neglect, followed his master to and fro, to the confusion of the dancers. Some mirthful comments followed; and Jean heard the poet say to his partner—or, as I should imagine, laughingly launch the remark to the company at large—that "he wished he could get any of the lasses to like him as well as his dog." Some time after, as the girl was bleaching clothes on Mauchline green, Robert chanced to go by, still accompanied by his dog; and the dog, "scouring in long excursion," scampered with four black paws across the linen. This brought the two into conversation; when Jean, with a somewhat hoydenish advance, inquired if "he had yet got any of the lasses to like him as well as his dog?"

It is one of the misfortunes of the professional Don Juan that his honour forbids him to refuse battle; he is in life like the Roman soldier upon duty, or like the sworn physician who must attend on all diseases. Burns accepted the provocation; hungry hope reawakened in his heart; here was a girl—pretty, simple at least, if not honestly stupid, and plainly not averse to his attentions: it seemed to him once more as if love might here be waiting him. Had he but known the truth! for this facile and empty-headed girl had nothing more in view than a flirtation; and her heart, from the first and on to the end of her story, was engaged by another man. Burns once more commenced the celebrated process of "battering himself into a warm affection;" and the proofs of his success are to be found in many verses of the period. Nor did he succeed with himself only; Jean, with her heart still elsewhere, succumbed to his fascination, and early in the next year the natural consequence became manifest. It was a heavy stroke for this unfortunate couple. They had trifled with life, and were now rudely reminded of life's serious issues. Jean awoke to the ruin of her hopes; the best she had now to expect was marriage with a man who was a stranger to her dearest thoughts; she might now be glad if she could get what she would never have chosen. As for Burns, at the stroke of the calamity he recognised that his voyage of discovery had led him into a wrong hemisphere—that he was not, and never had been, really in love with Jean. Hear him in the pressure of the hour. "Against two things," he writes, "I am as fixed as fate—staying at home, and owning her conjugally. The first, by heaven, I will not do!—the last, by hell, I will never do!" And then he adds, perhaps already in a more relenting temper: "If you see Jean, tell her I will meet her, so God help me in my hour of need." They met accordingly; and Burns, touched with her misery, came down from these heights of independence, and gave her a written acknowledgment of marriage. It is the punishment of Don Juanism to create continually false positions—relations in life which are wrong in themselves, and which it is equally wrong to break or to perpetuate. This was such a case. Worldly Wiseman would have laughed and gone his way; let us be glad that Burns was better counselled by his heart. When we discover that we can be no longer true, the next best is to be kind. I daresay he came away from that interview not very content, but with a glorious conscience; and as he went homeward, he would sing his favourite, "How are Thy servants blest, O Lord!" Jean, on the other hand, armed with her "lines," confided her position to the master-mason, her father, and his wife. Burns and his brother were then in a fair way to ruin themselves in their farm; the poet was an execrable match for any well-to-do country lass; and perhaps old Armour had an inkling of a previous attachment on his daughter's part. At least, he was not so much incensed by her slip from virtue as by the marriage which had been designed to cover it. Of this he would not hear a word. Jean, who had besought the acknowledgment only to appease her parents, and not at all from any violent inclination to the poet, readily gave up the paper for destruction; and all parties imagined, although wrongly, that the marriage was thus dissolved. To a proud man like Burns here was a crushing blow. The concession which had been wrung from his pity was now publicly thrown back in his teeth. The Armour family preferred disgrace to his connection. Since the promise, besides, he had doubtless been busy "battering himself" back again into his affection for the girl; and the blow would not only take him in his vanity, but wound him at the heart.

He relieved himself in verse; but for such a smarting affront manuscript poetry was insufficient to console him. He must find a more powerful remedy in good flesh and blood, and after this discomfiture, set forth again at once upon his voyage of discovery in quest of love. It is perhaps one of the most touching things in human nature, as it is a commonplace of psychology, that when a man has just lost hope or confidence in one love, he is then most eager to find and lean upon another. The universe could not be yet exhausted; there must be hope and love waiting for him somewhere; and so, with his head down, this poor, insulted poet ran once more upon his fate. There was an innocent and gentle Highland nursery-maid at service in a neighbouring family; and he had soon battered himself and her into a warm affection and a secret engagement. Jean's marriage lines had not been destroyed till March 13, 1786; yet all was settled between Burns and Mary Campbell by Sunday, May 14, when they met for the last time, and said farewell with rustic solemnities upon the banks of Ayr. They each wet their hands in a stream, and, standing one on either bank, held a Bible between them as they vowed eternal faith. Then they exchanged Bibles, on one of which Burns, for greater security, had inscribed texts as to the binding nature of an oath; and surely, if ceremony can do aught to fix the wandering affections, here were two people united for life. Mary came of a superstitious family, so that she perhaps insisted on these rites; but they must have been eminently to the taste of Burns at this period; for nothing would seem superfluous, and no oath great enough, to stay his tottering constancy.

Events of consequence now happened thickly in the poet's life. His book was announced; the Armours sought to summon him at law for the aliment of the child; he lay here and there in hiding to correct the sheets; he was under an engagement for Jamaica, where Mary was to join him as his wife; now, he had "orders within three weeks at latest to repair aboard the Nancy, Captain Smith;" now his chest was already on the road to Greenock; and now, in the wild autumn weather on the moorland, he measures verses of farewell:—

"The bursting tears my heart declare;

Farewell the bonny banks of Ayr!"

But the great master dramatist had secretly another intention for the piece; by the most violent and complicated solution, in which death and birth and sudden fame all play a part as interposing deities, the act-drop fell upon a scene of transformation. Jean was brought to bed of twins, and, by an amicable arrangement, the Burnses took the boy to bring up by hand, while the girl remained with her mother. The success of the book was immediate and emphatic; it put £20 at once into the author's purse; and he was encouraged upon all hands to go to Edinburgh and push his success in a second and larger edition. Third and last in these series of interpositions, a letter came one day to Mossgiel Farm for Robert. He went to the window to read it; a sudden change came over his face, and he left the room without a word. Years afterwards, when the story began to leak out, his family understood that he had then learned the death of Highland Mary. Except in a few poems and a few dry indications purposely misleading as to date, Burns himself made no reference to this passage of his life; it was an adventure of which, for I think sufficient reasons, he desired to bury the details. Of one thing we may be glad: in after years he visited the poor girl's mother, and left her with the impression that he was "a real warm-hearted chield."

Perhaps a month after he received this intelligence, he set out for Edinburgh on a pony he had borrowed from a friend. The town that winter was "agog with the ploughman poet." Robertson, Dugald Stewart, Blair, "Duchess Gordon and all the gay world," were of his acquaintance. Such a revolution is not to be found in literary history. He was now, it must be remembered, twenty-seven years of age; he had fought since his early boyhood an obstinate battle against poor soil, bad seed, and inclement seasons, wading deep in Ayrshire mosses, guiding the plough in the furrow wielding "the thresher's weary flingin'-tree;" and his education, his diet, and his pleasures, had been those of a Scotch countryman. Now he stepped forth suddenly among the polite and learned. We can see him as he then was, in his boots and buckskins, his blue coat and waistcoat striped with buff and blue, like a farmer in his Sunday best; the heavy ploughman's figure firmly planted on its burly legs; his face full of sense and shrewdness, and with a somewhat melancholy air of thought, and his large dark eye "literally glowing" as he spoke. "I never saw such another eye in a human head," says Walter Scott, "though I have seen the most distinguished men of my time." With men, whether they were lords or omnipotent critics, his manner was plain, dignified, and free from bashfulness or affectation. If he made a slip, he had the social courage to pass on and refrain from explanation. He was not embarrassed in this society, because he read and judged the men; he could spy snobbery in a titled lord; and, as for the critics, he dismissed their system in an epigram. "These gentlemen," said he, "remind me of some spinsters in my country who spin their thread so fine that it is neither fit for weft nor woof." Ladies, on the other hand, surprised him; he was scarce commander of himself in their society; he was disqualified by his acquired nature as a Don Juan; and he, who had been so much at his ease with country lasses, treated the town dames to an extreme of deference. One lady, who met him at a ball, gave Chambers a speaking sketch of his demeanour. "His manner was not prepossessing—scarcely, she thinks, manly or natural. It seemed as if he affected a rusticity or landertness, so that when he said the music was 'bonnie, bonnie,' it was like the expression of a child." These would be company manners; and doubtless on a slight degree of intimacy the affectation would grow less. And his talk to women had always "a turn either to the pathetic or humorous, which engaged the attention particularly."

The Edinburgh magnates (to conclude this episode at once) behaved well to Burns from first to last. Were heaven-born genius to revisit us in similar guise, I am not venturing too far when I say that he need expect neither so warm a welcome nor such solid help. Although Burns was only a peasant, and one of no very elegant reputation as to morals, he was made welcome to their homes. They gave him a great deal of good advice, helped him to some five hundred pounds of ready money, and got him, as soon as he asked it, a place in the Excise. Burns, on his part, bore the elevation with perfect dignity; and with perfect dignity returned, when the time had come, into a country privacy of life. His powerful sense never deserted him, and from the first he recognised that his Edinburgh popularity was but an ovation and the affair of a day. He wrote a few letters in a high-flown, bombastic vein of gratitude; but in practice he suffered no man to intrude upon his self-respect. On the other hand, he never turned his back, even for a moment, on his old associates; and he was always ready to sacrifice an acquaintance to a friend, although the acquaintance were a duke. He would be a bold man who should promise similar conduct in equally exacting circumstances. It was, in short, an admirable appearance on the stage of life—socially successful, intimately self-respecting, and like a gentleman from first to last.

In the present study, this must only be taken by the way, while we return to Burns's love affairs. Even on the road to Edinburgh he had seized upon the opportunity of a flirtation, and had carried the "battering" so far that when next he moved from town, it was to steal two days with this anonymous fair

one. The exact importance to Burns of this affair may be gathered from the
song in which he commemorated its occurrence. "I love the dear lassie,"
he sings, "because she loves me;" or, in the tongue of prose: "Finding an
opportunity, I did not hesitate to profit by it, and even now, if it returned, I
should not hesitate to profit by it again." A love thus founded has no interest
for mortal man. Meantime, early in the winter, and only once, we find him
regretting Jean in his correspondence. "Because"—such is his reason—
"because he does not think he will ever meet so delicious an armful again;"
and then, after a brief excursion into verse, he goes straight on to describe
a new episode in the voyage of discovery with the daughter of a Lothian
farmer for a heroine. I must ask the reader to follow all these references to
his future wife; they are essential to the comprehension of Burns's character
and fate. In June, we find him back at Mauchline, a famous man. There,
the Armour family greeted him with a "mean, servile compliance," which
increased his former disgust. Jean was not less compliant; a second time
the poor girl submitted to the fascination of the man whom she did not
love, and whom she had so cruelly insulted little more than a year ago; and,
though Burns took advantage of her weakness, it was in the ugliest and most
cynical spirit, and with a heart absolutely indifferent. Judge of this by a letter
written some twenty days after his return—a letter to my mind among the
most degrading in the whole collection—a letter which seems to have been
inspired by a boastful, libertine bagman. "I am afraid," it goes, "I have almost
ruined one source, the principal one, indeed, of my former happiness—the
eternal propensity I always had to fall in love. My heart no more glows
with feverish rapture; I have no paradisiacal evening interviews." Even the
process of "battering" has failed him, you perceive. Still he had some one
in his eye—a lady, if you please, with a fine figure and elegant manners, and
who had "seen the politest quarters in Europe." "I frequently visited her,"
he writes, "and after passing regularly the intermediate degrees between the
distant formal bow and the familiar grasp round the waist, I ventured, in my
careless way, to talk of friendship in rather ambiguous terms; and after her
return to —, I wrote her in the same terms. Miss, construing my remarks
further than even I intended, flew off in a tangent of female dignity and
reserve, like a mounting lark in an April morning; and wrote me an answer

which measured out very completely what an immense way I had to travel before I could reach the climate of her favours. But I am an old hawk at the sport, and wrote her such a cool, deliberate, prudent reply, as brought my bird from her aerial towerings, pop, down to my foot, like Corporal Trim's hat." I avow a carnal longing, after this transcription, to buffet the Old Hawk about the ears. There is little question that to this lady he must have repeated his addresses, and that he was by her (Miss Chalmers) eventually, though not at all unkindly, rejected. One more detail to characterise the period. Six months after the date of this letter, Burns, back in Edinburgh, is served with a writ in meditatione fugæ, on behalf of some Edinburgh fair one, probably of humble rank, who declared an intention of adding to his family.

About the beginning of December (1787), a new period opens in the story of the poet's random affections. He met at a tea party one Mrs. Agnes M'Lehose, a married woman of about his own age, who, with her two children, had been deserted by an unworthy husband. She had wit, could use her pen, and had read Werther with attention. Sociable, and even somewhat frisky, there was a good, sound, human kernel in the woman; a warmth of love, strong dogmatic religious feeling, and a considerable, but not authoritative, sense of the proprieties. Of what biographers refer to daintily as "her somewhat voluptuous style of beauty," judging from the silhouette in Mr. Scott Douglas's invaluable edition, the reader will be fastidious if he does not approve. Take her for all in all, I believe she was the best woman Burns encountered. The pair took a fancy for each other on the spot; Mrs. M'Lehose, in her turn, invited him to tea; but the poet, in his character of the Old Hawk, preferred a tête-à-tête, excused himself at the last moment, and offered a visit instead. An accident confined him to his room for nearly a month, and this led to the famous Clarinda and Sylvander correspondence. It was begun in simple sport; they are already at their fifth or sixth exchange, when Clarinda writes: "It is really curious so much fun passing between two persons who saw each other only once;" but it is hardly safe for a man and woman in the flower of their years to write almost daily, and sometimes in terms too ambiguous, sometimes in terms too plain, and generally in terms too warm, for mere acquaintance. The exercise partakes a little of the nature of battering, and danger may be apprehended when next they meet. It is difficult to give any account of this remarkable correspondence; it is too far away from us, and perhaps, not yet far enough, in point of time and manner; the imagination is baffled by these stilted literary utterances, warming, in bravura passages, into downright truculent nonsense. Clarinda has one famous sentence in which she bids Sylvander connect the thought of his mistress with the changing phases of the year; it was enthusiastically admired by the swain, but on the modern mind produces mild amazement and alarm. "Oh, Clarinda," writes Burns, "shall we not meet in a state—some yet unknown state—of being, where the lavish hand of Plenty shall minister to the highest wish of Benevolence, and where the chill north wind of Prudence shall never blow over the flowery field of Enjoyment?" The design may be that of an Old Hawk, but the style is more suggestive of a Bird of Paradise. It is sometimes hard to fancy they are not gravely making fun of each other as they write. Religion, poetry, love, and charming sensibility, are the current topics. "I am delighted, charming Clarinda, with your honest enthusiasm for religion," writes Burns; and the pair entertained a fiction that this was their "favourite subject." "This is Sunday," writes the lady, "and not a word on our favourite subject. O fy 'divine Clarinda!'" I suspect, although quite unconsciously on the part of the lady, who was bent on his redemption, they but used the favourite subject as a stalking-horse. In the meantime, the sportive acquaintance was ripening steadily into a genuine passion. Visits took place, and then became frequent. Clarinda's friends were hurt and suspicious; her clergyman interfered; she herself had smart attacks of conscience, but her heart had gone from her control; it was altogether his, and she "counted all things but loss—heaven excepted—that she might win and keep him." Burns himself was transported while in her neighbourhood, but his transports somewhat rapidly declined during an absence. I am tempted to imagine that, womanlike, he took on the colour of his mistress's feeling; that he could not but heat himself at the fire of her unaffected passion; but that, like one who should leave the hearth upon a winter's night, his temperature soon fell when he was out of sight, and in a word, though he could share the symptoms, that he had never shared the disease. At the same time, amid the fustian of the letters there are forcible and true expressions, and the love verses that he wrote upon Clarinda are among the most moving in the language.

We are approaching the solution. In mid-winter, Jean, once more in the family way, was turned out of doors by her family; and Burns had her received and cared for in the house of a friend. For he remained to the last imperfect in his character of Don Juan, and lacked the sinister courage to desert his victim. About the middle of February (1788), he had to tear himself from his Clarinda and make a journey into the south-west on business. Clarinda gave him two shirts for his little son. They were daily to meet in prayer at an appointed hour. Burns, too late for the post at Glasgow, sent her a letter by parcel that she might not have to wait. Clarinda on her part writes, this time with a beautiful simplicity: "I think the streets look deserted-like since Monday; and there's a certain insipidity in good kind folks I once enjoyed not a little. Miss Wardrobe supped here on Monday. She once named you, which kept me from falling asleep. I drank your health in a glass of ale—as the lasses do at Hallowe'en—'in to mysel'.'" Arrived at Mauchline, Burns installed Jean Armour in a lodging, and prevailed on Mrs. Armour to promise her help and countenance in the approaching confinement. This was kind at least; but hear his expressions: "I have taken her a room; I have taken her to my arms; I have given her a mahogany bed; I have given her a guinea. . . . I swore her privately and solemnly never to attempt any claim on me as a husband, even though anybody should persuade her she had such a claim—which she has not, neither during my life nor after my death. She did all this like a good girl." And then he took advantage of the situation. To Clarinda he wrote: "I this morning called for a certain woman. I am disgusted with her; I cannot endure her;" and he accused her of "tasteless insipidity, vulgarity of soul, and mercenary fawning." This was already in March; by the thirteenth of that month he was back in Edinburgh. On the 17th, he wrote to Clarinda: "Your hopes, your fears, your cares, my love, are mine; so don't mind them. I will take you in my hand through the dreary wilds of this world, and scare away the ravening bird or beast that would annoy you." Again, on the 21st: "Will you open, with satisfaction and delight, a letter from a man who loves you, who has loved you, and who will love you, to death, through death, and for ever. . . . How rich am I to have such a treasure as you! . . . 'The Lord God knoweth,' and, perhaps, 'Israel he shall know,' my love and your merit. Adieu, Clarinda! I am going to remember you in my prayers." By the 7th of April, seventeen days later he had already decided to make Jean Armour publicly his wife.

A more astonishing stage-trick is not to be found. And yet his conduct is seen, upon a nearer examination, to be grounded both in reason and in kindness. He was now about to embark on a solid worldly career; he had taken a farm; the affair with Clarinda, however gratifying to his heart, was too contingent to offer any great consolation to a man like Burns, to whom marriage must have seemed the very dawn of hope and self-respect. This is to regard the question from its lowest aspect; but there is no doubt that he entered on this new period of his life with a sincere determination to do right. He had just helped his brother with a loan of a hundred and eighty pounds; should he do nothing for the poor girl whom he had ruined? It was true he could not do as he did without brutally wounding Clarinda; that was the punishment of his bygone fault; he was, as he truly says, "damned with a choice only of different species of error and misconduct." To be professional Don Juan, to accept the provocation of any lively lass upon the village green, may thus lead a man through a series of detestable words and actions, and land him at last in an undesired and most unsuitable union for life. If he had been strong enough to refrain or bad enough to persevere in evil; if he had only not been Don Juan at all, or been Don Juan altogether, there had been some possible road for him throughout this troublesome world; but a man, alas! who is equally at the call of his worse and better instincts, stands among changing events without foundation or resource. [71]

Downward Course.

It may be questionable whether any marriage could have tamed Burns; but it is at least certain that there was no hope for him in the marriage he contracted. He did right, but then he had done wrong before; it was, as I said, one of those relations in life which it seems equally wrong to break or to perpetuate. He neither loved nor respected his wife. "God knows," he writes, "my choice was as random as blind man's buff." He consoles himself by the thought that he has acted kindly to her; that she "has the most sacred enthusiasm of attachment to him;" that she has a good figure; that she has a "wood-note wild," "her voice rising with ease to B natural," no less. The effect on the reader is one of unmingled pity for both parties concerned. This was not the wife who (in his own words) could "enter into his favourite studies or relish his favourite authors;" this was not even a wife, after the affair of the marriage lines, in whom a husband could joy to place his trust. Let her manage a farm with sense, let her voice rise to B natural all day long, she would still be a peasant to her lettered lord, and an object of pity rather than of equal affection. She could now be faithful, she could now be forgiving, she could now be generous even to a pathetic and touching degree; but coming from one who was unloved, and who had scarce shown herself worthy of the sentiment, these were all virtues thrown away, which could neither change her husband's heart nor affect the inherent destiny of their relation. From the outset, it was a marriage that had no root in nature; and we find him, ere long, lyrically regretting Highland Mary, renewing correspondence with Clarinda in the warmest language, on doubtful terms with Mrs. Riddel, and on terms unfortunately beyond any question with Anne Park.

Alas! this was not the only ill circumstance in his future. He had been idle for some eighteen months, superintending his new edition, hanging on to settle with the publisher, travelling in the Highlands with Willie Nichol, or philandering with Mrs. M'Lehose; and in this period the radical part of the man had suffered irremediable hurt. He had lost his habits of industry, and formed the habit of pleasure. Apologetical biographers assure us of the contrary; but from the first, he saw and recognised the danger for himself; his mind, he writes, is "enervated to an alarming degree" by idleness and dissipation; and again, "my mind has been vitiated with idleness." It never fairly recovered. To business he could bring the required diligence and attention without difficulty; but he was thenceforward incapable, except in rare instances, of that superior effort of concentration which is required for serious literary work. He may be said, indeed, to have worked no more, and only amused himself with letters. The man who had written a volume of masterpieces in six months, during the remainder of his life rarely found courage for any more sustained effort than a song. And the nature of the songs is itself characteristic of these idle later years; for they are often as polished and elaborate as his earlier works were frank, and headlong, and colloquial; and this sort of verbal elaboration in short flights is, for a man of literary turn, simply the most agreeable of pastimes. The change in manner coincides exactly with the Edinburgh visit. In 1786 he had written the Address to a Louse, which may be taken as an extreme instance of the first manner; and already, in 1787, we come upon the rosebud pieces to Miss Cruikshank, which are extreme examples of the second. The change was, therefore, the direct and very natural consequence of his great change in life; but it is not the less typical of his loss of moral courage that he should have given up all larger ventures, nor the less melancholy that a man who first attacked literature with a hand that seemed capable of moving mountains, should have spent his later years in whittling cherry-stones.

Meanwhile, the farm did not prosper; he had to join to it the salary of an exciseman; at last he had to give it up, and rely altogether on the latter resource. He was an active officer; and, though he sometimes tempered severity with mercy, we have local testimony oddly representing the public feeling of the period, that, while "in everything else he was a perfect gentleman, when he met with anything seizable he was no better than any other gauger."

There is but one manifestation of the man in these last years which need delay us: and that was the sudden interest in politics which arose from his sympathy with the great French Revolution. His only political feeling had been hitherto a sentimental Jacobitism, not more or less respectable than that of Scott, Aytoun, and the rest of what George Borrow has nicknamed the "Charlie over the water" Scotchmen. It was a sentiment almost entirely literary and picturesque in its origin, built on ballads and the adventures of the Young Chevalier; and in Burns it is the more excusable, because he lay out of the way of active politics in his youth. With the great French Revolution, something living, practical, and feasible appeared to him for the first time in this realm of human action. The young ploughman who had desired so earnestly to rise, now reached out his sympathies to a whole nation animated with the same desire. Already in 1788 we find the old Jacobitism hand in hand with the new popular doctrine, when, in a letter of indignation against the zeal of a Whig clergyman, he writes: "I daresay the American Congress in 1776 will be allowed to be as able and as enlightened as the English Convention was in 1688; and that their posterity will celebrate the centenary of their deliverance from us, as duly and sincerely as we do ours from the oppressive measures of the wrong-headed house of Stuart." As time wore on, his sentiments grew more pronounced and even violent; but there was a basis of sense and generous feeling to his hottest excess. What he asked was a fair chance for the individual in life; an open road to success and distinction for all classes of men. It was in the same spirit that he had helped to found a public library in the parish where his farm was situated, and that he sang his fervent snatches against tyranny and tyrants. Witness, were it alone, this verse:—

> "Here's freedom to him that wad read,
>
> Here's freedom to him that wad write;
>
> There's nane ever feared that the truth should be heard
>
> But them wham the truth wad indite."

Yet his enthusiasm for the cause was scarce guided by wisdom. Many stories are preserved of the bitter and unwise words he used in country coteries; how he proposed Washington's health as an amendment to Pitt's, gave as a toast "the last verse of the last chapter of Kings," and celebrated Dumouriez in a doggrel impromptu full of ridicule and hate. Now his sympathies would inspire him with Scots, wha hae; now involve him in a drunken broil with a loyal officer, and consequent apologies and explanations, hard to offer for a man of Burns's stomach. Nor was this the front of his offending. On February 27, 1792, he took part in the capture of an armed smuggler, bought at the subsequent sale four carronades, and despatched them with a letter to the French Assembly. Letter and guns were stopped at Dover by the English officials; there was trouble for Burns with his superiors; he was reminded firmly, however delicately, that, as a paid official, it was his duty to obey and to be silent; and all the blood of this poor, proud, and falling man must have rushed to his head at the humiliation. His letter to Mr. Erskine, subsequently Earl of Mar, testifies, in its turgid, turbulent phrases, to a perfect passion of alarmed self-respect and vanity. He had been muzzled, and muzzled, when all was said, by his paltry salary as an exciseman; alas! had he not a family to keep? Already, he wrote, he looked forward to some such judgment from a hackney scribbler as this: "Burns, notwithstanding the fanfaronnade of independence to be found in his works, and after having been held forth to view and to public estimation as a man of some genius, yet, quite destitute of resources within himself to support his borrowed dignity, he dwindled into a paltry exciseman, and shrunk out the rest of his insignificant existence in the meanest of pursuits, and among the vilest of mankind." And then on he goes, in a style of rhodomontade, but filled with living indignation, to declare his right to a political opinion, and his willingness to shed his blood for the political birthright of his sons. Poor, perturbed spirit! he was indeed exercised in vain; those who share and those who differ from his sentiments about the Revolution, alike understand and sympathise with him in this painful strait; for poetry and human manhood are lasting like the race, and politics, which are but a wrongful striving after right, pass and change from year to year and age to age. The Twa Dogs has already outlasted the constitution of Siéyès and the policy of the Whigs; and Burns is better known among English-speaking races than either Pitt or Fox.

Meanwhile, whether as a man, a husband, or a poet, his steps led downward. He knew, knew bitterly, that the best was out of him; he refused to make another volume, for he felt that it would be a disappointment; he grew petulantly alive to criticism, unless he was sure it reached him from a friend. For his songs, he would take nothing; they were all that he could do; the proposed Scotch play, the proposed series of Scotch tales in verse, all had gone to water; and in a fling of pain and disappointment, which is surely noble with the nobility of a viking, he would rather stoop to borrow than to accept money for these last and inadequate efforts of his muse. And this desperate abnegation rises at times near to the height of madness; as when he pretended that he had not written, but only found and published, his immortal Auld Lang Syne. In the same spirit he became more scrupulous as an artist; he was doing so little, he would fain do that little well; and about two months before his death, he asked Thomson to send back all his manuscripts for revisal, saying that he would rather write five songs to his taste than twice that number otherwise. The battle of his life was lost; in forlorn efforts to do well, in desperate submissions to evil, the last years flew by. His temper is dark and explosive, launching epigrams, quarrelling with his friends, jealous of young puppy officers. He tries to be a good father; he boasts himself a libertine. Sick, sad, and jaded, he can refuse no occasion of temporary pleasure, no opportunity to shine; and he who had once refused the invitations of lords and ladies is now whistled to the inn by any curious stranger. His death (July 21, 1796), in his thirty-seventh year, was indeed a kindly dispensation. It is the fashion to say he died of drink; many a man has drunk more and yet lived with reputation, and reached a good age. That drink and debauchery helped to destroy his constitution, and were the means of his unconscious suicide, is doubtless true; but he had failed in life, had lost his power of work, and was already married to the poor, unworthy, patient Jean, before he had shown his inclination to convivial nights, or at least before that inclination had become dangerous either to his health or his self-respect. He had trifled with life, and must pay the penalty. He had chosen to be Don Juan, he had grasped at temporary pleasures, and substantial happiness and solid industry had passed him by. He died of being Robert Burns, and there is no levity in such a statement of the case; for shall we not, one and all, deserve a similar epitaph?

Works.

The somewhat cruel necessity which has lain upon me throughout this paper only to touch upon those points in the life of Burns where correction or amplification seemed desirable, leaves me little opportunity to speak of the works which have made his name so famous. Yet, even here, a few observations seem necessary.

At the time when the poet made his appearance and great first success, his work was remarkable in two ways. For, first, in an age when poetry had become abstract and conventional, instead of continuing to deal with shepherds, thunderstorms, and personifications, he dealt with the actual circumstances of his life, however matter-of-fact and sordid these might be. And, second, in a time when English versification was particularly stiff, lame, and feeble, and words were used with ultra-academical timidity, he wrote verses that were easy, racy, graphic, and forcible, and used language with absolute tact and courage as it seemed most fit to give a clear impression. If you take even those English authors whom we know Burns to have most admired and studied, you will see at once that he owed them nothing but a warning. Take Shenstone, for instance, and watch that elegant author as he tries to grapple with the facts of life. He has a description, I remember, of a gentleman engaged in sliding or walking on thin ice, which is a little miracle of incompetence. You see my memory fails me, and I positively cannot recollect whether his hero was sliding or walking; as though a writer should describe a skirmish, and the reader, at the end, be still uncertain whether it were a charge of cavalry or a slow and stubborn advance of foot. There could be no such ambiguity in Burns; his work is at the opposite pole from such indefinite and stammering performances; and a whole lifetime passed in the study of Shenstone would only lead a man further and further from writing the Address to a Louse. Yet Burns, like most great artists, proceeded from a school and continued a tradition; only the school and tradition were Scotch, and not English. While the English language was becoming daily more pedantic and inflexible, and English letters more colourless and slack, there was another dialect in the sister country, and a different school of poetry tracing its descent, through King James I., from Chaucer. The dialect alone accounts for much; for it was then written colloquially, which kept it fresh and supple; and, although not shaped for heroic flights, it was a direct and vivid medium for all that had to do with social life. Hence, whenever Scotch poets left their laborious imitations of bad English verses, and fell back on their own dialect, their style would kindle, and they would write of their convivial and somewhat gross existences with pith and point. In Ramsay, and far more in the poor lad Fergusson, there was mettle, humour, literary courage, and a power of saying what they wished to say definitely and brightly, which in the latter case should have justified great anticipations. Had Burns died at the same age as Fergusson, he would have left us literally nothing worth remark. To Ramsay and to Fergusson, then, he was indebted in a very uncommon degree, not only following their tradition and using their measures, but directly and avowedly imitating their pieces. The same tendency to borrow a hint, to work on some one else's foundation, is notable in Burns from first to last, in the period of song-writing as well as in that of the early poems; and strikes one oddly in a man of such deep originality, who left so strong a print on all he touched, and whose work is so greatly distinguished by that character of "inevitability" which Wordsworth denied to Goethe.

When we remember Burns's obligations to his predecessors, we must never forget his immense advances on them. They had already "discovered" nature; but Burns discovered poetry—a higher and more intense way of thinking of the things that go to make up nature, a higher and more ideal key of words in which to speak of them. Ramsay and Fergusson excelled at making a popular—or shall we say vulgar?—sort of society verses, comical and prosaic, written, you would say, in taverns while a supper party waited for its laureate's word; but on the appearance of Burns, this coarse and laughing literature was touched to finer issues, and learned gravity of thought and natural pathos.

What he had gained from his predecessors was a direct, speaking style, and to walk on his own feet instead of on academical stilts. There was never a man of letters with more absolute command of his means; and we may say of him, without excess, that his style was his slave. Hence that energy of epithet, so concise and telling, that a foreigner is tempted to explain it by some special richness or aptitude in the dialect he wrote. Hence that Homeric justice and completeness of description which gives us the very physiognomy of nature, in body and detail, as nature is. Hence, too, the unbroken literary quality of his best pieces, which keeps him from any slip into the weariful trade of word-painting, and presents everything, as everything should be presented by the art of words, in a clear, continuous medium of thought. Principal Shairp, for instance, gives us a paraphrase of one tough verse of the original; and for those who know the Greek poets only by paraphrase, this has the very quality they are accustomed to look for and admire in Greek. The contemporaries of Burns were surprised that he should visit so many celebrated mountains and waterfalls, and not seize the opportunity to make a poem. Indeed, it is not for those who have a true command of the art of words, but for peddling, professional amateurs, that these pointed occasions are most useful and inspiring. As those who speak French imperfectly are glad to dwell on any topic they may have talked upon or heard others talk upon before, because they know appropriate words for it in French, so the dabbler in verse rejoices to behold a waterfall, because he has learned the sentiment and knows appropriate words for it in poetry. But the dialect of Burns was fitted to deal with any subject; and whether it was a stormy night, a shepherd's collie, a sheep struggling in the snow, the conduct of cowardly soldiers in the field, the gait and cogitations of a drunken man, or only a village cockcrow in the morning, he could find language to give it freshness, body, and relief. He was always ready to borrow the hint of a design, as though he had a difficulty in commencing—a difficulty, let us say, in choosing a subject out of a world which seemed all equally living and significant to him; but once he had the subject chosen, he could cope with nature single-handed, and make every stroke a triumph. Again, his absolute mastery in his art enabled him to express each and all of his different humours, and to pass smoothly and congruously from one to another. Many men invent a dialect for only one side of their nature—perhaps their pathos or their humour, or the delicacy of their senses—and, for lack of a medium, leave all the others unexpressed. You meet such an one, and find him in conversation full of thought, feeling, and experience, which he has lacked the art to employ in his writings. But Burns was not thus hampered in the practice of the literary art; he could throw the whole weight of his nature into his work, and impregnate it from end to end. If Doctor Johnson, that stilted and accomplished stylist, had lacked the sacred Boswell, what should we have known of him? and how should we have delighted in his acquaintance as we do? Those who spoke with Burns tell us how much we have lost who did not. But I think they exaggerate their privilege: I think we have the whole Burns in our possession set forth in his consummate verses.

It was by his style, and not by his matter, that he affected Wordsworth and the world. There is, indeed, only one merit worth considering in a man of letters—that he should write well; and only one damning fault—that he should write ill. We are little the better for the reflections of the sailor's parrot in the story. And so, if Burns helped to change the course of literary history, it was by his frank, direct, and masterly utterance, and not by his homely choice of subjects. That was imposed upon him, not chosen upon a principle. He wrote from his own experience, because it was his nature so to do, and the tradition of the school from which he proceeded was fortunately not opposed to homely subjects. But to these homely subjects he communicated the rich commentary of his nature; they were all steeped in Burns; and they interest us not in themselves, but because they have been passed through the spirit of so genuine and vigorous a man. Such is the stamp of living literature; and there was never any more alive than that of Burns.

What a gust of sympathy there is in him sometimes flowing out in byways hitherto unused, upon mice, and flowers, and the devil himself; sometimes speaking plainly between human hearts; sometimes ringing out in exultation like a peal of bells! When we compare the Farmer's Salutation to his Auld Mare Maggie, with the clever and inhumane production of half a century earlier, The Auld Man's Mare's dead, we see in a nutshell the spirit of the change introduced by Burns. And as to its manner, who that has read it can forget how the collie, Luath, in the Twa Dogs, describes and enters into the merry-making in the cottage?

> "The luntin' pipe an' sneeshin' mill,
>
> Are handed round wi' richt guid will;
>
> The canty auld folks crackin' crouse,
>
> The young anes rantin' through the house—
>
> My heart has been sae fain to see them
>
> That I for joy hae barkit wi' them."

It was this ardent power of sympathy that was fatal to so many women, and, through Jean Armour, to himself at last. His humour comes from him in a stream so deep and easy that I will venture to call him the best of humorous poets. He turns about in the midst to utter a noble sentiment or a trenchant remark on human life, and the style changes and rises to the occasion. I think it is Principal Shairp who says, happily, that Burns would have been no Scotchman if he had not loved to moralise; neither, may we add, would he have been his father's son; but (what is worthy of note) his moralisings are to a large extent the moral of his own career. He was among the least impersonal of artists. Except in the Jolly Beggars, he shows no gleam of dramatic instinct. Mr. Carlyle has complained that Tam o' Shanter is, from the absence of this quality, only a picturesque and external piece of work; and I may add that in the Twa Dogs it is precisely in the infringement of dramatic propriety that a great deal of the humour of the speeches depends for its existence and effect. Indeed, Burns was so full of his identity that it breaks forth on every page; and there is scarce an appropriate remark either in praise or blame of his own conduct, but he has put it himself into verse. Alas! for the tenor of these remarks! They are, indeed, his own pitiful apology for such a marred existence and talents so misused and stunted; and they seem to prove for ever how small a part is played by reason in the conduct of man's affairs. Here was one, at least, who with unfailing judgment predicted his own fate; yet his knowledge could not avail him, and with open eyes he must fulfil his tragic destiny. Ten years before the end he had written his epitaph; and neither subsequent events, nor the critical eyes of posterity, have shown us a word in it to alter. And, lastly, has he not put in for himself the last unanswerable plea?—

> "Then gently scan your brother man,
>
> Still gentler sister woman;
>
> Though they may gang a kennin wrang,
>
> To step aside is human:
>
> One point must still be greatly dark—"

One? Alas! I fear every man and woman of us is "greatly dark" to all their neighbours, from the day of birth until death removes them, in their greatest virtues as well as in their saddest faults; and we, who have been trying to read the character of Burns, may take home the lesson and be gentle in our thoughts.

WALT WHITMAN.

Of late years the name of Walt Whitman has been a good deal bandied about in books and magazines. It has become familiar both in good and ill repute. His works have been largely bespattered with praise by his admirers, and cruelly mauled and mangled by irreverent enemies. Now, whether his poetry is good or bad as poetry, is a matter that may admit of a difference of opinion without alienating those who differ. We could not keep the peace with a man who should put forward claims to taste and yet depreciate the choruses in Samson Agonistes; but, I think, we may shake hands with one who sees no more in Walt Whitman's volume, from a literary point of view, than a farrago of incompetent essays in a wrong direction. That may not be at all our own opinion. We may think that, when a work contains many unforgettable phrases, it cannot be altogether devoid of literary merit. We may even see passages of a high poetry here and there among its eccentric contents. But when all is said, Walt Whitman is neither a Milton nor a Shakespeare; to appreciate his works is not a condition necessary to salvation; and I would not disinherit a son upon the question, nor even think much the worse of a critic, for I should always have an idea what he meant.

What Whitman has to say is another affair from how he says it. It is not possible to acquit any one of defective intelligence, or else stiff prejudice, who is not interested by Whitman's matter and the spirit it represents. Not as a poet, but as what we must call (for lack of a more exact expression) a prophet, he occupies a curious and prominent position. Whether he may greatly influence the future or not, he is a notable symptom of the present. As a sign of the times, it would be hard to find his parallel. I should hazard a large wager, for instance, that he was not unacquainted with the works of Herbert Spencer; and yet where, in all the history books, shall we lay our hands on two more incongruous contemporaries? Mr. Spencer so decorous—I had almost said, so dandy—in dissent; and Whitman, like a large shaggy dog, just unchained, scouring the beaches of the world and baying at the moon. And when was an echo more curiously like a satire, than when Mr. Spencer found his Synthetic Philosophy reverberated from the other shores of the Atlantic in the "barbaric yawp" of Whitman?

I.

Whitman, it cannot be too soon explained, writes up to a system. He was a theoriser about society before he was a poet. He first perceived something wanting, and then sat down squarely to supply the want. The reader, running over his works, will find that he takes nearly as much pleasure in critically expounding his theory of poetry as in making poems. This is as far as it can be from the case of the spontaneous village minstrel dear to elegy, who has no theory whatever, although sometimes he may have fully as much poetry as Whitman. The whole of Whitman's work is deliberate and preconceived. A man born into a society comparatively new, full of conflicting elements and interests, could not fail, if he had any thoughts at all, to reflect upon the tendencies around him. He saw much good and evil on all sides, not yet settled down into some more or less unjust compromise as in older nations, but still in the act of settlement. And he could not but wonder what it would turn out; whether the compromise would be very just or very much the reverse, and give great or little scope for healthy human energies. From idle wonder to active speculation is but a step; and he seems to have been early struck with the inefficacy of literature and its extreme unsuitability to the conditions. What he calls "Feudal Literature" could have little living action on the tumult of American democracy; what he calls the "Literature of Wo," meaning the whole tribe of Werther and Byron, could have no action for good in any time or place. Both propositions, if art had none but a direct moral influence, would be true enough; and as this seems to be Whitman's view, they were true enough for him. He conceived the idea of a Literature which was to inhere in the life of the present; which was to be, first, human, and next, American; which was to be brave and cheerful as per contract; to give culture in a popular and poetical presentment; and, in so doing, catch and stereotype some democratic ideal of humanity which should be equally natural to all grades of wealth and education, and suited, in one of his favourite phrases, to "the average man." To the formation of some such literature as this his poems are to be regarded as so many contributions, one sometimes explaining, sometimes superseding, the other: and the whole together not so much a finished work as a body of suggestive hints. He does not profess to have built the castle, but he pretends he has traced the lines of the foundation. He has not made the poetry, but he flatters himself he has done something towards making the poets.

His notion of the poetic function is ambitious, and coincides roughly with what Schopenhauer has laid down as the province of the metaphysician. The poet is to gather together for men, and set in order, the materials of their existence. He is "The Answerer;" he is to find some way of speaking about life that shall satisfy, if only for the moment, man's enduring astonishment at his own position. And besides having an answer ready, it is he who shall provoke the question. He must shake people out of their indifference, and force them to make some election in this world, instead of sliding dully forward in a dream. Life is a business we are all apt to mismanage; either living recklessly from day to day, or suffering ourselves to be gulled out of our moments by the inanities of custom. We should despise a man who gave as little activity and forethought to the conduct of any other business. But in this, which is the one thing of all others, since it contains them all, we cannot see the forest for the trees. One brief impression obliterates another. There is something stupefying in the recurrence of unimportant things. And it is only on rare provocations that we can rise to take an outlook beyond daily concerns, and comprehend the narrow limits and great possibilities of our existence. It is the duty of the poet to induce such moments of clear sight. He is the declared enemy of all living by reflex action, of all that is done betwixt sleep and waking, of all the pleasureless pleasurings and imaginary duties in which we coin away our hearts and fritter invaluable years. He has to electrify his readers into an instant unflagging activity, founded on a wide and eager observation of the world, and make them direct their ways by a superior prudence, which has little or nothing in common with the maxims of the copy-book. That many of us lead such lives as they would heartily disown after two hours' serious reflection on the subject is, I am afraid, a true, and, I am sure, a very galling thought. The Enchanted Ground of dead-alive respectability is next, upon the map, to the Beulah of considerate virtue. But there they all slumber and take their rest in the middle of God's beautiful and wonderful universe; the drowsy heads have nodded together in the same position since first their fathers fell asleep; and not even the sound of the last trumpet can wake them to a single active thought.

The poet has a hard task before him to stir up such fellows to a sense of their own and other people's principles in life.

And it happens that literature is, in some ways, but an indifferent means to such an end. Language is but a poor bull's-eye lantern wherewith to show off the vast cathedral of the world; and yet a particular thing once said in words is so definite and memorable, that it makes us forget the absence of the many which remain unexpressed; like a bright window in a distant view, which dazzles and confuses our sight of its surroundings. There are not words enough in all Shakespeare to express the merest fraction of a man's experience in an hour. The speed of the eyesight and the hearing, and the continual industry of the mind, produce, in ten minutes, what it would require a laborious volume to shadow forth by comparisons and roundabout approaches. If verbal logic were sufficient, life would be as plain sailing as a piece of Euclid. But, as a matter of fact, we make a travesty of the simplest process of thought when we put it into words for the words are all coloured and forsworn, apply inaccurately, and bring with them, from former uses ideas of praise and blame that have nothing to do with the question in hand. So we must always see to it nearly, that we judge by the realities of life and not by the partial terms that represent them in man's speech; and at times of choice, we must leave words upon one side, and act upon those brute convictions, unexpressed and perhaps inexpressible, which cannot be flourished in an argument, but which are truly the sum and fruit of our experience. Words are for communication, not for judgment. This is what every thoughtful man knows for himself, for only fools and silly schoolmasters push definitions over far into the domain of conduct; and the majority of women, not learned in these scholastic refinements, live all-of-a-piece and unconsciously, as a tree grows, without caring to put a name upon their acts or motives. Hence, a new difficulty for Whitman's scrupulous and argumentative poet; he must do more than waken up the sleepers to his words; he must persuade them to look over the book and at life with their own eyes.

This side of truth is very present to Whitman; it is this that he means when he tells us that "To glance with an eye confounds the learning of all times." But he is not unready. He is never weary of descanting on the undebatable conviction that is forced upon our minds by the presence of other men, of animals, or of inanimate things. To glance with an eye, were it only at a chair or a park railing, is by far a more persuasive process, and brings us to a far more exact conclusion, than to read the works of all the logicians extant. If both, by a large allowance, may be said to end in certainty, the certainty in the one case transcends the other to an incalculable degree. If people see a lion, they run away; if they only apprehend a deduction, they keep wandering around in an experimental humour. Now, how is the poet to convince like nature, and not like books? Is there no actual piece of nature that he can show the man to his face, as he might show him a tree if they were walking together? Yes, there is one: the man's own thoughts. In fact, if the poet is to speak efficaciously, he must say what is already in his hearer's mind. That, alone, the hearer will believe; that, alone, he will be able to apply intelligently to the facts of life. Any conviction, even if it be a whole system or a whole religion, must pass into the condition of commonplace, or postulate, before it becomes fully operative. Strange excursions and high-flying theories may interest, but they cannot rule behaviour. Our faith is not the highest truth that we perceive, but the highest that we have been able to assimilate into the very texture and method of our thinking. It is not, therefore, by flashing before a man's eyes the weapons of dialectic; it is not by induction, deduction, or construction; it is not by forcing him on from one stage of reasoning to another, that the man will be effectually renewed. He cannot be made to believe anything; but he can be made to see that he has always believed it. And this is the practical canon. It is when the reader cries, "Oh, I know!" and is, perhaps, half irritated to see how nearly the author has forestalled his own thoughts, that he is on the way to what is called in theology a Saving Faith.

Here we have the key to Whitman's attitude. To give a certain unity of ideal to the average population of America—to gather their activities about some conception of humanity that shall be central and normal, if only for the moment—the poet must portray that population as it is. Like human law, human poetry is simply declaratory. If any ideal is possible, it must be already in the thoughts of the people; and, by the same reason, in the thoughts of the poet, who is one of them. And hence Whitman's own formula: "The poet is individual—he is complete in himself: the others are as good as he; only he sees it, and they do not." To show them how good they are, the poet must study his fellow-countrymen and himself somewhat like a traveller on the hunt for his book of travels. There is a sense, of course, in which all true books are books of travel; and all genuine poets must run their risk of being charged with the traveller's exaggeration; for to whom are such books more surprising than to those whose own life is faithfully and smartly pictured? But this danger is all upon one side; and you may judiciously flatter the portrait without any likelihood of the sitter's disowning it for a faithful likeness. And so Whitman has reasoned: that by drawing at first hand from himself and his neighbours, accepting without shame the inconsistencies and brutalities that go to make up man, and yet treating the whole in a high, magnanimous spirit, he would make sure of belief, and at the same time encourage people forward by the means of praise.

II.

We are accustomed nowadays to a great deal of puling over the circumstances in which we are placed. The great refinement of many poetical gentlemen has rendered them practically unfit for the jostling and ugliness of life, and they record their unfitness at considerable length. The bold and awful poetry of Job's complaint produces too many flimsy imitators; for there is always something consolatory in grandeur, but the symphony transposed for the piano becomes hysterically sad. This literature of woe, as Whitman calls it, this Maladie de René, as we like to call it in Europe, is in many ways a most humiliating and sickly phenomenon. Young gentlemen with three or four hundred a year of private means look down from a pinnacle of doleful experience on all the grown and hearty men who have dared to say a good word for life since the beginning of the world. There is no prophet but the melancholy Jacques, and the blue devils dance on all our literary wires.

It would be a poor service to spread culture, if this be its result, among the comparatively innocent and cheerful ranks of men. When our little poets have to be sent to look at the ploughman and learn wisdom, we must be careful how we tamper with our ploughmen. Where a man in not the best of circumstances preserves composure of mind, and relishes ale and tobacco, and his wife and children, in the intervals of dull and unremunerative labour; where a man in this predicament can afford a lesson by the way to what are called his intellectual superiors, there is plainly something to be lost, as well as something to be gained, by teaching him to think differently. It is better to leave him as he is than to teach him whining. It is better that he should go without the cheerful lights of culture, if cheerless doubt and paralysing sentimentalism are to be the consequence. Let us, by all means, fight against that hide-bound stolidity of sensation and sluggishness of mind which blurs and decolorises for poor natures the wonderful pageant of consciousness; let us teach people, as much as we can, to enjoy, and they will learn for themselves to sympathise; but let us see to it, above all, that we give these lessons in a brave, vivacious note, and build the man up in courage while we demolish its substitute, indifference.

Whitman is alive to all this. He sees that, if the poet is to be of any help, he must testify to the livableness of life. His poems, he tells us, are to be "hymns of the praise of things." They are to make for a certain high joy in living, or what he calls himself "a brave delight fit for freedom's athletes." And he has had no difficulty in introducing his optimism: it fitted readily enough with his system; for the average man is truly a courageous person and truly fond of living. One of Whitman's remarks upon this head is worth quotation, as he is there perfectly successful, and does precisely what he designs to do throughout: Takes ordinary and even commonplace circumstances; throws them out, by a happy turn of thinking, into significance and something like beauty; and tacks a hopeful moral lesson to the end.

"The passionate tenacity of hunters, woodmen, early risers, cultivators of gardens and orchards and fields, he says, the love of healthy women for the manly form, seafaring persons, drivers of horses, the passion for light and the open air,—all is an old unvaried sign of the unfailing perception of beauty, and of a residence of the poetic in outdoor people."

There seems to me something truly original in this choice of trite examples. You will remark how adroitly Whitman begins, hunters and woodmen being confessedly romantic. And one thing more. If he had said

75

"the love of healthy men for the female form," he would have said almost a silliness; for the thing has never been dissembled out of delicacy, and is so obvious as to be a public nuisance. But by reversing it, he tells us something not unlike news; something that sounds quite freshly in words; and, if the reader be a man, gives him a moment of great self-satisfaction and spiritual aggrandisement. In many different authors you may find passages more remarkable for grammar, but few of a more ingenious turn, and none that could be more to the point in our connection. The tenacity of many ordinary people in ordinary pursuits is a sort of standing challenge to everybody else. If one man can grow absorbed in delving his garden, others may grow absorbed and happy over something else. Not to be upsides in this with any groom or gardener, is to be very meanly organised. A man should be ashamed to take his food if he has not alchemy enough in his stomach to turn some of it into intense and enjoyable occupation.

Whitman tries to reinforce this cheerfulness by keeping up a sort of outdoor atmosphere of sentiment. His book, he tells us, should be read "among the cooling influences of external nature;" and this recommendation, like that other famous one which Hawthorne prefixed to his collected tales, is in itself a character of the work. Every one who has been upon a walking or a boating tour, living in the open air, with the body in constant exercise and the mind in fallow, knows true ease and quiet. The irritating action of the brain is set at rest; we think in a plain, unfeverish temper; little things seem big enough, and great things no longer portentous; and the world is smilingly accepted as it is. This is the spirit that Whitman inculcates and parades. He thinks very ill of the atmosphere of parlours or libraries. Wisdom keeps school outdoors. And he has the art to recommend this attitude of mind by simply pluming himself upon it as a virtue; so that the reader, to keep the advantage over his author which most readers enjoy, is tricked into professing the same view. And this spirit, as it is his chief lesson, is the greatest charm of his work. Thence, in spite of an uneven and emphatic key of expression, something trenchant and straightforward, something simple and surprising, distinguishes his poems. He has sayings that come home to one like the Bible. We fall upon Whitman, after the works of so many men who write better, with a sense of relief from strain, with a sense of touching nature, as when one passes out of the flaring, noisy thoroughfares of a great city into what he himself has called, with unexcelled imaginative justice of language, "the huge and thoughtful night." And his book in consequence, whatever may be the final judgment of its merit, whatever may be its influence on the future, should be in the hands of all parents and guardians as a specific for the distressing malady of being seventeen years old. Green-sickness yields to his treatment as to a charm of magic; and the youth, after a short course of reading, ceases to carry the universe upon his shoulders.

III.

Whitman is not one of those who can be deceived by familiarity. He considers it just as wonderful that there are myriads of stars, as that one man should rise from the dead. He declares "a hair on the back of his hand just as curious as any special revelation." His whole life is to him what it was to Sir Thomas Browne, one perpetual miracle. Everything is strange, everything unaccountable, everything beautiful; from a bug to the moon, from the sight of the eyes to the appetite for food. He makes it his business to see things as if he saw them for the first time, and professes astonishment on principle. But he has no leaning towards mythology; avows his contempt for what he calls "unregenerate poetry;" and does not mean by nature

> "The smooth walks, trimmed hedges, butterflies, posies, and nightingales of the English poets, but the whole orb, with its geologic history, the Kosmos, carrying fire and snow, that rolls through the illimitable areas, light as a feather though weighing billions of tons."

Nor is this exhaustive; for in his character of idealist all impressions, all thoughts, trees and people, love and faith, astronomy, history, and religion, enter upon equal terms into his notion of the universe. He is not against religion; not, indeed, against any religion. He wishes to drag with a larger net, to make a more comprehensive synthesis, than any or than all of them put together. In feeling after the central type of man, he must embrace all eccentricities; his cosmology must subsume all cosmologies, and the feelings that gave birth to them; his statement of facts must include all religion and all irreligion, Christ and Boodha, God and the devil. The world as it is, and the whole world as it is, physical, and spiritual, and historical, with its good and bad, with its manifold inconsistencies, is what he wishes to set forth, in strong, picturesque, and popular lineaments, for the understanding of the average man. One of his favourite endeavours is to get the whole matter into a nutshell; to knock the four corners of the universe, one after another, about his readers' ears; to hurry him, in breathless phrases, hither and thither, back and forward, in time and space; to focus all this about his own momentary personality; and then, drawing the ground from under his feet, as if by some cataclysm of nature, to plunge him into the unfathomable abyss sown with enormous suns and systems, and among the inconceivable numbers and magnitudes and velocities of the heavenly bodies. So that he concludes by striking into us some sense of that disproportion of things which Shelley has illuminated by the ironical flash of these eight words: The desire of the moth for the star.

The same truth, but to what a different purpose! Whitman's moth is mightily at his ease about all the planets in heaven, and cannot think too highly of our sublunary tapers. The universe is so large that imagination flags in the effort to conceive it; but here, in the meantime, is the world under our feet, a very warm and habitable corner. "The earth, that is sufficient; I do not want the constellations any nearer," he remarks. And again: "Let your soul stand cool and composed," says he, "before a million universes." It is the language of a transcendental common sense, such as Thoreau held and sometimes uttered. But Whitman, who has a somewhat vulgar inclination for technical talk and the jargon of philosophy, is not content with a few pregnant hints; he must put the dots upon his i's; he must corroborate the songs of Apollo by some of the darkest talk of human metaphysic. He tells his disciples that they must be ready "to confront the growing arrogance of Realism." Each person is, for himself, the keystone and the occasion of this universal edifice. "Nothing, not God," he says, "is greater to one than oneself is;" a statement with an irreligious smack at the first sight; but like most startling sayings, a manifest truism on a second. He will give effect to his own character without apology; he sees "that the elementary laws never apologise." "I reckon," he adds, with quaint colloquial arrogance, "I reckon I behave no prouder than the level I plant my house by, after all." The level follows the law of its being; so, unrelentingly, will he; everything, every person, is good in his own place and way; God is the maker of all and all are in one design. For he believes in God, and that with a sort of blasphemous security. "No array of terms," quoth he, "no array of terms can say how much at peace I am about God and about death." There certainly never was a prophet who carried things with a higher hand; he gives us less a body of dogmas than a series of proclamations by the grace of God; and language, you will observe, positively fails him to express how far he stands above the highest human doubts and trepidations.

But next in order of truths to a person's sublime conviction of himself, comes the attraction of one person for another, and all that we mean by the word love:—

"The dear love of man for his comrade—the attraction of friend for friend,

Of the well-married husband and wife, of children and parents,

Of city for city and land for land."

The solitude of the most sublime idealist is broken in upon by other people's faces; he sees a look in their eyes that corresponds to something in his own heart; there comes a tone in their voices which convicts him of a startling weakness for his fellow-creatures. While he is hymning the ego and commercing with God and the universe, a woman goes below his window; and at the turn of her skirt, or the colour of her eyes, Icarus is recalled from heaven by the run. Love is so startlingly real that it takes rank upon an equal footing of reality with the consciousness of personal existence. We are as heartily persuaded of the identity of those we love as of our own identity. And so sympathy pairs with self-assertion, the two gerents of human life on earth; and Whitman's ideal man must not only be strong, free, and self-reliant in himself, but his freedom must be bounded and his strength perfected by the most intimate, eager, and long-suffering love for others. To some extent this is taking away with the left hand what has been so generously given with the right. Morality has been ceremoniously extruded from the door only to be brought in again by the window. We are told, on one page, to do as we please; and on the next we are sharply upbraided for not having done as the author pleases. We are first assured that we are the finest fellows in the world in our own right; and then it appears that we are only fine fellows in so far as we practise a most quixotic code of morals. The disciple who saw himself in clear ether a moment before is plunged down again among the fogs and complications of duty. And this is all the more overwhelming because Whitman insists not only on love between sex and sex, and between friends of the same sex, but in the field of the less intense political sympathies; and his ideal man must not only be a generous friend but a conscientious voter into the bargain.

His method somewhat lessens the difficulty. He is not, the reader will remember, to tell us how good we ought to be, but to remind us how good we are. He is to encourage us to be free and kind, by proving that we are free and kind already. He passes our corporate life under review, to show that it is upheld by the very virtues of which he makes himself the advocate. "There is no object so soft," he says somewhere in his big, plain way, "there is no object so soft but it makes a hub for the wheel'd universe." Rightly understood, it is on the softest of all objects, the sympathetic heart, that the wheel of society turns easily and securely as on a perfect axle. There is no room, of course, for doubt or discussion, about conduct, where every one is to follow the law of his being with exact compliance. Whitman hates doubt, deprecates discussion, and discourages to his utmost the craving, carping sensibilities of the conscience. We are to imitate, to use one of his absurd and happy phrases, "the satisfaction and aplomb of animals." If he preaches a sort of ranting Christianity in morals, a fit consequent to the ranting optimism of his cosmology, it is because he declares it to be the original deliverance of the human heart; or at least, for he would be honestly historical in method, of the human heart as at present Christianised. His is a morality without a prohibition; his policy is one of encouragement all round. A man must be a born hero to come up to Whitman's standard in the practice of any of the positive virtues; but of a negative virtue, such as temperance or chastity, he has so little to say, that the reader need not be surprised if he drops a word or two upon the other side. He would lay down nothing that would be a clog; he would prescribe nothing that cannot be done ruddily, in a heat. The great point is to get people under way. To the faithful Whitmanite this would be justified by the belief that God made all, and that all was good; the prophet, in this doctrine, has only to cry "Tally-ho," and mankind will break into a gallop on the road to El Dorado. Perhaps, to another class of minds, it may look like the result of the somewhat cynical reflection that you will not make a kind man out of one who is unkind by any precepts under heaven; tempered by the belief that, in natural circumstances, the large majority is well disposed. Thence it would follow, that if you can only get every one to feel more warmly and act more courageously, the balance of results will be for good.

So far, you see, the doctrine is pretty coherent as a doctrine; as a picture of man's life it is incomplete and misleading, although eminently cheerful. This he is himself the first to acknowledge; for if he is prophetic in anything, it is in his noble disregard of consistency. "Do I contradict myself?" he asks somewhere; and then pat comes the answer, the best answer ever given in print, worthy of a sage, or rather of a woman: "Very well, then, I contradict myself." with this addition, not so feminine and perhaps not altogether so satisfactory: "I am large—I contain multitudes." Life, as a matter of fact, partakes largely of the nature of tragedy. The gospel according to Whitman, even if it be not so logical, has this advantage over the gospel according to Pangloss, that it does not utterly disregard the existence of temporal evil. Whitman accepts the fact of disease and wretchedness like an honest man; and instead of trying to qualify it in the interest of his optimism, sets himself to spur people up to be helpful. He expresses a conviction, indeed, that all will be made up to the victims in the end; that "what is untried and afterward" will fail no one, not even "the old man who has lived without purpose and feels it with bitterness worse than gall." But this is not to palliate our sense of what is hard or melancholy in the present. Pangloss, smarting under one of the worst things that ever was supposed to come from America, consoled himself with the reflection that it was the price we have to pay for cochineal. And with that murderous parody, logical optimism and the praises of the best of possible words went irrevocably out of season, and have been no more heard of in the mouths of reasonable men. Whitman spares us all allusions to the cochineal; he treats evil and sorrow in a spirit almost as of welcome; as an old sea-dog might have welcomed the sight of the enemy's topsails off the Spanish Main. There, at least, he seems to say, is something obvious to be done. I do not know many better things in literature than the brief pictures,—brief and vivid like things seen by lightning,—with which he tries to stir up the world's heart upon the side of mercy. He braces us, on the one hand, with examples of heroic duty and helpfulness; on the other, he touches us with pitiful instances of people needing help. He knows how to make the heart beat at a brave story; to inflame us with just resentment over the hunted slave; to stop our mouths for shame when he tells of the drunken prostitute. For all the afflicted, all the weak, all the wicked, a good word is said in a spirit which I can only call one of ultra-Christianity; and however wild, however contradictory, it may be in parts, this at least may be said for his book, as it may be said of the Christian Gospels, that no one will read it, however respectable, but he gets a knock upon his conscience; no one however fallen, but he finds a kindly and supporting welcome.

IV.

Nor has he been content with merely blowing the trumpet for the battle of well-doing; he has given to his precepts the authority of his own brave example. Naturally a grave, believing man, with little or no sense of humour, he has succeeded as well in life as in his printed performances. The spirit that was in him has come forth most eloquently in his actions. Many who have only read his poetry have been tempted to set him down as an ass, or even as a charlatan; but I never met any one who had known him personally who did not profess a solid affection and respect for the man's character. He practises as he professes; he feels deeply that Christian love for all men, that toleration, that cheerful delight in serving others, which he often celebrates in literature with a doubtful measure of success. And perhaps, out of all his writings, the best and the most human and convincing passages are to be found in "these soil'd and creas'd little livraisons, each composed of a sheet or two of paper, folded small to carry in the pocket, and fastened with a pin," which he scribbled during the war by the bedsides of the wounded or in the excitement of great events. They are hardly literature in the formal meaning of the word; he has left his jottings for the most part as he made them; a homely detail, a word from the lips of a dying soldier, a business memorandum, the copy of a letter-short, straightforward to the point, with none of the trappings of composition; but they breathe a profound sentiment, they give us a vivid look at one of the sides of life, and they make us acquainted with a man whom it is an honour to love.

Whitman's intense Americanism, his unlimited belief in the future of These States (as, with reverential capitals, he loves to call them), made the war a period of great trial to his soul. The new virtue, Unionism, of which he is the sole inventor, seemed to have fallen into premature unpopularity. All that he loved, hoped, or hated, hung in the balance. And the game of war was not only momentous to him in its issues; it sublimated his spirit by its heroic displays, and tortured him intimately by the spectacle of its horrors. It was a theatre, it was a place of education, it was like a season of religious revival. He watched Lincoln going daily to his work; he studied and fraternised with young soldiery passing to the front; above all, he walked the hospitals, reading the Bible, distributing clean clothes, or apples, or tobacco; a patient, helpful, reverend man, full of kind speeches.

His memoranda of this period are almost bewildering to read. From one point of view they seem those of a district visitor; from another, they look like the formless jottings of an artist in the picturesque. More than one woman, on whom I tried the experiment, immediately claimed the writer for a fellow-woman. More than one literary purist might identify him as a shoddy newspaper correspondent without the necessary faculty of style. And yet the story touches home; and if you are of the weeping order of mankind, you will certainly find your eyes fill with tears, of which you have no reason to be ashamed. There is only one way to characterise a work of this order, and that is to quote. Here is a passage from a letter to a mother, unknown to Whitman, whose son died in hospital:—

"Frank, as far as I saw, had everything requisite in surgical treatment, nursing, etc. He had watches much of the time. He was so good and well-behaved, and affectionate, I myself liked him very much. I was in the habit of coming in afternoons and sitting by him, and he liked to have me—liked to put out his arm and lay his hand on my knee—would keep it so a long while. Toward the last he was more restless and flighty at night—often fancied himself with his regiment—by his talk sometimes seem'd as if his feelings were hurt by being blamed by his officers for something he was entirely innocent of—said 'I never in my life was thought capable of such a thing, and never was.' At other times he would fancy himself talking as it seem'd to children or such like, his relatives, I suppose, and giving them good advice; would talk to them a long while. All the time he was out of his head not one single bad word, or thought, or idea escaped him. It was remark'd that many a man's conversation in his senses was not half so good as Frank's delirium.

"He was perfectly willing to die—he had become very weak, and had suffer'd a good deal, and was perfectly resign'd, poor boy. I do not know his past life, but I feel as if it must have been good. At any rate what I saw of him here, under the most trying circumstances, with a painful wound, and among strangers, I can say that he behaved so brave, so composed, and so sweet and affectionate, it could not be surpassed. And now, like many other noble and good men, after serving his country as a soldier, he has yielded up his young life at the very outset in her service. Such things are gloomy—yet there is a text, 'God doeth all things well,' the meaning of which, after due time, appears to the soul.

"I thought perhaps a few words, though from a stranger, about your son, from one who was with him at the last, might be worth while, for I loved the young man, though I but saw him immediately to lose him."

It is easy enough to pick holes in the grammar of this letter, but what are we to say of its profound goodness and tenderness? It is written as though he had the mother's face before his eyes, and saw her wincing in the flesh at every word. And what, again, are we to say of its sober truthfulness, not exaggerating, not running to phrases, not seeking to make a hero out of what was only an ordinary but good and brave young man? Literary reticence is not Whitman's stronghold; and this reticence is not literary, but humane; it is not that of a good artist but that of a good man. He knew that what the mother wished to hear about was Frank; and he told her about her Frank as he was.

V.

Something should be said of Whitman's style, for style is of the essence of thinking. And where a man is so critically deliberate as our author, and goes solemnly about his poetry for an ulterior end, every indication is worth notice. He has chosen a rough, unrhymed, lyrical verse; sometimes instinct with a fine processional movement; often so rugged and careless that it can only be described by saying that he has not taken the trouble to write prose. I believe myself that it was selected principally because it was easy to write, although not without recollections of the marching measures of some of the prose in our English Old Testament. According to Whitman, on the other hand, "the time has arrived to essentially break down the barriers of form between Prose and Poetry . . . for the most cogent purposes of those great inland states, and for Texas, and California, and Oregon;"—a statement which is among the happiest achievements of American humour. He calls his verses "recitatives," in easily followed allusion to a musical form. "Easily-written, loose-fingered chords," he cries, "I feel the thrum of your climax and close." Too often, I fear, he is the only one who can perceive the rhythm; and in spite of Mr. Swinburne, a great part of his work considered as verses is poor bald stuff. Considered, not as verse, but as speech, a great part of it is full of strange and admirable merits. The right detail is seized; the right word, bold and trenchant, is thrust into its place. Whitman has small regard to literary decencies, and is totally free from literary timidities. He is neither afraid of being slangy nor of being dull; nor, let me add, of being ridiculous. The result is a most surprising compound of plain grandeur, sentimental affectation, and downright nonsense. It would be useless to follow his detractors and give instances of how bad he can be at his worst; and perhaps it would be not much wiser to give extracted specimens of how happily he can write when he is at his best. These come in to most advantage in their own place; owing something, it may be, to the offset of their curious surroundings. And one thing is certain, that no one can appreciate Whitman's excellences until he has grown accustomed to his faults. Until you are content to pick poetry out of his pages almost as you must pick it out of a Greek play in Bohn's translation, your gravity will be continually upset, your ears perpetually disappointed, and the whole book will be no more to you than a particularly flagrant production by the Poet Close.

A writer of this uncertain quality was, perhaps, unfortunate in taking for thesis the beauty of the world as it now is, not only on the hill-tops but in the factory; not only by the harbour full of stately ships, but in the magazine of the hopelessly prosaic hatter. To show beauty in common things is the work of the rarest tact. It is not to be done by the wishing. It is easy to posit as a theory, but to bring it home to men's minds is the problem of literature, and is only accomplished by rare talent, and in comparatively rare instances. To bid the whole world stand and deliver, with a dogma in one's right hand by way of pistol; to cover reams of paper in a galloping, headstrong vein; to cry louder and louder over everything as it comes up, and make no distinction in one's enthusiasm over the most incomparable matters; to prove one's entire want of sympathy for the jaded, literary palate, by calling, not a spade a spade, but a hatter a hatter, in a lyrical apostrophe;—this, in spite of all the airs of inspiration, is not the way to do it. It may be very wrong, and very wounding to a respectable branch of industry, but the word "hatter" cannot be used seriously in emotional verse; not to understand this, is to have no literary tact; and I would, for his own sake, that this were the only inadmissible expression with which Whitman had bedecked his pages. The book teems with similar comicalities; and, to a reader who is determined to take it from that side only, presents a perfect carnival of fun.

A good deal of this is the result of theory playing its usual vile trick upon the artist. It is because he is a Democrat that Whitman must have in the hatter. If you may say Admiral, he reasons, why may you not say Hatter? One man is as good as another, and it is the business of the "great poet" to show poetry in the life of the one as well as the other. A most incontrovertible sentiment surely, and one which nobody would think of controverting, where—and here is the point—where any beauty has been shown. But how, where that is not the case? where the hatter is simply introduced, as God made him and as his fellow-men have miscalled him, at the crisis of a high-flown rhapsody? And what are we to say, where a man of Whitman's notable capacity for putting things in a bright, picturesque, and novel way, simply gives up the attempt, and indulges, with apparent exultation, in an inventory of trades or implements, with no more colour or coherence than so many index-words out of a dictionary? I do not know that we can say anything, but that it is a prodigiously amusing exhibition for a line or so. The worst of it is, that Whitman must have known better. The man is a great critic, and, so far as I can make out, a good one; and how much criticism does it require to know that capitulation is not description, or that fingering on a dumb keyboard, with whatever show of sentiment and execution, is not at all the same thing as discoursing music? I wish I could believe he was quite honest with us; but, indeed, who was ever quite honest who wrote a book for a purpose? It is a flight beyond the reach of human magnanimity.

One other point, where his means failed him, must be touched upon, however shortly. In his desire to accept all facts loyally and simply, it fell within his programme to speak at some length and with some plainness on what is, for I really do not know what reason, the most delicate of subjects. Seeing in that one of the most serious and interesting parts of life, he was aggrieved that it should be looked upon as ridiculous or shameful. No one speaks of maternity with his tongue in his cheek; and Whitman made a bold push to set the sanctity of fatherhood beside the sanctity of motherhood, and introduce this also among the things that can be spoken of without either a blush or a wink. But the Philistines have been too strong; and, to say truth, Whitman has rather played the fool. We may be thoroughly conscious that his end is improving; that it would be a good thing if a window were opened on these close privacies of life; that on this subject, as on all others, he now and then lets fall a pregnant saying. But we are not satisfied. We feel that he was not the man for so difficult an enterprise. He loses our sympathy in the character of a poet by attracting too much of our attention in that of a Bull in a China Shop. And where, by a little more art, we might have been solemnised ourselves, it is too often Whitman alone who is solemn in the face of an audience somewhat indecorously amused.

VI.

Lastly, as most important, after all, to human beings in our disputable state, what is that higher prudence which was to be the aim and issue of these deliberate productions?

Whitman is too clever to slip into a succinct formula. If he could have adequately said his say in a single proverb, it is to be presumed he would not have put himself to the trouble of writing several volumes. It was his programme to state as much as he could of the world with all its contradictions, and leave the upshot with God who planned it. What he has made of the world and the world's meanings is to be found at large in his poems. These altogether give his answers to the problems of belief and conduct; in many ways righteous and high-spirited, in some ways loose and contradictory. And yet there are two passages from the preface to the Leaves of Grass which do pretty well condense his teaching on all essential points, and yet preserve a measure of his spirit.

"This is what you shall do," he says in the one, "love the earth, and sun, and animals, despise riches, give alms to every one that asks, stand up for the stupid and crazy, devote your income and labour to others, hate tyrants, argue not concerning God, have patience and indulgence towards the people, take off your hat to nothing known or unknown, or to any man or number of men; go freely with powerful uneducated persons, and with the young, and mothers of families, read these leaves (his own works) in the open air every season of every year of your life; re-examine all you have been told at school or church, or in any book, and dismiss whatever insults your own soul."

"The prudence of the greatest poet," he adds in the other—and the greatest poet is, of course, himself—"knows that the young man who composedly perilled his life and lost it, has done exceeding well for himself; while the man who has not perilled his life, and retains it to old age in riches and ease, has perhaps achieved nothing for himself worth mentioning; and that only that person has no great prudence to learn, who has learnt to prefer real long-lived things, and favours body and soul the same, and perceives the indirect surely following the direct, and what evil or good he does leaping onward and waiting to meet him again, and who in his spirit, in any emergency whatever, neither hurries nor avoids death."

There is much that is Christian in these extracts, startlingly Christian.

Any reader who bears in mind Whitman's own advice and "dismisses whatever insults his own soul" will find plenty that is bracing, brightening, and chastening to reward him for a little patience at first. It seems hardly possible that any being should get evil from so healthy a book as the Leaves of Grass, which is simply comical wherever it falls short of nobility; but if there be any such, who cannot both take and leave, who cannot let a single opportunity pass by without some unworthy and unmanly thought, I should have as great difficulty, and neither more nor less, in recommending the works of Whitman as in lending them Shakespeare, or letting them go abroad outside of the grounds of a private asylum.

HENRY DAVID THOREAU: HIS CHARACTER AND OPINIONS.

I.

Thoreau's thin, penetrating, big-nosed face, even in a bad woodcut, conveys some hint of the limitations of his mind and character. With his almost acid sharpness of insight, with his almost animal dexterity in act, there went none of that large, unconscious geniality of the world's heroes. He was not easy, not ample, not urbane, not even kind; his enjoyment was hardly smiling, or the smile was not broad enough to be convincing; he had no waste lands nor kitchen-midden in his nature, but was all improved and sharpened to a point. "He was bred to no profession," says Emerson; "he never married; he lived alone; he never went to church; he never voted; he refused to pay a tax to the State; he ate no flesh, he drank no wine, he never knew the use of tobacco and, though a naturalist, he used neither trap nor gun. When asked at dinner what dish he preferred, he answered, 'the nearest.'" So many negative superiorities begin to smack a little of the prig. From his later works he was in the habit of cutting out the humorous passages, under the impression that they were beneath the dignity of his moral muse; and there we see the prig stand public and confessed. It was "much easier," says Emerson acutely, much easier for Thoreau to say no than yes; and that is a characteristic which depicts the man. It is a useful accomplishment to be able to say no, but surely it is the essence of amiability to prefer to say yes where it is possible. There is something wanting in the man who does not hate himself whenever he is constrained to say no. And there was a great deal wanting in this born dissenter. He was almost shockingly devoid of weaknesses; he had not enough of them to be truly polar with humanity; whether you call him demi-god or demi-man, he was at least not altogether one of us, for he was not touched with a feeling of our infirmities. The world's heroes have room for all positive qualities, even those which are disreputable, in the capacious theatre of their dispositions. Such can live many lives; while a Thoreau can live but one, and that only with perpetual foresight.

He was no ascetic, rather an Epicurean of the nobler sort; and he had this one great merit, that he succeeded so far as to be happy. "I love my fate to the core and rind," he wrote once; and even while he lay dying, here is what he dictated (for it seems he was already too feeble to control the pen): "You ask particularly after my health. I suppose that I have not many months to live, but of course know nothing about it. I may say that I am enjoying existence as much as ever, and regret nothing." It is not given to all to bear so clear a testimony to the sweetness of their fate, nor to any without courage and wisdom; for this world in itself is but a painful and uneasy place of residence, and lasting happiness, at least to the self-conscious, comes only from within. Now Thoreau's content and ecstasy in living was, we may say, like a plant that he had watered and tended with womanish solicitude; for there is apt to be something unmanly, something almost dastardly, in a life that does not move with dash and freedom, and that fears the bracing contact of the world. In one word, Thoreau was a skulker. He did not wish virtue to go out of him among his fellow-men, but slunk into a corner to hoard it for himself. He left all for the sake of certain virtuous self-indulgences. It is true that his tastes were noble; that his ruling passion was to keep himself unspotted from the world; and that his luxuries were all of the same healthy order as cold tubs and early rising. But a man may be both coldly cruel in the pursuit of goodness, and morbid even in the pursuit of health. I cannot lay my hands on the passage in which he explains his abstinence from tea and coffee, but I am sure I have the meaning correctly. It is this; He thought it bad economy and worthy of no true virtuoso to spoil the natural rapture of the morning with such muddy stimulants; let him but see the sun rise, and he was already sufficiently inspirited for the labours of the day. That may be reason good enough to abstain from tea; but when we go on to find the same man, on the same or similar grounds, abstain from nearly everything that his neighbours innocently and pleasurably use, and from the rubs and trials of human society itself into the bargain, we recognise that valetudinarian healthfulness which is more delicate than sickness itself. We need have no respect for a state of artificial training. True health is to be able to do without it. Shakespeare, we can imagine, might begin the day upon a quart of ale, and yet enjoy the sunrise to the full as much as Thoreau, and commemorate his enjoyment in vastly better verses. A man who must separate himself from his neighbours' habits in order to be happy, is in much the same case with one who requires to take opium for the same purpose. What we want to see is one who can breast into the world, do a man's work, and still preserve his first and pure enjoyment of existence.

Thoreau's faculties were of a piece with his moral shyness; for they were all delicacies. He could guide himself about the woods on the darkest night by the touch of his feet. He could pick up at once an exact dozen of pencils by the feeling, pace distances with accuracy, and gauge cubic contents by the eye. His smell was so dainty that he could perceive the fœtor of dwelling-houses as he passed them by at night; his palate so unsophisticated that, like a child, he disliked the taste of wine—or perhaps, living in America, had never tasted any that was good; and his knowledge of nature was so complete and curious that he could have told the time of year, within a day or so, by the aspect of the plants. In his dealings with animals, he was the original of Hawthorne's Donatello. He pulled the woodchuck out of its hole by the tail; the hunted fox came to him for protection; wild squirrels have been seen to nestle in his waistcoat; he would thrust his arm into a pool and bring forth a bright, panting fish, lying undismayed in the palm of his hand. There were few things that he could not do. He could make a house, a boat, a pencil, or a book. He was a surveyor, a scholar, a natural historian. He could run, walk, climb, skate, swim, and manage a boat. The smallest occasion served to display his physical accomplishment; and a manufacturer, from merely observing his dexterity with the window of a railway carriage, offered him a situation on the spot. "The only fruit of much living," he observes, "is the ability to do some slight thing better." But such was the exactitude of his senses, so alive was he in every fibre, that it seems as if the maxim should be changed in his case, for he could do most things with unusual perfection. And perhaps he had an approving eye to himself when he wrote: "Though the youth at last grows indifferent, the laws of the universe are not indifferent, but are for ever on the side of the most sensitive."

II.

Thoreau had decided, it would seem, from the very first to lead a life of self-improvement: the needle did not tremble as with richer natures, but pointed steadily north; and as he saw duty and inclination in one, he turned all his strength in that direction. He was met upon the threshold by a common difficulty. In this world, in spite of its many agreeable features, even the most sensitive must undergo some drudgery to live. It is not possible to devote your time to study and meditation without what are quaintly but happily denominated private means; these absent, a man must contrive to earn his bread by some service to the public such as the public cares to pay him for; or, as Thoreau loved to put it, Apollo must serve Admetus. This was to Thoreau even a sourer necessity than it is to most; there was a love of freedom, a strain of the wild man, in his nature, that rebelled with violence against the yoke of custom; and he was so eager to cultivate himself and to be happy in his own society, that he could consent with difficulty even to the interruptions of friendship. "Such are my engagements to myself that I dare not promise," he once wrote in answer to an invitation; and the italics are his own. Marcus Aurelius found time to study virtue, and between whiles to conduct the imperial affairs of Rome; but Thoreau is so busy improving himself, that he must think twice about a morning call. And now imagine him condemned for eight hours a day to some uncongenial and unmeaning business! He shrank from the very look of the mechanical in life; all should, if possible, be sweetly spontaneous and swimmingly progressive. Thus he learned to make lead-pencils, and, when he had gained the best certificate and his friends began to congratulate him on his establishment in life, calmly announced that he should never make another. "Why should I?" said he "I would not do again what I have done once." For when a thing has once been done as well as it wants to be, it is of no further interest to the self-improver. Yet in after years, and when it became needful to support his family, he returned patiently to this mechanical art—a step more than worthy of himself.

The pencils seem to have been Apollo's first experiment in the service of Admetus; but others followed. "I have thoroughly tried school-keeping," he writes, "and found that my expenses were in proportion, or rather out of proportion, to my income; for I was obliged to dress and train, not to say think and believe, accordingly, and I lost my time into the bargain. As I did not teach for the benefit of my fellow-men, but simply for a livelihood, this was a failure. I have tried trade, but I found that it would take ten years to get under way in that, and that then I should probably be on my way to the devil." Nothing, indeed, can surpass his scorn for all so-called business. Upon that subject gall squirts from him at a touch. "The whole enterprise of this nation is not illustrated by a thought," he writes; "it is not warmed by a sentiment; there is nothing in it for which a man should lay down his life, nor even his gloves." And again: "If our merchants did not most of them fail, and the banks too, my faith in the old laws of this world would be staggered. The statement that ninety-six in a hundred doing such business surely break down is perhaps the sweetest fact that statistics have revealed." The wish was probably father to the figures; but there is something enlivening in a hatred of so genuine a brand, hot as Corsican revenge, and sneering like Voltaire.

Pencils, school-keeping, and trade being thus discarded one after another, Thoreau, with a stroke of strategy, turned the position. He saw his way to get his board and lodging for practically nothing; and Admetus never got less work out of any servant since the world began. It was his ambition to be an oriental philosopher; but he was always a very Yankee sort of oriental. Even in the peculiar attitude in which he stood to money, his system of personal economics, as we may call it, he displayed a vast amount of truly down-East calculation, and he adopted poverty like a piece of business. Yet his system is based on one or two ideas which, I believe, come naturally to all thoughtful youths, and are only pounded out of them by city uncles. Indeed, something essentially youthful distinguishes all Thoreau's knock-down blows at current opinion. Like the posers of a child, they leave the orthodox in a kind of speechless agony. These know the thing is nonsense. They are sure there must be an answer, yet somehow cannot find it. So it is with his system of economy. He cuts through the subject on so new a plane that the accepted arguments apply no longer; he attacks it in a new dialect where there are no catchwords ready made for the defender; after you have been boxing for years on a polite, gladiatorial convention, here is an assailant who does not scruple to hit below the belt.

"The cost of a thing," says he, "is the amount of what I will call life which is required to be exchanged for it, immediately or in the long run." I have been accustomed to put it to myself, perhaps more clearly, that the price we have to pay for money is paid in liberty. Between these two ways of it, at least, the reader will probably not fail to find a third definition of his own; and it follows, on one or other, that a man may pay too dearly for his livelihood, by giving, in Thoreau's terms, his whole life for it, or, in mine, bartering for it the whole of his available liberty, and becoming a slave till death. There are two questions to be considered—the quality of what we buy, and the price we have to pay for it. Do you want a thousand a year, a two thousand a year, or a ten thousand a year livelihood? and can you afford the one you want? It is a matter of taste; it is not in the least degree a question of duty, though commonly supposed so. But there is no authority for that view anywhere. It is nowhere in the Bible. It is true that we might do a vast amount of good if we were wealthy, but it is also highly improbable; not many do; and the art of growing rich is not only quite distinct from that of doing good, but the practice of the one does not at all train a man for practising the other. "Money might be of great service to me," writes Thoreau; "but the difficulty now is that I do not improve my opportunities, and therefore I am not prepared to have my opportunities increased." It is a mere illusion that, above a certain income, the personal desires will be satisfied and leave a wider margin for the generous impulse. It is as difficult to be generous, or anything else, except perhaps a member of Parliament, on thirty thousand as on two hundred a year.

Now Thoreau's tastes were well defined. He loved to be free, to be master of his times and seasons, to indulge the mind rather than the body; he preferred long rambles to rich dinners, his own reflections to the consideration of society, and an easy, calm, unfettered, active life among green trees to dull toiling at the counter of a bank. And such being his inclination he determined to gratify it. A poor man must save off something; he determined to save off his livelihood. "When a man has attained those things which are necessary to life," he writes, "there is another alternative than to obtain the superfluities; he may adventure on life now, his vacation from humbler toil having commenced." Thoreau would get shelter, some kind of covering for his body, and necessary daily bread; even these he should get as cheaply as possible; and then, his vacation from humbler toil having commenced, devote himself to oriental philosophers, the study of nature, and the work of self-improvement.

Prudence, which bids us all go to the ant for wisdom and hoard against the day of sickness, was not a favourite with Thoreau. He preferred that other, whose name is so much misappropriated: Faith. When he had secured the necessaries of the moment, he would not reckon up possible accidents or torment himself with trouble for the future. He had no toleration for the man "who ventures to live only by the aid of the mutual insurance company, which has promised to bury him decently." He would trust himself a little to the world. "We may safely trust a good deal more than we do," says he. "How much is not done by us! or what if we had been taken sick?" And then, with a stab of satire, he describes contemporary mankind in a phrase: "All the day long on the alert, at night we unwillingly say our prayers and commit ourselves to uncertainties." It is not likely that the public will be much affected by Thoreau, when they blink the direct injunctions of the religion they profess; and yet, whether we will or no, we make the same hazardous ventures; we back our own health and the honesty of our neighbours for all that we are worth; and it is chilling to think how many must lose their wager.

In 1845, twenty-eight years old, an age by which the liveliest have usually declined into some conformity with the world, Thoreau, with a capital of something less than five pounds and a borrowed axe, walked forth into the woods by Walden Pond, and began his new experiment in life. He built himself a dwelling, and returned the axe, he says with characteristic and workman-like pride, sharper than when he borrowed it; he reclaimed a patch, where he cultivated beans, peas, potatoes, and sweet corn; he had his bread to bake, his farm to dig, and for the matter of six weeks in the summer he worked at surveying, carpentry, or some other of his numerous dexterities, for hire.

For more than five years, this was all that he required to do for his support, and he had the winter and most of the summer at his entire disposal. For six weeks of occupation, a little cooking and a little gentle hygienic gardening, the man, you may say, had as good as stolen his livelihood. Or we must rather allow that he had done far better; for the thief himself is continually and busily occupied; and even one born to inherit a million will have more calls upon his time than Thoreau. Well might he say, "What old people tell you-you cannot do, you try and find you can." And how surprising is his conclusion: "I am convinced that to maintain oneself on this earth is not a hardship, but a pastime, if we will live simply and wisely; as the pursuits of simpler nations are still the sports of the more artificial."

When he had enough of that kind of life, he showed the same simplicity in giving it up as in beginning it. There are some who could have done the one, but, vanity forbidding, not the other; and that is perhaps the story of the hermits; but Thoreau made no fetish of his own example, and did what he wanted squarely. And five years is long enough for an experiment and to prove the success of transcendental Yankeeism. It is not his frugality which is worthy of note; for, to begin with, that was inborn, and therefore inimitable by others who are differently constituted; and again, it was no new thing, but has often been equalled by poor Scotch students at the universities. The point is the sanity of his view of life, and the insight with which he recognised the position of money, and thought out for himself the problem of riches and a livelihood. Apart from his eccentricities, he had perceived, and was acting on, a truth of universal application. For money enters in two different characters into the scheme of life. A certain amount, varying with the number and empire of our desires, is a true necessary to each one of us in the present order of society; but beyond that amount, money is a commodity to be bought or not to be bought, a luxury in which we may either indulge or stint ourselves, like any other. And there are many luxuries that we may legitimately prefer to it, such as a grateful conscience, a country life, or the woman of our inclination. Trite, flat, and obvious as this conclusion may appear, we have only to look round us in society to see how scantily it has been recognised; and perhaps even ourselves, after a little reflection, may decide to spend a trifle less for money, and indulge ourselves a trifle more in the article of freedom.

III.

"To have done anything by which you earned money merely," says Thoreau, "is to be" (have been, he means) "idle and worse." There are two passages in his letters, both, oddly enough, relating to firewood, which must be brought together to be rightly understood. So taken, they contain between them the marrow of all good sense on the subject of work in its relation to something broader than mere livelihood. Here is the first: "I suppose I have burned up a good-sized tree to-night—and for what? I settled with Mr. Tarbell for it the other day; but that wasn't the final settlement. I got off cheaply from him. At last one will say: 'Let us see, how much wood did you burn, sir?' And I shall shudder to think that the next question will be, 'What did you do while you were warm?'" Even after we have settled with Admetus in the person of Mr. Tarbell, there comes, you see, a further question. It is not enough to have earned our livelihood. Either the earning itself should have been serviceable to mankind, or something else must follow. To live is sometimes very difficult, but it is never meritorious in itself; and we must have a reason to allege to our own conscience why we should continue to exist upon this crowded earth.

If Thoreau had simply dwelt in his house at Walden, a lover of trees, birds, and fishes, and the open air and virtue, a reader of wise books, an idle, selfish self-improver, he would have managed to cheat Admetus, but, to cling to metaphor, the devil would have had him in the end. Those who can avoid toil altogether and dwell in the Arcadia of private means, and even those who can, by abstinence, reduce the necessary amount of it to some six weeks a year, having the more liberty, have only the higher moral obligation to be up and doing in the interest of man.

The second passage is this: "There is a far more important and warming heat, commonly lost, which precedes the burning of the wood. It is the smoke of industry, which is incense. I had been so thoroughly warmed in body and spirit, that when at length my fuel was housed, I came near selling it to the ashman, as if I had extracted all its heat." Industry is, in itself and when properly chosen, delightful and profitable to the worker; and when your toil has been a pleasure, you have not, as Thoreau says, "earned money merely," but money, health, delight, and moral profit, all in one. "We must heap up a great pile of doing for a small diameter of being," he says in another place; and then exclaims, "How admirably the artist is made to accomplish his self-culture by devotion to his art!" We may escape uncongenial toil, only to devote ourselves to that which is congenial. It is only to transact some higher business that even Apollo dare play the truant from Admetus. We must all work for the sake of work; we must all work, as Thoreau says again, in any "absorbing pursuit—it does not much matter what, so it be honest;" but the most profitable work is that which combines into one continued effort the largest proportion of the powers and desires of a man's nature; that into which he will plunge with ardour, and from which he will desist with reluctance; in which he will know the weariness of fatigue, but not that of satiety; and which will be ever fresh, pleasing, and stimulating to his taste. Such work holds a man together, braced at all points; it does not suffer him to doze or wander; it keeps him actively conscious of himself, yet raised among superior interests; it gives him the profit of industry with the pleasures of a pastime. This is what his art should be to the true artist, and that to a degree unknown in other and less intimate pursuits. For other professions stand apart from the human business of life; but an art has its seat at the centre of the artist's doings and sufferings, deals directly with his experiences, teaches him the lessons of his own fortunes and mishaps, and becomes a part of his biography. So says Goethe:

> "Spät erklingt was früh erklang;
>
> Glück und Unglück wird Gesang."

Now Thoreau's art was literature; and it was one of which he had conceived most ambitiously. He loved and believed in good books. He said well, "Life is not habitually seen from any common platform so truly and unexaggerated as in the light of literature." But the literature he loved was of the heroic order. "Books, not which afford us a cowering enjoyment, but in which each thought is of unusual daring; such as an idle man cannot read, and a timid one would not be entertained by, which even make us dangerous to existing institutions—such I call good books." He did not think them easy to be read. "The heroic books," he says, "even if printed in the character of our mother-tongue, will always be in a language dead to degenerate times; and we must laboriously seek the meaning of each word and line, conjecturing a larger sense than common use permits out of what wisdom and valour and generosity we have." Nor does he suppose that such books are easily written. "Great prose, of equal elevation, commands our respect more than great verse," says he, "since it implies a more permanent and level height, a life more pervaded with the grandeur of the thought. The poet often only makes an irruption, like the Parthian, and is off again, shooting while he retreats; but the prose writer has conquered like a Roman and settled colonies." We may ask ourselves, almost with dismay, whether such works exist at all but in the imagination of the student. For the bulk of the best of books is apt to be made up with ballast; and those in which energy of thought is combined with any stateliness of utterance may be almost counted on the fingers. Looking round in English for a book that should answer Thoreau's two demands of a style like poetry and sense that shall be both original and inspiriting, I come to Milton's Areopagitica, and can name no other instance for the moment. Two things at least are plain: that if a man will condescend to nothing more commonplace in the way of reading, he must not look to have a large library; and that if he proposes himself to write in a similar vein, he will find his work cut out for him.

Thoreau composed seemingly while he walked, or at least exercise and composition were with him intimately connected; for we are told that "the length of his walk uniformly made the length of his writing." He speaks in one place of "plainness and vigour, the ornaments of style," which is rather too paradoxical to be comprehensively, true.

In another he remarks: "As for style of writing, if one has anything to say it drops from him simply as a stone falls to the ground." We must conjecture a very large sense indeed for the phrase "if one has anything to say." When truth flows from a man, fittingly clothed in style and without conscious effort, it is because the effort has been made and the work practically completed before he sat down to write. It is only out of fulness of thinking that expression drops perfect like a ripe fruit; and when Thoreau wrote so nonchalantly at his desk, it was because he had been vigorously active during his walk. For neither clearness compression, nor beauty of language, come to any living creature till after a busy and a prolonged acquaintance with the subject on hand. Easy writers are those who, like Walter Scott, choose to remain contented with a less degree of perfection than is legitimately within the compass of their powers. We hear of Shakespeare and his clean manuscript; but in face of the evidence of the style itself and of the various editions of Hamlet, this merely proves that Messrs. Hemming and Condell were unacquainted with the common enough phenomenon called a fair copy. He who would recast a tragedy already given to the world must frequently and earnestly have revised details in the study. Thoreau himself, and in spite of his protestations, is an instance of even extreme research in one direction; and his effort after heroic utterance is proved not only by the occasional finish, but by the determined exaggeration of his style. "I trust you realise what an exaggerator I am— that I lay myself out to exaggerate," he writes. And again, hinting at the explanation: "Who that has heard a strain of music feared lest he should speak extravagantly any more for ever?" And yet once more, in his essay on Carlyle, and this time with his meaning well in hand: "No truth, we think, was ever expressed but with this sort of emphasis, that for the time there seemed to be no other." Thus Thoreau was an exaggerative and a parabolical writer, not because he loved the literature of the East, but from a desire that people should understand and realise what he was writing. He was near the truth upon the general question; but in his own particular method, it appears to me, he wandered. Literature is not less a conventional art than painting or sculpture; and it is the least striking, as it is the most comprehensive of the three. To hear a strain of music to see a beautiful woman, a river, a great city, or a starry night, is to make a man despair of his Lilliputian arts in language. Now, to gain that emphasis which seems denied to us by the very nature of the medium, the proper method of literature is by selection, which is a kind of negative exaggeration. It is the right of the literary artist, as Thoreau was on the point of seeing, to leave out whatever does not suit his purpose. Thus we extract the pure gold; and thus the well-written story of a noble life becomes, by its very omissions, more thrilling to the reader. But to go beyond this, like Thoreau, and to exaggerate directly, is to leave the saner classical tradition, and to put the reader on his guard. And when you write the whole for the half, you do not express your thought more forcibly, but only express a different thought which is not yours.

Thoreau's true subject was the pursuit of self-improvement combined with an unfriendly criticism of life as it goes on in our societies; it is there that he best displays the freshness and surprising trenchancy of his intellect;

it is there that his style becomes plain and vigorous, and therefore, according to his own formula, ornamental. Yet he did not care to follow this vein singly, but must drop into it by the way in books of a different purport. Walden, or Life in the Woods, A Week on the Concord and Merrimack Rivers, The Maine Woods,—such are the titles he affects. He was probably reminded by his delicate critical perception that the true business of literature is with narrative; in reasoned narrative, and there alone, that art enjoys all its advantages, and suffers least from its defects. Dry precept and disembodied disquisition, as they can only be read with an effort of abstraction, can never convey a perfectly complete or a perfectly natural impression. Truth, even in literature, must be clothed with flesh and blood, or it cannot tell its whole story to the reader. Hence the effect of anecdote on simple minds; and hence good biographies and works of high, imaginative art, are not only far more entertaining, but far more edifying, than books of theory or precept. Now Thoreau could not clothe his opinions in the garment of art, for that was not his talent; but he sought to gain the same elbow-room for himself, and to afford a similar relief to his readers, by mingling his thoughts with a record of experience.

Again, he was a lover of nature. The quality which we should call mystery in a painting, and which belongs so particularly to the aspect of the external world and to its influence upon our feelings, was one which he was never weary of attempting to reproduce in his books. The seeming significance of nature's appearances, their unchanging strangeness to the senses, and the thrilling response which they waken in the mind of man, continued to surprise and stimulate his spirits. It appeared to him, I think, that if we could only write near enough to the facts, and yet with no pedestrian calm, but ardently, we might transfer the glamour of reality direct upon our pages; and that, if it were once thus captured and expressed, a new and instructive relation might appear between men's thoughts and the phenomena of nature. This was the eagle that he pursued all his life long, like a schoolboy with a butterfly net. Hear him to a friend: "Let me suggest a theme for you—to state to yourself precisely and completely what that walk over the mountains amounted to for you, returning to this essay again and again until you are satisfied that all that was important in your experience is in it. Don't suppose that you can tell it precisely the first dozen times you try, but at 'em again; especially when, after a sufficient pause you suspect that you are touching the heart or summit of the matter, reiterate your blows there, and account for the mountain to yourself. Not that the story need be long, but it will take a long while to make it short." Such was the method, not consistent for a man whose meanings were to "drop from him as a stone falls to the ground." Perhaps the most successful work that Thoreau ever accomplished in this direction is to be found in the passages relating to fish in the Week. These are remarkable for a vivid truth of impression and a happy suitability of language, not frequently surpassed.

Whatever Thoreau tried to do was tried in fair, square prose, with sentences solidly built, and no help from bastard rhythms. Moreover, there is a progression—I cannot call it a progress—in his work towards a more and more strictly prosaic level, until at last he sinks into the bathos of the prosy. Emerson mentions having once remarked to Thoreau: "Who would not like to write something which all can read, like Robinson Crusoe? and who does not see with regret that his page is not solid with a right materialistic treatment which delights everybody?" I must say in passing that it is not the right materialistic treatment which delights the world in Robinson, but the romantic and philosophic interest of the fable. The same treatment does quite the reverse of delighting us when it is applied, in Colonel Jack, to the management of a plantation. But I cannot help suspecting Thoreau to have been influenced either by this identical remark or by some other closely similar in meaning. He began to fall more and more into a detailed materialistic treatment; he went into the business doggedly, as one who should make a guide-book; he not only chronicled what had been important in his own experience, but whatever might have been important in the experience of anybody else; not only what had affected him, but all that he saw or heard. His ardour had grown less, or perhaps it was inconsistent with a right materialistic treatment to display such emotions as he felt; and, to complete the eventful change, he chose, from a sense of moral dignity, to gut these later works of the saving quality of humour. He was not one of those authors who have learned, in his own words, "to leave out their dulness." He inflicts his full quantity upon the reader in such books as Cape Cod, or The Yankee in

Canada. Of the latter he confessed that he had not managed to get much of himself into it. Heaven knows he had not, nor yet much of Canada, we may hope. "Nothing," he says somewhere, "can shock a brave man but dulness." Well, there are few spots more shocking to the brave than the pages of The Yankee in Canada.

There are but three books of his that will be read with much pleasure: the Week, Walden, and the collected letters. As to his poetry, Emerson's word shall suffice for us, it is so accurate and so prettily said: "The thyme and majoram are not yet honey." In this, as in his prose, he relied greatly on the goodwill of the reader, and wrote throughout in faith. It was an exercise of faith to suppose that many would understand the sense of his best work, or that any could be exhilarated by the dreary chronicling of his worst. "But," as he says, "the gods do not hear any rude or discordant sound, as we learn from the echo; and I know that the nature towards which I launch these sounds is so rich that it will modulate anew and wonderfully improve my rudest strain."

IV.

"What means the fact," he cries, "that a soul which has lost all hope for itself can inspire in another listening soul such an infinite confidence in it, even while it is expressing its despair?" The question is an echo and an illustration of the words last quoted; and it forms the key-note of his thoughts on friendship. No one else, to my knowledge, has spoken in so high and just a spirit of the kindly relations; and I doubt whether it be a drawback that these lessons should come from one in many ways so unfitted to be a teacher in this branch. The very coldness and egoism of his own intercourse gave him a clearer insight into the intellectual basis of our warm, mutual tolerations; and testimony to their worth comes with added force from one who was solitary and disobliging, and of whom a friend remarked, with equal wit and wisdom, "I love Henry, but I cannot like him."

He can hardly be persuaded to make any distinction between love and friendship; in such rarefied and freezing air, upon the mountain-tops of meditation, had he taught himself to breathe. He was, indeed, too accurate an observer not to have remarked that "there exists already a natural disinterestedness and liberality" between men and women; yet, he thought, "friendship is no respecter of sex." Perhaps there is a sense in which the words are true; but they were spoken in ignorance; and perhaps we shall have put the matter most correctly, if we call love a foundation for a nearer and freer degree of friendship than can be possible without it. For there are delicacies, eternal between persons of the same sex, which are melted and disappear in the warmth of love.

To both, if they are to be right, he attributes the same nature and condition. "We are not what we are," says he, "nor do we treat or esteem each other for such, but for what we are capable of being." "A friend is one who incessantly pays us the compliment of expecting all the virtues from us, and who can appreciate them in us." "The friend asks no return but that his friend will religiously accept and wear and not disgrace his apotheosis of him." "It is the merit and preservation of friendship that it takes place on a level higher than the actual characters of the parties would seem to warrant." This is to put friendship on a pedestal indeed; and yet the root of the matter is there; and the last sentence, in particular, is like a light in a dark place, and makes many mysteries plain. We are different with different friends; yet if we look closely we shall find that every such relation reposes on some particular apotheosis of oneself; with each friend, although we could not distinguish it in words from any other, we have at least one special reputation to preserve: and it is thus that we run, when mortified, to our friend or the woman that we love, not to hear ourselves called better, but to be better men in point of fact. We seek this society to flatter ourselves with our own good conduct. And hence any falsehood in the relation, any incomplete or perverted understanding, will spoil even the pleasure of these visits. Thus says Thoreau again: "Only lovers know the value of truth." And yet again: "They ask for words and deeds, when a true relation is word and deed."

But it follows that since they are neither of them so good as the other hopes, and each is, in a very honest manner, playing a part above his powers, such an intercourse must often be disappointing to both. "We may bid farewell sooner than complain," says Thoreau, "for our complaint is too well grounded to be uttered." "We have not so good a right to hate any as our friend."

"It were treason to our love

And a sin to God above,

One iota to abate

Of a pure, impartial hate."

Love is not blind, nor yet forgiving. "O yes, believe me," as the song says, "Love has eyes!" The nearer the intimacy, the more cuttingly do we feel the unworthiness of those we love; and because you love one, and would die for that love to-morrow, you have not forgiven, and you never will forgive, that friend's misconduct. If you want a person's faults, go to those who love him. They will not tell you, but they know. And herein lies the magnanimous courage of love, that it endures this knowledge without change.

It required a cold, distant personality like that of Thoreau, perhaps, to recognise and certainly to utter this truth; for a more human love makes it a point of honour not to acknowledge those faults of which it is most conscious. But his point of view is both high and dry. He has no illusions; he does not give way to love any more than to hatred, but preserves them both with care like valuable curiosities. A more bald-headed picture of life, if I may so express myself, has seldom been presented. He is an egoist; he does not remember, or does not think it worth while to remark, that, in these near intimacies, we are ninety-nine times disappointed in our beggarly selves for once that we are disappointed in our friend; that it is we who seem most frequently undeserving of the love that unites us; and that it is by our friend's conduct that we are continually rebuked and yet strengthened for a fresh endeavour. Thoreau is dry, priggish, and selfish. It is profit he is after in these intimacies; moral profit, certainly, but still profit to himself. If you will be the sort of friend I want, he remarks naïvely, "my education cannot dispense with your society." His education! as though a friend were a dictionary. And with all this, not one word about pleasure, or laughter, or kisses, or any quality of flesh and blood. It was not inappropriate, surely, that he had such close relations with the fish. We can understand the friend already quoted, when he cried: "As for taking his arm, I would as soon think of taking the arm of an elm-tree!"

As a matter of fact he experienced but a broken enjoyment in his intimacies. He says he has been perpetually on the brink of the sort of intercourse he wanted, and yet never completely attained it. And what else had he to expect when he would not, in a happy phrase of Carlyle's, "nestle down into it"? Truly, so it will be always if you only stroll in upon your friends as you might stroll in to see a cricket match; and even then not simply for the pleasure of the thing, but with some afterthought of self-improvement, as though you had come to the cricket match to bet. It was his theory that people saw each other too frequently, so that their curiosity was not properly whetted, nor had they anything fresh to communicate; but friendship must be something else than a society for mutual improvement—indeed, it must only be that by the way, and to some extent unconsciously; and if Thoreau had been a man instead of a manner of elm-tree, he would have felt that he saw his friends too seldom, and have reaped benefits unknown to his philosophy from a more sustained and easy intercourse. We might remind him of his own words about love: "We should have no reserve; we should give the whole of ourselves to that business. But commonly men have not imagination enough to be thus employed about a human being, but must be coopering a barrel, forsooth." Ay, or reading oriental philosophers. It is not the nature of the rival occupation, it is the fact that you suffer it to be a rival, that renders loving intimacy impossible. Nothing is given for nothing in this world; there can be no true love, even on your own side, without devotion; devotion is the exercise of love, by which it grows; but if you will give enough of that, if you will pay the price in a sufficient "amount of what you call life," why then, indeed, whether with wife or comrade, you may have months and even years of such easy, natural, pleasurable, and yet improving intercourse as shall make time a moment and kindness a delight.

The secret of his retirement lies not in misanthropy, of which he had no tincture, but part in his engrossing design of self-improvement and part in the real deficiencies of social intercourse. He was not so much difficult about his fellow human beings as he could not tolerate the terms of their association. He could take to a man for any genuine qualities, as we see by his admirable sketch of the Canadian woodcutter in Walden; but he would not consent, in his own words, to "feebly fabulate and paddle in the social slush."

107

It seemed to him, I think, that society is precisely the reverse of friendship, in that it takes place on a lower level than the characters of any of the parties would warrant us to expect. The society talk of even the most brilliant man is of greatly less account than what you will get from him in (as the French say) a little committee. And Thoreau wanted geniality; he had not enough of the superficial, even at command; he could not swoop into a parlour and, in the naval phrase, "cut out" a human being from that dreary port; nor had he inclination for the task. I suspect he loved books and nature as well and near as warmly as he loved his fellow-creatures,—a melancholy, lean degeneration of the human character.

"As for the dispute about solitude and society," he thus sums up: "Any comparison is impertinent. It is an idling down on the plain at the base of the mountain instead of climbing steadily to its top. Of course you will be glad of all the society you can get to go up with? Will you go to glory with me? is the burden of the song. It is not that we love to be alone, but that we love to soar, and when we do soar the company grows thinner and thinner till there is none at all. It is either the tribune on the plain, a sermon on the mount, or a very private ecstasy still higher up. Use all the society that will abet you." But surely it is no very extravagant opinion that it is better to give than to receive, to serve than to use our companions; and above all, where there is no question of service upon either side, that it is good to enjoy their company like a natural man. It is curious and in some ways dispiriting that a writer may be always best corrected out of his own mouth; and so, to conclude, here is another passage from Thoreau which seems aimed directly at himself: "Do not be too moral; you may cheat yourself out of much life so. . . . All fables, indeed, have their morals; but the innocent enjoy the story."

V.

"The only obligation," says he, "which I have a right to assume is to do at any time what I think right." "Why should we ever go abroad, even across the way, to ask a neighbour's advice?" "There is a nearer neighbour within, who is incessantly telling us how we should behave. But we wait for the neighbour without to tell us of some false, easier way." "The greater part of what my neighbours call good I believe in my soul to be bad." To be what we are, and to become what we are capable of becoming, is the only end of life. It is "when we fall behind ourselves" that "we are cursed with duties and the neglect of duties." "I love the wild," he says, "not less than the good." And again: "The life of a good man will hardly improve us more than the life of a freebooter, for the inevitable laws appear as plainly in the infringement as in the observance, and" (mark this) "our lives are sustained by a nearly equal expense of virtue of some kind." Even although he were a prig, it will be owned he could announce a startling doctrine. "As for doing good," he writes elsewhere, "that is one of the professions that are full. Moreover, I have tried it fairly, and, strange as it may seem, am satisfied that it does not agree with my constitution. Probably I should not conscientiously and deliberately forsake my particular calling to do the good which society demands of me, to save the universe from annihilation; and I believe that a like but infinitely greater steadfastness elsewhere is all that now preserves it. If you should ever be betrayed into any of these philanthropies, do not let your left hand know what your right hand does, for it is not worth knowing." Elsewhere he returns upon the subject, and explains his meaning thus: "If I ever did a man any good in their sense, of course it was something exceptional and insignificant compared with the good or evil I am constantly doing by being what I am."

There is a rude nobility, like that of a barbarian king, in this unshaken confidence in himself and indifference to the wants, thoughts, or sufferings of others. In his whole works I find no trace of pity. This was partly the result of theory, for he held the world too mysterious to be criticised, and asks conclusively: "What right have I to grieve who have not ceased to wonder?" But it sprang still more from constitutional indifference and superiority; and he grew up healthy, composed, and unconscious from among life's horrors, like a green bay-tree from a field of battle. It was from this lack in himself that he failed to do justice to the spirit of Christ; for while he could glean more meaning from individual precepts than any score of Christians, yet he conceived life in such a different hope, and viewed it with such contrary emotions, that the sense and purport of the doctrine as a whole seems to have passed him by or left him unimpressed. He could understand the idealism of the Christian view, but he was himself so unaffectedly unhuman that he did not recognise the human intention and essence of that teaching. Hence he complained that Christ did not leave us a rule that was proper and sufficient for this world, not having conceived the nature of the rule that was laid down; for things of that character that are sufficiently unacceptable become positively non-existent to the mind. But perhaps we shall best appreciate the defect in Thoreau by seeing it supplied in the case of Whitman. For the one, I feel confident, is the disciple of the other; it is what Thoreau clearly whispered that Whitman so uproariously bawls; it is the same doctrine, but with how immense a difference! the same argument, but used to what a new conclusion! Thoreau had plenty of humour until he tutored himself out of it, and so forfeited that best birthright of a sensible man; Whitman, in that respect, seems to have been sent into the world naked and unashamed; and yet by a strange consummation, it is the theory of the former that is arid, abstract, and claustral. Of these two philosophies so nearly identical at bottom, the one pursues Self-improvement—a churlish, mangy dog; the other is up with the morning, in the best of health, and following the nymph Happiness, buxom, blithe, and debonair. Happiness, at least, is not solitary; it joys to communicate; it loves others, for it depends on them for its existence; it sanctions and encourages to all delights that are not unkind in themselves; if it lived to a thousand, it would not make excision of a single humorous passage; and while the self-improver dwindles towards the prig, and, if he be not of an excellent constitution may even grow deformed into an Obermann, the very name and appearance of a happy man breathe of good-nature, and help the rest of us to live.

In the case of Thoreau, so great a show of doctrine demands some outcome in the field of action. If nothing were to be done but build a shanty beside Walden Pond, we have heard altogether too much of these declarations of independence. That the man wrote some books is nothing to the purpose, for the same has been done in a suburban villa. That he kept himself happy is perhaps a sufficient excuse, but it is disappointing to the reader. We may be unjust, but when a man despises commerce and philanthropy alike, and has views of good so soaring that he must take himself apart from mankind for their cultivation, we will not be content without some striking act. It was not Thoreau's fault if he were not martyred; had the occasion come, he would have made a noble ending. As it is, he did once seek to interfere in the world's course; he made one practical appearance on the stage of affairs; and a strange one it was, and strangely characteristic of the nobility and the eccentricity of the man. It was forced on him by his calm but radical opposition to negro slavery. "Voting for the right is doing nothing for it," he saw; "it is only expressing to men feebly your desire that it should prevail." For his part, he would not "for an instant recognise that political organisation for his government which is the slave's government also." "I do not hesitate to say," he adds, "that those who call themselves Abolitionists should at once effectually withdraw their support, both in person and property, from the government of Massachusetts." That is what he did: in 1843 he ceased to pay the poll-tax. The highway-tax he paid, for he said he was as desirous to be a good neighbour as to be a bad subject; but no more poll-tax to the State of Massachusetts. Thoreau had now seceded, and was a polity unto himself; or, as he explains it with admirable sense, "In fact, I quietly declare war with the State after my fashion, though I will still make what use and get what advantage of her I can, as is usual in such cases." He was put in prison; but that was a part of his design. "Under a government which imprisons any unjustly, the true place for a just man is also a prison. I know this well, that if one thousand, if one hundred, if ten men whom I could name—ay, if one HONEST man, in this State of Massachusetts, ceasing to hold slaves, were actually to withdraw from this copartnership, and be locked up in the county gaol therefor, it would be the abolition of slavery in America. For it matters not how small the beginning may seem to be; what is once well done is done for ever." Such was his theory of civil disobedience.

And the upshot? A friend paid the tax for him; continued year by year to pay it in the sequel; and Thoreau was free to walk the woods unmolested. It was a fiasco, but to me it does not seem laughable; even those who joined in the laughter at the moment would be insensibly affected by this quaint instance of a good man's horror for injustice. We may compute the worth of that one night's imprisonment as outweighing half a hundred voters at some subsequent election: and if Thoreau had possessed as great a power of persuasion as (let us say) Falstaff, if he had counted a party however small, if his example had been followed by a hundred or by thirty of his fellows, I cannot but believe it would have greatly precipitated the era of freedom and justice. We feel the misdeeds of our country with so little fervour, for we are not witnesses to the suffering they cause; but when we see them wake an active horror in our fellow-man, when we see a neighbour prefer to lie in prison rather than be so much as passively implicated in their perpetration, even the dullest of us will begin to realise them with a quicker pulse.

Not far from twenty years later, when Captain John Brown was taken at Harper's Ferry, Thoreau was the first to come forward in his defence. The committees wrote to him unanimously that his action was premature. "I did not send to you for advice," said he, "but to announce that I was to speak." I have used the word "defence;" in truth he did not seek to defend him, even declared it would be better for the good cause that he should die; but he praised his action as I think Brown would have liked to hear it praised.

Thus this singularly eccentric and independent mind, wedded to a character of so much strength, singleness, and purity, pursued its own path of self-improvement for more than half a century, part gymnosophist, part backwoodsman; and thus did it come twice, though in a subaltern attitude, into the field of political history.

NOTE.—For many facts in the above essay, among which I may mention the incident of the squirrel, I am indebted to *Thoreau: His Life and Aims,* by J. A. Page, or, as is well known, Dr. Japp.

YOSHIDA-TORAJIRO

The name at the head of this page is probably unknown to the English reader, and yet I think it should become a household word like that of Garibaldi or John Brown. Some day soon, we may expect to hear more fully the details of Yoshida's history, and the degree of his influence in the transformation of Japan; even now there must be Englishmen acquainted with the subject, and perhaps the appearance of this sketch may elicit something more complete and exact. I wish to say that I am not, rightly speaking, the author of the present paper: I tell the story on the authority of an intelligent Japanese gentleman, Mr. Taiso Masaki, who told it me with an emotion that does honour to his heart; and though I have taken some pains, and sent my notes to him to be corrected, this can be no more than an imperfect outline.

Yoshida-Torajiro was son to the hereditary military instructor of the house of Choshu. The name you are to pronounce with an equality of accent on the different syllables, almost as in French, the vowels as in Italian, but the consonants in the English manner—except the j, which has the French sound, or, as it has been cleverly proposed to write it, the sound of zh. Yoshida was very learned in Chinese letters, or, as we might say, in the classics, and in his father's subject; fortification was among his favourite studies, and he was a poet from his boyhood. He was born to a lively and intelligent patriotism; the condition of Japan was his great concern; and while he projected a better future, he lost no opportunity of improving his knowledge of her present state. With this end he was continually travelling in his youth, going on foot and sometimes with three days' provision on his back, in the brave, self-helpful manner of all heroes. He kept a full diary while he was thus upon his journeys, but it is feared that these notes have been destroyed. If their value were in any respect such as we have reason to expect from the man's character, this would be a loss not easy to exaggerate. It is still wonderful to the Japanese how far he contrived to push these explorations; a cultured gentleman of that land and period would leave a complimentary poem wherever he had been hospitably entertained; and a friend of Mr. Masaki, who was likewise a great wanderer, has found such traces of Yoshida's passage in very remote regions of Japan.

Politics is perhaps the only profession for which no preparation is thought necessary; but Yoshida considered otherwise, and he studied the miseries of his fellow-countrymen with as much attention and research as though he had been going to write a book instead of merely to propose a remedy. To a man of his intensity and singleness, there is no question but that this survey was melancholy in the extreme. His dissatisfaction is proved by the eagerness with which he threw himself into the cause of reform; and what would have discouraged another braced Yoshida for his task. As he professed the theory of arms, it was firstly the defences of Japan that occupied his mind. The external feebleness of that country was then illustrated by the manners of overriding barbarians, and the visits of big barbarian war ships: she was a country beleaguered. Thus the patriotism of Yoshida took a form which may be said to have defeated itself: he had it upon him to keep out these all-powerful foreigners, whom it is now one of his chief merits to have helped to introduce; but a man who follows his own virtuous heart will be always found in the end to have been fighting for the best. One thing leads naturally to another in an awakened mind, and that with an upward progress from effect to cause. The power and knowledge of these foreigners were things inseparable; by envying them their military strength, Yoshida came to envy them their culture; from the desire to equal them in the first, sprang his desire to share with them in the second; and thus he is found treating in the same book of a new scheme to strengthen the defences of Kioto and of the establishment, in the same city, of a university of foreign teachers. He hoped, perhaps, to get the good of other lands without their evil; to enable Japan to profit by the knowledge of the barbarians, and still keep her inviolate with her own arts and virtues. But whatever was the precise nature of his hope, the means by which it was to be accomplished were both difficult and obvious. Some one with eyes and understanding must break through the official cordon, escape into the new world, and study this other civilisation on the spot. And who could be better suited for the business? It was not without danger, but he was without fear. It needed preparation and insight; and what had he done since he was a child but prepare himself with the best culture of

Japan, and acquire in his excursions the power and habit of observing?

He was but twenty-two, and already all this was clear in his mind, when news reached Choshu that Commodore Perry was lying near to Yeddo. Here, then, was the patriot's opportunity. Among the Samurai of Choshu, and in particular among the councillors of the Daimio, his general culture, his views, which the enlightened were eager to accept, and, above all, the prophetic charm, the radiant persuasion of the man, had gained him many and sincere disciples. He had thus a strong influence at the provincial Court; and so he obtained leave to quit the district, and, by way of a pretext, a privilege to follow his profession in Yeddo. Thither he hurried, and arrived in time to be too late: Perry had weighed anchor, and his sails had vanished from the waters of Japan. But Yoshida, having put his hand to the plough, was not the man to go back; he had entered upon this business, and, please God, he would carry it through; and so he gave up his professional career and remained in Yeddo to be at hand against the next opportunity. By this behaviour he put himself into an attitude towards his superior, the Daimio of Choshu, which I cannot thoroughly explain. Certainly, he became a Ronyin, a broken man, a feudal outlaw; certainly he was liable to be arrested if he set foot upon his native province; yet I am cautioned that "he did not really break his allegiance," but only so far separated himself as that the prince could no longer be held accountable for his late vassal's conduct. There is some nicety of feudal custom here that escapes my comprehension.

In Yeddo, with this nondescript political status, and cut off from any means of livelihood, he was joyfully supported by those who sympathised with his design. One was Sákuma-Shozan, hereditary retainer of one of the Shogun's councillors, and from him he got more than money or than money's worth. A steady, respectable man, with an eye to the world's opinion, Sákuma was one of those who, if they cannot do great deeds in their own person, have yet an ardour of admiration for those who can, that recommends them to the gratitude of history. They aid and abet greatness more, perhaps, than we imagine. One thinks of them in connection with Nicodemus, who visited our Lord by night. And Sákuma was in a position to help Yoshida more practically than by simple countenance; for he could read Dutch, and was eager to communicate what he knew.

While the young Ronyin thus lay studying in Yeddo, news came of a Russian ship at Nangasaki. No time was to be lost. Sákuma contributed "a long copy of encouraging verses;" and off set Yoshida on foot for Nangasaki. His way lay through his own province of Choshu; but, as the highroad to the south lay apart from the capital, he was able to avoid arrest. He supported himself, like a trouvère, by his proficiency in verse. He carried his works along with him, to serve as an introduction. When he reached a town he would inquire for the house of any one celebrated for swordsmanship, or poetry, or some of the other acknowledged forms of culture; and there, on giving a taste of his skill, he would be received and entertained, and leave behind him, when he went away, a compliment in verse. Thus he travelled through the Middle Ages on his voyage of discovery into the nineteenth century. When he reached Nangasaki he was once more too late. The Russians were gone. But he made a profit on his journey in spite of fate, and stayed awhile to pick up scraps of knowledge from the Dutch interpreters—a low class of men, but one that had opportunities; and then, still full of purpose, returned to Yeddo on foot, as he had come.

It was not only his youth and courage that supported him under these successive disappointments, but the continual affluence of new disciples. The man had the tenacity of a Bruce or a Columbus, with a pliability that was all his own. He did not fight for what the world would call success; but for "the wages of going on." Check him off in a dozen directions, he would find another outlet and break forth. He missed one vessel after another, and the main work still halted; but so long as he had a single Japanese to enlighten and prepare for the better future, he could still feel that he was working for Japan. Now, he had scarce returned from Nangasaki, when he was sought out by a new inquirer, the most promising of all. This was a common soldier, of the Hemming class, a dyer by birth, who had heard vaguely [179] of Yoshida's movements, and had become filled with wonder as to their design. This was a far different inquirer from Sákuma-Shozan, or the councillors of the Daimio of Choshu. This was no two-sworded gentleman, but the common stuff of the country, born in low traditions and unimproved by books; and

116

yet that influence, that radiant persuasion that never failed Yoshida in any circumstance of his short life, enchanted, enthralled, and converted the common soldier, as it had done already with the elegant and learned. The man instantly burned up into a true enthusiasm; his mind had been only waiting for a teacher; he grasped in a moment the profit of these new ideas; he, too, would go to foreign, outlandish parts, and bring back the knowledge that was to strengthen and renew Japan; and in the meantime, that he might be the better prepared, Yoshida set himself to teach, and he to learn, the Chinese literature. It is an episode most honourable to Yoshida, and yet more honourable still to the soldier, and to the capacity and virtue of the common people of Japan.

And now, at length, Commodore Perry returned to Simoda. Friends crowded round Yoshida with help, counsels, and encouragement. One presented him with a great sword, three feet long and very heavy, which, in the exultation of the hour, he swore to carry throughout all his wanderings, and to bring back—a far-travelled weapon—to Japan. A long letter was prepared in Chinese for the American officers; it was revised and corrected by Sákuma, and signed by Yoshida, under the name of Urinaki-Manji, and by the soldier under that of Ichigi-Koda. Yoshida had supplied himself with a profusion of materials for writing; his dress was literally stuffed with paper which was to come back again enriched with his observations, and make a great and happy kingdom of Japan. Thus equipped, this pair of emigrants set forward on foot from Yeddo, and reached Simoda about nightfall. At no period within history can travel have presented to any European creature the same face of awe and terror as to these courageous Japanese. The descent of Ulysses into hell is a parallel more near the case than the boldest expedition in the Polar circles. For their act was unprecedented; it was criminal; and it was to take them beyond the pale of humanity into a land of devils. It is not to be wondered at if they were thrilled by the thought of their unusual situation; and perhaps the soldier gave utterance to the sentiment of both when he sang, "in Chinese singing" (so that we see he had already profited by his lessons), these two appropriate verses:

"We do not know where we are to sleep to-night,

117

In a thousand miles of desert where we can see no human smoke."

In a little temple, hard by the sea-shore, they lay down to repose; sleep overtook them as they lay; and when they awoke, "the east was already white" for their last morning in Japan. They seized a fisherman's boat and rowed out—Perry lying far to sea because of the two tides. Their very manner of boarding was significant of determination; for they had no sooner caught hold upon the ship than they kicked away their boat to make return impossible. And now you would have thought that all was over. But the Commodore was already in treaty with the Shogun's Government; it was one of the stipulations that no Japanese was to be aided in escaping from Japan; and Yoshida and his followers were handed over as prisoners to the authorities at Simoda. That night he who had been to explore the secrets of the barbarian slept, if he might sleep at all, in a cell too short for lying down at full length, and too low for standing upright. There are some disappointments too great for commentary.

Sákuma, implicated by his handwriting, was sent into his own province in confinement, from which he was soon released. Yoshida and the soldier suffered a long and miserable period of captivity, and the latter, indeed, died, while yet in prison, of a skin disease. But such a spirit as that of Yoshida-Torajiro is not easily made or kept a captive; and that which cannot be broken by misfortune you shall seek in vain to confine in a bastille. He was indefatigably active, writing reports to Government and treatises for dissemination. These latter were contraband; and yet he found no difficulty in their distribution, for he always had the jailor on his side. It was in vain that they kept changing him from one prison to another; Government by that plan only hastened the spread of new ideas; for Yoshida had only to arrive to make a convert. Thus, though he himself has laid by the heels, he confirmed and extended his party in the State.

At last, after many lesser transferences, he was given over from the prisons of the Shogun to those of his own superior, the Daimio of Choshu. I conceive it possible that he may then have served out his time for the attempt to leave Japan, and was now resigned to the provincial Government on a lesser count, as a Ronyin or feudal rebel. But, however that may be, the change was of great importance to Yoshida; for by the influence of his admirers in the

Daimio's council, he was allowed the privilege, underhand, of dwelling in his own house. And there, as well to keep up communication with his fellow-reformers as to pursue his work of education, he received boys to teach. It must not be supposed that he was free; he was too marked a man for that; he was probably assigned to some small circle, and lived, as we should say, under police surveillance; but to him, who had done so much from under lock and key, this would seem a large and profitable liberty.

It was at this period that Mr. Masaki was brought into personal contact with Yoshida; and hence, through the eyes of a boy of thirteen, we get one good look at the character and habits of the hero. He was ugly and laughably disfigured with the smallpox; and while nature had been so niggardly with him from the first, his personal habits were even sluttish. His clothes were wretched; when he ate or washed he wiped his hands upon his sleeves; and as his hair was not tied more than once in the two months, it was often disgusting to behold. With such a picture, it is easy to believe that he never married. A good teacher, gentle in act, although violent and abusive in speech, his lessons were apt to go over the heads of his scholars and to leave them gaping, or more often laughing. Such was his passion for study that he even grudged himself natural repose; and when he grew drowsy over his books he would, if it was summer, put mosquitoes up his sleeve; and, if it was winter, take off his shoes and run barefoot on the snow. His handwriting was exceptionally villainous; poet though he was, he had no taste for what was elegant; and in a country where to write beautifully was not the mark of a scrivener but an admired accomplishment for gentlemen, he suffered his letters to be jolted out of him by the press of matter and the heat of his convictions. He would not tolerate even the appearance of a bribe; for bribery lay at the root of much that was evil in Japan, as well as in countries nearer home; and once when a merchant brought him his son to educate, and added, as was customary, [185] a little private sweetener, Yoshida dashed the money in the giver's face, and launched into such an outbreak of indignation as made the matter public in the school. He was still, when Masaki knew him, much weakened by his hardships in prison; and the presentation sword, three feet long, was too heavy for him to wear without distress; yet he would always gird it on when he went to dig in his garden. That is a touch which qualifies the man. A weaker nature would have shrunk from the sight of what only commemorated a failure. But he was of Thoreau's mind, that if you can "make your failure tragical by courage, it will not differ from success." He could look back without confusion to his enthusiastic promise. If events had been contrary, and he found himself unable to carry out that purpose—well, there was but the more reason to be brave and constant in another; if he could not carry the sword into barbarian lands, it should at least be witness to a life spent entirely for Japan.

This is the sight we have of him as he appeared to schoolboys, but not related in the schoolboy spirit. A man so careless of the graces must be out of court with boys and women. And, indeed, as we have all been more or less to school, it will astonish no one that Yoshida was regarded by his scholars as a laughing-stock. The schoolboy has a keen sense of humour. Heroes he learns to understand and to admire in books; but he is not forward to recognise the heroic under the traits of any contemporary man, and least of all in a brawling, dirty, and eccentric teacher. But as the years went by, and the scholars of Yoshida continued in vain to look around them for the abstractly perfect, and began more and more to understand the drift of his instructions, they learned to look back upon their comic school-master as upon the noblest of mankind.

The last act of this brief and full existence was already near at hand. Some of his work was done; for already there had been Dutch teachers admitted into Nangasaki, and the country at large was keen for the new learning. But though the renaissance had begun, it was impeded and dangerously threatened by the power of the Shogun. His minister—the same who was afterwards assassinated in the snow in the very midst of his bodyguard—not only held back pupils from going to the Dutchmen, but by spies and detectives, by imprisonment and death, kept thinning out of Japan the most intelligent and active spirits. It is the old story of a power upon its last legs—learning to the bastille, and courage to the block; when there are none left but sheep and donkeys, the State will have been saved. But a man must not think to cope with a Revolution; nor a minister, however fortified with guards, to hold in check a country that had given birth to such men as Yoshida and his soldier-follower. The violence of the ministerial Tarquin only served to direct attention to the illegality of his master's rule; and people began to turn their allegiance from Yeddo and the Shogun to the long-forgotten Mikado in his seclusion at Kioto. At this juncture, whether in consequence or not, the relations between these two rulers became strained; and the Shogun's minister set forth for Kioto to put another affront upon the rightful sovereign. The circumstance was well fitted to precipitate events. It was a piece of religion to defend the Mikado; it was a plain piece of political righteousness to oppose a tyrannical and bloody usurpation. To Yoshida the moment for action seemed to have arrived. He was himself still confined in Choshu. Nothing was free but his intelligence; but with that he sharpened a sword for the Shogun's minister. A party of his followers were to waylay the tyrant at a village on the Yeddo and Kioto road, present him with a petition, and put him to the sword. But Yoshida and his friends were closely observed; and the too great expedition of two of the conspirators, a boy of eighteen and his brother, wakened the suspicion of the authorities, and led to a full discovery of the plot and the arrest of all who were concerned.

In Yeddo, to which he was taken, Yoshida was thrown again into a strict confinement. But he was not left destitute of sympathy in this last hour of trial. In the next cell lay one Kusákabé, a reformer from the southern highlands of Satzuma. They were in prison for different plots indeed, but for the same intention; they shared the same beliefs and the same aspirations for Japan; many and long were the conversations they held through the prison wall, and dear was the sympathy that soon united them. It fell first to the lot of Kusákabé to pass before the judges; and when sentence had been pronounced he was led towards the place of death below Yoshida's window. To turn the head would have been to implicate his fellow-prisoner; but he threw him a look from his eye, and bade him farewell in a loud voice, with these two Chinese verses:—

"It is better to be a crystal and be broken,

Than to remain perfect like a tile upon the housetop."

So Kusákabé, from the highlands of Satzuma, passed out of the theatre of this world. His death was like an antique worthy's.

A little after, and Yoshida too must appear before the Court. His last scene was of a piece with his career, and fitly crowned it. He seized on the opportunity of a public audience, confessed and gloried in his design, and, reading his auditors a lesson in the history of their country, told at length the illegality of the Shogun's power and the crimes by which its exercise was sullied. So, having said his say for once, he was led forth and executed, thirty-one years old.

A military engineer, a bold traveller (at least in wish), a poet, a patriot, a schoolmaster, a friend to learning, a martyr to reform,—there are not many men, dying at seventy, who have served their country in such various characters. He was not only wise and provident in thought, but surely one of the fieriest of heroes in execution. It is hard to say which is most remarkable—his capacity for command, which subdued his very jailors; his hot, unflagging zeal; or his stubborn superiority to defeat. He failed in each particular enterprise that he attempted; and yet we have only to look at his country to see how complete has been his general success. His friends and pupils made the majority of leaders in that final Revolution, now some twelve years old; and many of them are, or were until the other day, high placed among the rulers of Japan. And when we see all round us these brisk intelligent students, with their strange foreign air, we should never forget how Yoshida marched afoot from Choshu to Yeddo, and from Yeddo to Nangasaki, and from Nangasaki back again to Yeddo; how he boarded the American ship, his dress stuffed with writing material; nor how he languished in prison, and finally gave his death, as he had formerly given all his life and strength and leisure, to gain for his native land that very benefit which she now enjoys so largely. It is better to be Yoshida and perish, than to be only Sákuma and yet save the hide. Kusákabé, of Satzuma, has said the word: it is better to be a crystal and be broken.

I must add a word; for I hope the reader will not fail to perceive that this is as much the story of a heroic people as that of a heroic man. It is not enough to remember Yoshida; we must not forget the common soldier, nor Kusákabé, nor the boy of eighteen, Nomura, of Choshu, whose eagerness betrayed the plot. It is exhilarating to have lived in the same days with these great-hearted gentlemen. Only a few miles from us, to speak by the proportion of the universe, while I was droning over my lessons, Yoshida was goading himself to be wakeful with the stings of the mosquito; and while you were grudging a penny income tax, Kusákabé was stepping to death with a noble sentence on his lips.

FRANÇOIS VILLON, STUDENT, POET, AND HOUSEBREAKER.

Perhaps one of the most curious revolutions in literary history is the sudden bull's-eye light cast by M. Longnon on the obscure existence of François Villon. [192] His book is not remarkable merely as a chapter of biography exhumed after four centuries. To readers of the poet it will recall, with a flavour of satire, that characteristic passage in which he bequeaths his spectacles—with a humorous reservation of the case—to the hospital for blind paupers known as the Fifteen-Score. Thus equipped, let the blind paupers go and separate the good from the bad in the cemetery of the Innocents! For his own part the poet can see no distinction. Much have the dead people made of their advantages. What does it matter now that they have lain in state beds and nourished portly bodies upon cakes and cream! Here they all lie, to be trodden in the mud; the large estate and the small, sounding virtue and adroit or powerful vice, in very much the same condition; and a bishop not to be distinguished from a lamp-lighter with even the strongest spectacles.

Such was Villon's cynical philosophy. Four hundred years after his death, when surely all danger might be considered at an end, a pair of critical spectacles have been applied to his own remains; and though he left behind him a sufficiently ragged reputation from the first, it is only after these four hundred years that his delinquencies have been finally tracked home, and we can assign him to his proper place among the good or wicked. It is a staggering thought, and one that affords a fine figure of the imperishability of men's acts, that the stealth of the private inquiry office can be carried so far back into the dead and dusty past. We are not so soon quit of our concerns as Villon fancied. In the extreme of dissolution, when not so much as a man's name is remembered, when his dust is scattered to the four winds, and perhaps the very grave and the very graveyard where he was laid to rest have been forgotten, desecrated, and buried under populous towns,—even in this extreme let an antiquary fall across a sheet of manuscript, and the name will be recalled, the old infamy will pop out into daylight like a toad out of a fissure in the rock, and the shadow of the shade of what was once a man will be heartily pilloried by his descendants. A little while ago and Villon was almost totally forgotten; then he was revived for the sake of his verses; and now he is being revived with a vengeance in the detection of his misdemeanours. How unsubstantial is this projection of a man's existence, which can lie in abeyance for centuries and then be brushed up again and set forth for the consideration of posterity by a few dips in an antiquary's inkpot! This precarious tenure of fame goes a long way to justify those (and they are not few) who prefer cakes and cream in the immediate present.

A Wild Youth.

François de Montcorbier, alias François des Loges, alias François Villon, alias Michel Mouton, Master of Arts in the University of Paris, was born in that city in the summer of 1431. It was a memorable year for France on other and higher considerations. A great-hearted girl and a poor-hearted boy made, the one her last, the other his first appearance on the public stage of that unhappy country. On the 30th of May the ashes of Joan of Arc were thrown into the Seine, and on the 2d of December our Henry Sixth made his Joyous Entry dismally enough into disaffected and depopulating Paris. Sword and fire still ravaged the open country. On a single April Saturday twelve hundred persons, besides children, made their escape out of the starving capital. The hangman, as is not uninteresting to note in connection with Master Francis, was kept hard at work in 1431; on the last of April and on the 4th of May alone, sixty-two bandits swung from Paris gibbets. [195] A more confused or troublous time it would have been difficult to select for a start in life. Not even a man's nationality was certain; for the people of Paris there was no such thing as a Frenchman. The English were the English indeed, but the French were only the Armagnacs, whom, with Joan of Arc at their head, they had beaten back from under their ramparts not two years before. Such public sentiment as they had centred about their dear Duke of Burgundy, and the dear Duke had no more urgent business than to keep out of their neighbourhood. . . . At least, and whether he liked it or not, our disreputable troubadour was tubbed and swaddled as a subject of the English crown.

We hear nothing of Villon's father except that he was poor and of mean extraction. His mother was given piously, which does not imply very much in an old Frenchwoman, and quite uneducated. He had an uncle, a monk in an abbey at Angers, who must have prospered beyond the family average, and was reported to be worth five or six hundred crowns. Of this uncle and his money-box the reader will hear once more. In 1448 Francis became a student of the University of Paris; in 1450 he took the degree of Bachelor, and in 1452 that of Master of Arts. His bourse, or the sum paid weekly for his board, was of the amount of two sous. Now two sous was about the price of a pound of salt butter in the bad times of 1417; it was the price of half-a-pound in the worse times of 1419; and in 1444, just four years before Villon joined the University, it seems to have been taken as the average wage for a day's manual labour. [196] In short, it cannot have been a very profuse allowance to keep a sharp-set lad in breakfast and supper for seven mortal days; and Villon's share of the cakes and pastry and general good cheer, to which he is never weary of referring, must have been slender from the first.

The educational arrangements of the University of Paris were, to our way of thinking, somewhat incomplete. Worldly and monkish elements were presented in a curious confusion, which the youth might disentangle for himself. If he had an opportunity, on the one hand, of acquiring much hair-drawn divinity and a taste for formal disputation, he was put in the way of much gross and flaunting vice upon the other. The lecture room of a scholastic doctor was sometimes under the same roof with establishments of a very different and peculiarly unedifying order. The students had extraordinary privileges, which by all accounts they abused extraordinarily. And while some condemned themselves to an almost sepulchral regularity and seclusion, others fled the schools, swaggered in the street "with their thumbs in their girdle," passed the night in riot, and behaved themselves as the worthy forerunners of Jehan Frollo in the romance of Notre Dame de Paris. Villon tells us himself that he was among the truants, but we hardly needed his avowal. The burlesque erudition in which he sometimes indulged implies no more than the merest smattering of knowledge; whereas his acquaintance with blackguard haunts and industries could only have been acquired by early and consistent impiety and idleness. He passed his degrees, it is true; but some of us who have been to modern universities will make their own reflections on the value of the test. As for his three pupils, Colin

Laurent, Girard Gossouyn, and Jehan Marceau—if they were really his pupils in any serious sense—what can we say but God help them! And sure enough, by his own description, they turned out as ragged, rowdy, and ignorant as was to be looked for from the views and manners of their rare preceptor.

At some time or other, before or during his university career, the poet was adopted by Master Guillaume de Villon, chaplain of Saint Benoît-le-Bétourné near the Sorbonne. From him he borrowed the surname by which he is known to posterity. It was most likely from his house, called the Porte Rouge, and situated in a garden in the cloister of St. Benoît, that Master Francis heard the bell of the Sorbonne ring out the Angelus while he was finishing his Small Testament at Christmastide in 1456. Towards this benefactor he usually gets credit for a respectable display of gratitude. But with his trap and pitfall style of writing, it is easy to make too sure. His sentiments are about as much to be relied on as those of a professional beggar; and in this, as in so many other matters, he comes towards us whining and piping the eye, and goes off again with a whoop and his finger to his nose. Thus, he calls Guillaume de Villon his "more than father," thanks him with a great show of sincerity for having helped him out of many scrapes, and bequeaths him his portion of renown. But the portion of renown which belonged to a young thief, distinguished (if, at the period when he wrote this legacy, he was distinguished at all) for having written some more or less obscene and scurrilous ballads, must have been little fitted to gratify the self-respect or increase the reputation of a benevolent ecclesiastic. The same remark applies to a subsequent legacy of the poet's library, with specification of one work which was plainly neither decent nor devout. We are thus left on the horns of a dilemma. If the chaplain was a godly, philanthropic personage, who had tried to graft good principles and good behaviour on this wild slip of an adopted son, these jesting legacies would obviously cut him to the heart. The position of an adopted son towards his adoptive father is one full of delicacy; where a man lends his name he looks for great consideration. And this legacy of Villon's portion of renown may be taken as the mere fling of an unregenerate scapegrace who has wit enough to recognise in his own shame the readiest weapon of offence against a prosy benefactor's feelings. The gratitude of Master Francis figures, on this reading, as a frightful minus quantity. If, on the other hand, those jests were given and taken in good humour, the whole relation between the pair degenerates into the unedifying complicity of a debauched old chaplain and a witty and dissolute young scholar. At this rate the house with the red door may have rung with the most mundane minstrelsy; and it may have been below its roof that Villon, through a hole in the plaster, studied, as he tells us, the leisures of a rich ecclesiastic.

It was, perhaps, of some moment in the poet's life that he should have inhabited the cloister of Saint Benoît. Three of the most remarkable among his early acquaintances are Catherine de Vausselles, for whom he entertained a short-lived affection and an enduring and most unmanly resentment; Regnier de Montigny, a young blackguard of good birth; and Colin de Cayeux, a fellow with a marked aptitude for picking locks. Now we are on a foundation of mere conjecture, but it is at least curious to find that two of the canons of Saint Benoît answered respectively to the names of Pierre de Vaucel and Etienne de Montigny, and that there was a householder called Nicolas de Cayeux in a street—the Rue des Poirées—in the immediate neighbourhood of the cloister. M. Longnon is almost ready to identify Catherine as the niece of Pierre; Regnier as the nephew of Etienne, and Colin as the son of Nicolas. Without going so far, it must be owned that the approximation of names is significant. As we go on to see the part played by each of these persons in the sordid melodrama of the poet's life, we shall come to regard it as even more notable. Is it not Clough who has remarked that, after all, everything lies in juxtaposition? Many a man's destiny has been settled by nothing apparently more grave than a pretty face on the opposite side of the street and a couple of bad companions round the corner.

Catherine de Vausselles (or de Vaucel—the change is within the limits of Villon's licence) had plainly delighted in the poet's conversation; near neighbours or not, they were much together and Villon made no secret of his court, and suffered himself to believe that his feeling was repaid in kind. This may have been an error from the first, or he may have estranged her by subsequent misconduct or temerity. One can easily imagine Villon an impatient wooer. One thing, at least, is sure: that the affair terminated in a manner bitterly humiliating to Master Francis. In presence of his lady-love, perhaps under her window and certainly with her connivance, he was unmercifully thrashed by one Noë le Joly—beaten, as he says himself, like dirty linen on the washing-board. It is characteristic that his malice had notably increased between the time when he wrote the Small Testament immediately on the back of the occurrence, and the time when he wrote the Large Testament five years after. On the latter occasion nothing is too bad for his "damsel with the twisted nose," as he calls her. She is spared neither hint nor accusation, and he tells his messenger to accost her with the vilest insults. Villon, it is thought, was out of Paris when these amenities escaped his pen; or perhaps the strong arm of Noë le Joly would have been again in requisition. So ends the love story, if love story it may properly be called. Poets are not necessarily fortunate in love; but they usually fall among more romantic circumstances and bear their disappointment with a better grace.

The neighbourhood of Regnier de Montigny and Colin de Cayeux was probably more influential on his after life than the contempt of Catherine. For a man who is greedy of all pleasures, and provided with little money and less dignity of character, we may prophesy a safe and speedy voyage downward. Humble or even truckling virtue may walk unspotted in this life. But only those who despise the pleasures can afford to despise the opinion of the world. A man of a strong, heady temperament, like Villon, is very differently tempted. His eyes lay hold on all provocations greedily, and his heart flames up at a look into imperious desire; he is snared and broached-to by anything and everything, from a pretty face to a piece of pastry in a cookshop window; he will drink the rinsing of the wine cup, stay the latest at the tavern party; tap at the lit windows, follow the sound of singing, and beat the whole neighbourhood for another reveller, as he goes reluctantly homeward; and grudge himself every hour of sleep as a black empty period in which he cannot follow after pleasure. Such a person is lost if he have not dignity, or, failing that, at least pride, which is its shadow and in many ways its substitute. Master Francis, I fancy, would follow his own eager instincts without much spiritual struggle. And we soon find him fallen among thieves in sober, literal earnest, and counting as acquaintances the most disreputable people he could lay his hands on: fellows who stole ducks in Paris Moat; sergeants of the criminal court, and archers of the watch; blackguards who slept at night under the butchers' stalls, and for whom the aforesaid archers peered about carefully with lanterns; Regnier de Montigny, Colin de Cayeux, and their crew, all bound on a favouring breeze towards the gallows; the disorderly abbess of Port Royal, who went about at fair time with soldiers and thieves, and conducted her abbey on the queerest principles, and most likely Perette Mauger, the great Paris receiver of stolen goods, not yet dreaming, poor woman! of the last scene of her career when Henry Cousin, executor of the high justice, shall bury her, alive and most reluctant, in front of the new Montigny gibbet. [204] Nay, our friend soon began to take a foremost rank in this society. He could string off verses, which is always an agreeable talent; and he could make himself useful in many other ways. The whole ragged army of Bohemia, and whosoever loved good cheer without at all loving to work and pay for it, are addressed in contemporary verses as the "Subjects of François Villon." He was a good genius to all hungry and unscrupulous persons; and became the hero of a whole legendary cycle of tavern tricks and cheateries. At best, these were doubtful levities, rather too thievish for a schoolboy, rather too gamesome for a thief. But he would not linger long in this equivocal border land. He must soon have complied with his surroundings. He was one who would go where the cannikin clinked, not caring who should pay; and from supping in the wolves' den, there is but a step to hunting with the pack. And here, as I am on the chapter of his degradation, I shall say all I mean to say about its darkest expression, and be done with it for good. Some charitable critics see no more than a jeu d'esprit, a graceful and trifling exercise of the imagination, in the grimy ballad of Fat Peg (Grosse Margot). I am not able to follow these gentlemen to this polite extreme. Out of all Villon's works that ballad stands forth in flaring reality, gross and ghastly, as a thing written in a contraction of disgust. M. Longnon shows us more and more clearly at every page that we are to read our poet literally, that his names are the names of real persons, and the events he chronicles were actual events. But even if the tendency of criticism had run the other way, this ballad would have gone far to prove itself. I can well understand the reluctance of worthy persons in this matter; for of course it is unpleasant to think of a man of genius as one who held, in the words of Marina to Boult—

"A place, for which the pained'st fiend

Of hell would not in reputation change."

But beyond this natural unwillingness, the whole difficulty of the case springs from a highly virtuous ignorance of life. Paris now is not so different from the Paris of then; and the whole of the doings of Bohemia are not written in the sugar-candy pastorals of Murger. It is really not at all surprising that a young man of the fifteenth century, with a knack of making verses, should accept his bread upon disgraceful terms. The race of those who do is not extinct; and some of them to this day write the prettiest verses imaginable. . . . After this, it were impossible for Master Francis to fall lower: to go and steal for himself would be an admirable advance from every point of view, divine or human.

And yet it is not as a thief, but as a homicide, that he makes his first appearance before angry justice. On June 5, 1455, when he was about twenty-four, and had been Master of Arts for a matter of three years, we behold him for the first time quite definitely. Angry justice had, as it were, photographed him in the act of his homicide; and M. Longnon, rummaging among old deeds, has turned up the negative and printed it off for our instruction. Villon had been supping—copiously we may believe—and sat on a stone bench in front of the Church of St. Benoît, in company with a priest called Gilles and a woman of the name of Isabeau. It was nine o'clock, a mighty late hour for the period, and evidently a fine summer's night. Master Francis carried a mantle, like a prudent man, to keep him from the dews (serain), and had a sword below it dangling from his girdle. So these three dallied in front of St. Benoît, taking their pleasure (pour soy esbatre). Suddenly there arrived upon the scene a priest, Philippe Chermoye or Sermaise, also with sword and cloak, and accompanied by one Master Jehan le Mardi. Sermaise, according to Villon's account, which is all we have to go upon, came up blustering and denying God; as Villon rose to make room for him upon the bench, thrust him rudely back into his place; and finally drew his sword and cut open his lower lip, by what I should imagine was a very clumsy stroke. Up to this point, Villon professes to have been a model of courtesy, even of feebleness: and the brawl, in his version, reads like the fable of the wolf and the lamb.

But now the lamb was roused; he drew his sword, stabbed Sermaise in the groin, knocked him on the head with a big stone, and then, leaving him to his fate, went away to have his own lip doctored by a barber of the name of Fouquet. In one version, he says that Gilles, Isabeau, and Le Mardi ran away at the first high words, and that he and Sermaise had it out alone; in another, Le Mardi is represented as returning and wresting Villon's sword from him: the reader may please himself. Sermaise was picked up, lay all that night in the prison of Saint Benoît, where he was examined by an official of the Châtelet and expressly pardoned Villon, and died on the following Saturday in the Hôtel Dieu.

This, as I have said, was in June. Not before January of the next year could Villon extract a pardon from the king; but while his hand was in, he got two. One is for "François des Loges, alias (autrement dit) de Villon;" and the other runs in the name of François de Montcorbier. Nay, it appears there was a further complication; for in the narrative of the first of these documents, it is mentioned that he passed himself off upon Fouquet, the barber-surgeon, as one Michel Mouton. M. Longnon has a theory that this unhappy accident with Sermaise was the cause of Villon's subsequent irregularities; and that up to that moment he had been the pink of good behaviour. But the matter has to my eyes a more dubious air. A pardon necessary for Des Loges and another for Montcorbier? and these two the same person? and one or both of them known by the alias of Villon, however honestly come by? and lastly, in the heat of the moment, a fourth name thrown out with an assured countenance? A ship is not to be trusted that sails under so many colours. This is not the simple bearing of innocence. No—the young master was already treading crooked paths; already, he would start and blench at a hand upon his shoulder, with the look we know so well in the face of Hogarth's Idle Apprentice; already, in the blue devils, he would see Henry Cousin, the executor of high justice, going in dolorous procession towards Montfaucon, and hear the wind and the birds crying around Paris gibbet.

A Gang of Thieves.

In spite of the prodigious number of people who managed to get hanged, the fifteenth century was by no means a bad time for criminals. A great confusion of parties and great dust of fighting favoured the escape of private housebreakers and quiet fellows who stole ducks in Paris Moat. Prisons were leaky; and as we shall see, a man with a few crowns in his pocket and perhaps some acquaintance among the officials, could easily slip out and become once more a free marauder. There was no want of a sanctuary where he might harbour until troubles blew by; and accomplices helped each other with more or less good faith. Clerks, above all, had remarkable facilities for a criminal way of life; for they were privileged, except in cases of notorious incorrigibility, to be plucked from the hands of rude secular justice and tried by a tribunal of their own. In 1402, a couple of thieves, both clerks of the University, were condemned to death by the Provost of Paris. As they were taken to Montfaucon, they kept crying "high and clearly" for their benefit of clergy, but were none the less pitilessly hanged and gibbeted. Indignant Alma Mater interfered before the king; and the Provost was deprived of all royal offices, and condemned to return the bodies and erect a great stone cross, on the road from Paris to the gibbet graven with the effigies of these two holy martyrs. [210] We shall hear more of the benefit of clergy; for after this the reader will not be surprised to meet with thieves in the shape of tonsured clerks, or even priests and monks.

To a knot of such learned pilferers our poet certainly belonged; and by turning over a few more of M. Longnon's negatives, we shall get a clear idea of their character and doings. Montigny and De Cayeux are names already known; Guy Tabary, Petit-Jehan, Dom Nicolas, little Thibault, who was both clerk and goldsmith, and who made picklocks and melted plate for himself and his companions—with these the reader has still to become acquainted. Petit-Jehan and De Cayeux were handy fellows and enjoyed a useful pre-eminence in honour of their doings with the picklock. "Dictus des Cahyeus est fortis operator crochetorum," says Tabary's interrogation, "sed dictus Petit-Jehan, ejus socius, est forcius operator." But the flower of the flock was little Thibault; it was reported that no lock could stand before him; he had a persuasive hand; let us salute capacity wherever we may find it. Perhaps the term gang is not quite properly applied to the persons whose fortunes we are now about to follow; rather they were independent malefactors, socially intimate, and occasionally joining together for some serious operation just as modern stockjobbers form a syndicate for an important loan. Nor were they at all particular to any branch of misdoing. They did not scrupulously confine themselves to a single sort of theft, as I hear is common among modern thieves. They were ready for anything, from pitch-and-toss to manslaughter. Montigny, for instance, had neglected neither of these extremes, and we find him accused of cheating at games of hazard on the one hand, and on the other of the murder of one Thevenin Pensete in a house by the Cemetery of St. John. If time had only spared us some particulars, might not this last have furnished us with the matter of a grisly winter's tale?

At Christmas-time in 1456, readers of Villon will remember that he was engaged on the Small Testament. About the same period, circa festum nativitatis Domini, he took part in a memorable supper at the Mule Tavern, in front of the Church of St. Mathurin. Tabary, who seems to have been very much Villon's creature, had ordered the supper in the course of the afternoon. He was a man who had had troubles in his time and languished in the Bishop of Paris's prisons on a suspicion of picking locks; confiding, convivial, not very astute—who had copied out a whole improper romance with his own right hand. This supper-party was to be his first introduction to De Cayeux and Petit-Jehan, which was probably a matter of some concern to the poor man's muddy wits; in the sequel, at least, he speaks of both with an undisguised respect, based on professional inferiority in the matter of picklocks. Dom Nicolas, a Picardy monk, was the fifth and last at table. When supper had been despatched and fairly washed down, we may suppose, with white Baigneux or red Beaune, which were favourite wines among the fellowship, Tabary was solemnly sworn over to secrecy on the night's performances; and the party left the Mule and proceeded to an unoccupied house belonging to Robert de Saint-Simon. This, over a low wall, they entered without difficulty. All but Tabary took off their upper garments; a ladder was found and applied to the high wall which separated Saint-Simon's house from the court of the College of Navarre; the four fellows in their shirt-sleeves (as we might say) clambered over in a twinkling; and Master Guy Tabary remained alone beside the overcoats. From the court the burglars made their way into the vestry of the chapel, where they found a large chest, strengthened with iron bands and closed with four locks. One of these locks they picked, and then, by levering up the corner, forced the other three. Inside was a small coffer, of walnut wood, also barred with iron, but fastened with only three locks, which were all comfortably picked by way of the keyhole. In the walnut coffer—a joyous sight by our thieves' lantern—were five hundred crowns of gold. There was some talk of opening the aumries, where, if they had only known, a booty eight or nine times greater lay ready to their hand; but one of the party (I have a humorous suspicion it was Dom Nicolas, the Picardy monk) hurried them away. It was ten o'clock when they mounted the ladder; it was about midnight before Tabary beheld them coming back. To him they gave ten crowns, and promised a share of a two-crown dinner on the morrow; whereat we may suppose his mouth watered. In course of time, he got wind of the real amount of their booty and understood how scurvily he had been used; but he seems to have borne no malice. How could he, against such superb operators as Petit-Jehan and De Cayeux; or a person like Villon, who could have made a new improper romance out of his own head, instead of merely copying an old one with mechanical right hand?

The rest of the winter was not uneventful for the gang. First they made a demonstration against the Church of St. Mathurin after chalices, and were ignominiously chased away by barking dogs. Then Tabary fell out with Casin Chollet, one of the fellows who stole ducks in Paris Moat, who subsequently became a sergeant of the Châtelet and distinguished himself by misconduct, followed by imprisonment and public castigation, during the wars of Louis Eleventh. The quarrel was not conducted with a proper regard to the king's peace, and the pair publicly belaboured each other until the police stepped in, and Master Tabary was cast once more into the prisons of the Bishop. While he still lay in durance, another job was cleverly executed by the band in broad daylight, at the Augustine Monastery. Brother Guillaume Coiffier was beguiled by an accomplice to St. Mathurin to say mass; and during his absence, his chamber was entered and five or six hundred crowns in money and some silver plate successfully abstracted. A melancholy man was Coiffier on his return! Eight crowns from this adventure were forwarded by little Thibault to the incarcerated Tabary; and with these he bribed the jailor and reappeared in Paris taverns. Some time before or shortly after this, Villon set out for Angers, as he had promised in the Small Testament. The object of this excursion was not merely to avoid the presence of his cruel mistress or the strong arm of Noë le Joly, but to plan a deliberate robbery on his uncle the monk. As soon as he had properly studied the ground, the others were to go over in force from Paris—picklocks and all—and away with my uncle's strongbox! This throws a comical sidelight on his own accusation against his relatives, that they had "forgotten natural duty" and disowned him because he was poor. A poor relation is a distasteful circumstance at the best, but a poor relation who plans deliberate robberies against those of his blood, and trudges hundreds of weary leagues to put them into execution, is surely a little on the wrong side of toleration. The uncle at Angers may have been monstrously undutiful; but the nephew from Paris was upsides with him.

On the 23d April, that venerable and discreet person, Master Pierre Marchand, Curate and Prior of Paray-le-Monial, in the diocese of Chartres, arrived in Paris and put up at the sign of the Three Chandeliers, in the Rue de la Huchette. Next day, or the day after, as he was breakfasting at the sign of the Armchair, he fell into talk with two customers, one of whom was a priest and the other our friend Tabary. The idiotic Tabary became mighty confidential as to his past life. Pierre Marchand, who was an acquaintance of Guillaume Coiffier's and had sympathised with him over his loss, pricked up his ears at the mention of picklocks, and led on the transcriber of improper romances from one thing to another, until they were fast friends. For picklocks the Prior of Paray professed a keen curiosity; but Tabary, upon some late alarm, had thrown all his into the Seine. Let that be no difficulty, however, for was there not little Thibault, who could make them of all shapes and sizes, and to whom Tabary, smelling an accomplice, would be only too glad to introduce his new acquaintance? On the morrow, accordingly, they met; and Tabary, after having first wet his whistle at the prior's expense, led him to Notre Dame and presented him to four or five "young companions," who were keeping sanctuary in the church. They were all clerks, recently escaped, like Tabary himself, from the episcopal prisons. Among these we may notice Thibault, the operator, a little fellow of twenty-six, wearing long hair behind. The Prior expressed, through Tabary, his anxiety to become their accomplice and altogether such as they were (de leur sorte et de leurs complices). Mighty polite they showed themselves, and made him many fine speeches in return. But for all that, perhaps because they had longer heads than Tabary, perhaps

136

because it is less easy to wheedle men in a body, they kept obstinately to generalities and gave him no information as to their exploits, past, present, or to come. I suppose Tabary groaned under this reserve; for no sooner were he and the Prior out of the church than he fairly emptied his heart to him, gave him full details of many hanging matters in the past, and explained the future intentions of the band. The scheme of the hour was to rob another Augustine monk, Robert de la Porte, and in this the Prior agreed to take a hand with simulated greed. Thus, in the course of two days, he had turned this wineskin of a Tabary inside out. For a while longer the farce was carried on; the Prior was introduced to Petit-Jehan, whom he describes as a little, very smart man of thirty, with a black beard and a short jacket; an appointment was made and broken in the de la Porte affair; Tabary had some breakfast at the Prior's charge and leaked out more secrets under the influence of wine and friendship; and then all of a sudden, on the 17th of May, an alarm sprang up, the Prior picked up his skirts and walked quietly over to the Châtelet to make a deposition, and the whole band took to their heels and vanished out of Paris and the sight of the police.

Vanish as they like, they all go with a clog about their feet. Sooner or later, here or there, they will be caught in the fact, and ignominiously sent home. From our vantage of four centuries afterwards, it is odd and pitiful to watch the order in which the fugitives are captured and dragged in.

Montigny was the first. In August of that same year, he was laid by the heels on many grievous counts; sacrilegious robberies, frauds, incorrigibility, and that bad business about Thevenin Pensete in the house by the cemetery of St. John. He was reclaimed by the ecclesiastical authorities as a clerk; but the claim was rebutted on the score of incorrigibility, and ultimately fell to the ground; and he was condemned to death by the Provost of Paris. It was a very rude hour for Montigny, but hope was not yet over. He was a fellow of some birth; his father had been king's pantler; his sister, probably married to some one about the Court, was in the family way, and her health would be endangered if the execution was proceeded with. So down comes Charles the Seventh with letters of mercy, commuting the penalty to a year in a dungeon on bread and water, and a pilgrimage to the shrine of St. James in

Galicia. Alas! the document was incomplete; it did not contain the full tale of Montigny's enormities; it did not recite that he had been denied benefit of clergy, and it said nothing about Thevenin Pensete. Montigny's hour was at hand. Benefit of clergy, honourable descent from king's pantler, sister in the family way, royal letters of commutation—all were of no avail. He had been in prison in Rouen, in Tours, in Bordeaux, and four times already in Paris; and out of all these he had come scatheless; but now he must make a little excursion as far as Montfaucon with Henry Cousin, executor of high justice. There let him swing among the carrion crows.

About a year later, in July 1458, the police laid hands on Tabary. Before the ecclesiastical commissary he was twice examined, and, on the latter occasion, put to the question ordinary and extraordinary. What a dismal change from pleasant suppers at the Mule, where he sat in triumph with expert operators and great wits! He is at the lees of life, poor rogue; and those fingers which once transcribed improper romances are now agonisingly stretched upon the rack. We have no sure knowledge, but we may have a shrewd guess of the conclusion. Tabary, the admirer, would go the same way as those whom he admired.

The last we hear of is Colin de Cayeux. He was caught in autumn 1460, in the great Church of St. Leu d'Esserens, which makes so fine a figure in the pleasant Oise valley between Creil and Beaumont. He was reclaimed by no less than two bishops; but the Procureur for the Provost held fast by incorrigible Colin. 1460 was an ill-starred year: for justice was making a clean sweep of "poor and indigent persons, thieves, cheats, and lockpickers," in the neighbourhood of Paris; [220a] and Colin de Cayeux, with many others, was condemned to death and hanged. [220b]

Villon and the Gallows.

Villon was still absent on the Angers expedition when the Prior of Paray sent such a bombshell among his accomplices; and the dates of his return and arrest remain undiscoverable. M. Campaux plausibly enough opined for the autumn of 1457, which would make him closely follow on Montigny, and the first of those denounced by the Prior to fall into the toils. We may suppose, at least, that it was not long thereafter; we may suppose him competed for between lay and clerical Courts; and we may suppose him alternately pert and impudent, humble and fawning, in his defence. But at the end of all supposing, we come upon some nuggets of fact. For first, he was put to the question by water. He who had tossed off so many cups of white Baigneux or red Beaune, now drank water through linen folds, until his bowels were flooded and his heart stood still. After so much raising of the elbow, so much outcry of fictitious thirst, here at last was enough drinking for a lifetime. Truly, of our pleasant vices, the gods make whips to scourge us. And secondly he was condemned to be hanged. A man may have been expecting a catastrophe for years, and yet find himself unprepared when it arrives. Certainly, Villon found, in this legitimate issue of his career, a very staggering and grave consideration. Every beast, as he says, clings bitterly to a whole skin. If everything is lost, and even honour, life still remains; nay, and it becomes, like the ewe lamb in Nathan's parable, as dear as all the rest. "Do you fancy," he asks, in a lively ballad, "that I had not enough philosophy under my hood to cry out: 'I appeal'? If I had made any bones about the matter, I should have been planted upright in the fields, by the St. Denis Road"— Montfaucon being on the way to St. Denis. An appeal to Parliament, as we saw in the case of Colin de Cayeux, did not necessarily lead to an acquittal or a commutation; and while the matter was pending, our poet had ample opportunity to reflect on his position. Hanging is a sharp argument, and to swing with many others on the gibbet adds a horrible corollary for the imagination. With the aspect of Montfaucon he was well acquainted; indeed, as the neighbourhood appears to have been sacred to junketing and nocturnal picnics of wild young men and women, he had probably studied it under all varieties of hour and weather. And now, as he lay in prison waiting the mortal push, these different aspects crowded back on his imagination with a new and startling significance; and he wrote a ballad, by way of epitaph for himself and his companions, which remains unique in the annals of mankind. It is, in the highest sense, a piece of his biography:—

"La pluye nous a debuez et lavez,

Et le soleil dessechez et noirciz;

Pies, corbeaulx, nous ont les yeux cavez,

Et arrachez la barbe et les sourcilz.

Jamais, nul temps, nous ne sommes rassis;

Puis ça, puis là, comme le vent varie,

A son plaisir sans cesser nous charie,

Plus becquetez d'oiscaulx que dez à couldre.

Ne soyez donc de nostre confrairie,

Mais priez Dieu que tous nous vueille absouldre."

Here is some genuine thieves' literature after so much that was spurious; sharp as an etching, written with a shuddering soul. There is an intensity of consideration in the piece that shows it to be the transcript of familiar thoughts. It is the quintessence of many a doleful nightmare on the straw, when he felt himself swing helpless in the wind, and saw the birds turn about him, screaming and menacing his eyes.

And, after all, the Parliament changed his sentence into one of banishment; and to Roussillon, in Dauphiny, our poet must carry his woes without delay. Travellers between Lyons and Marseilles may remember a station on the line, some way below Vienne, where the Rhone fleets seaward between vine-clad hills. This was Villon's Siberia. It would be a little warm in summer perhaps, and a little cold in winter in that draughty valley between two great mountain fields; but what with the hills, and the racing river, and the fiery Rhone wines, he was little to be pitied on the conditions of his exile. Villon, in a remarkably bad ballad, written in a breath, heartily thanked and fulsomely belauded the Parliament; the envoi, like the proverbial postscript of a lady's letter, containing the pith of his performance in a request for three days' delay to settle his affairs and bid his friends farewell. He was probably not followed out of Paris, like Antoine Fradin, the popular preacher, another exile of a few years later, by weeping multitudes; [224] but I daresay one or two rogues of his acquaintance would keep him company for a mile or so on the south road, and drink a bottle with him before they turned. For banished people, in those days, seem to have set out on their own responsibility, in their own guard, and at their own expense. It was no joke to make one's way from Paris to Roussillon alone and penniless in the fifteenth century. Villon says he left a rag of his tails on every bush. Indeed, he must have had many a weary tramp, many a slender meal, and many a to-do with blustering captains of the Ordonnance. But with one of his light fingers, we may fancy that he took as good as he gave; for every rag of his tail, he would manage to indemnify himself upon the population in the shape of food, or wine, or ringing money; and his route would be traceable across France and Burgundy by housewives and inn-keepers lamenting over petty thefts, like the track of a single human locust. A strange figure he must have cut in the eyes of the good country people: this ragged, blackguard city poet, with a smack of the Paris student, and a smack of the Paris street arab, posting along the highways, in rain or sun, among the green fields and vineyards. For himself, he had no taste for rural loveliness; green fields and vineyards would be mighty indifferent to Master Francis; but he would often have his tongue in his cheek at the simplicity of rustic dupes, and often, at city gates, he might stop to contemplate the gibbet with its swinging bodies, and hug himself on his escape.

How long he stayed at Roussillon, how far he became the protégé of the Bourbons, to whom that town belonged, or when it was that he took part, under the auspices of Charles of Orleans, in a rhyming tournament to be referred to once again in the pages of the present volume, are matters that still remain in darkness, in spite of M. Longnon's diligent rummaging among archives. When we next find him, in summer 1461, alas! he is once more in durance: this time at Méun-sur-Loire, in the prisons of Thibault d'Aussigny, Bishop of Orleans. He had been lowered in a basket into a noisome pit, where he lay, all summer, gnawing hard crusts and railing upon fate. His teeth, he says, were like the teeth of a rake: a touch of haggard portraiture all the more real for being excessive and burlesque, and all the more proper to the man for being a caricature of his own misery. His eyes were "bandaged with thick walls." It might blow hurricanes overhead; the lightning might leap in high heaven; but no word of all this reached him in his noisome pit. "Il n'entre, ou gist, n'escler ni tourbillon." Above all, he was fevered with envy and anger at the freedom of others; and his heart flowed over into curses as he thought of Thibault d'Aussigny, walking the streets in God's sunlight, and blessing people with extended fingers. So much we find sharply lined in his own poems. Why he was cast again into prison—how he had again managed to shave the gallows—this we know not, nor, from the destruction of authorities, are we ever likely to learn. But on October 2d, 1461, or some day immediately preceding, the new King, Louis Eleventh, made his joyous entry into Méun. Now it was a part of the formality on such occasions for the new King to liberate certain prisoners; and so the basket was let down into Villon's pit, and hastily did Master Francis scramble in, and was most joyfully hauled up, and shot out, blinking and tottering, but once more a free man, into the blessed sun and wind. Now or never is the time for verses! Such a happy revolution would turn the head of a stocking-weaver, and set him jingling rhymes. And so—after a voyage to Paris, where he finds Montigny and De Cayeux clattering, their bones upon the gibbet, and his three pupils roystering in Paris streets, "with their thumbs under their girdles,"—down sits Master Francis to write his Large Testament, and perpetuate his name in a sort of glorious ignominy.

The Large Testament.

Of this capital achievement and, with it, of Villon's style in general, it is here the place to speak. The Large Testament is a hurly-burly of cynical and sentimental reflections about life, jesting legacies to friends and enemies, and, interspersed among these many admirable ballades, both serious and absurd. With so free a design, no thought that occurred to him would need to be dismissed without expression; and he could draw at full length the portrait of his own bedevilled soul, and of the bleak and blackguardly world which was the theatre of his exploits and sufferings. If the reader can conceive something between the slap-dash inconsequence of Byron's Don Juan and the racy humorous gravity and brief noble touches that distinguish the vernacular poems of Burns, he will have formed some idea of Villon's style. To the latter writer—except in the ballades, which are quite his own, and can be paralleled from no other language known to me—he bears a particular resemblance. In common with Burns he has a certain rugged compression, a brutal vivacity of epithet, a homely vigour, a delight in local personalities, and an interest in many sides of life, that are often despised and passed over by more effete and cultured poets. Both also, in their strong, easy colloquial way, tend to become

142

difficult and obscure; the obscurity in the case of Villon passing at times into the absolute darkness of cant language. They are perhaps the only two great masters of expression who keep sending their readers to a glossary.

"Shall we not dare to say of a thief," asks Montaigne, "that he has a handsome leg?" It is a far more serious claim that we have to put forward in behalf of Villon. Beside that of his contemporaries, his writing, so full of colour, so eloquent, so picturesque, stands out in an almost miraculous isolation. If only one or two of the chroniclers could have taken a leaf out of his book, history would have been a pastime, and the fifteenth century as present to our minds as the age of Charles Second. This gallows-bird was the one great writer of his age and country, and initiated modern literature for France. Boileau, long ago, in the period of perukes and snuff-boxes, recognised him as the first articulate poet in the language; and if we measure him, not by priority of merit, but living duration of influence, not on a comparison with obscure forerunners, but with great and famous successors, we shall instal this ragged and disreputable figure in a far higher niche in glory's temple than was ever dreamed of by the critic. It is, in itself, a memorable fact that, before 1542, in the very dawn of printing, and while modern France was in the making, the works of Villon ran through seven different editions. Out of him flows much of Rabelais; and through Rabelais, directly and indirectly, a deep, permanent, and growing inspiration. Not only his style, but his callous pertinent way of looking upon the sordid and ugly sides of life, becomes every day a more specific feature in the literature of France. And only the other year, a work of some power appeared in Paris, and appeared with infinite scandal, which owed its whole inner significance and much of its outward form to the study of our rhyming thief.

The world to which he introduces us is, as before said, blackguardly and bleak. Paris swarms before us, full of famine, shame, and death; monks and the servants of great lords hold high wassail upon cakes and pastry; the poor man licks his lips before the baker's window; people with patched eyes sprawl all night under the stalls; chuckling Tabary transcribes an improper romance; bare-bosomed lasses and ruffling students swagger in the streets; the drunkard goes stumbling homewards; the graveyard is full of bones; and away on Montfaucon, Colin de Cayeux and Montigny hang draggled in the rain. Is there nothing better to be seen than sordid misery and worthless joys? Only where the poor old mother of the poet kneels in church below painted windows, and makes tremulous supplication to the Mother of God.

In our mixed world, full of green fields and happy lovers, where not long before, Joan of Arc had led one of the highest and noblest lives in the whole story of mankind, this was all worth chronicling that our poet could perceive. His eyes were indeed sealed with his own filth. He dwelt all his life in a pit more noisome than the dungeon at Méun. In the moral world, also, there are large phenomena not cognisable out of holes and corners. Loud winds blow, speeding home deep-laden ships and sweeping rubbish from the earth; the lightning leaps and cleans the face of heaven; high purposes and brave passions shake and sublimate men's spirits; and meanwhile, in the narrow dungeon of his soul, Villon is mumbling crusts and picking vermin.

Along with this deadly gloom of outlook, we must take another characteristic of his work: its unrivalled insincerity. I can give no better similitude of this quality than I have given already: that he comes up with a whine, and runs away with a whoop and his finger to his nose. His pathos is that of a professional mendicant who should happen to be a man of genius; his levity that of a bitter street arab, full of bread. On a first reading, the pathetic passages preoccupy the reader, and he is cheated out of an alms in the shape of sympathy. But when the thing is studied the illusion fades away: in the transitions, above all, we can detect the evil, ironical temper of the man; and instead of a flighty work, where many crude but genuine feelings tumble together for the mastery as in the lists of tournament, we are tempted to think of the Large Testament as of one long-drawn epical grimace, pulled by a merry-andrew, who has found a certain despicable eminence over human respect and human affections by perching himself astride upon the gallows. Between these two views, at best, all temperate judgments will be found to fall; and rather, as I imagine, towards the last.

There were two things on which he felt with perfect and, in one case, even threatening sincerity.

The first of these was an undisguised envy of those richer than himself.

He was for ever drawing a parallel, already exemplified from his own words, between the happy life of the well-to-do and the miseries of the poor. Burns, too proud and honest not to work, continued through all reverses to sing of poverty with a light, defiant note. Béranger waited till he was himself beyond the reach of want, before writing the Old Vagabond or Jacques. Samuel Johnson, although he was very sorry to be poor, "was a great arguer for the advantages of poverty" in his ill days. Thus it is that brave men carry their crosses, and smile with the fox burrowing in their vitals. But Villon, who had not the courage to be poor with honesty, now whiningly implores our sympathy, now shows his teeth upon the dung-heap with an ugly snarl. He envies bitterly, envies passionately. Poverty, he protests, drives men to steal, as hunger makes the wolf sally from the forest. The poor, he goes on, will always have a carping word to say, or, if that outlet be denied, nourish rebellious thoughts. It is a calumny on the noble army of the poor. Thousands in a small way of life, ay, and even in the smallest, go through life with tenfold as much honour and dignity and peace of mind, as the rich gluttons whose dainties and state-beds awakened Villon's covetous temper. And every morning's sun sees thousands who pass whistling to their toil. But Villon was the "mauvais pauvre" defined by Victor Hugo, and, in its English expression, so admirably stereotyped by Dickens. He was the first wicked sansculotte. He is the man of genius with the moleskin cap. He is mighty pathetic and beseeching here in the street, but I would not go down a dark road with him for a large consideration.

The second of the points on which he was genuine and emphatic was common to the middle ages; a deep and somewhat snivelling conviction of the transitory nature of this life and the pity and horror of death. Old age and the grave, with some dark and yet half-sceptical terror of an after-world— these were ideas that clung about his bones like a disease. An old ape, as he says, may play all the tricks in its repertory, and none of them will tickle an audience into good humour. "Tousjours vieil synge est desplaisant." It is not the old jester who receives most recognition at a tavern party, but the young fellow, fresh and handsome, who knows the new slang, and carries off his vice with a certain air. Of this, as a tavern jester himself, he would be pointedly conscious. As for the women with whom he was best acquainted,

145

his reflections on their old age, in all their harrowing pathos, shall remain in the original for me. Horace has disgraced himself to something the same tune; but what Horace throws out with an ill-favoured laugh, Villon dwells on with an almost maudlin whimper.

It is in death that he finds his truest inspiration in the swift and sorrowful change that overtakes beauty; in the strange revolution by which great fortunes and renowns are diminished to a handful of churchyard dust; and in the utter passing away of what was once lovable and mighty. It is in this that the mixed texture of his thought enables him to reach such poignant and terrible effects, and to enchance pity with ridicule, like a man cutting capers to a funeral march. It is in this, also, that he rises out of himself into the higher spheres of art. So, in the ballade by which he is best known, he rings the changes on names that once stood for beautiful and queenly women, and are now no more than letters and a legend. "Where are the snows of yester year?" runs the burden. And so, in another not so famous, he passes in review the different degrees of bygone men, from the holy Apostles and the golden Emperor of the East, down to the heralds, pursuivants, and trumpeters, who also bore their part in the world's pageantries and ate greedily at great folks' tables: all this to the refrain of "So much carry the winds away!" Probably, there was some melancholy in his mind for a yet lower grade, and Montigny and Colin de Cayeux clattering their bones on Paris gibbet. Alas, and with so pitiful an experience of life, Villon can offer us nothing but terror and lamentation about death! No one has ever more skilfully communicated his own disenchantment; no one ever blown a more ear-piercing note of sadness. This unrepentant thief can attain neither to Christian confidence, nor to the spirit of the bright Greek saying, that whom the gods love die early. It is a poor heart, and a poorer age, that cannot accept the conditions of life with some heroic readiness.

* * * * *

The date of the Large Testament is the last date in the poet's biography. After having achieved that admirable and despicable performance, he disappears into the night from whence he came. How or when he died, whether decently in bed or trussed up to a gallows, remains a riddle for foolhardy commentators. It appears his health had suffered in the pit at Méun; he was thirty years of age and quite bald; with the notch in his under lip where Sermaise had struck him with the sword, and what wrinkles the reader may imagine. In default of portraits, this is all I have been able to piece together, and perhaps even the baldness should be taken as a figure of his destitution. A sinister dog, in all likelihood, but with a look in his eye, and the loose flexile mouth that goes with wit and an overweening sensual temperament. Certainly the sorriest figure on the rolls of fame.

CHARLES OF ORLEANS.

For one who was no great politician, nor (as men go) especially wise, capable or virtuous, Charles of Orleans is more than usually enviable to all who love that better sort of fame which consists in being known not widely, but intimately. "To be content that time to come should know there was such a man, not caring whether they knew more of him, or to subsist under naked denominations, without deserts or noble acts," is, says Sir Thomas Browne, a frigid ambition. It is to some more specific memory that youth looks forward in its vigils. Old kings are sometimes disinterred in all the emphasis of life, the hands untainted by decay, the beard that had so often wagged in camp or senate still spread upon the royal bosom; and in busts and pictures, some similitude of the great and beautiful of former days is handed down. In this way, public curiosity may be gratified, but hardly any private aspiration after fame. It is not likely that posterity will fall in love with us, but not impossible that it may respect or sympathise; and so a man would rather leave behind him the portrait of his spirit than a portrait of his face, figura animi magis quam corporis. Of those who have thus survived themselves most completely, left a sort of personal seduction behind them in the world, and retained, after death, the art of making friends, Montaigne and Samuel Johnson certainly stand first. But we have portraits of all sorts of men, from august Cæsar to the king's dwarf; and all sorts of portraits, from a Titian treasured in the Louvre to a profile over the grocer's chimney shelf. And so in a less degree, but no less truly, than the spirit of Montaigne lives on in the delightful Essays, that of Charles of Orleans survives in a few old songs and old account-books; and it is still in the choice of the reader to make this duke's acquaintance, and, if their humours suit, become his friend.

I.

His birth—if we are to argue from a man's parents—was above his merit. It is not merely that he was the grandson of one king, the father of another, and the uncle of a third; but something more specious was to be looked for from the son of his father, Louis de Valois, Duke of Orleans, brother to the mad king Charles VI., lover of Queen Isabel, and the leading patron of art and one of the leading politicians in France. And the poet might have inherited yet higher virtues from his mother, Valentina of Milan, a very pathetic figure of the age, the faithful wife of an unfaithful husband, and the friend of a most unhappy king. The father, beautiful, eloquent, and accomplished, exercised a strange fascination over his contemporaries; and among those who dip nowadays into the annals of the time there are not many—and these few are little to be envied—who can resist the fascination of the mother. All mankind owe her a debt of gratitude because she brought some comfort into the life of the poor madman who wore the crown of France.

Born (May 1391) of such a noble stock, Charles was to know from the first all favours of nature and art. His father's gardens were the admiration of his contemporaries; his castles were situated in the most agreeable parts of France, and sumptuously adorned. We have preserved, in an inventory of 1403, the description of tapestried rooms where Charles may have played in childhood. [238] "A green room, with the ceiling full of angels, and the dossier of shepherds and shepherdesses seeming (faisant contenance) to eat nuts and cherries. A room of gold, silk and worsted, with a device of little children in a river, and the sky full of birds. A room of green tapestry, showing a knight and lady at chess in a pavilion. Another green room, with shepherdesses in a trellised garden worked in gold and silk. A carpet representing cherry-trees, where there is a fountain, and a lady gathering cherries in a basin." These were some of the pictures over which his fancy might busy itself of an afternoon, or at morning as he lay awake in bed. With our deeper and more logical sense of life, we can have no idea how large a space in the attention of mediæval men might be occupied by such figured hangings on the wall. There was something timid and purblind in the view they had of the world. Morally, they saw nothing outside of traditional axioms; and little of the physical aspect of things entered vividly into their mind, beyond what was to be seen on church windows and the walls and floors of palaces. The reader will remember how Villon's mother conceived of heaven and hell and took all her scanty stock of theology from the stained glass that threw its light upon her as she prayed. And there is scarcely a detail of external effect in the chronicles and romances of the time, but might have been borrowed at second hand from a piece of tapestry. It was a stage in the history of mankind which we may see paralleled, to some extent, in the first infant school, where the representations of lions and elephants alternate round the wall with moral verses and trite presentments of the lesser virtues. So that to live in a house of many pictures was tantamount, for the time, to a liberal education in itself.

At Charles's birth an order of knighthood was inaugurated in his honour. At nine years old, he was a squire; at eleven, he had the escort of a chaplain and a schoolmaster; at twelve, his uncle the king made him a pension of twelve thousand livres d'or. [240a] He saw the most brilliant and the most learned persons of France, in his father's Court; and would not fail to notice that these brilliant and learned persons were one and all engaged in rhyming. Indeed, if it is difficult to realise the part played by pictures, it is perhaps even more difficult to realise that played by verses in the polite and active history of the age. At the siege of Pontoise, English and French exchanged defiant ballades over the walls. [240b] If a scandal happened, as in the loathsome thirty-third story of the Cent Nouvelles Nouvelles, all the wits must make rondels and chansonettes, which they would hand from one to another with an unmanly sneer. Ladies carried their favourite's ballades in their girdles. [241a] Margaret of Scotland, all the world knows already, kissed Alain Chartier's lips in honour of the many virtuous thoughts and golden sayings they had uttered; but it is not so well known, that this princess was herself the most industrious of poetasters, that she is supposed to have hastened her death by her literary vigils, and sometimes wrote as many as twelve rondels in the day. [241b] It was in rhyme, even, that the young Charles should learn his lessons. He might get all manner of instruction in the truly noble art of the chase, not without a smack of ethics by the way, from the compendious didactic poem of Gace de la Bigne. Nay, and it was in rhyme that he should learn rhyming: in the verses of his father's Maître d'Hôtel, Eustache Deschamps, which treated of "l'art de dictier et de faire chançons, ballades, virelais et rondeaux," along with many other matters worth attention, from the courts of Heaven to the misgovernment of France. [241c] At this rate, all knowledge is to be had in a goody, and the end of it is an old song. We need not wonder when we hear from Monstrelet that Charles was a very well educated person. He could string Latin texts together by the hour, and make ballades and rondels better than Eustache Deschamps himself. He had seen a mad king who would not change his clothes, and a drunken emperor who could not keep his hand from the wine-cup. He had spoken a great deal with jesters and fiddlers, and with the profligate lords who helped his father to waste the revenues of France. He had seen ladies dance on into broad daylight, and much burning of torches and waste of dainties and good wine. [242a] And when all is said, it was no very helpful preparation for the battle of life. "I believe Louis XI.," writes Comines, "would not have saved himself, if he had not been very differently brought up from such other lords as I have seen educated in this country; for these were taught nothing but to play the jackanapes with finery and fine words." [242b] I am afraid Charles took such lessons to heart, and conceived of life as a season principally for junketing and war. His view of the whole duty of man, so empty, vain, and wearisome to us, was yet sincerely and consistently held. When he came in his ripe years to compare the glory of two kingdoms, England and France, it was on three points only,—pleasures, valour, and riches,—that he cared to measure them; and in the very outset of that tract he speaks of the life of the great as passed, "whether in arms, as in assaults, battles, and sieges, or in jousts and tournaments, in high and stately festivities and in funeral solemnities." [243]

When he was no more than thirteen, his father had him affianced to Isabella, virgin-widow of our Richard II. and daughter of his uncle Charles VI.; and, two years after (June 29, 1406), the cousins were married at Compiègne, he fifteen, she seventeen years of age. It was in every way a most desirable match. The bride brought five hundred thousand francs of dowry. The ceremony was of the utmost magnificence, Louis of Orleans figuring in crimson velvet, adorned with no less than seven hundred and ninety-five pearls, gathered together expressly for this occasion. And no doubt it must have been very gratifying for a young gentleman of fifteen, to play the chief part in a pageant so gaily put upon the stage. Only, the bridegroom might have been a little older; and, as ill-luck would have it, the bride herself was of this way of thinking, and would not be consoled for the loss of her title as queen, or the contemptible age of her new husband. Pleuroit fort ladite Isabeau; the said Isabella wept copiously. [244] It is fairly debatable whether Charles was much to be pitied when, three years later (September 1409), this odd marriage was dissolved by death. Short as it was, however, this connection left a lasting stamp upon his mind; and we find that, in the last decade of his life, and after he had remarried for perhaps the second time, he had not yet forgotten or forgiven the violent death of Richard II. "Ce mauvais cas"—that ugly business, he writes, has yet to be avenged.

The marriage festivity was on the threshold of evil days. The great rivalry between Louis of Orleans and John the Fearless, Duke of Burgundy, had been forsworn with the most reverend solemnities. But the feud was only in abeyance, and John of Burgundy still conspired in secret. On November 23, 1407—in that black winter when the frost lasted six-and-sixty days on end—a summons from the king reached Louis of Orleans at the Hôtel Barbette, where he had been supping with Queen Isabel. It was seven or eight in the evening, and the inhabitants of the quarter were abed. He set forth in haste, accompanied by two squires riding on one horse, a page, and a few varlets running with torches. As he rode, he hummed to himself and trifled with his glove. And so riding, he was beset by the bravoes of his enemy and slain. My lord of Burgundy set an ill precedent in this deed, as he found some years after on the bridge of Montereau; and even in the meantime he did not profit quietly by his rival's death. The horror of the other princes seems to have perturbed himself; he avowed his guilt in the council, tried to brazen it out, finally lost heart and fled at full gallop, cutting bridges behind him, towards Bapaume and Lille. And so there we have the head of one faction, who had just made himself the most formidable man in France, engaged in a remarkably hurried journey, with black care on the pillion. And meantime, on the other side, the widowed duchess came to Paris in appropriate mourning, to demand justice for her husband's death. Charles VI., who was then in a lucid interval, did probably all that he could, when he raised up the kneeling suppliant with kisses and smooth words. Things were at a dead-lock. The criminal might be in the sorriest fright, but he was still the greatest of vassals. Justice was easy to ask and not difficult to promise; how it was to be executed was another question. No one in France was strong enough to punish John of Burgundy; and perhaps no one, except the widow, very sincere in wishing to punish him.

She, indeed, was eaten up of zeal; but the intensity of her eagerness wore her out; and she died about a year after the murder, of grief and indignation, unrequited love and unsatisfied resentment. It was during the last months of her life that this fiery and generous woman, seeing the soft hearts of her own children, looked with envy on a certain natural son of her husband's destined to become famous in the sequel as the Bastard of Orleans, or the brave Dunois. "You were stolen from me," she said; "it is you who are fit to avenge your father." These are not the words of ordinary mourning, or of an ordinary woman. It is a saying, over which Balzac would have rubbed his episcopal hands. That the child who was to avenge her husband had not been born out of her body, was a thing intolerable to Valentina of Milan; and the expression of this singular and tragic jealousy is preserved to us by a rare chance, in such straightforward and vivid words as we are accustomed to hear only on the stress of actual life, or in the theatre. In history—where we see things as in a glass darkly, and the fashion of former times is brought before us, deplorably adulterated and defaced, fitted to very vague and pompous words, and strained through many men's minds of everything personal or precise—this speech of the widowed duchess startles a reader, somewhat as the footprint startled Robinson Crusoe. A human voice breaks in upon the silence of the study, and the student is aware of a fellow-creature in his world of documents. With such a clue in hand, one may imagine how this wounded lioness would spur and exasperate the resentment of her children, and what would be the last words of counsel and command she left behind her.

With these instancies of his dying mother—almost a voice from the tomb—still tingling in his ears, the position of young Charles of Orleans, when he was left at the head of that great house, was curiously similar to that of Shakspeare's Hamlet. The times were out of joint; here was a murdered father to avenge on a powerful murderer; and here, in both cases, a lad of inactive disposition born to set these matters right. Valentina's commendation of Dunois involved a judgment on Charles, and that judgment was exactly correct. Whoever might be, Charles was not the man to avenge his father. Like Hamlet, this son of a dear father murdered was sincerely grieved at heart. Like Hamlet, too, he could unpack his heart with words, and wrote a most eloquent letter to the king, complaining that what was denied to him would not be denied "to the lowest born and poorest man on earth."

Even in his private hours he strove to preserve a lively recollection of his injury, and keep up the native hue of resolution. He had gems engraved with appropriate legends, hortatory or threatening: "Dieu le scet," God knows it; or "Souvenez-vous de —" Remember! [248] It is only towards the end that the two stories begin to differ; and in some points the historical version is the more tragic. Hamlet only stabbed a silly old councillor behind the arras; Charles of Orleans trampled France for five years under the hoofs of his banditti. The miscarriage of Hamlet's vengeance was confined, at widest, to the palace; the ruin wrought by Charles of Orleans was as broad as France.

Yet the first act of the young duke is worthy of honourable mention. Prodigal Louis had made enormous debts; and there is a story extant, to illustrate how lightly he himself regarded these commercial obligations. It appears that Louis, after a narrow escape he made in a thunder-storm, had a smart access of penitence, and announced he would pay his debts on the following Sunday. More than eight hundred creditors presented themselves, but by that time the devil was well again, and they were shown the door with more gaiety than politeness. A time when such cynical dishonesty was possible for a man of culture is not, it will be granted, a fortunate epoch for creditors. When the original debtor was so lax, we may imagine how an heir would deal with the incumbrances of his inheritance. On the death of Philip the Forward, father of that John the Fearless whom we have seen at work, the widow went through the ceremony of a public renunciation of goods; taking off her purse and girdle, she left them on the grave, and thus, by one notable act, cancelled her husband's debts and defamed his honour. The conduct of young Charles of Orleans was very different. To meet the joint liabilities of his father and mother (for Valentina also was lavish), he had to sell or pledge a quantity of jewels; and yet he would not take advantage of a pretext, even legally valid, to diminish the amount. Thus, one Godefroi Lefèvre, having disbursed many odd sums for the late duke, and received or kept no vouchers, Charles ordered that he should be believed upon his oath. [249] To a modern mind this seems as honourable to his father's memory as if John the Fearless had been hanged as high as Haman. And as things fell out, except a recantation from the University of Paris, which had justified the murder out of party feeling, and various other purely paper reparations, this was about the outside of what Charles was to effect in that direction. He lived five years, and grew up from sixteen to twenty-one, in the midst of the most horrible civil war, or series of civil wars, that ever devastated France; and from first to last his wars were ill-starred, or else his victories useless. Two years after the murder (March 1409), John the Fearless having the upper hand for the moment, a shameful and useless reconciliation took place, by the king's command, in the church of Our Lady at Chartres. The advocate of the Duke of Burgundy stated that Louis of Orleans had been killed "for the good of the king's person and realm." Charles and his brothers, with tears of shame, under protest, pour ne pas desobéir au roi, forgave their father's murderer and swore peace upon the missal. It was, as I say, a shameful and useless ceremony; the very greffier, entering it in his register, wrote in the margin, "Pax, pax, inquit Propheta, et non est Pax." [250] Charles was soon after allied with the abominable Bernard d'Armagnac, even betrothed or married to a daughter of his, called by a name that sounds like a contradiction in terms, Bonne d'Armagnac. From that time forth, throughout all this monstrous period—a very nightmare in the history of France—he is no more than a stalking-horse for the ambitious Gascon. Sometimes the smoke lifts, and you can see him for the twinkling of an eye, a very pale figure; at one moment there is a rumour he will be crowned king; at another, when the uproar has subsided, he will be heard still crying out for justice; and the next (1412), he is showing himself to the applauding populace on the same horse with John of Burgundy. But these are exceptional seasons, and, for the most part, he merely rides at the Gascon's bridle over devastated France. His very party go, not by the name of Orleans, but by the name of Armagnac. Paris is in the hands of the butchers: the peasants have taken to the woods. Alliances are made and broken as if in a country dance; the English called in, now by this one, now by the other. Poor people sing in church, with white faces and lamentable music: "Domine Jesu, parce populo tuo, dirige in viam pacis principes." And the end and upshot of the whole affair for Charles of Orleans is another peace with John the Fearless. France is once more tranquil, with the tranquillity of ruin; he may ride home again to Blois, and look, with what countenance he may, on those gems he had got engraved in the early days of his resentment, "Souvenez-vous de —" Remember! He has killed Polonius, to be sure; but the king is never a penny the worse.

155

II.

From the battle of Agincourt (Oct. 1415) dates the second period of Charles's life. The English reader will remember the name of Orleans in the play of Henry V.; and it is at least odd that we can trace a resemblance between the puppet and the original. The interjection, "I have heard a sonnet begin so to one's mistress" (Act iii. scene 7), may very well indicate one who was already an expert in that sort of trifle; and the game of proverbs he plays with the Constable in the same scene, would be quite in character for a man who spent many years of his life capping verses with his courtiers. Certainly, Charles was in the great battle with five hundred lances (say, three thousand men), and there he was made prisoner as he led the van. According to one story, some ragged English archer shot him down; and some diligent English Pistol, hunting ransoms on the field of battle, extracted him from under a heap of bodies and retailed him to our King Henry. He was the most important capture of the day, and used with all consideration. On the way to Calais, Henry sent him a present of bread and wine (and bread, you will remember, was an article of luxury in the English camp), but Charles would neither eat nor drink. Thereupon, Henry came to visit him in his quarters. "Noble cousin," said he, "how are you?" Charles replied that he was well. "Why, then, do you neither eat nor drink?" And then with some asperity, as I imagine, the young duke told him that "truly he had no inclination for food." And our Henry improved the occasion with something of a snuffle, assuring his prisoner that God had fought against the French on account of their manifold sins and transgressions. Upon this there supervened the agonies of a rough sea passage; and many French lords, Charles, certainly, among the number, declared they would rather endure such another defeat than such another sore trial on shipboard. Charles, indeed, never forgot his sufferings. Long afterwards, he declared his hatred to a seafaring life, and willingly yielded to England the empire of the seas, "because there is danger and loss of life, and God knows what pity when it storms; and sea-sickness is for many people hard to bear; and the rough life that must be led is little suitable for the nobility:" [253] which, of all babyish utterances that ever fell from any public man, may surely bear the bell. Scarcely disembarked, he followed his victor, with such wry face as we may fancy, through the streets of holiday London. And then the doors closed upon his last day of garish life for more than a quarter of a century. After a boyhood passed in the dissipations of a luxurious court or in the camp of war, his ears still stunned and his cheeks still burning from his enemies' jubilations; out of all this ringing of English bells and singing of English anthems, from among all these shouting citizens in scarlet cloaks, and beautiful virgins attired in white, he passed into the silence and solitude of a political prison. [254]

His captivity was not without alleviations. He was allowed to go hawking, and he found England an admirable country for the sport; he was a favourite with English ladies, and admired their beauty; and he did not lack for money, wine, or books; he was honourably imprisoned in the strongholds of great nobles, in Windsor Castle and the Tower of London. But when all is said, he was a prisoner for five-and-twenty years. For five-and-twenty years he could not go where he would, or do what he liked, or speak with any but his gaolers. We may talk very wisely of alleviations; there is only one alleviation for which the man would thank you: he would thank you to open the door. With what regret Scottish James I. bethought him (in the next room perhaps to Charles) of the time when he rose "as early as the day." What would he not have given to wet his boots once more with morning dew, and follow his vagrant fancy among the meadows? The only alleviation to the misery of constraint lies in the disposition of the prisoner. To each one this place of discipline brings his own lesson. It stirs Latude or Baron Trenck into heroic action; it is a hermitage for pious and conformable spirits. Béranger tells us he found prison life, with its regular hours and long evenings, both pleasant and profitable. The Pilgrim's Progress and Don Quixote were begun in prison. It was after they were become (to use the words of one of them), "Oh, worst imprisonment—the dungeon of themselves!" that Homer and Milton worked so hard and so well for the profit of mankind. In the year 1415 Henry V. had two distinguished prisoners, French Charles of Orleans and Scottish James I., who whiled away the hours of their captivity with rhyming. Indeed, there can be no better pastime for a lonely man than the mechanical exercise of verse. Such intricate forms as Charles had been used to from childhood, the ballade with its scanty rhymes; the rondel, with the recurrence first of the whole, then of half the burthen, in thirteen verses, seem to have been invented for the prison and the sick bed. The common Scotch saying, on the sight of anything operose and finical, "he must have had little to do that made that!" might be put as epigraph on all the song books of old France. Making such sorts of verse belongs to the same class of pleasures as guessing acrostics or "burying proverbs." It is almost purely formal, almost purely verbal. It must be done gently and gingerly. It keeps the mind occupied a long time, and never so intently as to be distressing; for anything like strain is against the very nature of the craft. Sometimes things go easily, the refrains fall into their place as if of their own accord, and it becomes something of the nature of an intellectual tennis; you must make your poem as the rhymes will go, just as you must strike your ball as your adversary played it. So that these forms are suitable rather for those who wish to make verses, than for those who wish to express opinions. Sometimes, on the other hand, difficulties arise: rival verses come into a man's head, and fugitive words elude his memory. Then it is that he enjoys at the same time the deliberate pleasures of a connoisseur comparing wines, and the ardour of the chase. He may have been sitting all day long in prison with folded hands; but when he goes to bed, the retrospect will seem animated and eventful.

Besides confirming himself as an habitual maker of verses, Charles acquired some new opinions during his captivity. He was perpetually reminded of the change that had befallen him. He found the climate of England cold and "prejudicial to the human frame;" he had a great contempt for English fruit and English beer; even the coal fires were unpleasing in his eyes. [257a] He was rooted up from among his friends and customs and the places that had known him. And so in this strange land he began to learn the love of his own. Sad people all the world over are like to be moved when the wind is in some particular quarter. So Burns preferred when it was in the west, and blew to him from his mistress; so the girl in the ballade, looking south to Yarrow, thought it might carry a kiss betwixt her and her gallant; and so we find Charles singing of the "pleasant wind that comes from France." [257b] One day, at "Dover-on-the-Sea," he looked across the straits, and saw the sandhills about Calais. And it happened to him, he tells us in a ballade, to remember his happiness over there in the past; and he was both sad and merry at the recollection, and could not have his fill of gazing on the shores of

France. [257c] Although guilty of unpatriotic acts, he had never been exactly unpatriotic in feeling. But his sojourn in England gave, for the time at least, some consistency to what had been a very weak and ineffectual prejudice. He must have been under the influence of more than usually solemn considerations, when he proceeded to turn Henry's puritanical homily after Agincourt into a ballade, and reproach France, and himself by implication, with pride, gluttony, idleness, unbridled covetousness, and sensuality. [258a] For the moment, he must really have been thinking more of France than of Charles of Orleans.

And another lesson he learned. He who was only to be released in case of peace, begins to think upon the disadvantages of war. "Pray for peace," is his refrain: a strange enough subject for the ally of Bernard d'Armagnac. [258b] But this lesson was plain and practical; it had one side in particular that was specially attractive for Charles; and he did not hesitate to explain it in so many words. "Everybody," he writes—I translate roughly—"everybody should be much inclined to peace, for everybody has a deal to gain by it." [258c]

Charles made laudable endeavours to acquire English, and even learned to write a rondel in that tongue of quite average mediocrity. [259a] He was for some time billeted on the unhappy Suffolk, who received fourteen shillings and fourpence a day for his expenses; and from the fact that Suffolk afterwards visited Charles in France while he was negotiating the marriage of Henry VI., as well as the terms of that nobleman's impeachment, we may believe there was some not unkindly intercourse between the prisoner and his gaoler: a fact of considerable interest when we remember that Suffolk's wife was the granddaughter of the poet Geoffrey Chaucer. [259b] Apart from this, and a mere catalogue of dates and places, only one thing seems evident in the story of Charles's captivity. It seems evident that, as these five-and-twenty years drew on, he became less and less resigned. Circumstances were against the growth of such a feeling. One after another of his fellow-prisoners was ransomed and went home. More than once he was himself permitted to visit France; where he worked on abortive treaties and showed himself more eager for his own deliverance than for the profit of his native land.

Resignation may follow after a reasonable time upon despair; but if a man is persecuted by a series of brief and irritating hopes, his mind no more attains to a settled frame of resolution, than his eye would grow familiar with a night of thunder and lightning. Years after, when he was speaking at the trial of that Duke of Alençon, who began life so hopefully as the boyish favourite of Joan of Arc, he sought to prove that captivity was a harder punishment than death. "For I have had experience myself," he said; "and in my prison of England, for the weariness, danger, and displeasure in which I then lay, I have many a time wished I had been slain at the battle where they took me." [260] This is a flourish, if you will, but it is something more. His spirit would sometimes rise up in a fine anger against the petty desires and contrarieties of life. He would compare his own condition with the quiet and dignified estate of the dead; and aspire to lie among his comrades on the field of Agincourt, as the Psalmist prayed to have the wings of a dove and dwell in the uttermost parts of the sea. But such high thoughts came to Charles only in a flash.

John the Fearless had been murdered in his turn on the bridge of Montereau so far back as 1419. His son, Philip the Good—partly to extinguish the feud, partly that he might do a popular action, and partly, in view of his ambitious schemes, to detach another great vassal from the throne of France—had taken up the cause of Charles of Orleans, and negotiated diligently for his release. In 1433 a Burgundian embassy was admitted to an interview with the captive duke, in the presence of Suffolk. Charles shook hands most affectionately with the ambassadors. They asked after his health. "I am well enough in body," he replied, "but far from well in mind. I am dying of grief at having to pass the best days of my life in prison, with none to sympathise." The talk falling on the chances of peace, Charles referred to Suffolk if he were not sincere and constant in his endeavours to bring it about. "If peace depended on me," he said, "I should procure it gladly, were it to cost me my life seven days after." We may take this as showing what a large price he set, not so much on peace, as on seven days of freedom. Seven days!—he would make them seven years in the employment. Finally, he assured the ambassadors of his good will to Philip of Burgundy; squeezed one of them by the hand and nipped him twice in the arm to signify things unspeakable before Suffolk; and two days after sent them Suffolk's barber, one

Jean Carnet, a native of Lille, to testify more freely of his sentiments. "As I speak French," said this emissary, "the Duke of Orleans is more familiar with me than with any other of the household; and I can bear witness he never said anything against Duke Philip." [262a] It will be remembered that this person, with whom he was so anxious to stand well, was no other than his hereditary enemy, the son of his father's murderer. But the honest fellow bore no malice, indeed not he. He began exchanging ballades with Philip, whom he apostrophises as his companion, his cousin, and his brother. He assures him that, soul and body, he is altogether Burgundian; and protests that he has given his heart in pledge to him. Regarded as the history of a vendetta, it must be owned that Charles's life has points of some originality. And yet there is an engaging frankness about these ballades which disarms criticism. [262b] You see Charles throwing himself headforemost into the trap; you hear Burgundy, in his answers begin to inspire him with his own prejudices, and draw melancholy pictures of the misgovernment of France. But Charles's own spirits are so high and so amiable, and he is so thoroughly convinced his cousin is a fine fellow, that one's scruples are carried away in the torrent of his happiness and gratitude. And his would be a sordid spirit who would not clap hands at the consummation (Nov. 1440); when Charles, after having sworn on the Sacrament that he would never again bear arms against England, and pledged himself body and soul to the unpatriotic faction in his own country, set out from London with a light heart and a damaged integrity.

In the magnificent copy of Charles's poems, given by our Henry VII. to Elizabeth of York on the occasion of their marriage, a large illumination figures at the head of one of the pages, which, in chronological perspective, is almost a history of his imprisonment. It gives a view of London with all its spires, the river passing through the old bridge and busy with boats. One side of the White Tower has been taken out, and we can see, as under a sort of shrine, the paved room where the duke sits writing. He occupies a high-backed bench in front of a great chimney; red and black ink are before him; and the upper end of the apartment is guarded by many halberdiers, with the red cross of England on their breast. On the next side of the tower he appears again, leaning out of window and gazing on the river; doubtless there blows just then "a pleasant wind from out the land of France," and some ship comes up the river: "the ship of good news." At the door we find him yet again; this time embracing a messenger, while a groom stands by holding two saddled horses. And yet further to the left, a cavalcade defiles out of the tower; the duke is on his way at last towards "the sunshine of France."

III.

During the five-and-twenty years of his captivity, Charles had not lost in the esteem of his fellow-countrymen. For so young a man, the head of so great a house, and so numerous a party, to be taken prisoner as he rode in the vanguard of France, and stereotyped for all men in this heroic attitude, was to taste untimeously the honours of the grave. Of him, as of the dead, it would be ungenerous to speak evil; what little energy he had displayed would be remembered with piety, when all that he had done amiss was courteously forgotten. As English folk looked for Arthur; as Danes awaited the coming of Ogier; as Somersetshire peasants or sergeants of the Old Guard expected the return of Monmouth or Napoleon; the countrymen of Charles of Orleans looked over the straits towards his English prison with desire and confidence. Events had so fallen out while he was rhyming ballades, that he had become the type of all that was most truly patriotic. The remnants of his old party had been the chief defenders of the unity of France. His enemies of Burgundy had been notoriously favourers and furtherers of English domination. People forgot that his brother still lay by the heels for an unpatriotic treaty with England, because Charles himself had been taken prisoner patriotically fighting against it. That Henry V. had left special orders against his liberation, served to increase the wistful pity with which he was regarded. And when, in defiance of all contemporary virtue, and against express pledges, the English carried war into their prisoner's fief, not only France, but all thinking men in Christendom, were roused to indignation against the oppressors, and sympathy with the victim. It was little wonder if he came to bulk somewhat largely in the imagination of the best of those at home. Charles le Boutteillier, when (as the story goes) he slew Clarence at Beaugé, was only seeking an exchange for Charles of Orleans. [265a] It was one of Joan of Arc's declared intentions to deliver the captive duke. If there was no other way, she meant to cross the seas and bring him home by force. And she professed before her judges a sure knowledge that Charles of Orleans

162

was beloved of God. [265b]

Alas! it was not at all as a deliverer that Charles returned to France. He was nearly fifty years old. Many changes had been accomplished since, at twenty-three, he was taken on the field of Agincourt. But of all these he was profoundly ignorant, or had only heard of them in the discoloured reports of Philip of Burgundy. He had the ideas of a former generation, and sought to correct them by the scandal of a factious party. With such qualifications he came back eager for the domination, the pleasures, and the display that befitted his princely birth. A long disuse of all political activity combined with the flatteries of his new friends to fill him with an overweening conceit of his own capacity and influence. If aught had gone wrong in his absence, it seemed quite natural men should look to him for its redress. Was not King Arthur come again?

The Duke of Burgundy received him with politic honours. He took his guest by his foible for pageantry, all the easier as it was a foible of his own; and Charles walked right out of prison into much the same atmosphere of trumpeting and bell-ringing as he had left behind when he went in. Fifteen days after his deliverance he was married to Mary of Cleves, at St. Omer. The marriage was celebrated with the usual pomp of the Burgundian court; there were joustings, and illuminations, and animals that spouted wine; and many nobles dined together, comme en brigade, and were served abundantly with many rich and curious dishes. [267a] It must have reminded Charles not a little of his first marriage at Compiègne; only then he was two years the junior of his bride, and this time he was five-and-thirty years her senior. It will be a fine question which marriage promises more: for a boy of fifteen to lead off with a lass of seventeen, or a man of fifty to make a match of it with a child of fifteen. But there was something bitter in both. The lamentations of Isabella will not have been forgotten. As for Mary, she took up with one Jaquet de la Lain, a sort of muscular Methody of the period, with a huge appetite for tournaments, and a habit of confessing himself the last thing before he went to bed. [267b] With such a hero, the young duchess's amours were most likely innocent; and in all other ways she was a suitable partner for the duke, and well fitted to enter into his pleasures.

When the festivities at Saint Omer had come to an end, Charles and his wife set forth by Ghent and Tournay. The towns gave him offerings of money as he passed through, to help in the payment of his ransom. From all sides, ladies and gentlemen thronged to offer him their services; some gave him their sons for pages, some archers for a bodyguard; and by the time he reached Tournay, he had a following of 300 horse. Everywhere he was received as though he had been the King of France. [268] If he did not come to imagine himself something of the sort, he certainly forgot the existence of any one with a better claim to the title. He conducted himself on the hypothesis that Charles VII. was another Charles VI. He signed with enthusiasm that treaty of Arras, which left France almost at the discretion of Burgundy. On December 18 he was still no farther than Bruges, where he entered into a private treaty with Philip; and it was not until January 14, ten weeks after he disembarked in France, and attended by a ruck of Burgundian gentlemen, that he arrived in Paris and offered to present himself before Charles VII. The king sent word that he might come, if he would, with a small retinue, but not with his present following; and the duke, who was mightily on his high horse after all the ovations he had received, took the king's attitude amiss, and turned aside into Touraine, to receive more welcome and more presents, and be convoyed by torchlight into faithful cities.

And so you see, here was King Arthur home again, and matters nowise mended in consequence. The best we can say is, that this last stage of Charles's public life was of no long duration. His confidence was soon knocked out of him in the contact with others. He began to find he was an earthen vessel among many vessels of brass; he began to be shrewdly aware that he was no King Arthur. In 1442, at Limoges, he made himself the spokesman of the malcontent nobility. The king showed himself humiliatingly indifferent to his counsels, and humiliatingly generous towards his necessities. And there, with some blushes, he may be said to have taken farewell of the political stage. A feeble attempt on the county of Asti is scarce worth the name of exception. Thenceforward let Ambition wile whom she may into the turmoil of events, our duke will walk cannily in his well-ordered garden, or sit by the fire to touch the slender reed. [269]

IV.

If it were given each of us to transplant his life wherever he pleased in time or space, with all the ages and all the countries of the world to choose from, there would be quite an instructive diversity of taste. A certain sedentary majority would prefer to remain where they were. Many would choose the Renaissance; many some stately and simple period of Grecian life; and still more elect to pass a few years wandering among the villages of Palestine with an inspired conductor. For some of our quaintly vicious contemporaries, we have the decline of the Roman Empire and the reign of Henry III. of France. But there are others not quite so vicious, who yet cannot look upon the world with perfect gravity, who have never taken the categorical imperative to wife, and have more taste for what is comfortable than for what is magnanimous and high; and I can imagine some of these casting their lot in the Court of Blois during the last twenty years of the life of Charles of Orleans.

The duke and duchess, their staff of officers and ladies, and the high-born and learned persons who were attracted to Blois on a visit, formed a society for killing time and perfecting each other in various elegant accomplishments, such as we might imagine for an ideal watering-place in the Delectable Mountains. The company hunted and went on pleasure-parties; they played chess, tables, and many other games. What we now call the history of the period passed, I imagine, over the heads of these good people much as it passes over our own. News reached them, indeed, of great and joyful import. William Peel received eight livres and five sous from the duchess, when he brought the first tidings that Rouen was recaptured from the English. [271a] A little later and the duke sang, in a truly patriotic vein, the deliverance of Guyenne and Normandy. [271b] They were liberal of rhymes and largesse, and welcomed the prosperity of their country much as they welcomed the coming of spring, and with no more thought of collaborating towards the event. Religion was not forgotten in the Court of Blois. Pilgrimages were agreeable and picturesque excursions. In those days a well-served chapel was something like a good vinery in our own, an opportunity for display and the source of mild enjoyments. There was probably something of his rooted delight in pageantry, as well as a good deal of gentle piety, in the feelings with which Charles gave dinner every Friday to thirteen poor people, served them himself, and washed their feet with his own hands. [271c] Solemn affairs would interest Charles and his courtiers from their trivial side. The duke perhaps cared less for the deliverance of Guyenne and Normandy than for his own verses on the occasion; just as Dr. Russell's correspondence in The Times was among the most material parts of the Crimean War for that talented correspondent. And I think it scarcely cynical to suppose that religion as well as patriotism was principally cultivated as a means of filling up the day.

It was not only messengers fiery red with haste and charged with the destiny of nations, who were made welcome at the gates of Blois. If any man of accomplishment came that way, he was sure of an audience, and something for his pocket. The courtiers would have received Ben Jonson like Drummond of Hawthornden, and a good pugilist like Captain Barclay. They were catholic, as none but the entirely idle can be catholic. It might be Pierre, called Dieu d'amours, the juggler; or it might be three high English minstrels; or the two men, players of ghitterns, from the kingdom of Scotland, who sang the destruction of the Turks; or again Jehan Rognelet, player of instruments of music, who played and danced with his wife and two children; they would each be called into the castle to give a taste of his proficiency before my lord the duke. [272] Sometimes the performance was of a more personal interest, and produced much the same sensations as are felt on an English green on the arrival of a professional cricketer, or round an English billiard table during a match between Roberts and Cooke. This was when Jehan Nègre, the Lombard, came to Blois and played chess against all these chess-players, and won much money from my lord and his intimates; or when Baudet Harenc of Chalons made ballades before all these ballade-makers. [273]

It will not surprise the reader to learn they were all makers of ballades and rondels. To write verses for May day, seems to have been as much a matter of course, as to ride out with the cavalcade that went to gather hawthorn. The choice of Valentines was a standing challenge, and the courtiers pelted each other with humorous and sentimental verses as in a literary carnival. If an indecorous adventure befell our friend Maistre Estienne le Gout, my lord the duke would turn it into the funniest of rondels, all the rhymes being the names of the cases of nouns or the moods of verbs; and Maistre Estienne would make reply in similar fashion, seeking to prune the story of its more humiliating episodes. If Frédet was too long away from Court, a rondel went to upbraid him; and it was in a rondel that Frédet would excuse himself. Sometimes two or three, or as many as a dozen, would set to work on the same refrain, the same idea, or in the same macaronic jargon. Some of the poetasters were heavy enough; others were not wanting in address; and the duchess herself was among those who most excelled. On one occasion eleven competitors made a ballade on the idea,

"I die of thirst beside the fountain's edge"

(Je meurs de soif emprès de la fontaine).

These eleven ballades still exist; and one of them arrests the attention rather from the name of the author than from any special merit in itself. It purports to be the work of François Villon; and so far as a foreigner can judge (which is indeed a small way), it may very well be his. Nay, and if any one thing is more probable than another, in the great tabula rasa, or unknown land, which we are fain to call the biography of Villon, it seems probable enough that he may have gone upon a visit to Charles of Orleans. Where Master Baudet Harenc, of Chalons, found a sympathetic, or perhaps a derisive audience (for who can tell nowadays the degree of Baudet's excellence in his art?), favour would not be wanting for the greatest ballade-maker of all time. Great as would seem the incongruity, it may have pleased Charles to own a sort of kinship with ragged singers, and whimsically regard himself as one of the confraternity of poets. And he would have other grounds of intimacy with Villon. A room looking upon Windsor gardens is a different matter from Villon's dungeon at Méun; yet each in his own degree had been tried in prison. Each in his own way also, loved the good things of this life and the service of the Muses. But the same gulf that separated Burns from his Edinburgh patrons would separate the singer of Bohemia from the rhyming duke. And it is hard to imagine that Villon's training amongst thieves, loose women, and vagabond students, had fitted him to move in a society of any dignity and courtliness. Ballades are very admirable things; and a poet is doubtless a most interesting visitor. But among the courtiers of Charles, there would be considerable regard for the proprieties of etiquette; and even a duke will sometimes have an eye to his teaspoons. Moreover, as a poet, I can conceive he may have disappointed expectation. It need surprise nobody if Villon's ballade on the theme,

"I die of thirst beside the fountain's edge,"

was but a poor performance. He would make better verses on the lee-side of a flagon at the sign of the Pomme du Pin, than in a cushioned settle in the halls of Blois.

Charles liked change of place. He was often not so much travelling as making a progress; now to join the king for some great tournament; now to visit King René, at Tarascon, where he had a study of his own and saw all manner of interesting things—oriental curios, King René painting birds, and, what particularly pleased him, Triboulet, the dwarf jester, whose skull-cap was no bigger than an orange. [276a] Sometimes the journeys were set about on horseback in a large party, with the fourriers sent forward to prepare a lodging at the next stage. We find almost Gargantuan details of the provision made by these officers against the duke's arrival, of eggs and butter and bread, cheese and peas and chickens, pike and bream and barbel, and wine both white and red. [276b] Sometimes he went by water in a barge, playing chess or tables with a friend in the pavilion, or watching other vessels as they went before the wind. [276c] Children ran along the bank, as they do to this day on the Crinan Canal; and when Charles threw in money, they would dive and bring it up. [276d] As he looked on at their exploits, I wonder whether that room of gold and silk and worsted came back into his memory, with the device of little children in a river, and the sky full of birds?

He was a bit of a book-fancier, and had vied with his brother Angoulême in bringing back the library of their grandfather Charles V., when Bedford put it up for sale in London. [277a] The duchess had a library of her own; and we hear of her borrowing romances from ladies in attendance on the blue-stocking Margaret of Scotland. [277b] Not only were books collected, but new books were written at the court of Blois. The widow of one Jean Fougère, a bookbinder, seems to have done a number of odd commissions for the bibliophilous count. She it was who received three vellum-skins to bind the duchess's Book of Hours, and who was employed to prepare parchment for the use of the duke's scribes. And she it was who bound in vermilion leather the great manuscript of Charles's own poems, which was presented to him by his secretary, Anthony Astesan, with the text in one column, and Astesan's Latin version in the other. [277c]

Such tastes, with the coming of years, would doubtless take the place of many others. We find in Charles's verse much semi-ironical regret for other days, and resignation to growing infirmities. He who had been "nourished in the schools of love," now sees nothing either to please or displease him. Old age has imprisoned him within doors, where he means to take his ease, and let younger fellows bestir themselves in life. He had written (in earlier days, we may presume) a bright and defiant little poem in praise of solitude. If they would but leave him alone with his own thoughts and happy recollections, he declared it was beyond the power of melancholy to affect him. But now, when his animal strength has so much declined that he sings the discomforts of winter instead of the inspirations of spring, and he has no longer any appetite for life, he confesses he is wretched when alone, and, to keep his mind from grievous thoughts, he must have many people around him, laughing, talking, and singing. [278]

While Charles was thus falling into years, the order of things, of which he was the outcome and ornament, was growing old along with him. The semi-royalty of the princes of the blood was already a thing of the past; and when Charles VII. was gathered to his fathers, a new king reigned in France, who seemed every way the opposite of royal. Louis XI. had aims that were incomprehensible, and virtues that were inconceivable to his contemporaries. But his contemporaries were able enough to appreciate his sordid exterior, and his cruel and treacherous spirit. To the whole nobility of France he was a fatal and unreasonable phenomenon. All such courts as that of Charles at Blois, or his friend René's in Provence, would soon be made impossible; interference was the order of the day; hunting was already abolished; and who should say what was to go next? Louis, in fact, must have appeared to Charles primarily in the light of a kill-joy. I take it, when missionaries land in South Sea Islands and lay strange embargo on the simplest things in life, the islanders will not be much more puzzled and irritated than Charles of Orleans at the policy of the Eleventh Louis. There was one thing, I seem to apprehend, that had always particularly moved him; and that was, any proposal to punish a person of his acquaintance. No matter what treason he may have made or meddled with, an Alençon or an Armagnac was sure to find Charles reappear from private life, and do his best to get him pardoned. He knew them quite well. He had made rondels with them. They were charming people in every way. There must certainly be some mistake. Had not he himself made anti-national treaties almost before he was out of his nonage? And for the matter of that, had not every one else done the like? Such are some of the thoughts by which he might explain to himself his aversion to such extremities; but it was on a deeper basis that the feeling probably reposed. A man of his temper could not fail to be impressed at the thought of disastrous revolutions in the fortunes of those he knew. He would feel painfully the tragic contrast, when those who had everything to make life valuable were deprived of life itself. And it was shocking to the clemency of his spirit, that sinners should be hurried before their judge without a fitting interval for penitence and satisfaction. It was this feeling which brought him at last, a poor, purblind blue-bottle of the later autumn, into collision with "the universal spider," Louis XI. He took up the defence of the Duke of Brittany at Tours. But Louis was then in no humour to hear Charles's texts and Latin sentiments; he had his back to the wall, the future of France was at stake; and if all the old men in the world had crossed his path, they would have had the rough side of his tongue like Charles of Orleans. I have found nowhere what he said, but it seems it was monstrously to the point, and so rudely conceived that the old duke never recovered the indignity. He got home as far as Amboise, sickened, and died two days after (Jan. 4, 1465), in the seventy-fourth year of his age. And so a whiff of pungent prose stopped the issue of melodious rondels to the end of time.

V.

The futility of Charles's public life was of a piece throughout. He never succeeded in any single purpose he set before him; for his deliverance from England, after twenty-five years of failure and at the cost of dignity and consistency, it would be ridiculously hyperbolical to treat as a success. During the first part of his life he was the stalking horse of Bernard d'Armagnac; during the second, he was the passive instrument of English diplomatists; and before he was well entered on the third, he hastened to become the dupe and catspaw of Burgundian treason. On each of these occasions, a strong and not dishonourable personal motive determined his behaviour. In 1407 and the following years, he had his father's murder uppermost in his mind. During his English captivity, that thought was displaced by a more immediate desire for his own liberation. In 1440 a sentiment of gratitude to Philip of Burgundy blinded him to all else, and led him to break with the tradition of his party and his own former life. He was born a great vassal, and he conducted himself like a private gentleman. He began life in a showy and brilliant enough fashion, by the light of a petty personal chivalry. He was not without some tincture of patriotism; but it was resolvable into two parts: a preference for life among his fellow-countrymen, and a barren point of honour. In England, he could comfort himself by the reflection that "he had been taken while loyally doing his devoir," without any misgiving as to his conduct in the previous years, when he had prepared the disaster of Agincourt by wasteful feud. This unconsciousness of the larger interests is perhaps most happily exampled out of his own mouth. When Alençon stood accused of betraying Normandy into the hands of the English, Charles made a speech in his defence, from which I have already quoted more than once. Alençon, he said, had professed a great love and trust towards him; "yet did he give no great proof thereof, when he sought to betray Normandy; whereby he would have made me lose an estate of 10,000 livres a year, and might have occasioned the destruction of the kingdom and of all us Frenchmen." These are the words of one, mark you, against whom Gloucester warned the English Council because of his "great subtility and cautelous disposition." It is not hard to excuse the impatience of Louis XI., if such stuff was foisted on him by way of political deliberation.

This incapacity to see things with any greatness, this obscure and narrow view was fundamentally characteristic of the man as well as of the epoch. It is not even so striking in his public life, where he failed, as in his poems, where he notably succeeded. For wherever we might expect a poet to be unintelligent, it certainly would not be in his poetry. And Charles is unintelligent even there. Of all authors whom a modern may still read and read over again with pleasure, he has perhaps the least to say. His poems seem to bear testimony rather to the fashion of rhyming, which distinguished the age, than to any special vocation in the man himself. Some of them are drawing-room exercises and the rest seem made by habit. Great writers are struck with something in nature or society, with which they become pregnant and longing; they are possessed with an idea, and cannot be at peace until they have put it outside of them in some distinct embodiment. But with Charles literature was an object rather than a mean; he was one who loved bandying words for its own sake; the rigidity of intricate metrical forms stood him in lieu of precise thought; instead of communicating truth, he observed the laws of a game; and when he had no one to challenge at chess or rackets, he made verses in a wager against himself. From the very idleness of the man's mind, and not from intensity of feeling, it happens that all his poems are more or less autobiographical. But they form an autobiography singularly bald and uneventful. Little is therein recorded beside sentiments. Thoughts, in any true sense, he had none to record. And if we can gather that he had been a prisoner in England, that he had lived in the Orleannese, and that he hunted and went in parties of pleasure, I believe it is about as much definite experience as is to be found in all these five hundred pages of autobiographical verse. Doubtless, we find here and there a complaint on the progress of the infirmities of age. Doubtless, he feels the great change of the year, and distinguishes winter from spring; winter as the time of snow and the fireside; spring as the return of grass and flowers, the time of St. Valentine's day and a beating heart. And he feels love after a fashion. Again and again, we learn that Charles of Orleans is in love, and hear him ring the changes through the whole gamut of dainty and tender sentiment. But there is never a spark of passion; and heaven alone knows whether there was any real woman in the matter, or the whole thing was an exercise in fancy. If these poems were indeed inspired by some living mistress, one would think he had never seen, never heard, and never touched her. There is nothing in any one of these so numerous love-songs to indicate who or what the lady was. Was she dark or fair, passionate or gentle like himself, witty or simple? Was it always one woman? or are there a dozen here immortalised in cold indistinction? The old English translator mentions gray eyes in his version of one of the amorous rondels; so far as I remember, he was driven by some emergency of the verse; but in the absence of all sharp lines of character and anything specific, we feel for the moment a sort of surprise, as though the epithet were singularly happy and unusual, or as though we had made our escape from cloudland into something tangible and sure. The measure of Charles's indifference to all that now preoccupies and excites a poet, is best given by a positive example. If, besides the coming of spring, any one external circumstance may be said to have struck his imagination, it was the despatch of fourriers, while on a journey, to prepare the night's lodging. This seems to be his favourite image; it reappears like the upas-tree in the early work of Coleridge: we may judge with what childish eyes he looked upon the world, if one of the sights which most impressed him was that of a man going to order dinner.

Although they are not inspired by any deeper motive than the common run of contemporaneous drawing-room verses, those of Charles of Orleans are executed with inimitable lightness and delicacy of touch. They deal with floating and colourless sentiments, and the writer is never greatly moved, but he seems always genuine. He makes no attempt to set off thin conceptions with a multiplicity of phrases. His ballades are generally thin and scanty of import; for the ballade presented too large a canvas, and he was preoccupied by technical requirements. But in the rondel he has put himself before all competitors by a happy knack and a prevailing distinction of manner. He is very much more of a duke in his verses than in his absurd and inconsequential career as a statesman; and how he shows himself a duke is precisely by the absence of all pretension, turgidity, or emphasis. He turns verses, as he would have come into the king's presence, with a quiet accomplishment of grace.

Théodore de Banville, the youngest poet of a famous generation now nearly extinct, and himself a sure and finished artist, knocked off, in his happiest vein, a few experiments in imitation of Charles of Orleans. I would recommend these modern rondels to all who care about the old duke, not only because they are delightful in themselves, but because they serve as a contrast to throw into relief the peculiarities of their model. When de Banville revives a forgotten form of verse—and he has already had the honour of reviving the ballade—he does it in the spirit of a workman choosing a good tool wherever he can find one, and not at all in that of the dilettante, who seeks to renew bygone forms of thought and make historic forgeries. With the ballade this seemed natural enough; for in connection with ballades the mind recurs to Villon, and Villon was almost more of a modern than de Banville himself. But in the case of the rondel, a comparison is challenged with Charles of Orleans, and the difference between two ages and two literatures is illustrated in a few poems of thirteen lines. Something, certainly, has been retained of the old movement; the refrain falls in time like a well-played bass; and the very brevity of the thing, by hampering and restraining the greater fecundity of the modern mind, assists the imitation. But de Banville's poems are full of form and colour; they smack racily of modern life, and own small kindred with the verse of other days, when it seems as if men walked by twilight, seeing little, and that with distracted eyes, and instead of blood, some thin and spectral fluid circulated in their veins. They might gird themselves for battle, make love, eat and drink, and acquit themselves manfully in all the external parts of life; but of the life that is within, and those processes by which we render ourselves an intelligent account of what we feel and do, and so represent experience that we for the first time make it ours, they had only a loose and troubled possession. They beheld or took part in great events, but there was no answerable commotion in their reflective being; and they passed throughout turbulent epochs in a sort of ghostly quiet and abstraction. Feeling seems to have been strangely disproportioned to the occasion, and words were laughably trivial and scanty to set forth the feeling even such as it was. Juvenal des Ursins chronicles calamity after calamity, with but one comment for them all: that "it was great pity." Perhaps, after too much of our florid literature, we find an adventitious charm in what is so different; and while the big drums are beaten every day by perspiring editors over the loss of a cock-boat or the rejection of a clause, and nothing is heard that is not proclaimed with sound of trumpet, it is not wonderful if we retire with pleasure into old books, and listen to authors who speak small and clear, as if in a private conversation. Truly this is so with Charles of Orleans. We are pleased to find a small man without the buskin, and obvious sentiments stated without affectation. If the sentiments are obvious, there is all the more chance we may have experienced the like. As we turn over the leaves, we may find ourselves in sympathy with some one or other of these staid joys and smiling sorrows. If we do we shall be strangely pleased, for there is a genuine pathos in these simple words, and the lines go with a lilt, and sing themselves to music of their own.

SAMUEL PEPYS.

In two books a fresh light has recently been thrown on the character and position of Samuel Pepys. Mr. Mynors Bright has given us a new transcription of the Diary, increasing it in bulk by near a third, correcting many errors, and completing our knowledge of the man in some curious and important points. We can only regret that he has taken liberties with the author and the public. It is no part of the duties of the editor of an established classic to decide what may or may not be "tedious to the reader." The book is either an historical document or not, and in condemning Lord Braybrooke Mr. Bright condemns himself. As for the time-honoured phrase, "unfit for publication," without being cynical, we may regard it as the sign of a precaution more or less commercial; and we may think, without being sordid, that when we purchase six huge and distressingly expensive volumes, we are entitled to be treated rather more like scholars and rather less like children. But Mr. Bright may rest assured: while we complain, we are still grateful. Mr. Wheatley, to divide our obligation, brings together, clearly and with no lost words, a body of illustrative material. Sometimes we might ask a little more; never, I think, less. And as a matter of fact, a great part of Mr. Wheatley's volume might be transferred, by a good editor of Pepys, to the margin of the text, for it is precisely what the reader wants.

In the light of these two books, at least, we have now to read our author. Between them they contain all we can expect to learn for, it may be, many years. Now, if ever we should be able to form some notion of that unparalleled figure in the annals of mankind—unparalleled for three good reasons: first, because he was a man known to his contemporaries in a halo of almost historical pomp, and to his remote descendants with an indecent familiarity, like a tap-room comrade; second, because he has outstripped all competitors in the art or virtue of a conscious honesty about oneself; and, third, because, being in many ways a very ordinary person, he has yet placed himself before the public eye with such a fulness and such an intimacy of detail as might be envied by a genius like Montaigne. Not then for his own sake only, but as a character in a unique position, endowed with a unique talent, and shedding a unique light upon the lives of the mass of mankind, he is surely worthy of prolonged and patient study.

The Diary.

That there should be such a book as Pepys's Diary is incomparably strange. Pepys, in a corrupt and idle period, played the man in public employments, toiling hard and keeping his honour bright. Much of the little good that is set down to James the Second comes by right to Pepys; and if it were little for a king, it is much for a subordinate. To his clear, capable head was owing somewhat of the greatness of England on the seas. In the exploits of Hawke, Rodney, or Nelson, this dead Mr. Pepys of the Navy Office had some considerable share. He stood well by his business in the appalling plague of 1666. He was loved and respected by some of the best and wisest men in England. He was President of the Royal Society; and when he came to die, people said of his conduct in that solemn hour—thinking it needless to say more—that it was answerable to the greatness of his life. Thus he walked in dignity, guards of soldiers sometimes attending him in his walks, subalterns bowing before his periwig; and when he uttered his thoughts they were suitable to his state and services. On February 8, 1668, we find him writing to Evelyn, his mind bitterly occupied with the late Dutch war, and some thoughts of the different story of the repulse of the Great Armada: "Sir, you will not wonder at the backwardness of my thanks for the present you made me, so many days since, of the Prospect of the Medway, while the Hollander rode master in it, when I have told you that the sight of it hath led me to such reflections on my particular interest, by my employment, in the reproach due to that miscarriage, as have given me little less disquiet than he is fancied to have who found his face in Michael Angelo's hell. The same should serve me also in excuse for my silence in celebrating your mastery shown in the design and draught, did not indignation rather than courtship urge me so far to commend them, as to wish the furniture of our House of Lords changed from the story of '88 to that of '67 (of Evelyn's designing), till the pravity of this were reformed to the temper of that age, wherein God Almighty found his blessings more operative than, I fear, he doth in ours his judgments."

This is a letter honourable to the writer, where the meaning rather than the words is eloquent. Such was the account he gave of himself to his contemporaries; such thoughts he chose to utter, and in such language: giving himself out for a grave and patriotic public servant. We turn to the same date in the Diary by which he is known, after two centuries, to his descendants. The entry begins in the same key with the letter, blaming the "madness of the House of Commons" and "the base proceedings, just the epitome of all our public proceedings in this age, of the House of Lords;" and then, without the least transition, this is how our diarist proceeds: "To the Strand, to my bookseller's, and there bought an idle, rogueish French book, L'escholle des Filles, which I have bought in plain binding, avoiding the buying of it better bound, because I resolve, as soon as I have read it, to burn it, that it may not stand in the list of books, nor among them, to disgrace them, if it should be found." Even in our day, when responsibility is so much more clearly apprehended, the man who wrote the letter would be notable; but what about the man, I do not say who bought a roguish book, but who was ashamed of doing so, yet did it, and recorded both the doing and the shame in the pages of his daily journal?

We all, whether we write or speak, must somewhat drape ourselves when we address our fellows; at a given moment we apprehend our character and acts by some particular side; we are merry with one, grave with another, as befits the nature and demands of the relation. Pepys's letter to Evelyn would have little in common with that other one to Mrs. Knipp which he signed by the pseudonym of Dapper Dicky; yet each would be suitable to the character of his correspondent. There is no untruth in this, for man, being a Protean animal, swiftly shares and changes with his company and surroundings; and these changes are the better part of his education in the world. To strike a posture once for all, and to march through life like a drum-major, is to be highly disagreeable to others and a fool for oneself into the bargain. To Evelyn and to Knipp we understand the double facing; but to whom was he posing in the Diary, and what, in the name of astonishment, was the nature of the pose? Had he suppressed all mention of the book, or had he bought it, gloried in the act, and cheerfully recorded his glorification, in either case we should have made him out. But no; he is full of precautions to conceal the "disgrace" of the purchase, and yet speeds to chronicle the whole affair in pen and ink. It is a sort of anomaly in human action, which we can exactly parallel from another part of the Diary.

Mrs. Pepys had written a paper of her too just complaints against her husband, and written it in plain and very pungent English. Pepys, in an agony lest the world should come to see it, brutally seizes and destroys the tell-tale document; and then—you disbelieve your eyes—down goes the whole story with unsparing truth and in the cruellest detail. It seems he has no design but to appear respectable, and here he keeps a private book to prove he was not. You are at first faintly reminded of some of the vagaries of the morbid religious diarist; but at a moment's thought the resemblance disappears. The design of Pepys is not at all to edify; it is not from repentance that he chronicles his peccadilloes, for he tells us when he does repent, and, to be just to him, there often follows some improvement. Again, the sins of the religious diarist are of a very formal pattern, and are told with an elaborate whine. But in Pepys you come upon good, substantive misdemeanours; beams in his eye of which he alone remains unconscious; healthy outbreaks of the animal nature, and laughable subterfuges to himself that always command belief and often engage the sympathies.

Pepys was a young man for his age, came slowly to himself in the world, sowed his wild oats late, took late to industry, and preserved till nearly forty the headlong gusto of a boy. So, to come rightly at the spirit in which the Diary was written, we must recall a class of sentiments which with most of us are over and done before the age of twelve. In our tender years we still preserve a freshness of surprise at our prolonged existence; events make an impression out of all proportion to their consequence; we are unspeakably touched by our own past adventures, and look forward to our future personality with sentimental interest. It was something of this, I think, that clung to Pepys. Although not sentimental in the abstract, he was sweetly sentimental about himself. His own past clung about his heart, an evergreen. He was the slave of an association. He could not pass by Islington, where his father used to carry him to cakes and ale, but he must light at the "King's Head" and eat and drink "for remembrance of the old house sake." He counted it good fortune to lie a night at Epsom to renew his old walks, "where Mrs. Hely and I did use to walk and talk, with whom I had the first sentiments of love and pleasure in a woman's company, discourse and taking her by the hand, she being a pretty woman." He goes about weighing up the Assurance, which lay near Woolwich underwater, and cries in a parenthesis, "Poor ship, that I have been twice merry in, in Captain Holland's time;" and after revisiting the Naseby, now changed into the Charles, he confesses "it was a great pleasure to myself to see the ship that I began my good fortune in." The stone that he was cut for he preserved in a case; and to the Turners he kept alive such gratitude for their assistance that for years, and after he had begun to mount himself into higher zones, he continued to have that family to dinner on the anniversary of the operation. Not Hazlitt nor Rousseau had a more romantic passion for their past, although at times they might express it more romantically; and if Pepys shared with them this childish fondness, did not Rousseau, who left behind him the Confessions, or Hazlitt, who wrote the Liber Amoris, and loaded his essays with loving personal detail, share with Pepys in his unwearied egotism? For the two things go hand in hand; or, to be more exact, it is the first that makes the second either possible or pleasing.

But, to be quite in sympathy with Pepys, we must return once more to the experience of children. I can remember to have written, in the fly-leaf of more than one book, the date and the place where I then was—if, for instance, I was ill in bed or sitting in a certain garden; these were jottings for my future self; if I should chance on such a note in after years, I thought it would cause me a particular thrill to recognise myself across the intervening distance. Indeed, I might come upon them now, and not be moved one tittle—which shows that I have comparatively failed in life, and grown older than Samuel Pepys. For in the Diary we can find more than one such note of perfect childish egotism; as when he explains that his candle is going out, "which makes me write thus slobberingly;" or as in this incredible particularity, "To my study, where I only wrote thus much of this day's passages to this *, and so out again;" or lastly, as here, with more of circumstance: "I staid up till the bellman came by with his bell under my window, as I was writing of this very line, and cried, 'Past one of the clock, and a cold, frosty, windy morning.'" Such passages are not to be misunderstood. The appeal to Samuel Pepys years hence is unmistakable. He desires that dear, though unknown, gentleman keenly to realise his predecessor; to remember why a passage was uncleanly written; to recall (let us fancy, with a sigh) the tones of the bellman, the chill of the early, windy morning, and the very line his own romantic self was scribing at the moment. The man, you will perceive, was making reminiscences—a sort of pleasure by ricochet, which comforts many in distress, and turns some others into sentimental libertines: and the whole book, if you will but look at it in that way, is seen to be a work of art to Pepys's own address.

Here, then, we have the key to that remarkable attitude preserved by him throughout his Diary, to that unflinching—I had almost said, that unintelligent—sincerity which makes it a miracle among human books. He was not unconscious of his errors—far from it; he was often startled into shame, often reformed, often made and broke his vows of change. But whether he did ill or well, he was still his own unequalled self; still that entrancing ego of whom alone he cared to write; and still sure of his own affectionate indulgence, when the parts should be changed, and the Writer come to read what he had written. Whatever he did, or said, or thought, or suffered, it was still a trait of Pepys, a character of his career; and as, to himself, he was more interesting than Moses or than Alexander, so all should be faithfully set down. I have called his Diary a work of art. Now when the artist has found something, word or deed, exactly proper to a favourite character in play or novel, he will neither suppress nor diminish it, though the remark be silly or the act mean. The hesitation of Hamlet, the credulity of Othello, the baseness of Emma Bovary, or the irregularities of Mr. Swiveller, caused neither disappointment nor disgust to their creators. And so with Pepys and his adored protagonist: adored not blindly, but with trenchant insight and enduring, human toleration. I have gone over and over the greater part of the Diary; and the points where, to the most suspicious scrutiny, he has seemed not perfectly sincere, are so few, so doubtful, and so petty, that I am ashamed to name them. It may be said that we all of us write such a diary in airy characters upon our brain; but I fear there is a distinction to be made; I fear that as we render to our consciousness an account of our daily fortunes and behaviour, we too often weave a tissue of romantic compliments and dull excuses; and even if Pepys were the ass and coward that men call him, we must take rank as sillier and more cowardly than he. The bald truth about oneself, what we are all too timid to admit when we are not too dull to see it, that was what he saw clearly and set down unsparingly.

It is improbable that the Diary can have been carried on in the same single spirit in which it was begun. Pepys was not such an ass, but he must have perceived, as he went on, the extraordinary nature of the work he was producing. He was a great reader, and he knew what other books were like. It must, at least, have crossed his mind that some one might ultimately decipher the manuscript, and he himself, with all his pains and pleasures, be resuscitated in some later day; and the thought, although discouraged, must have warmed his heart. He was not such an ass, besides, but he must have been conscious of the deadly explosives, the gun-cotton and the giant powder, he was hoarding in his drawer. Let some contemporary light upon the journal, and Pepys was plunged for ever in social and political disgrace. We can trace the growth of his terrors by two facts. In 1660, while the Diary was still in its youth, he tells about it, as a matter of course, to a lieutenant in the navy; but in 1669, when it was already near an end, he could have bitten his tongue out, as the saying is, because he had let slip his secret to one so grave and friendly as Sir William Coventry. And from two other facts I think we may infer that he had entertained, even if he had not acquiesced in, the thought of a far-distant publicity. The first is of capital importance: the Diary was not destroyed. The second—that he took unusual precautions to confound the cipher in "rogueish" passages—proves, beyond question, that he was thinking of some other reader besides himself. Perhaps while his friends were admiring the "greatness of his behaviour" at the approach of death, he may have had a twinkling hope of immortality. Mens cujusque is est quisque, said his chosen motto; and, as he had stamped his mind with every crook and foible in the pages of the Diary, he might feel that what he left behind him was indeed himself. There is perhaps no other instance so remarkable of the desire of man for publicity and an enduring name. The greatness of his life was open, yet he longed to communicate its smallness also; and, while contemporaries bowed before him, he must buttonhole posterity with the news that his periwig was once alive with nits. But this thought, although I cannot doubt he had it, was neither his first nor his deepest; it did not colour one word that he wrote; and the Diary, for as long as he kept it, remained what it was when he began, a private pleasure for himself. It was his bosom secret; it added a zest to all his pleasures; he lived in and for it, and might well write these solemn words, when he closed that confidant for ever: "And so I betake myself to that course which is almost as much as to see myself go into the grave; for which, and all the discomforts that will accompany my being blind, the good God prepare me."

A Liberal Genius.

Pepys spent part of a certain winter Sunday, when he had taken physic, composing "a song in praise of a liberal genius (such as I take my own to be) to all studies and pleasures." The song was unsuccessful, but the Diary is, in a sense, the very song that he was seeking; and his portrait by Hales, so admirably reproduced in Mynors Bright's edition, is a confirmation of the Diary. Hales, it would appear, had known his business; and though he put his sitter to a deal of trouble, almost breaking his neck "to have the portrait full of shadows," and draping him in an Indian gown hired expressly for the purpose, he was preoccupied about no merely picturesque effects, but to portray the essence of the man. Whether we read the picture by the Diary or the Diary by the picture, we shall at least agree that Hales was among the number of those who can "surprise the manners in the face." Here we have a mouth pouting, moist with desires; eyes greedy, protuberant, and yet apt for weeping too; a nose great alike in character and dimensions; and altogether a most fleshly, melting countenance. The face is attractive by its promise of reciprocity. I have used the word greedy, but the reader must not suppose that he can change it for that closely kindred one of hungry, for there is here no aspiration, no waiting for better things, but an animal joy in all that comes. It could never be the face of an artist; it is the face of a viveur—kindly, pleased and pleasing, protected from excess and upheld in contentment by the shifting versatility of his desires. For a single desire is more rightly to be called a lust; but there is health in a variety, where one may balance and control another.

The whole world, town or country, was to Pepys a garden of Armida. Wherever he went, his steps were winged with the most eager expectation;

whatever he did, it was done with the most lively pleasure. An insatiable curiosity in all the shows of the world and all the secrets of knowledge, filled him brimful of the longing to travel, and supported him in the toils of study. Rome was the dream of his life; he was never happier than when he read or talked of the Eternal City. When he was in Holland, he was "with child" to see any strange thing. Meeting some friends and singing with them in a palace near the Hague, his pen fails him to express his passion of delight, "the more so because in a heaven of pleasure and in a strange country." He must go to see all famous executions. He must needs visit the body of a murdered man, defaced "with a broad wound," he says, "that makes my hand now shake to write of it." He learned to dance, and was "like to make a dancer." He learned to sing, and walked about Gray's Inn Fields "humming to myself (which is now my constant practice) the trillo." He learned to play the lute, the flute, the flageolet, and the theorbo, and it was not the fault of his intention if he did not learn the harpsichord or the spinet. He learned to compose songs, and burned to give forth "a scheme and theory of music not yet ever made in the world." When he heard "a fellow whistle like a bird exceeding well," he promised to return another day and give an angel for a lesson in the art. Once, he writes, "I took the Bezan back with me, and with a brave gale and tide reached up that night to the Hope, taking great pleasure in learning the seamen's manner of singing when they sound the depths." If he found himself rusty in his Latin grammar, he must fall to it like a schoolboy. He was a member of Harrington's Club till its dissolution, and of the Royal Society before it had received the name. Boyle's Hydrostatics was "of infinite delight" to him, walking in Barnes Elms. We find him comparing Bible concordances, a captious judge of sermons, deep in Descartes and Aristotle. We find him, in a single year, studying timber and the measurement of timber; tar and oil, hemp, and the process of preparing cordage; mathematics and accounting; the hull and the rigging of ships from a model; and "looking and improving himself of the (naval) stores with"—hark to the fellow!—"great delight." His familiar spirit of delight was not the same with Shelley's; but how true it was to him through life! He is only copying something, and behold, he "takes great pleasure to rule the lines, and have the capital words wrote with red ink;" he has only had his coal-cellar emptied and cleaned, and behold, "it do please him exceedingly." A hog's harslett is "a piece of meat he loves." He cannot ride home in my Lord Sandwich's coach, but he must exclaim, with breathless gusto, "his noble, rich coach." When he is bound for a supper party, he anticipates a "glut of pleasure." When he has a new watch, "to see my childishness," says he, "I could not forbear carrying it in my hand and seeing what o'clock it was an hundred times." To go to Vauxhall, he says, and "to hear the nightingales and other birds, hear fiddles, and there a harp and here a Jew's trump, and here laughing, and there fine people walking, is mighty divertising." And the nightingales, I take it, were particularly dear to him; and it was again "with great pleasure" that he paused to hear them as he walked to Woolwich, while the fog was rising and the April sun broke through.

He must always be doing something agreeable, and, by preference, two agreeable things at once. In his house he had a box of carpenter's tools, two dogs, an eagle, a canary, and a blackbird that whistled tunes, lest, even in that full life, he should chance upon an empty moment. If he had to wait for a dish of poached eggs, he must put in the time by playing on the flageolet; if a sermon were dull, he must read in the book of Tobit or divert his mind with sly advances on the nearest women. When he walked, it must be with a book in his pocket to beguile the way in case the nightingales were silent; and even along the streets of London, with so many pretty faces to be spied for and dignitaries to be saluted, his trail was marked by little debts "for wine, pictures, etc.," the true headmark of a life intolerant of any joyless passage. He had a kind of idealism in pleasure; like the princess in the fairy story, he was conscious of a rose-leaf out of place. Dearly as he loved to talk, he could not enjoy nor shine in a conversation when he thought himself unsuitably dressed. Dearly as he loved eating, he "knew not how to eat alone;" pleasure for him must heighten pleasure; and the eye and ear must be flattered like the palate ere he avow himself content. He had no zest in a good dinner when it fell to be eaten "in a bad street and in a periwig-maker's house;" and a collation was spoiled for him by indifferent music. His body was indefatigable, doing him yeoman's service in this breathless chase of pleasures. On April 11, 1662, he mentions that he went to bed "weary, which I seldom am;" and already over thirty, he would sit up all night cheerfully to see a comet. But it is never pleasure that exhausts the pleasure-seeker; for in that career, as in all others, it is failure that kills. The man who enjoys so wholly and bears so impatiently the slightest widowhood from joy, is just the man to lose a night's rest over some paltry question of his right to fiddle on the leads, or to be "vexed to the blood" by a solecism in his wife's attire; and we find in consequence that he was always peevish when he was hungry, and that his head "aked mightily" after a dispute. But nothing could divert him from his aim in life; his remedy in care was the same as his delight in prosperity; it was with pleasure, and with pleasure only, that he sought to drive out sorrow; and, whether he was jealous of his wife or skulking from a bailiff, he would equally take refuge in the theatre. There, if the house be full and the company noble, if the songs be tunable, the actors perfect, and the play diverting, this odd hero of the secret Diary, this private self-adorer, will speedily be healed of his distresses.

Equally pleased with a watch, a coach, a piece of meat, a tune upon the fiddle, or a fact in hydrostatics, Pepys was pleased yet more by the beauty, the worth, the mirth, or the mere scenic attitude in life of his fellow-creatures. He shows himself throughout a sterling humanist. Indeed, he who loves himself, not in idle vanity, but with a plenitude of knowledge, is the best equipped of all to love his neighbours. And perhaps it is in this sense that charity may be most properly said to begin at home. It does not matter what quality a person has: Pepys can appreciate and love him for it. He "fills his eyes" with the beauty of Lady Castlemaine; indeed, he may be said to dote upon the thought of her for years; if a woman be good-looking and not painted, he will walk miles to have another sight of her; and even when a lady by a mischance spat upon his clothes, he was immediately consoled when he had observed that she was pretty. But, on the other hand, he is delighted to see Mrs. Pett upon her knees, and speaks thus of his Aunt James: "a poor, religious, well-meaning, good soul, talking of nothing but God Almighty, and that with so much innocence that mightily pleased me." He is taken with Pen's merriment and loose songs, but not less taken with the sterling worth of Coventry. He is jolly with a drunken sailor, but listens with interest and patience, as he rides the Essex roads, to the story of a Quaker's spiritual trials and convictions. He lends a critical ear to the discourse of kings and royal dukes. He spends an evening at Vauxhall with "Killigrew and young Newport—loose company," says he, "but worth a man's being in for once, to know the nature of it, and their manner of talk and lives." And when a rag-boy lights him home, he examines him about his business and other ways of livelihood for destitute children. This is almost half-way to the beginning of philanthropy; had it only been the fashion, as it is at present, Pepys had perhaps been a man famous for good deeds. And it is through this quality that he rises, at times, superior to his surprising egotism; his interest in the love affairs of others is, indeed, impersonal; he is filled with concern for my Lady Castlemaine, whom he only knows by sight, shares in her very jealousies, joys with her in her successes; and it is not untrue, however strange it seems in his abrupt presentment, that he loved his maid Jane because she was in love with his man Tom.

Let us hear him, for once, at length: "So the women and W. Hewer and I walked upon the Downes, where a flock of sheep was; and the most pleasant and innocent sight that ever I saw in my life. We found a shepherd and his little boy reading, far from any houses or sight of people, the Bible to him; so I made the boy read to me, which he did with the forced tone that children do usually read, that was mighty pretty; and then I did give him something, and went to the father, and talked with him. He did content himself mightily in my liking his boy's reading, and did bless God for him, the most like one of the old patriarchs that ever I saw in my life, and it brought those thoughts of the old age of the world in my mind for two or three days after. We took notice of his woolen knit stockings of two colours mixed, and of his shoes shod with iron, both at the toe and heels, and with great nails in the soles of his feet, which was mighty pretty; and taking notice of them, 'Why,' says the poor man, 'the downes, you see, are full of stones, and we are faine to shoe ourselves thus; and these,' says he, 'will make the stones fly till they ring before me.' I did give the poor man something, for which he was mighty thankful, and I tried to cast stones with his horne crooke. He values his dog mightily, that would turn a sheep any way which he would have him, when he goes to fold them; told me there was about eighteen score sheep in his flock, and that he hath four shillings a week the year round for keeping of them; and Mrs. Turner, in the common fields here, did gather one of the prettiest nosegays that ever I saw in my life."

187

And so the story rambles on to the end of that day's pleasuring; with cups of milk, and glowworms, and people walking at sundown with their wives and children, and all the way home Pepys still dreaming "of the old age of the world" and the early innocence of man. This was how he walked through life, his eyes and ears wide open, and his hand, you will observe, not shut; and thus he observed the lives, the speech, and the manners of his fellow-men, with prose fidelity of detail and yet a lingering glamour of romance.

It was "two or three days after" that he extended this passage in the pages of his journal, and the style has thus the benefit of some reflection. It is generally supposed that, as a writer, Pepys must rank at the bottom of the scale of merit. But a style which is indefatigably lively, telling, and picturesque through six large volumes of everyday experience, which deals with the whole matter of a life, and yet is rarely wearisome, which condescends to the most fastidious particulars, and yet sweeps all away in the forthright current of the narrative,—such a style may be ungrammatical, it may be inelegant, it may be one tissue of mistakes, but it can never be devoid of merit. The first and the true function of the writer has been thoroughly performed throughout; and though the manner of his utterance may be childishly awkward, the matter has been transformed and assimilated by his unfeigned interest and delight. The gusto of the man speaks out fierily after all these years. For the difference between Pepys and Shelley, to return to that half-whimsical approximation, is one of quality but not one of degree; in his sphere, Pepys felt as keenly, and his is the true prose of poetry—prose because the spirit of the man was narrow and earthly, but poetry because he was delightedly alive. Hence, in such a passage as this about the Epsom shepherd, the result upon the reader's mind is entire conviction and unmingled pleasure. So, you feel, the thing fell out, not otherwise; and you would no more change it than you would change a sublimity of Shakespeare's, a homely touch of Bunyan's, or a favoured reminiscence of your own.

There never was a man nearer being an artist, who yet was not one. The tang was in the family; while he was writing the journal for our enjoyment in his comely house in Navy Gardens, no fewer than two of his cousins were tramping the fens, kit under arm, to make music to the country girls. But he himself, though he could play so many instruments and pass judgment in so many fields of art, remained an amateur. It is not given to any one so keenly to enjoy, without some greater power to understand. That he did not like Shakespeare as an artist for the stage may be a fault, but it is not without either parallel or excuse. He certainly admired him as a poet; he was the first beyond mere actors on the rolls of that innumerable army who have got "To be or not to be" by heart. Nor was he content with that; it haunted his mind; he quoted it to himself in the pages of the Diary, and, rushing in where angels fear to tread, he set it to music. Nothing, indeed, is more notable than the heroic quality of the verses that our little sensualist in a periwig chose out to marry with his own mortal strains. Some gust from brave Elizabethan times must have warmed his spirit, as he sat tuning his sublime theorbo. "To be or not to be. Whether 'tis nobler"—"Beauty retire, thou dost my pity move"—"It is decreed, nor shall thy fate, O Rome;"— open and dignified in the sound, various and majestic in the sentiment, it was no inapt, as it was certainly no timid, spirit that selected such a range of themes. Of "Gaze not on Swans," I know no more than these four words; yet that also seems to promise well. It was, however, on a probable suspicion, the work of his master, Mr. Berkenshaw—as the drawings that figure at the breaking up of a young ladies' seminary are the work of the professor attached to the establishment. Mr. Berkenshaw was not altogether happy in his pupil. The amateur cannot usually rise into the artist, some leaven of the world still clogging him; and we find Pepys behaving like a pickthank to the man who taught him composition. In relation to the stage, which he so warmly loved and understood, he was not only more hearty, but more generous to others. Thus he encounters Colonel Reames, "a man," says he, "who understands and loves a play as well as I, and I love him for it." And again, when he and his wife had seen a most ridiculous insipid piece, "Glad we were," he writes, "that Betterton had no part in it." It is by such a zeal and loyalty to those who labour for his delight that the amateur grows worthy of the artist. And it should be kept in mind that, not only in art, but in morals, Pepys rejoiced to recognise his betters. There was not one speck of envy in the whole human-hearted egotist.

189

Respectability.

When writers inveigh against respectability, in the present degraded meaning of the word, they are usually suspected of a taste for clay pipes and beer cellars; and their performances are thought to hail from the Owl's Nest of the comedy. They have something more, however, in their eye than the dulness of a round million dinner parties that sit down yearly in old England. For to do anything because others do it, and not because the thing is good, or kind, or honest in its own right, is to resign all moral control and captaincy upon yourself, and go post-haste to the devil with the greater number. We smile over the ascendency of priests; but I had rather follow a priest than what they call the leaders of society. No life can better than that of Pepys illustrate the dangers of this respectable theory of living. For what can be more untoward than the occurrence, at a critical period and while the habits are still pliable, of such a sweeping transformation as the return of Charles the Second? Round went the whole fleet of England on the other tack; and while a few tall pintas, Milton or Pen, still sailed a lonely course by the stars and their own private compass, the cock-boat, Pepys, must go about with the majority among "the stupid starers and the loud huzzas."

The respectable are not led so much by any desire of applause as by a positive need for countenance. The weaker and the tamer the man, the more will he require this support; and any positive quality relieves him, by just so much, of this dependence. In a dozen ways, Pepys was quite strong enough to please himself without regard for others; but his positive qualities were not co-extensive with the field of conduct; and in many parts of life he followed, with gleeful precision, in the footprints of the contemporary Mrs. Grundy. In morals, particularly, he lived by the countenance of others; felt a slight from another more keenly than a meanness in himself; and then first repented when he was found out. You could talk of religion or morality to such a man; and by the artist side of him, by his lively sympathy and apprehension, he could rise, as it were dramatically, to the significance of what you said. All that matter in religion which has been nicknamed other-worldliness was strictly in his gamut; but a rule of life that should make a man rudely virtuous, following right in good report and ill report, was foolishness and a stumbling-block to Pepys. He was much thrown across the Friends; and nothing can be more instructive than his attitude towards these most interesting people of that age. I have mentioned how he conversed with one as he rode; when he saw some brought from a meeting under arrest, "I would to God," said he, "they would either conform, or be more wise and not be catched;" and to a Quaker in his own office he extended a timid though effectual protection. Meanwhile there was growing up next door to him that beautiful nature William Pen. It is odd that Pepys condemned him for a fop; odd, though natural enough when you see Pen's portrait, that Pepys was jealous of him with his wife. But the cream of the story is when Pen publishes his Sandy Foundation Shaken, and Pepys has it read aloud by his wife. "I find it," he says, "so well writ as, I think, it is too good for him ever to have writ it; and it is a serious sort of book, and not fit for everybody to read." Nothing is more galling to the merely respectable than to be brought in contact with religious ardour. Pepys had his own foundation, sandy enough, but dear to him from practical considerations, and he would read the book with true uneasiness of spirit; for conceive the blow if, by some plaguy accident, this Pen were to convert him! It was a different kind of doctrine that he judged profitable for himself and others. "A good sermon of Mr. Gifford's at our church, upon 'Seek ye first the kingdom of heaven.' A very excellent and persuasive, good and moral sermon. He showed, like a wise man, that righteousness is a surer moral way of being rich than sin and villainy." It is thus that respectable people desire to have their Greathearts address them, telling, in mild accents, how you may make the best of both worlds, and be a moral hero without courage, kindness, or troublesome reflection; and thus the Gospel, cleared of Eastern metaphor, becomes a manual of worldly prudence, and a handybook for Pepys and the successful merchant.

The respectability of Pepys was deeply grained. He has no idea of truth except for the Diary. He has no care that a thing shall be, if it but appear; gives out that he has inherited a good estate, when he has seemingly got nothing but a lawsuit; and is pleased to be thought liberal when he knows he has been mean. He is conscientiously ostentatious. I say conscientiously, with reason. He could never have been taken for a fop, like Pen, but arrayed himself in a manner nicely suitable to his position. For long he hesitated to assume the famous periwig; for a public man should travel gravely with the fashions not foppishly before, nor dowdily behind, the central movement of his age. For long he durst not keep a carriage; that, in his circumstances would have been improper; but a time comes, with the growth of his fortune, when the impropriety has shifted to the other side, and he is "ashamed to be seen in a hackney." Pepys talked about being "a Quaker or some very melancholy thing;" for my part, I can imagine nothing so melancholy, because nothing half so silly, as to be concerned about such problems. But so respectability and the duties of society haunt and burden their poor devotees; and what seems at first the very primrose path of life, proves difficult and thorny like the rest. And the time comes to Pepys, as to all the merely respectable, when he must not only order his pleasures, but even clip his virtuous movements, to the public pattern of the age. There was some juggling among officials to avoid direct taxation; and Pepys, with a noble impulse, growing ashamed of this dishonesty, designed to charge himself with £1000; but finding none to set him an example, "nobody of our ablest merchants" with this moderate liking for clean hands, he judged it "not decent;" he feared it would "be thought vain glory;" and, rather than appear singular, cheerfully remained a thief. One able merchant's countenance, and Pepys had dared to do an honest act! Had he found one brave spirit, properly recognised by society, he might have gone far as a disciple. Mrs. Turner, it is true, can fill him full of sordid scandal, and make him believe, against the testimony of his senses, that Pen's venison pasty stank like the devil; but, on the other hand, Sir William Coventry can raise him by a word into another being. Pepys, when he is with Coventry, talks in the vein of an old Roman. What does he care for office or emolument? "Thank God, I have enough of my own," says he, "to buy me a good book and a good fiddle, and I have a good wife." And again, we find this pair projecting an old age when an ungrateful country shall have dismissed them from the field of public service; Coventry living retired in a fine house, and Pepys dropping in, "it may be, to read a chapter of Seneca."

Under this influence, the only good one in his life, Pepys continued zealous and, for the period, pure in his employment. He would not be "bribed to be unjust," he says, though he was "not so squeamish as to refuse a present after," suppose the king to have received no wrong. His new arrangement for the victualling of Tangier he tells us with honest complacency, will save the king a thousand and gain Pepys three hundred pounds a year,—a statement which exactly fixes the degree of the age's enlightenment. But for his industry and capacity no praise can be too high. It was an unending struggle for the man to stick to his business in such a garden of Armida as he found this life; and the story of his oaths, so often broken, so courageously renewed, is worthy rather of admiration that the contempt it has received.

Elsewhere, and beyond the sphere of Coventry's influence, we find him losing scruples and daily complying further with the age. When he began the journal, he was a trifle prim and puritanic; merry enough, to be sure, over his private cups, and still remembering Magdalene ale and his acquaintance with Mrs. Ainsworth of Cambridge. But youth is a hot season with all; when a man smells April and May he is apt at times to stumble; and in spite of a disordered practice, Pepys's theory, the better things that he approved and followed after, we may even say were strict. Where there was "tag, rag, and bobtail, dancing, singing, and drinking," he felt "ashamed, and went away;" and when he slept in church, he prayed God forgive him. In but a little while we find him with some ladies keeping each other awake "from spite," as though not to sleep in church were an obvious hardship; and yet later he calmly passes the time of service, looking about him, with a perspective glass, on all the pretty women. His favourite ejaculation, "Lord!" occurs but once that I have observed in 1660, never in '61, twice in '62, and at least five times in '63; after which the "Lords" may be said to pullulate like herrings, with here and there a solitary "damned," as it were a whale among the shoal. He and his wife, once filled with dudgeon by some innocent freedoms at a marriage, are soon content to go pleasuring with my Lord Brouncker's mistress, who was not even, by his own account, the most discreet of mistresses. Tag, rag, and bobtail, dancing, singing, and drinking, become his natural element; actors and actresses and drunken, roaring courtiers are to be found in his society; until the man grew so involved with Saturnalian manners and companions that he was shot almost unconsciously into the grand domestic crash of 1668.

That was the legitimate issue and punishment of years of staggering walk and conversation. The man who has smoked his pipe for half a century in a

193

powder magazine finds himself at last the author and the victim of a hideous disaster. So with our pleasant-minded Pepys and his peccadilloes. All of a sudden, as he still trips dexterously enough among the dangers of a double-faced career, thinking no great evil, humming to himself the trillo, Fate takes the further conduct of that matter from his hands, and brings him face to face with the consequences of his acts. For a man still, after so many years, the lover, although not the constant lover, of his wife,—for a man, besides, who was so greatly careful of appearances,—the revelation of his infidelities was a crushing blow. The tears that he shed, the indignities that he endured, are not to be measured. A vulgar woman, and now justly incensed, Mrs. Pepys spared him no detail of suffering. She was violent, threatening him with the tongs; she was careless of his honour, driving him to insult the mistress whom she had driven him to betray and to discard; worst of all, she was hopelessly inconsequent, in word and thought and deed, now lulling him with reconciliations, and anon flaming forth again with the original anger. Pepys had not used his wife well; he had wearied her with jealousies, even while himself unfaithful; he had grudged her clothes and pleasures, while lavishing both upon himself; he had abused her in words; he had bent his fist at her in anger; he had once blacked her eye; and it is one of the oddest particulars in that odd Diary of his, that, while the injury is referred to once in passing, there is no hint as to the occasion or the manner of the blow. But now, when he is in the wrong, nothing can exceed the long-suffering affection of this impatient husband. While he was still sinning and still undiscovered, he seems not to have known a touch of penitence stronger than what might lead him to take his wife to the theatre, or for an airing, or to give her a new dress, by way of compensation. Once found out, however, and he seems to himself to have lost all claim to decent usage. It is perhaps the strongest instance of his externality. His wife may do what she pleases, and though he may groan, it will never occur to him to blame her; he has no weapon left but tears and the most abject submission. We should perhaps have respected him more had he not given way so utterly—above all, had he refused to write, under his wife's dictation, an insulting letter to his unhappy fellow-culprit, Miss Willet; but somehow I believe we like him better as he was.

The death of his wife, following so shortly after, must have stamped the impression of this episode upon his mind. For the remaining years of his long life we have no Diary to help us, and we have seen already how little stress is to be laid upon the tenor of his correspondence; but what with the recollection of the catastrophe of his married life, what with the natural influence of his advancing years and reputation, it seems not unlikely that the period of gallantry was at an end for Pepys; and it is beyond a doubt that he sat down at last to an honoured and agreeable old age among his books and music, the correspondent of Sir Isaac Newton, and, in one instance at least the poetical counsellor of Dryden. Through all this period, that Diary which contained the secret memoirs of his life, with all its inconsistencies and escapades, had been religiously preserved; nor, when he came to die, does he appear to have provided for its destruction. So we may conceive him faithful to the end to all his dear and early memories; still mindful of Mrs. Hely in the woods at Epsom; still lighting at Islington for a cup of kindness to the dead; still, if he heard again that air that once so much disturbed him, thrilling at the recollection of the love that bound him to his wife.

JOHN KNOX AND HIS RELATIONS TO WOMEN.

I.—The Controversy about Female Rule.

When first the idea became widely spread among men that the Word of God, instead of being truly the foundation of all existing institutions, was rather a stone which the builders had rejected, it was but natural that the consequent havoc among received opinions should be accompanied by the generation of many new and lively hopes for the future. Somewhat as in the early days of the French Revolution, men must have looked for an immediate and universal improvement in their condition. Christianity, up to that time, had been somewhat of a failure politically. The reason was now obvious, the capital flaw was detected, the sickness of the body politic traced at last to its efficient cause. It was only necessary to put the Bible thoroughly into practice, to set themselves strenuously to realise in life the Holy Commonwealth, and all abuses and iniquities would surely pass away. Thus, in a pageant played at Geneva in the year 1523, the world was represented as a sick man at the end of his wits for help, to whom his doctor recommends Lutheran specifics. [329] The Reformers themselves had set their affections in a different world, and professed to look for the finished result of their endeavours on the other side of death. They took no interest in politics as such; they even condemned political action as Antichristian: notably, Luther in the case of the Peasants' War. And yet, as the purely religious question was inseparably complicated with political difficulties, and they had to make opposition, from day to day, against principalities and powers, they were led, one after another, and again and again, to leave the sphere which was more strictly their own, and meddle, for good and evil, with the affairs of State. Not much was to be expected from interference in such a spirit. Whenever a minister found himself galled or hindered, he would be inclined to suppose some contravention of the Bible. Whenever Christian liberty was restrained (and Christian liberty for each individual would be about coextensive with what he wished to do), it was obvious that the State was Antichristian. The great thing, and the one thing, was to push the Gospel and the Reformers' own interpretation of it. Whatever helped was good; whatever hindered was evil; and if this simple classification proved inapplicable over the whole field, it was no business of his to stop and reconcile incongruities. He had more pressing concerns on hand; he had to save souls; he had to be about his Father's business. This short-sighted view resulted in a doctrine that was actually Jesuitical in application. They had no serious ideas upon politics, and they were ready, nay, they seemed almost bound, to adopt and support whichever ensured for the moment the greatest benefit to the souls of their fellow-men. They were dishonest in all sincerity. Thus Labitte, in the introduction to a book [330a] in which he exposes the hypocritical democracy of the Catholics under the League, steps aside for a moment to stigmatise the hypocritical democracy of the Protestants. And nowhere was this expediency in political questions more apparent than about the question of female sovereignty. So much was this the case that one James Thomasius, of Leipsic, wrote a little paper [330b] about the religious partialities of those who took part in the controversy, in which some of these learned disputants cut a very sorry figure.

Now Knox has been from the first a man well hated; and it is somewhat characteristic of his luck that he figures here in the very forefront of the list of partial scribes who trimmed their doctrine with the wind in all good conscience, and were political weathercocks out of conviction. Not only has Thomasius mentioned him, but Bayle has taken the hint from Thomasius, and dedicated a long note to the matter at the end of his article on the Scotch Reformer. This is a little less than fair. If any one among the evangelists of that period showed more serious political sense than another, it was assuredly Knox; and even in this very matter of female rule, although I do not suppose any one nowadays will feel inclined to endorse his sentiments, I confess I can make great allowance for his conduct. The controversy, besides, has an interest of its own, in view of later controversies.

John Knox, from 1556 to 1559, was resident in Geneva, as minister, jointly with Goodman, of a little church of English refugees. He and his congregation were banished from England by one woman, Mary Tudor, and proscribed in Scotland by another, the Regent Mary of Guise. The coincidence was tempting: here were many abuses centring about one abuse; here was Christ's Gospel persecuted in the two kingdoms by one anomalous power. He had not far to go to find the idea that female government was anomalous. It was an age, indeed, in which women, capable and incapable, played a conspicuous part upon the stage of European history; and yet their rule, whatever may have been the opinion of here and there a wise man or enthusiast, was regarded as an anomaly by the great bulk of their contemporaries. It was defended as an anomaly. It, and all that accompanied and sanctioned it, was set aside as a single exception; and no one thought of reasoning down from queens and extending their privileges to ordinary women. Great ladies, as we know, had the privilege of entering into monasteries and cloisters, otherwise forbidden to their sex. As with one thing, so with another. Thus, Margaret of Navarre wrote books with great acclamation, and no one, seemingly, saw fit to call her conduct in question; but Mademoiselle de Gournay, Montaigne's adopted daughter, was in a controversy with the world as to whether a woman might be an author without incongruity. Thus, too, we have Théodore Agrippa d'Aubigné writing to his daughters about the learned women of his century, and cautioning them, in conclusion, that the study of letters was unsuited to ladies of a middling station, and should be reserved for princesses. [333a] And once more, if we desire to see the same principle carried to ludicrous extreme, we shall find that Reverend Father in God the Abbot of Brantôme, claiming, on the authority of some lord of his acquaintance, a privilege, or rather a duty, of free love for great princesses, and carefully excluding other ladies from the same gallant dispensation. [333b] One sees the spirit in which these immunities were granted; and how they were but the natural consequence of that awe for courts and kings that made the last writer tell us, with simple wonder, how Catherine de Medici would "laugh her fill just like another" over the humours of pantaloons and zanies. And such servility was, of all things, what would touch most nearly the republican spirit of Knox. It was not difficult for him to set aside this weak scruple of loyalty. The lantern of his analysis did not always shine with a very serviceable light; but he had the virtue, at least, to carry it into many places of fictitious holiness, and was not abashed by the tinsel divinity that hedged kings and queens from his contemporaries. And so he could put the proposition in the form already mentioned: there was Christ's Gospel persecuted in the two kingdoms by one anomalous power plainly, then, the "regiment of women" was Antichristian. Early in 1558 he communicated this discovery to the world, by publishing at Geneva his notorious book—The First Blast of the Trumpet against the Monstrous Regiment of Women. [334]

As a whole, it is a dull performance; but the preface, as is usual with Knox, is both interesting and morally fine. Knox was not one of those who are humble in the hour of triumph; he was aggressive even when things were at their worst. He had a grim reliance in himself, or rather in his mission; if he were not sure that he was a great man, he was at least sure that he was one set apart to do great things. And he judged simply that whatever passed in his mind, whatever moved him to flee from persecution instead of constantly facing it out, or, as here, to publish and withhold his name from the title-page of a critical work, would not fail to be of interest, perhaps of benefit, to the world. There may be something more finely sensitive in the modern humour, that tends more and more to withdraw a man's personality from the lessons he inculcates or the cause that he has espoused; but there is a loss herewith of wholesome responsibility; and when we find in the works of Knox, as in the Epistles of Paul, the man himself standing nakedly forward, courting and anticipating criticism, putting his character, as it were, in pledge for the sincerity of his doctrine, we had best waive the question of delicacy, and make our acknowledgments for a lesson of courage, not unnecessary in these days of anonymous criticism, and much light, otherwise unattainable, on the spirit in which great movements were initiated and carried forward. Knox's personal revelations are always interesting; and, in the case of the "First Blast," as I have said, there is no exception to the rule. He begins by stating the solemn responsibility of all who are watchmen over God's flock; and all are watchmen (he goes on to explain, with that fine breadth of spirit that characterises him even when, as here, he shows himself most narrow), all are watchmen "whose eyes God doth open, and whose conscience he pricketh to admonish the ungodly." And with the full consciousness of this great duty before him, he sets himself to answer the scruples of timorous or worldly-minded people. How can a man repent, he asks, unless the nature of his transgression is made plain to him? "And therefore I say," he continues, "that of necessity it is that this monstriferous empire of women (which among all enormities that this day do abound upon the face of the whole earth, is most detestable and damnable) be openly and plainly declared to the world, to the end that some may repent and be saved." To those who think the doctrine useless, because it cannot be expected to amend those princes whom it would dispossess if once accepted, he makes answer in a strain that shows him at his greatest. After having instanced how the rumour of Christ's censures found its way to Herod in his own court, "even so," he continues, "may the sound of our weak trumpet, by the support of some wind (blow it from the south, or blow it from the north, it is of no matter), come to the ears of the chief offenders. But whether it do or not, yet dare we not cease to blow as God will give strength. For we are debtors to more than to princes, to wit, to the great multitude of our brethren, of whom, no doubt, a great number have heretofore offended by error and ignorance."

It is for the multitude, then, he writes; he does not greatly hope that his trumpet will be audible in palaces, or that crowned women will submissively discrown themselves at his appeal; what he does hope, in plain English, is to encourage and justify rebellion; and we shall see, before we have done, that he can put his purpose into words as roundly as I can put it for him. This he sees to be a matter of much hazard; he is not "altogether so brutish and insensible, but that he has laid his account what the finishing of the work may cost." He knows that he will find many adversaries, since "to the most part of men, lawful and godly appeareth whatsoever antiquity hath received." He looks for opposition, "not only of the ignorant multitude, but of the wise, politic, and quiet spirits of the earth." He will be called foolish, curious, despiteful, and a sower of sedition; and one day, perhaps, for all he is now nameless, he may be attainted of treason. Yet he has "determined to obey God, notwithstanding that the world shall rage thereat." Finally, he makes some excuse for the anonymous appearance of this first instalment: it is his purpose thrice to blow the trumpet in this matter, if God so permit; twice he intends to do it without name; but at the last blast to take the odium upon himself, that all others may be purged.

Thus he ends the preface, and enters upon his argument with a

200

secondary title: "The First Blast to awake Women degenerate." We are in the land of assertion without delay. That a woman should bear rule, superiority, dominion or empire over any realm, nation, or city, he tells us, is repugnant to nature, contumely to God, and a subversion of good order. Women are weak, frail, impatient, feeble, and foolish. God has denied to woman wisdom to consider, or providence to foresee, what is profitable to a commonwealth. Women have been ever lightly esteemed; they have been denied the tutory of their own sons, and subjected to the unquestionable sway of their husbands; and surely it is irrational to give the greater where the less has been withheld, and suffer a woman to reign supreme over a great kingdom who would be allowed no authority by her own fireside. He appeals to the Bible; but though he makes much of the first transgression and certain strong texts in Genesis and Paul's Epistles, he does not appeal with entire success. The cases of Deborah and Huldah can be brought into no sort of harmony with his thesis. Indeed, I may say that, logically, he left his bones there; and that it is but the phantom of an argument that he parades thenceforward to the end. Well was it for Knox that he succeeded no better; it is under this very ambiguity about Deborah that we shall find him fain to creep for shelter before he is done with the regiment of women. After having thus exhausted Scripture, and formulated its teaching in the somewhat blasphemous maxim that the man is placed above the woman, even as God above the angels, he goes on triumphantly to adduce the testimonies of Tertullian, Augustine, Ambrose, Basil, Chrysostom, and the Pandects; and having gathered this little cloud of witnesses about him, like pursuivants about a herald, he solemnly proclaims all reigning women to be traitoresses and rebels against God; discharges all men thenceforward from holding any office under such monstrous regiment, and calls upon all the lieges with one consent to "study to repress the inordinate pride and tyranny" of queens. If this is not treasonable teaching, one would be glad to know what is; and yet, as if he feared he had not made the case plain enough against himself, he goes on to deduce the startling corollary that all oaths of allegiance must be incontinently broken. If it was sin thus to have sworn even in ignorance, it were obstinate sin to continue to respect them after fuller knowledge. Then comes the peroration, in which he cries aloud against the cruelties of that cursed Jezebel of England—that horrible monster Jezebel of England; and after having predicted sudden destruction to her rule and to the rule of all crowned women, and warned all men that if they presume to defend the same when any "noble heart" shall be raised up to vindicate the liberty of his country, they shall not fail to perish themselves in the ruin, he concludes with a last rhetorical flourish: "And therefore let all men be advertised, for the Trumpet hath once blown."

The capitals are his own. In writing, he probably felt the want of some such reverberation of the pulpit under strong hands as he was wont to emphasise his spoken utterances withal; there would seem to him a want of passion in the orderly lines of type; and I suppose we may take the capitals as a mere substitute for the great voice with which he would have given it forth, had we heard it from his own lips. Indeed, as it is, in this little strain of rhetoric about the trumpet, this current allusion to the fall of Jericho, that alone distinguishes his bitter and hasty production, he was probably right, according to all artistic canon, thus to support and accentuate in conclusion the sustained metaphor of a hostile proclamation. It is curious, by the way, to note how favourite an image the trumpet was with the Reformer. He returns to it again and again; it is the Alpha and Omega of his rhetoric; it is to him what a ship is to the stage sailor; and one would almost fancy he had begun the world as a trumpeter's apprentice. The partiality is surely characteristic. All his life long he was blowing summonses before various Jerichos, some of which fell duly, but not all. Wherever he appears in history his speech is loud, angry, and hostile; there is no peace in his life, and little tenderness; he is always sounding hopefully to the front for some rough enterprise.

And as his voice had something of the trumpet's hardness, it had something also of the trumpet's warlike inspiration. So Randolph, possibly fresh from the sound of the Reformer's preaching, writes of him to Cecil:— "Where your honour exhorteth us to stoutness, I assure you the voice of one man is able, in an hour, to put more life in us than six hundred trumpets continually blustering in our ears." [341]

Thus was the proclamation made. Nor was it long in wakening all the echoes of Europe. What success might have attended it, had the question decided been a purely abstract question, it is difficult to say. As it was, it was to stand or fall, not by logic, but by political needs and sympathies. Thus, in France, his doctrine was to have some future, because Protestants suffered there under the feeble and treacherous regency of Catherine de Medici; and thus it was to have no future anywhere else, because the Protestant interest was bound up with the prosperity of Queen Elizabeth. This stumbling-block lay at the very threshold of the matter; and Knox, in the text of the "First Blast," had set everybody the wrong example and gone to the ground himself. He finds occasion to regret "the blood of innocent Lady Jane Dudley." But Lady Jane Dudley, or Lady Jane Grey, as we call her, was a would-be traitoress and rebel against God, to use his own expressions. If, therefore, political and religious sympathy led Knox himself into so grave a partiality, what was he to expect from his disciples?

If the trumpet gave so ambiguous a sound, who could heartily prepare himself for the battle? The question whether Lady Jane Dudley was an innocent martyr, or a traitoress against God, whose inordinate pride and tyranny had been effectually repressed, was thus left altogether in the wind; and it was not, perhaps, wonderful if many of Knox's readers concluded that all right and wrong in the matter turned upon the degree of the sovereign's orthodoxy and possible helpfulness to the Reformation. He should have been the more careful of such an ambiguity of meaning, as he must have known well the lukewarm indifference and dishonesty of his fellow-reformers in political matters. He had already, in 1556 or 1557, talked the matter over with his great master, Calvin, in "a private conversation;" and the interview [342] must have been truly distasteful to both parties. Calvin, indeed, went a far way with him in theory, and owned that the "government of women was a deviation from the original and proper order of nature, to be ranked, no less than slavery, among the punishments consequent upon the fall of man." But, in practice, their two roads separated. For the Man of Geneva saw difficulties in the way of the Scripture proof in the cases of Deborah and Huldah, and in the prophecy of Isaiah that queens should be the nursing mothers of the Church. And as the Bible was not decisive, he thought the subject should be let alone, because, "by custom and public consent and long practice, it has been established that realms and principalities may descend to females by hereditary right, and it would not be lawful to unsettle governments which are ordained by the peculiar providence of God." I imagine Knox's ears must have burned during this interview. Think of him listening dutifully to all this—how it would not do to meddle with anointed kings—how there was a peculiar providence in these great affairs; and then think of his own peroration, and the "noble heart" whom he looks for "to vindicate the liberty of his country;" or his answer to Queen Mary, when she asked him who he was, to interfere in the affairs of Scotland:—"Madam, a subject born within the same!" Indeed, the two doctors who differed at this private conversation represented, at the moment, two principles of enormous import in the subsequent history of Europe. In Calvin we have represented that passive obedience, that toleration of injustice and absurdity, that holding back of the hand from political affairs as from something unclean, which lost France, if we are to believe M. Michelet, for the Reformation; a spirit necessarily fatal in the long run to the existence of any sect that may profess it; a suicidal doctrine that survives among us to this day in narrow views of personal duty, and the low political morality of many virtuous men. In Knox, on the other hand, we see foreshadowed the whole Puritan Revolution and the scaffold of Charles I.

There is little doubt in my mind that this interview was what caused Knox to print his book without a name. [344] It was a dangerous thing to contradict the Man of Geneva, and doubly so, surely, when one had had the advantage of correction from him in a private conversation; and Knox had his little flock of English refugees to consider. If they had fallen into bad odour at Geneva, where else was there left to flee to? It was printed, as I said, in 1558; and, by a singular mal-à-propos, in that same year Mary died, and Elizabeth succeeded to the throne of England. And just as the accession of Catholic Queen Mary had condemned female rule in the eyes of Knox, the accession of Protestant Queen Elizabeth justified it in the eyes of his colleagues. Female rule ceases to be an anomaly, not because Elizabeth can "reply to eight ambassadors in one day in their different languages," but because she represents for the moment the political future of the Reformation. The exiles troop back to England with songs of praise in their mouths. The bright occidental star, of which we have all read in the Preface to the Bible, has risen over the darkness of Europe. There is a thrill of hope through the persecuted

Churches of the Continent. Calvin writes to Cecil, washing his hands of Knox and his political heresies. The sale of the "First Blast" is prohibited in Geneva; and along with it the bold book of Knox's colleague, Goodman—a book dear to Milton—where female rule was briefly characterised as a "monster in nature and disorder among men." [345a] Any who may ever have doubted, or been for a moment led away by Knox or Goodman, or their own wicked imaginations, are now more than convinced. They have seen the occidental star. Aylmer, with his eye set greedily on a possible bishopric, and "the better to obtain the favour of the new Queen," [345b] sharpens his pen to confound Knox by logic. What need? He has been confounded by facts. "Thus what had been to the refugees of Geneva as the very word of God, no sooner were they back in England than, behold! it was the word of the devil." [346a]

Now, what of the real sentiments of these loyal subjects of Elizabeth? They professed a holy horror for Knox's position: let us see if their own would please a modern audience any better, or was, in substance, greatly different.

John Aylmer, afterwards Bishop of London, published an answer to Knox, under the title of An Harbour for Faithful and true Subjects against the late Blown Blast, concerning the government of Women. [346b] And certainly he was a thought more acute, a thought less precipitate and simple, than his adversary. He is not to be led away by such captious terms as natural and unnatural. It is obvious to him that a woman's disability to rule is not natural in the same sense in which it is natural for a stone to fall or fire to burn. He is doubtful, on the whole, whether this disability be natural at all; nay, when he is laying it down that a woman should not be a priest, he shows some elementary conception of what many of us now hold to be the truth of the matter. "The bringing-up of women," he says, "is commonly such" that they cannot have the necessary qualifications, "for they are not brought up in learning in schools, nor trained in disputation." And even so, he can ask, "Are there not in England women, think you, that for learning and wisdom could tell their household and neighbours as good a tale as any Sir John there?" For all that, his advocacy is weak. If women's rule is not unnatural in a sense preclusive of its very existence, it is neither so convenient nor so profitable as the government of men. He holds England to be specially suitable for the government of women, because there the governor is more limited and restrained by the other members of the constitution than in other places; and this argument has kept his book from being altogether forgotten. It is only in hereditary monarchies that he will offer any defence of the anomaly. "If rulers were to be chosen by lot or suffrage, he would not that any women should stand in the election, but men only." The law of succession of crowns was a law to him, in the same sense as the law of evolution is a law to Mr. Herbert Spencer; and the one and the other counsels his readers, in a spirit suggestively alike, not to kick against the pricks or seek to be more wise than He who made them. [348] If God has put a female child into the direct line of inheritance, it is God's affair. His strength will be perfected in her weakness. He makes the Creator address the objectors in this not very flattering vein:—"I, that could make Daniel, a sucking babe, to judge better than the wisest lawyers; a brute beast to reprehend the folly of a prophet; and poor fishers to confound the great clerks of the world—cannot I make a woman to be a good ruler over you?" This is the last word of his reasoning. Although he was not altogether without Puritanic leaven, shown particularly in what he says of the incomes of Bishops, yet it was rather loyalty to the old order of things than any generous belief in the capacity of women, that raised up for them this clerical champion. His courtly spirit contrasts singularly with the rude, bracing republicanism of Knox. "Thy knee shall bow," he says, "thy cap shall off, thy tongue shall speak reverently of thy sovereign." For himself, his tongue is even more than reverent. Nothing can stay the issue of his eloquent adulation. Again and again, "the remembrance of Elizabeth's virtues" carries him away; and he has to hark back again to find the scent of his argument. He is repressing his vehement adoration throughout, until, when the end comes, and he feels his business at an end, he can indulge himself to his heart's content in indiscriminate laudation of his royal mistress. It is humorous to think that this illustrious lady, whom he here praises, among many other excellences, for the simplicity of her attire and the "marvellous meekness of her stomach," threatened him, years after, in no very meek terms, for a sermon against female vanity in dress, which she held as a reflection on herself. [349]

Whatever was wanting here in respect for women generally, there was no want of respect for the Queen; and one cannot very greatly wonder if these devoted servants looked askance, not upon Knox only, but on his little flock, as they came back to England tainted with disloyal doctrine. For them, as for him, the occidental star rose somewhat red and angry. As for poor Knox, his position was the saddest of all. For the juncture seemed to him of the highest importance; it was the nick of time, the flood-water of opportunity. Not only was there an opening for him in Scotland, a smouldering brand of civil liberty and religious enthusiasm which it should be for him to kindle into flame with his powerful breath but he had his eye seemingly on an object of even higher worth. For now, when religious sympathy ran so high that it could be set against national aversion, he wished to begin the fusion together of England and Scotland, and to begin it at the sore place. If once the open wound were closed at the Border, the work would be half done. Ministers placed at Berwick and such places might seek their converts equally on either side of the march; old enemies would sit together to hear the gospel of peace, and forget the inherited jealousies of many generations in the enthusiasm of a common faith; or—let us say better—a common heresy. For people are not most conscious of brotherhood when they continue languidly together in one creed, but when, with some doubt, with some danger perhaps, and certainly not without some reluctance, they violently break with the tradition of the past, and go forth from the sanctuary of their fathers to worship under the bare heaven. A new creed, like a new country, is an unhomely place of sojourn; but it makes men lean on one another and join hands. It was on this that Knox relied to begin the union of the English and the Scotch. And he had, perhaps, better means of judging than any even of his contemporaries. He knew the temper of both nations; and already during his two years' chaplaincy at Berwick, he had seen his scheme put to the proof. But whether practicable or not, the proposal does him much honour. That he should thus have sought to make a love-match of it between the two peoples, and tried to win their inclination towards a union instead of simply transferring them, like so many sheep, by a marriage, or testament, or private treaty, is thoroughly characteristic of what is best in the man. Nor was this all. He had, besides, to assure himself of English support, secret or avowed, for the reformation party in Scotland; a delicate affair, trenching upon treason. And so he had plenty to say to Cecil, plenty that he did not care to "commit to paper neither yet to the knowledge of many." But his miserable publication had shut the doors of England in his face. Summoned to Edinburgh by the confederate lords, he waited at Dieppe, anxiously praying for leave to journey through England. The most dispiriting tidings reach him. His messengers, coming from so obnoxious a quarter, narrowly escape imprisonment. His old congregation are coldly received, and even begin to look back again to their place of exile with regret. "My First Blast," he writes ruefully, "has blown from me all my friends of England." And then he adds, with a snarl, "The Second Blast, I fear, shall sound somewhat more sharp, except men be more moderate than I hear they are." [352a] But the threat is empty; there will never be a second blast—he has had enough of that trumpet. Nay, he begins to feel uneasily that, unless he is to be rendered useless for the rest of his life, unless he is to lose his right arm and go about his great work maimed and impotent, he must find some way of making his peace with England and the indignant Queen. The letter just quoted was written on the 6th of April 1559; and on the 10th, after he had cooled his heels for four days more about the streets of Dieppe, he gave in altogether, and writes a letter of capitulation to Cecil. In this letter, [352b] which he kept back until the 22d, still hoping that things would come right of themselves, he censures the great secretary for having "followed the world in the way of perdition," characterises him as "worthy of hell," and threatens him, if he be not found simple, sincere, and fervent in the cause of Christ's gospel, that he shall "taste of the same cup that politic heads have drunken in before him." This is all, I take it, out of respect for the Reformer's own position; if he is going to be humiliated, let others be humiliated first; like a child who will not take his medicine until he has made his nurse and his mother drink of it before him. "But I have, say you, written a treasonable book against the regiment and empire of women. . . . The writing of that book I will not deny; but to prove it treasonable I think it shall be hard. . . . It is hinted that my book shall be written against. If so be, sir, I greatly doubt they shall rather hurt nor (than) mend the matter." And here come the terms of capitulation; for he does not surrender unconditionally, even in this sore strait: "And yet if any," he goes on, "think me enemy to the person, or yet to the regiment, of her whom God hath now promoted, they are utterly deceived in me, for the miraculous work of God, comforting His afflicted by means of an infirm vessel, I do acknowledge, and the power of His most potent hand I will obey. More plainly to speak, if Queen Elizabeth shall confess, that the extraordinary dispensation of God's great mercy maketh that lawful unto her which both nature and God's law do deny to all women, then shall none in England be more willing to maintain her lawful authority than I shall be. But if (God's wondrous work set aside) she ground (as God forbid) the justness of her title upon consuetude, laws, or ordinances of men, then"—Then Knox will denounce her? Not so; he is more politic nowadays—then, he "greatly fears" that her ingratitude to God will not go long without punishment.

His letter to Elizabeth, written some few months later, was a mere amplification of the sentences quoted above. She must base her title entirely upon the extraordinary providence of God; but if she does this, "if thus, in God's presence, she humbles herself, so will he with tongue and pen justify her authority, as the Holy Ghost hath justified the same in Deborah, that blessed mother in Israel." [354] And so, you see, his consistency is preserved; he is merely applying the doctrine of the "First Blast." The argument goes thus: The regiment of women is, as before noted in our work, repugnant to nature, contumely to God, and a subversion of good order. It has nevertheless pleased God to raise up, as exceptions to this law, first Deborah, and afterward Elizabeth Tudor—whose regiment we shall proceed to celebrate.

There is no evidence as to how the Reformer's explanations were received, and indeed it is most probable that the letter was never shown to Elizabeth at all. For it was sent under cover of another to Cecil, and as it was not of a very courtly conception throughout, and was, of all things, what would most excite the Queen's uneasy jealousy about her title, it is like enough that the secretary exercised his discretion (he had Knox's leave in this case, and did not always wait for that, it is reputed) to put the letter harmlessly away beside other valueless or unpresentable State Papers. I wonder very much if he did the same with another, [355] written two years later, after Mary had come into Scotland, in which Knox almost seeks to make Elizabeth an accomplice with him in the matter of the "First Blast." The Queen of Scotland is going to have that work refuted, he tells her; and "though it were but foolishness in him to prescribe unto her Majesty what is to be done," he would yet remind her that Mary is neither so much alarmed about her own security, nor so generously interested in Elizabeth's, "that she would take such pains, unless her crafty counsel in so doing shot at a further mark." There is something really ingenious in this letter; it showed Knox in the double capacity of the author of the "First Blast" and the faithful friend of Elizabeth; and he combines them there so naturally, that one would scarcely imagine the two to be incongruous.

Twenty days later he was defending his intemperate publication to another queen—his own queen, Mary Stuart. This was on the first of those three interviews which he has preserved for us with so much dramatic vigour in the picturesque pages of his history. After he had avowed the authorship in his usual haughty style, Mary asked: "You think, then, that I have no just authority?" The question was evaded. "Please your Majesty," he answered, "that learned men in all ages have had their judgments free, and most commonly disagreeing from the common judgment of the world; such also have they published by pen and tongue; and yet notwithstanding they themselves have lived in the common society with others, and have borne patiently with the errors and imperfections which they could not amend." Thus did "Plato the philosopher:" thus will do John Knox. "I have communicated my judgment to the world: if the realm finds no inconvenience from the regiment of a woman, that which they approve, shall I not further disallow than within my own breast; but shall be as well content to live under your Grace, as Paul was to live under Nero. And my hope is, that so long as ye defile not your hands with the blood of the saints of God, neither I nor my book shall hurt either you or your authority." All this is admirable in wisdom and moderation, and, except that he might have hit upon a comparison less offensive than that with Paul and Nero, hardly to be bettered. Having said thus much, he feels he needs say no more; and so, when he is further pressed, he closes that part of the discussion with an astonishing sally. If he has been content to let this matter sleep, he would recommend her Grace to follow his example with thankfulness of heart; it is grimly to be understood which of them has most to fear if the question should be reawakened. So the talk wandered to other subjects. Only, when the Queen was summoned at last to dinner ("for it was afternoon") Knox made his salutation in this form of words: "I pray God, Madam, that you may be as much blessed within the Commonwealth of Scotland, if it be the pleasure of God, as ever Deborah was in the Commonwealth of Israel." [357] Deborah again.

But he was not yet done with the echoes of his own "First Blast." In 1571, when he was already near his end, the old controversy was taken up in one of a series of anonymous libels against the Reformer affixed, Sunday after Sunday, to the church door. The dilemma was fairly enough stated. Either his doctrine is false, in which case he is a "false doctor" and seditious; or, if it be true, why does he "avow and approve the contrare, I mean that regiment in the Queen of England's person; which he avoweth and approveth, not only praying for the maintenance of her estate, but also procuring her aid and support against his own native country?" Knox answered the libel, as his wont was, next Sunday, from the pulpit. He justified the "First Blast" with all the old arrogance; there is no drawing back there. The regiment of women is repugnant to nature, contumely to God, and a subversion of good order, as before. When he prays for the maintenance of Elizabeth's estate, he is only following the example of those prophets of God who warned and comforted the wicked kings of Israel; or of Jeremiah, who bade the Jews pray for the prosperity of Nebuchadnezzar. As for the Queen's aid, there is no harm in that: quia (these are his own words) quia omnia munda mundis: because to the pure all things are pure. One thing, in conclusion, he "may not pretermit" to give the lie in the throat to his accuser, where he charges him with seeking support against his native country. "What I have been to my country," said the old Reformer, "What I have been to my country, albeit this unthankful age will not know, yet the ages to come will be compelled to bear witness to the truth. And thus I cease, requiring of all men that have anything to oppone against me, that he may (they may) do it so plainly, as that I may make myself and all my doings manifest to the world. For to me it seemeth a thing unreasonable, that, in this my decrepit age, I shall be compelled to fight against shadows, and howlets that dare not abide the light." [359]

Now, in this, which may be called his Last Blast, there is as sharp speaking as any in the "First Blast" itself. He is of the same opinion to the end, you see, although he has been obliged to cloak and garble that opinion for political ends. He has been tacking indeed, and he has indeed been seeking the favour of a queen; but what man ever sought a queen's favour with a more virtuous purpose, or with as little courtly policy? The question of consistency is delicate, and must be made plain. Knox never changed his opinion about female rule, but lived to regret that he had published that opinion. Doubtless he had many thoughts so far out of the range of public sympathy, that he could only keep them to himself, and, in his own words, bear patiently with the errors and imperfections that he could not amend. For example, I make no doubt myself that, in his own heart, he did hold the shocking dogma attributed to him by more than one calumniator; and that, had the time been ripe, had there been aught to gain by it, instead of all to lose, he would have been the first to assert that Scotland was elective instead of hereditary—"elective as in the days of paganism," as one Thevet says in holy horror. [360] And yet, because the time was not ripe, I find no hint of such an idea in his collected works. Now, the regiment of women was another matter that he should have kept to himself; right or wrong, his opinion did not fit the moment; right or wrong, as Aylmer puts it, "the Blast was blown out of season." And this it was that he began to perceive after the accession of Elizabeth; not that he had been wrong, and that female rule was a good thing, for he had said from the first that "the felicity of some women in their empires" could not change the law of God and the nature of created things; not this, but that the regiment of women was one of those imperfections of society which must be borne with because yet they cannot be remedied. The thing had seemed so obvious to him, in his sense of unspeakable masculine superiority, and his fine contempt for what is only sanctioned by antiquity and common consent, he had imagined that, at the first hint, men would arise and shake off the debasing tyranny. He found himself wrong, and he showed that he could be moderate in his own fashion, and understood the spirit of true compromise. He came round to Calvin's position, in fact, but by a different way. And it derogates nothing from the merit of this wise attitude that it was the consequence of a change of interest. We are all taught by interest; and if the interest be not merely selfish, there is no wiser preceptor under heaven, and perhaps no sterner.

Such is the history of John Knox's connection with the controversy about female rule. In itself, this is obviously an incomplete study; not fully to be understood, without a knowledge of his private relations with the other sex, and what he thought of their position in domestic life. This shall be dealt with in another paper.

II.—Private Life.

To those who know Knox by hearsay only, I believe the matter of this paper will be somewhat astonishing. For the hard energy of the man in all public matters has possessed the imagination of the world; he remains for posterity in certain traditional phrases, browbeating Queen Mary, or breaking beautiful carved work in abbeys and cathedrals, that had long smoked themselves out and were no more than sorry ruins, while he was still quietly teaching children in a country gentleman's family. It does not consist with the common acceptation of his character to fancy him much moved, except with anger. And yet the language of passion came to his pen as readily, whether it was a passion of denunciation against some of the abuses that vexed his righteous spirit, or of yearning for the society of an absent friend. He was vehement in affection, as in doctrine. I will not deny that there may have been, along with his vehemence, something shifty, and for the moment only; that, like many men, and many Scotchmen, he saw the world and his own heart, not so much under any very steady, equable light, as by extreme flashes of passion, true for the moment, but not true in the long run. There does seem to me to be something of this traceable in the Reformer's utterances: precipitation and repentance, hardy speech and action somewhat circumspect, a strong tendency to see himself in a heroic light and to place a ready belief in the disposition of the moment. Withal he had considerable confidence in himself, and in the uprightness of his own disciplined emotions, underlying much sincere aspiration after spiritual humility. And it is this confidence that makes his intercourse with women so interesting to a modern. It would be easy, of course, to make fun of the whole affair, to picture him strutting vaingloriously among these inferior creatures, or compare a religious friendship in the sixteenth century with what was called, I think, a literary friendship in the eighteenth. But it is more just and profitable to recognise what there is sterling and human underneath all his theoretical affectations of superiority. Women, he has said in his "First Blast," are, "weak, frail, impatient, feeble, and foolish;" and yet it does not appear that he was himself any less dependent than other men upon the sympathy and affection of these weak, frail, impatient, feeble, and foolish creatures; it seems even as if he had been rather more dependent than most.

Of those who are to act influentially on their fellows, we should expect always something large and public in their way of life, something more or less urbane and comprehensive in their sentiment for others. We should not expect to see them spend their sympathy in idyls, however beautiful. We should not seek them among those who, if they have but a wife to their bosom, ask no more of womankind, just as they ask no more of their own sex, if they can find a friend or two for their immediate need. They will be quick to feel all the pleasures of our association—not the great ones alone, but all. They will know not love only, but all those other ways in which man and woman mutually make each other happy—by sympathy, by admiration, by the atmosphere they bear about them—down to the mere impersonal pleasure of passing happy faces in the street. For, through all this gradation, the difference of sex makes itself pleasurably felt. Down to the most lukewarm courtesies of life, there is a special chivalry due and a special pleasure received, when the two sexes are brought ever so lightly into contact. We love our mothers otherwise than we love our fathers; a sister is not as a brother to us; and friendship between man and woman, be it never so unalloyed and innocent, is not the same as friendship between man and man. Such friendship is not even possible for all. To conjoin tenderness for a woman that is not far short of passionate with such disinterestedness and beautiful gratuity of affection as there is between friends of the same sex, requires no ordinary disposition in the man. For either it would presuppose quite womanly delicacy of perception, and, as it were, a curiosity in shades of differing sentiment; or it would mean that he had accepted the large, simple divisions of society: a strong and positive spirit robustly virtuous, who has chosen a better part coarsely, and holds to it steadfastly, with all its consequences of pain to himself and others; as one who should go straight before him on a journey, neither tempted by wayside flowers nor very scrupulous of small lives under foot. It was in virtue of this latter disposition that Knox was capable of those intimacies with women that embellished his life; and we find him preserved for us in old letters as a man of many women friends; a man of some expansion toward the other sex; a man ever ready to comfort weeping women, and to weep along with them.

Of such scraps and fragments of evidence as to his private life and more intimate thoughts as have survived to us from all the perils that environ written paper, an astonishingly large proportion is in the shape of letters to women of his familiarity. He was twice married, but that is not greatly to the purpose; for the Turk, who thinks even more meanly of women than John Knox, is none the less given to marrying. What is really significant is quite apart from marriage. For the man Knox was a true man, and woman, the ewig-weibliche, was as necessary to him, in spite of all low theories, as ever she was to Goethe. He came to her in a certain halo of his own, as the minister of truth, just as Goethe came to her in a glory of art; he made himself necessary to troubled hearts and minds exercised in the painful complications that naturally result from all changes in the world's way of thinking; and those whom he had thus helped became dear to him, and were made the chosen companions of his leisure if they were at hand, or encouraged and comforted by letter if they were afar.

It must not be forgotten that Knox had been a presbyter of the old Church, and that the many women whom we shall see gathering around him, as he goes through life, had probably been accustomed, while still in the communion of Rome, to rely much upon some chosen spiritual director, so that the intimacies of which I propose to offer some account, while testifying to a good heart in the Reformer, testify also to a certain survival of the spirit of the confessional in the Reformed Church, and are not properly to be judged without this idea. There is no friendship so noble, but it is the product of the time; and a world of little finical observances, and little frail proprieties and fashions of the hour, go to make or to mar, to stint or to perfect, the union of spirits the most loving and the most intolerant of such interference. The trick of the country and the age steps in even between the mother and her child, counts out their caresses upon niggardly fingers, and says, in the voice of authority, that this one thing shall be a matter of confidence between them, and this other thing shall not. And thus it is that we must take into reckoning whatever tended to modify the social atmosphere in which Knox and his women friends met, and loved and trusted each other. To the man who had been their priest and was now their minister, women would be able to speak with a confidence quite impossible in these latter days; the women would be able to speak, and the man to hear. It was a beaten road just then; and I daresay we should be no less scandalised at their plain speech than they, if they could come back to earth, would be offended at our waltzes and worldly fashions. This, then, was the footing on which Knox stood with his many women friends. The reader will see, as he goes on, how much of warmth, of interest, and of that happy mutual dependence which is the very gist of friendship, he contrived to ingraft upon this somewhat dry relationship of penitent and confessor.

It must be understood that we know nothing of his intercourse with women (as indeed we know little at all about his life) until he came to Berwick in 1549, when he was already in the forty-fifth year of his age. At the same time it is just possible that some of a little group at Edinburgh, with whom he corresponded during his last absence, may have been friends of an older standing. Certainly they were, of all his female correspondents, the least personally favoured. He treats them throughout in a comprehensive sort of spirit that must at times have been a little wounding. Thus, he remits one of them to his former letters, "which I trust be common betwixt you and the rest of our sisters, for to me ye are all equal in Christ." [368] Another letter is a gem in this way. "Albeit" it begins, "albeit I have no particular matter to write unto you, beloved sister, yet I could not refrain to write these few lines to you in declaration of my remembrance of you. True it is that I have many whom I bear in equal remembrance before God with you, to whom at present I write nothing, either for that I esteem them stronger than you, and therefore they need the less my rude labours, or else because they have not provoked me by their writing to recompense their remembrance." [369a] His "sisters in Edinburgh" had evidently to "provoke" his attention pretty constantly; nearly all his letters are, on the face of them, answers to questions, and the answers are given with a certain crudity that I do not find repeated when he writes to those he really cares for. So when they consult him about women's apparel (a subject on which his opinion may be pretty correctly imagined by the ingenious reader for himself) he takes occasion to anticipate some of the most offensive matter of the "First Blast" in a style of real brutality. [369b] It is not merely that he tells them "the garments of women do declare their weakness and inability to execute the office of man," though that in itself is neither very wise nor very opportune in such a correspondence one would think; but if the reader will take the trouble to wade through the long, tedious sermon for himself, he will see proof enough that Knox neither loved, nor very deeply respected, the women he was then addressing. In very truth, I believe these Edinburgh sisters simply bored him. He had a certain interest in them as his children in the Lord; they were continually "provoking him by their writing;" and, if they handed his letters about, writing to them was as good a form of publication as was then open to him in Scotland. There is one letter, however, in this budget, addressed to the wife of Clerk-Register Mackgil, which is worthy of some further mention. The Clerk-Register had not opened his heart, it would appear, to the preaching of the Gospel, and Mrs. Mackgil has written, seeking the Reformer's prayers in his behalf. "Your husband," he answers, "is dear to me for that he is a man indued with some good gifts, but more dear for that he is your husband. Charity moveth me to thirst his illumination, both for his comfort and for the trouble which you sustain by his coldness, which justly may be called infidelity." He wishes her, however, not to hope too much; he can promise that his prayers will be earnest, but not that they will be effectual; it is possible that this is to be her "cross" in life; that "her head, appointed by God for her comfort, should be her enemy." And if this be so, well, there is nothing for it; "with patience she must abide God's merciful deliverance," taking heed only that she does not "obey manifest iniquity for the pleasure of any mortal man." [371a] I conceive this epistle would have given a very modified sort of pleasure to the Clerk-Register, had it chanced to fall into his hands. Compare its tenor— the dry resignation not without a hope of merciful deliverance therein recommended—with these words from another letter, written but the year before to two married women of London: "Call first for grace by Jesus, and thereafter communicate with your faithful husbands, and then shall God, I

217

doubt not, conduct your footsteps, and direct your counsels to His glory." [371b] Here the husbands are put in a very high place; we can recognise here the same hand that has written for our instruction how the man is set above the woman, even as God above the angels. But the point of the distinction is plain. For Clerk-Register Mackgil was not a faithful husband; displayed, indeed, towards religion a "coldness which justly might be called infidelity." We shall see in more notable instances how much Knox's conception of the duty of wives varies according to the zeal and orthodoxy of the husband.

As I have said, he may possibly have made the acquaintance of Mrs. Mackgil, Mrs. Guthrie, or some other, or all, of these Edinburgh friends while he was still Douglas of Longniddry's private tutor. But our certain knowledge begins in 1549. He was then but newly escaped from his captivity in France, after pulling an oar for nineteen months on the benches of the galley Nostre Dame; now up the rivers, holding stealthy intercourse with other Scottish prisoners in the castle of Rouen; now out in the North Sea, raising his sick head to catch a glimpse of the far-off steeples of St. Andrews. And now he was sent down by the English Privy Council as a preacher to Berwick-upon-Tweed; somewhat shaken in health by all his hardships, full of pains and agues, and tormented by gravel, that sorrow of great men; altogether, what with his romantic story, his weak health, and his great faculty of eloquence, a very natural object for the sympathy of devout women. At this happy juncture he fell into the company of a Mrs. Elizabeth Bowes, wife of Richard Bowes, of Aske, in Yorkshire, to whom she had borne twelve children. She was a religious hypochondriac, a very weariful woman, full of doubts and scruples, and giving no rest on earth either to herself or to those whom she honoured with her confidence. From the first time she heard Knox preach she formed a high opinion of him, and was solicitous ever after of his society. [373a] Nor was Knox unresponsive. "I have always delighted in your company," he writes, "and when labours would permit, you know I have not spared hours to talk and commune with you." Often when they had met in depression he reminds her, "God hath sent great comfort unto both." [373b] We can gather from such letters as are yet extant how close and continuous was their intercourse. "I think it best you remain till the morrow," he writes once, "and so shall we commune at large at afternoon.

This day you know to be the day of my study and prayer unto God; yet if your trouble be intolerable, or, if you think my presence may release your pain, do as the Spirit shall move you. . . . Your messenger found me in bed, after a sore trouble and most dolorous night, and so dolour may complain to dolour when we two meet. . . . And this is more plain than ever I spoke, to let you know you have a companion in trouble." [373c]   Once we have the curtain raised for a moment, and can look at the two together for the length of a phrase. "After the writing of this preceding," writes Knox, "your brother and mine, Harrie Wycliffe, did advertise me by writing, that your adversary (the devil) took occasion to trouble you because that I did start back from you rehearsing your infirmities. I remember myself so to have done, and that is my common on consuetude when anything pierceth or toucheth my heart. Call to your mind what I did standing at the cupboard at Alnwick. In very deed I thought that no creature had been tempted as I was; and when I heard proceed from your mouth the very same words that he troubles me with, I did wonder and from my heart lament your sore trouble, knowing in myself the dolour thereof." [374a]   Now intercourse of so very close a description, whether it be religious intercourse or not, is apt to displease and disquiet a husband; and we know incidentally from Knox himself that there was some little scandal about his intimacy with Mrs. Bowes. "The slander and fear of men," he writes, "has impeded me to exercise my pen so oft as I would; yea, very shame hath holden me from your company, when I was most surely persuaded that God had appointed me at that time to comfort and feed your hungry and afflicted soul. God in His infinite mercy," he goes on, "remove not only from me all fear that tendeth not to godliness, but from others suspicion to judge of me otherwise than it becometh one member to judge of another." [374b]   And the scandal, such as it was, would not be allayed by the dissension in which Mrs. Bowes seems to have lived with her family upon the matter of religion, and the countenance shown by Knox to her resistance. Talking of these conflicts, and her courage against "her own flesh and most inward affections, yea, against some of her most natural friends," he writes it, "to the praise of God, he has wondered at the bold constancy which he has found in her when his own heart was faint." [375a]

Now, perhaps in order to stop scandalous mouths, perhaps out of a desire to bind the much-loved evangelist nearer to her in the only manner possible, Mrs. Bowes conceived the scheme of marrying him to her fifth daughter, Marjorie; and the Reformer seems to have fallen in with it readily enough. It seems to have been believed in the family that the whole matter had been originally made up between these two, with no very spontaneous inclination on the part of the bride. [375b] Knox's idea of marriage, as I have said, was not the same for all men; but on the whole, it was not lofty. We have a curious letter of his, written at the request of Queen Mary, to the Earl of Argyle, on very delicate household matters; which, as he tells us, "was not well accepted of the said Earl." [375c] We may suppose, however, that his own home was regulated in a similar spirit. I can fancy that for such a man, emotional, and with a need, now and again, to exercise parsimony in emotions not strictly needful, something a little mechanical, something hard and fast and clearly understood, would enter into his ideal of a home. There were storms enough without, and equability was to be desired at the fireside even at a sacrifice of deeper pleasures. So, from a wife, of all women, he would not ask much. One letter to her which has come down to us is, I had almost said, conspicuous for coldness. [376] He calls her, as he called other female correspondents, "dearly beloved sister;" the epistle is doctrinal, and nearly the half of it bears, not upon her own case, but upon that of her mother. However, we know what Heine wrote in his wife's album; and there is, after all, one passage that may be held to intimate some tenderness, although even that admits of an amusingly opposite construction. "I think," he says, "I think this be the first letter I ever wrote to you." This, if we are to take it literally, may pair off with the "two or three children" whom Montaigne mentions having lost at nurse; the one is as eccentric in a lover as the other in a parent. Nevertheless, he displayed more energy in the course of his troubled wooing than might have been expected. The whole Bowes family, angry enough already at the influence he had obtained over the mother, set their faces obdurately against the match. And I daresay the opposition quickened his inclination. I find him writing to Mrs. Bowes that she need no further trouble herself about the marriage; it should now be his business altogether; it behoved him now to jeopard his life "for the comfort of his own flesh, both fear and friendship of all earthly creature laid aside." [377]

This is a wonderfully chivalrous utterance for a Reformer forty-eight years old; and it compares well with the leaden coquetries of Calvin, not much over thirty, taking this and that into consideration, weighing together dowries and religious qualifications and the instancy of friends, and exhibiting what M. Bungener calls "an honourable and Christian difficulty" of choice, in frigid indecisions and insincere proposals. But Knox's next letter is in a humbler tone; he has not found the negotiation so easy as he fancied; he despairs of the marriage altogether, and talks of leaving England,—regards not "what country consumes his wicked carcass." "You shall understand," he says, "that this sixth of November, I spoke with Sir Robert Bowes" (the head of the family, his bride's uncle) "in the matter you know, according to your request; whose disdainful, yea, despiteful, words hath so pierced my heart that my life is bitter to me. I bear a good countenance with a sore troubled heart, because he that ought to consider matters with a deep judgment is become not only a despiser, but also a taunter of God's messengers—God be merciful unto him! Amongst others his most unpleasing words, while that I was about to have declared my heart in the whole matter, he said, 'Away with your rhetorical reasons! for I will not be persuaded with them.' God knows I did use no rhetoric nor coloured speech; but would have spoken the truth, and that in most simple manner. I am not a good orator in my own cause; but what he would not be content to hear of me, God shall declare to him one day to his displeasure, unless he repent." [378] Poor Knox, you see, is quite commoved. It has been a very unpleasant interview. And as it is the only sample that we have of how things went with him during his courtship, we may infer that the period was not as agreeable for Knox as it has been for some others.

However, when once they were married, I imagine he and Marjorie Bowes hit it off together comfortably enough. The little we know of it may be brought together in a very short space. She bore him two sons. He seems to have kept her pretty busy, and depended on her to some degree in his work; so that when she fell ill, his papers got at once into disorder. [379a] Certainly she sometimes wrote to his dictation; and, in this capacity, he calls her "his left hand." [379b] In June 1559, at the headiest moment of the Reformation in Scotland, he writes regretting the absence of his helpful colleague, Goodman, "whose presence" (this is the not very grammatical form of his lament) "whose presence I more thirst, than she that is my own flesh." [379c] And this, considering the source and the circumstances, may be held as evidence of a very tender sentiment. He tells us himself in his history, on the occasion of a certain meeting at the Kirk of Field, that "he was in no small heaviness by reason of the late death of his dear bed-fellow, Marjorie Bowes." [379d] Calvin, condoling with him, speaks of her as "a wife whose like is not to be found everywhere" (that is very like Calvin), and again, as "the most delightful of wives." We know what Calvin thought desirable in a wife, "good humour, chastity, thrift, patience, and solicitude for her husband's health," and so we may suppose that the first Mrs. Knox fell not far short of this ideal.

The actual date of the marriage is uncertain but by September 1566, at the latest, the Reformer was settled in Geneva with his wife. There is no fear either that he will be dull; even if the chaste, thrifty, patient Marjorie should not altogether occupy his mind, he need not go out of the house to seek more female sympathy; for behold! Mrs. Bowes is duly domesticated with the young couple. Dr. M'Crie imagined that Richard Bowes was now dead, and his widow, consequently, free to live where she would; and where could she go more naturally than to the house of a married daughter? This, however, is not the case. Richard Bowes did not die till at least two years later. It is impossible to believe that he approved of his wife's desertion, after so many years of marriage, after twelve children had been born to them; and accordingly we find in his will, dated 1558, no mention either of her or of Knox's wife. [380] This is plain sailing. It is easy enough to understand the anger of Bowes against this interloper, who had come into a quiet family, married the daughter in spite of the father's opposition, alienated the wife from the husband and the husband's religion, supported her in a long course of resistance and rebellion, and, after years of intimacy, already too close and tender for any jealous spirit to behold without resentment, carried her away with him at last into a foreign land. But it is not quite easy to understand how, except out of sheer weariness and disgust, he was ever brought to agree to the arrangement. Nor is it easy to square the Reformer's conduct with his public teaching. We have, for instance, a letter by him, Craig, and Spottiswood, to the Archbishops of Canterbury and York, anent "a wicked and rebellious woman," one Anne Good, spouse to "John Barron, a minister of Christ

Jesus his evangel," who, "after great rebellion shown unto him, and divers admonitions given, as well by himself as by others in his name, that she should in no wise depart from this realm, nor from his house without his license, hath not the less stubbornly and rebelliously departed, separated herself from his society, left his house, and withdrawn herself from this realm." [381] Perhaps some sort of license was extorted, as I have said, from Richard Bowes, weary with years of domestic dissension; but setting that aside, the words employed with so much righteous indignation by Knox, Craig, and Spottiswood, to describe the conduct of that wicked and rebellious woman, Mrs. Barron, would describe nearly as exactly the conduct of the religious Mrs. Bowes. It is a little bewildering, until we recollect the distinction between faithful and unfaithful husbands; for Barron was "a minister of Christ Jesus his evangel," while Richard Bowes, besides being own brother to a despiser and taunter of God's messengers, is shrewdly suspected to have been "a bigoted adherent of the Roman Catholic faith," or, as Knox himself would have expressed it, "a rotten Papist."

You would have thought that Knox was now pretty well supplied with female society. But we are not yet at the end of the roll. The last year of his sojourn in England had been spent principally in London, where he was resident as one of the chaplains of Edward the Sixth; and here he boasts, although a stranger, he had, by God's grace, found favour before many. [382a] The godly women of the metropolis made much of him; once he writes to Mrs. Bowes that her last letter had found him closeted with three, and he and the three women were all in tears. [382b] Out of all, however, he had chosen two. "God," he writes to them, "brought us in such familiar acquaintance, that your hearts were incensed and kindled with a special care over me, as a mother useth to be over her natural child; and my heart was opened and compelled in your presence to be more plain than ever I was to any." [382c] And out of the two even he had chosen one, Mrs. Anne Locke, wife to Mr. Harry Locke, merchant, nigh to Bow Kirk, Cheapside, in London, as the address runs. If one may venture to judge upon such imperfect evidence, this was the woman he loved best. I have a difficulty in quite forming to myself an idea of her character. She may have been one of the three tearful visitors before alluded to; she may even have been that one of them who was so profoundly moved by some passages of Mrs. Bowes's letter, which the Reformer opened, and read aloud to them before they went. "O would to God," cried this impressionable matron, "would to God that I might speak with that person, for I perceive there are more tempted than I." [383] This may have been Mrs. Locke, as I say; but even if it were, we must not conclude from this one fact that she was such another as Mrs. Bowes. All the evidence tends the other way. She was a woman of understanding, plainly, who followed political events with interest, and to whom Knox thought it worth while to write, in detail, the history of his trials and successes. She was religious, but without that morbid perversity of spirit that made religion so heavy a burden for the poor-hearted Mrs. Bowes. More of her I do not find, save testimony to the profound affection that united her to the Reformer. So we find him writing to her from Geneva, in such terms as these:—"You write that your desire is earnest to see me. Dear sister, if I should express the thirst and languor which I have had for your presence, I should appear to pass measure. . . Yea, I weep and rejoice in remembrance of you; but that would evanish by the comfort of your presence, which I assure you is so dear to me, that if the charge of this little flock here, gathered together in Christ's name, did not impede me, my coming should prevent my letter." [384] I say that this was written from Geneva; and yet you will observe that it is no consideration for his wife or mother-in-law, only the charge of his little flock, that keeps him from setting out forthwith for London, to comfort himself with the dear presence of Mrs. Locke. Remember that was a certain plausible enough pretext for Mrs. Locke to come to Geneva—"the most perfect school of Christ that ever was on earth since the days of the Apostles"—for we are now under the reign of that "horrible monster Jezebel of England," when a lady of good orthodox sentiments was better out of London. It was doubtful, however, whether this was to be. She was detained in England, partly by circumstances unknown, "partly by empire of her head," Mr. Harry Locke, the Cheapside merchant. It is somewhat humorous to see Knox struggling for resignation, now that he has to do with a faithful husband (for Mr. Harry Locke was faithful). Had it been otherwise, "in my heart," he says, "I could have wished—yea," here he breaks out, "yea, and cannot cease to wish—that God would guide you to this place." [385] And after all, he had not long to wait, for, whether Mr. Harry

Locke died in the interval, or was wearied, he too, into giving permission, five months after the date of the letter last quoted, "Mrs. Anne Locke, Harry her son, and Anne her daughter, and Katharine her maid," arrived in that perfect school of Christ, the Presbyterian paradise, Geneva. So now, and for the next two years, the cup of Knox's happiness was surely full. Of an afternoon, when the bells rang out for the sermon, the shops closed, and the good folk gathered to the churches, psalm-book in hand, we can imagine him drawing near to the English chapel in quite patriarchal fashion, with Mrs. Knox and Mrs. Bowes and Mrs. Locke, James his servant, Patrick his pupil, and a due following of children and maids. He might be alone at work all morning in his study, for he wrote much during these two years; but at night, you may be sure there was a circle of admiring women, eager to hear the new paragraph, and not sparing of applause. And what work, among others, was he elaborating at this time, but the notorious "First Blast"? So that he may have rolled out in his big pulpit voice, how women were weak, frail, impatient, feeble, foolish, inconstant, variable, cruel, and lacking the spirit of counsel, and how men were above them, even as God is above the angels, in the ears of his own wife, and the two dearest friends he had on earth. But he had lost the sense of incongruity, and continued to despise in theory the sex he honoured so much in practice, of whom he chose his most intimate associates, and whose courage he was compelled to wonder at, when his own heart was faint.

We may say that such a man was not worthy of his fortune; and so, as he would not learn, he was taken away from that agreeable school, and his fellowship of women was broken up, not to be reunited. Called into Scotland to take at last that strange position in history which is his best claim to commemoration, he was followed thither by his wife and his mother-in-law. The wife soon died. The death of her daughter did not altogether separate Mrs. Bowes from Knox, but she seems to have come and gone between his house and England. In 1562, however, we find him characterised as "a sole man by reason of the absence of his mother-in-law, Mrs. Bowes," and a passport is got for her, her man, a maid, and "three horses, whereof two shall return," as well as liberty to take all her own money with her into Scotland. This looks like a definite arrangement; but whether she died at Edinburgh, or went back to England yet again, I cannot find.

With that great family of hers, unless in leaving her husband she had quarrelled with them all, there must have been frequent occasion for her presence, one would think. Knox at least survived her; and we possess his epigraph to their long intimacy, given to the world by him in an appendix to his latest publication. I have said in a former paper that Knox was not shy of personal revelations in his published works. And the trick seems to have grown on him. To this last tract, a controversial onslaught on a Scottish Jesuit, he prefixed a prayer, not very pertinent to the matter in hand, and containing references to his family which were the occasion of some wit in his adversary's answer; and appended what seems equally irrelevant, one of his devout letters to Mrs. Bowes, with an explanatory preface. To say truth, I believe he had always felt uneasily that the circumstances of this intimacy were very capable of misconstruction; and now, when he was an old man, taking "his good night of all the faithful in both realms," and only desirous "that without any notable sclander to the evangel of Jesus Christ, he might end his battle; for as the world was weary of him, so was he of it;"—in such a spirit it was not, perhaps, unnatural that he should return to this old story, and seek to put it right in the eyes of all men, ere he died. "Because that God," he says, "because that God now in His mercy hath put an end to the battle of my dear mother, Mistress Elizabeth Bowes, before that He put an end to my wretched life, I could not cease but declare to the world what was the cause of our great familiarity and long acquaintance; which was neither flesh nor blood, but a troubled conscience upon her part, which never suffered her to rest but when she was in the company of the faithful, of whom (from the first hearing of the word at my mouth) she judged me to be one. . . . Her company to me was comfortable (yea, honourable and profitable, for she was to me and mine a mother), but yet it was not without some cross; for besides trouble and fashery of body sustained for her, my mind was seldom quiet, for doing somewhat for the comfort of her troubled conscience." [388] He had written to her years before, from his first exile in Dieppe, that "only God's hand" could withhold him from once more speaking with her face to face; and now, when God's hand has indeed interposed, when there lies between them, instead of the voyageable straits, that great gulf over which no man can pass, this is the spirit in which he can look back upon their long acquaintance. She was a religious hypochondriac, it appears, whom, not without some cross and fashery of mind and body, he was good enough to tend. He might have given a truer character of their friendship, had he thought less of his own standing in public estimation, and more of the dead woman. But he was in all things, as Burke said of his son in that ever memorable passage, a public creature. He wished that even into this private place of his affections posterity should follow him with a complete approval; and he was willing, in order that this might be so, to exhibit the defects of his lost friend, and tell the world what weariness he had sustained through her unhappy disposition. There is something here that reminds one of Rousseau.

I do not think he ever saw Mrs. Locke after he left Geneva; but his correspondence with her continued for three years. It may have continued longer, of course, but I think the last letters we possess read like the last that would be written. Perhaps Mrs. Locke was then remarried, for there is much obscurity over her subsequent history. For as long as their intimacy was kept up, at least, the human element remains in the Reformer's life. Here is one passage, for example, the most likable utterance of Knox's that I can quote:—Mrs. Locke has been upbraiding him as a bad correspondent. "My remembrance of you," he answers, "is not so dead, but I trust it shall be fresh enough, albeit it be renewed by no outward token for one year. Of nature, I am churlish; yet one thing I ashame not to affirm, that familiarity once thoroughly contracted was never yet broken on my default. The cause may be that I have rather need of all, than that any have need of me. However it (that) be, it cannot be, as I say, the corporal absence of one year or two that can quench in my heart that familiar acquaintance in Christ Jesus, which half a year did engender, and almost two years did nourish and confirm. And therefore, whether I write or no, be assuredly persuaded that I have you in such memory as becometh the faithful to have of the faithful." [390] This is the truest touch of personal humility that I can remember to have seen in all the five volumes of the Reformer's collected works: it is no small honour to Mrs. Locke that his affection for her should have brought home to him this unwonted feeling of dependence upon others. Everything else in the course of the correspondence testifies to a good, sound, down-right sort of friendship between the two, less ecstatic than it was at first, perhaps, but serviceable and very equal. He gives her ample details as to the progress of the work of reformation; sends her the sheets of the Confession of Faith, "in quairs," as he calls it; asks her to assist him with her prayers, to collect money for the good cause in Scotland, and to send him books for himself—books by Calvin especially, one on Isaiah, and a new revised edition of the "Institutes." "I must be bold on your liberality," he writes, "not only in that, but in greater things as I shall need." [391a] On her part she applies to him for spiritual advice, not after the manner of the drooping Mrs. Bowes, but in a more positive spirit,—advice as to practical points, advice as to the Church of England, for instance, whose ritual he condemns as a "mingle-mangle." [391b] Just at the end she ceases to write, sends him "a token, without writing." "I understand your impediment," he answers, "and therefore I cannot complain. Yet if you understood the variety of my temptations, I doubt not but you would have written somewhat." [391c] One letter more, and then silence.

And I think the best of the Reformer died out with that correspondence. It is after this, of course, that he wrote that ungenerous description of his intercourse with Mrs. Bowes. It is after this, also, that we come to the unlovely episode of his second marriage. He had been left a widower at the age of fifty-five. Three years after, it occurred apparently to yet another pious parent to sacrifice a child upon the altar of his respect for the Reformer. In January 1563, Randolph writes to Cecil: "Your Honour will take it for a great wonder when I shall write unto you that Mr. Knox shall marry a very near kinswoman of the Duke's, a Lord's daughter, a young lass not above sixteen years of age." [392] He adds that he fears he will be laughed at for reporting so mad a story. And yet it was true; and on Palm Sunday, 1564, Margaret Stewart, daughter of Andrew Lord Stewart of Ochiltree, aged seventeen, was duly united to John Knox, Minister of St. Giles's Kirk, Edinburgh, aged fifty-nine,—to the great disgust of Queen Mary from family pride, and I would fain hope of many others for more humane considerations. "In this," as Randolph says, "I wish he had done otherwise." The Consistory of Geneva, "that most perfect school of Christ that ever was on earth since the days of the Apostles," were wont to forbid marriages on the ground of too great a disproportion in age. I cannot help wondering whether the old Reformer's conscience did not uneasily remind him, now and again, of this good custom of his religious metropolis, as he thought of the two-and-forty years that separated him from his poor bride. Fitly enough, we hear nothing of the second Mrs. Knox until she appears at her husband's deathbed, eight years after. She bore him three daughters in the interval; and I suppose the poor child's martyrdom was made as easy for her as might be. She was "extremely attentive to him" at the end, we read and he seems to have spoken to her with some confidence. Moreover, and this is very characteristic, he had copied out for her use a little volume of his own devotional letters to other women.

This is the end of the roll, unless we add to it Mrs. Adamson, who had delighted much in his company "by reason that she had a troubled conscience," and whose deathbed is commemorated at some length in the pages of his history. [393]

And now, looking back, it cannot be said that Knox's intercourse with women was quite of the highest sort. It is characteristic that we find him more alarmed for his own reputation than for the reputation of the women with whom he was familiar. There was a fatal preponderance of self in all his intimacies: many women came to learn from him, but he never condescended to become a learner in his turn. And so there is not anything idyllic in these intimacies of his; and they were never so renovating to his spirit as they might have been. But I believe they were good enough for the women. I fancy the women knew what they were about when so many of them followed after Knox. It is not simply because a man is always fully persuaded that he knows the right from the wrong and sees his way plainly through the maze of life, great qualities as these are, that people will love and follow him, and write him letters full of their "earnest desire for him" when he is absent. It is not over a man, whose one characteristic is grim fixity of purpose, that the hearts of women are "incensed and kindled with a special care," as it were over their natural children. In the strong quiet patience of all his letters to the weariful Mrs. Bowes, we may perhaps see one cause of the fascination he possessed for these religious women. Here was one whom you could besiege all the year round with inconsistent scruples and complaints; you might write to him on Thursday that you were so elated it was plain the devil was deceiving you, and again on Friday that you were so depressed it was plain God had cast you off for ever; and he would read all this patiently and sympathetically, and give you an answer in the most reassuring polysyllables, and all divided into heads—who knows?—like a treatise on divinity. And then, those easy tears of his. There are some women who like to see men crying; and here was this great-voiced, bearded man of God, who might be seen beating the solid pulpit every Sunday, and casting abroad his clamorous denunciations to the terror of all, and who on the Monday would sit in their parlours by the hour, and weep with them over their manifold trials and temptations. Nowadays, he would have to drink a dish of tea with all these penitents. . . . It sounds a little vulgar, as the past will do, if we look into it too closely. We could not let these great folk of old into our drawing-rooms. Queen Elizabeth would positively not be eligible for a housemaid. The old manners and the old customs go sinking from grade to grade, until, if some mighty emperor revisited the glimpses of the moon, he would not find any one of his way of thinking, any one he could strike hands with and talk to freely and without offence, save perhaps the porter at the end of the street, or the fellow with his elbows out who loafs all day before the public-house. So that this little note of vulgarity is not a thing to be dwelt upon; it is to be put away from us, as we recall the fashion of these old intimacies; so that we may only remember Knox as one who was very long-suffering with women, kind to them in his own way, loving them in his own way—and that not the worst way, if it was not the best—and once at least, if not twice, moved to his heart of hearts by a woman, and giving expression to the yearning he had for her society in words that none of us need be ashamed to borrow.

And let us bear in mind always that the period I have gone over in this essay begins when the Reformer was already beyond the middle age, and already broken in bodily health: it has been the story of an old man's friendships. This it is that makes Knox enviable. Unknown until past forty, he had then before him five-and-thirty years of splendid and influential life, passed through uncommon hardships to an uncommon degree of power, lived in his own country as a sort of king, and did what he would with the sound of his voice out of the pulpit. And besides all this, such a following of faithful women! One would take the first forty years gladly, if one could be sure of the last thirty. Most of us, even if, by reason of great strength and the dignity of gray hairs, we retain some degree of public respect in the latter days of our existence, will find a falling away of friends, and a solitude making itself round about us day by day, until we are left alone with the hired sick-nurse. For the attraction of a man's character is apt to be outlived, like the attraction of his body; and the power to love grows feeble in its turn, as well as the power to inspire love in others. It is only with a few rare natures that friendship is added to friendship, love to love, and the man keeps growing richer in affection—richer, I mean, as a bank may be said to grow richer, both giving and receiving more—after his head is white and his back weary, and he prepares to go down into the dust of death.

THE END.

FOOTNOTES

[0] Gaudeamus: Carmina vagorum selecta. Leipsic. Trübner. 1879.

[27] Prefatory letter to Peveril of the Peak.

[71] For the love affairs see, in particular, Mr. Scott Douglas's edition under the different dates.

[179] Yoshida, when on his way to Nangasaki, met the soldier and talked with him by the roadside; they then parted, but the soldier was so much struck by the words he heard, that on Yoshida's return he sought him out and declared his intention of devoting his life to the good cause. I venture, in the absence of the writer, to insert this correction, having been present when the story was told by Mr. Masaki.—F. J. And I, there being none to settle the difference, must reproduce both versions.—R. L. S.

[185] I understood that the merchant was endeavouring surreptitiously to obtain for his son instruction to which he was not entitled.—F. J.

[192] Etude Biographique sur François Villon. Paris: H. Menu.

[195] Bougeois de Paris, ed. Panthéon, pp. 688, 689.

[196] Bourgeois, pp. 627, 636, and 725.

[204] Chronìque Scandaleuse, ed. Panthéon, p. 237.

[210] Monstrelet: Panthéon Littéraire, p. 26.

[220a] Chron. Scand. ut supra.

[220b] Here and there, principally in the order of events, this article differs from M. Longnon's own reading of his material. The ground on which he defers the execution of Montigny and De Cayeux beyond the date of their trials seems insufficient. There is a law of parsimony for the construction of historical documents; simplicity is the first duty of narration; and hanged they were.

[224] Chron. Scand., p. 338.

[238] Champollion-Figeac's Louis et Charles d'Orléans, p. 348.

[240a] D'Héricault's admirable Memoir, prefixed to his edition of Charles's works, vol. i. p. xi.

[240b] Vallet de Viriville, Charles VII. et son Epoque, ii. 428, note 2.

[241a] See Lecoy de la Marche, Le Roi René, i. 167.

[241b] Vallet, Charles VII, ii. 85, 86, note 2.

[241c] Champollion-Figeac, 193–198.

[242a] Champollion-Figeac, 209.

[242b] The student will see that there are facts cited, and expressions borrowed, in this paragraph, from a period extending over almost the whole of Charles's life, instead of being confined entirely to his boyhood. As I do not believe there was any change, so I do not believe there is any anachronism involved.

[243] The Debate between the Heralds of France and England, translated and admirably edited by Mr. Henry Pyne. For the attribution of this tract to Charles, the reader is referred to Mr. Pyne's conclusive argument.

[244] Des Ursins.

[248] Michelet, iv. App. 179, p. 337.

[249] Champollion-Figeac, pp. 279–82.

[250] Michelet, iv. pp. 123–4.

[253] Debate between the Heralds.

[254] Sir H. Nicholas, Agincourt.

[257a] Debate between the Heralds.

[257b] Works (ed. d'Héricault), i. 43.

[257c] Ibid. 143.

[258a] Works (ed. d'Héricault), i. 190.

[258b] Ibid. 144.

[258c] Ibid. 158.

[259a] M. Champollion-Figeac gives many in his editions of Charles's works, most (as I should think) of very doubtful authenticity, or worse.

[259b] Rymer, x. 564. D'Héricault's Memoir, p. xli. Gairdner's Paston Letters, i. 27, 99.

[260] Champollion-Figeac, 377.

[262a] Dom Plancher, iv. 178–9.

[262b] Works, i. 157–63.

[265a] Vallet's Charles VII., i. 251.

[265b] Procès de Jeanne d'Arc, i. 133–55.

[267a] Monstrelet.

[267b] Vallet's Charles VII., iii. chap. i. But see the chronicle that bears Jaquet's name: a lean and dreary book.

[268] Monstrelet.

[269] D'Héricault's Memoir, xl. xli. Vallet, Charles VI., ii. 435.

[271a] Champollion-Figeac, 368.

[271b] Works, i. 115.

[271c] D'Héricault's Memoir, xlv.

[272] Champollion-Figeac, 381, 361, 381.

[273] Champollion-Figeac, 359,361.

[276a] Lecoy de la Marche, Roi René, ii. 155, 177.

[276b] Champollion-Figeac, chaps. v. and vi.

[276c] Ibid. 364; Works, i. 172.

[276d] Champollion-Figeac, 364: "Jeter de l'argent aux petis enfans qui estoient au long de Bourbon, pour les faire nonner en l'eau et aller querre l'argent au fond."

[277a] Champollion-Figeac, 387.

[277b] Nouvelle Biographie Didot, art. "Marie de Clèves." Vallet, Charles VII, iii. 85, note 1.

[277c] Champollion-Figeac, 383, 384–386.

[278] Works, ii. 57, 258.

[329] Gaberel's Eglist de Genève, i. 88.

[330a] La Démocratie chez les Prédicateurs de la Ligue.

[330b] Historia affectuum se immiscentium controversiæ de gynæcocratia. It is in his collected prefaces, Leipsic, 1683.

[333a] Œuvres de d'Aubigné, i. 449.

[333b] Dames Illustres, pp. 358–360.

[334] Works of John Knox, iv. 349.

[341] M'Crie's Life of Knox, ii. 41.

[342] Described by Calvin in a letter to Cecil, Knox's Works, vol. iv.

[344] It was anonymously published, but no one seems to have been in doubt about its authorship; he might as well have set his name to it, for all the good he got by holding it back.

[345a] Knox's Works, iv. 358.

[345b] Strype's Aylmer, p. 16.

[346a] It may interest the reader to know that these (so says Thomasius) are the "ipsissima verba Schlusselburgii."

[346b] I am indebted for a sight of this book to the kindness of Mr.

David Laing, the editor of Knox's Works.

[348] Social Statics, p. 64, etc.

[349] Hallam's Const. Hist. of England, i. 225, note m.

[352a] Knox to Mrs. Locke, 6th April 1559. Works, vi. 14.

[352b] Knox to Sir William Cecil, 10th April 1559. Works, ii. 16, or vi. 15.

[354] Knox to Queen Elizabeth, July. 20th, 1559. Works, vi. 47, or ii. 26.

[355] Knox to Queen Elizabeth, August 6th, 1561. Works, vi. 126.

[357] Knox's Works, ii. 278–280.

[359] Calderwood's History of the Kirk of Scotland, edition of the Wodrow Society, iii. 51–54.

[360] Bayle's Historical Dictionary, art. Knox, remark G.

[368] Works, iv. 244.

[369a] Works, iv. 246.

[369b] Ib. iv. 225.

[371a] Works, iv. 245.

[371b] Ib. iv. 221.

[373a] Works, vi. 514.

[373b] Ib. iii. 338.

[373c] Ib. iii. 352, 353.

[374a] Works, iii. 350.

[374b] Ib. iii. 390, 391.

[375a] Works, iii. 142.

[375b] Ib. iii. 378.

[375c] Ib. ii. 379.

[376] Works, iii. 394.

[377] Works, iii. 376.

[378] Works, iii. 378.

[379a] Works, vi. 104.

[379b] Ib. v. 5.

[379c] Ib. vi. 27.

[379d] Ib. ii. 138.

[380] Mr. Laing's preface to the sixth volume of Knox's Works, p. lxii.

[381] Works. vi. 534.

[382a] Works, iv. 220.

[382b] Ib. iii. 380.

[382c] Ib. iv. 220.

[383] Works, iii. 380.

[384] Works, iv. 238.

[385] Works, iv. 240.

[388] Works, vi. 513, 514.

[390] Works, vi. ii.

[391a] Works, vi. pp. 21. 101, 108, 130.

[391b] Ib. vi. 83.

[391c] Ib. vi. 129.

[392] Works, vi. 532.

[393] Works, i. 246.

TRAVELS WITH A DONKEY IN THE CÉVENNES

My Dear Sidney Colvin,

The journey which this little book is to describe was very agreeable and fortunate for me. After an uncouth beginning, I had the best of luck to the end. But we are all travellers in what John Bunyan calls the wilderness of this world—all, too, travellers with a donkey: and the best that we find in our travels is an honest friend. He is a fortunate voyager who finds many. We travel, indeed, to find them. They are the end and the reward of life. They keep us worthy of ourselves; and when we are alone, we are only nearer to the absent.

Every book is, in an intimate sense, a circular letter to the friends of him who writes it. They alone take his meaning; they find private messages, assurances of love, and expressions of gratitude, dropped for them in every corner. The public is but a generous patron who defrays the postage. Yet though the letter is directed to all, we have an old and kindly custom of addressing it on the outside to one. Of what shall a man be proud, if he is not proud of his friends? And so, my dear Sidney Colvin, it is with pride that I sign myself affectionately yours,

R. L. S.

VELAY

Many are the mighty things, and nought is more mighty than man. . . .
He masters by his devices the tenant of the fields.

SOPHOCLES.

Who hath loosed the bands of the wild ass?

JOB.

THE DONKEY, THE PACK, AND THE PACK-SADDLE

In a little place called Le Monastier, in a pleasant highland valley fifteen
miles from Le Puy, I spent about a month of fine days. Monastier is notable
for the making of lace, for drunkenness, for freedom of language, and for
unparalleled political dissension. There are adherents of each of the four
French parties—Legitimists, Orleanists, Imperialists, and Republicans—in
this little mountain-town; and they all hate, loathe, decry, and calumniate
each other. Except for business purposes, or to give each other the lie in
a tavern brawl, they have laid aside even the civility of speech. 'Tis a mere
mountain Poland. In the midst of this Babylon I found myself a rallying-
point; every one was anxious to be kind and helpful to the stranger. This was
not merely from the natural hospitality of mountain people, nor even from
the surprise with which I was regarded as a man living of his own free will in
Le Monastier, when he might just as well have lived anywhere else in this big
world; it arose a good deal from my projected excursion southward through
the Cevennes. A traveller of my sort was a thing hitherto unheard of in that
district. I was looked upon with contempt, like a man who should project a
journey to the moon, but yet with a respectful interest, like one setting forth
for the inclement Pole. All were ready to help in my preparations; a crowd
of sympathisers supported me at the critical moment of a bargain; not a step
was taken but was heralded by glasses round and celebrated by a dinner or a
breakfast.

It was already hard upon October before I was ready to set forth, and at the high altitudes over which my road lay there was no Indian summer to be looked for. I was determined, if not to camp out, at least to have the means of camping out in my possession; for there is nothing more harassing to an easy mind than the necessity of reaching shelter by dusk, and the hospitality of a village inn is not always to be reckoned sure by those who trudge on foot. A tent, above all for a solitary traveller, is troublesome to pitch, and troublesome to strike again; and even on the march it forms a conspicuous feature in your baggage. A sleeping-sack, on the other hand, is always ready—you have only to get into it; it serves a double purpose—a bed by night, a portmanteau by day; and it does not advertise your intention of camping out to every curious passer-by. This is a huge point. If a camp is not secret, it is but a troubled resting-place; you become a public character; the convivial rustic visits your bedside after an early supper; and you must sleep with one eye open, and be up before the day. I decided on a sleeping-sack; and after repeated visits to Le Puy, and a deal of high living for myself and my advisers, a sleeping-sack was designed, constructed, and triumphantly brought home.

This child of my invention was nearly six feet square, exclusive of two triangular flaps to serve as a pillow by night and as the top and bottom of the sack by day. I call it 'the sack,' but it was never a sack by more than courtesy: only a sort of long roll or sausage, green waterproof cart-cloth without and blue sheep's fur within. It was commodious as a valise, warm and dry for a bed. There was luxurious turning room for one; and at a pinch the thing might serve for two. I could bury myself in it up to the neck; for my head I trusted to a fur cap, with a hood to fold down over my ears and a band to pass under my nose like a respirator; and in case of heavy rain I proposed to make myself a little tent, or tentlet, with my waterproof coat, three stones, and a bent branch.

It will readily be conceived that I could not carry this huge package on my own, merely human, shoulders. It remained to choose a beast of burden. Now, a horse is a fine lady among animals, flighty, timid, delicate in eating, of tender health; he is too valuable and too restive to be left alone, so that you are chained to your brute as to a fellow galley-slave; a dangerous road puts him out of his wits; in short, he's an uncertain and exacting ally, and adds thirty-fold to the troubles of the voyager. What I required was something cheap and small and hardy, and of a stolid and peaceful temper; and all these requisites pointed to a donkey.

There dwelt an old man in Monastier, of rather unsound intellect according to some, much followed by street-boys, and known to fame as Father Adam. Father Adam had a cart, and to draw the cart a diminutive she-ass, not much bigger than a dog, the colour of a mouse, with a kindly eye and a determined under-jaw. There was something neat and high-bred, a quakerish elegance, about the rogue that hit my fancy on the spot. Our first interview was in Monastier market-place. To prove her good temper, one child after another was set upon her back to ride, and one after another went head over heels into the air; until a want of confidence began to reign in youthful bosoms, and the experiment was discontinued from a dearth of subjects. I was already backed by a deputation of my friends; but as if this were not enough, all the buyers and sellers came round and helped me in the bargain; and the ass and I and Father Adam were the centre of a hubbub for near half an hour. At length she passed into my service for the consideration of sixty-five francs and a glass of brandy. The sack had already cost eighty francs and two glasses of beer; so that Modestine, as I instantly baptized her, was upon all accounts the cheaper article. Indeed, that was as it should be; for she was only an appurtenance of my mattress, or self-acting bedstead on four castors.

I had a last interview with Father Adam in a billiard-room at the witching hour of dawn, when I administered the brandy. He professed himself greatly touched by the separation, and declared he had often bought white bread for the donkey when he had been content with black bread for himself; but this, according to the best authorities, must have been a flight of fancy. He had a name in the village for brutally misusing the ass; yet it is certain that he shed a tear, and the tear made a clean mark down one cheek.

By the advice of a fallacious local saddler, a leather pad was made for me with rings to fasten on my bundle; and I thoughtfully completed my kit and arranged my toilette. By way of armoury and utensils, I took a revolver, a little spirit-lamp and pan, a lantern and some halfpenny candles, a jack-knife and a large leather flask. The main cargo consisted of two entire changes of warm clothing—besides my travelling wear of country velveteen, pilot-coat, and knitted spencer—some books, and my railway-rug, which, being also in the form of a bag, made me a double castle for cold nights. The permanent larder was represented by cakes of chocolate and tins of Bologna sausage. All this, except what I carried about my person, was easily stowed into the sheepskin bag; and by good fortune I threw in my empty knapsack, rather for convenience of carriage than from any thought that I should want it on my journey. For more immediate needs I took a leg of cold mutton, a bottle of Beaujolais, an empty bottle to carry milk, an egg-beater, and a considerable quantity of black bread and white, like Father Adam, for myself and donkey, only in my scheme of things the destinations were reversed.

Monastrians, of all shades of thought in politics, had agreed in threatening me with many ludicrous misadventures, and with sudden death in many surprising forms. Cold, wolves, robbers, above all the nocturnal practical joker, were daily and eloquently forced on my attention. Yet in these vaticinations, the true, patent danger was left out. Like Christian, it was from my pack I suffered by the way. Before telling my own mishaps, let me in two words relate the lesson of my experience. If the pack is well strapped at the ends, and hung at full length—not doubled, for your life—across the pack-saddle, the traveller is safe. The saddle will certainly not fit, such is the imperfection of our transitory life; it will assuredly topple and tend to overset; but there are stones on every roadside, and a man soon learns the art of correcting any tendency to overbalance with a well-adjusted stone.

On the day of my departure I was up a little after five; by six, we began to load the donkey; and ten minutes after, my hopes were in the dust. The pad would not stay on Modestine's back for half a moment. I returned it to its maker, with whom I had so contumelious a passage that the street outside was crowded from wall to wall with gossips looking on and listening. The pad changed hands with much vivacity; perhaps it would be more descriptive to say that we threw it at each other's heads; and, at any rate, we were very warm and unfriendly, and spoke with a deal of freedom.

244

I had a common donkey pack-saddle—a barde, as they call it—fitted upon Modestine; and once more loaded her with my effects. The doubled sack, my pilot-coat (for it was warm, and I was to walk in my waistcoat), a great bar of black bread, and an open basket containing the white bread, the mutton, and the bottles, were all corded together in a very elaborate system of knots, and I looked on the result with fatuous content. In such a monstrous deck-cargo, all poised above the donkey's shoulders, with nothing below to balance, on a brand-new pack-saddle that had not yet been worn to fit the animal, and fastened with brand-new girths that might be expected to stretch and slacken by the way, even a very careless traveller should have seen disaster brewing. That elaborate system of knots, again, was the work of too many sympathisers to be very artfully designed. It is true they tightened the cords with a will; as many as three at a time would have a foot against Modestine's quarters, and be hauling with clenched teeth; but I learned afterwards that one thoughtful person, without any exercise of force, can make a more solid job than half-a-dozen heated and enthusiastic grooms. I was then but a novice; even after the misadventure of the pad nothing could disturb my security, and I went forth from the stable door as an ox goeth to the slaughter.

THE GREEN DONKEY-DRIVER

The bell of Monastier was just striking nine as I got quit of these preliminary troubles and descended the hill through the common. As long as I was within sight of the windows, a secret shame and the fear of some laughable defeat withheld me from tampering with Modestine. She tripped along upon her four small hoofs with a sober daintiness of gait; from time to time she shook her ears or her tail; and she looked so small under the bundle that my mind misgave me. We got across the ford without difficulty—there was no doubt about the matter, she was docility itself—and once on the other bank, where the road begins to mount through pine-woods, I took in my right hand the unhallowed staff, and with a quaking spirit applied it to the donkey. Modestine brisked up her pace for perhaps three steps, and then relapsed into her former minuet. Another application had the same effect, and so with the third. I am worthy the name of an Englishman, and it goes against my conscience to lay my hand rudely on a female. I desisted, and looked her all over from head to foot; the poor brute's knees were trembling

245

and her breathing was distressed; it was plain that she could go no faster on a hill. God forbid, thought I, that I should brutalise this innocent creature; let her go at her own pace, and let me patiently follow.

What that pace was, there is no word mean enough to describe; it was something as much slower than a walk as a walk is slower than a run; it kept me hanging on each foot for an incredible length of time; in five minutes it exhausted the spirit and set up a fever in all the muscles of the leg. And yet I had to keep close at hand and measure my advance exactly upon hers; for if I dropped a few yards into the rear, or went on a few yards ahead, Modestine came instantly to a halt and began to browse. The thought that this was to last from here to Alais nearly broke my heart. Of all conceivable journeys, this promised to be the most tedious. I tried to tell myself it was a lovely day; I tried to charm my foreboding spirit with tobacco; but I had a vision ever present to me of the long, long roads, up hill and down dale, and a pair of figures ever infinitesimally moving, foot by foot, a yard to the minute, and, like things enchanted in a nightmare, approaching no nearer to the goal.

In the meantime there came up behind us a tall peasant, perhaps forty years of age, of an ironical snuffy countenance, and arrayed in the green tail-coat of the country. He overtook us hand over hand, and stopped to consider our pitiful advance.

'Your donkey,' says he, 'is very old?'

I told him, I believed not.

Then, he supposed, we had come far.

I told him, we had but newly left Monastier.

'Et vous marchez comme ça!' cried he; and, throwing back his head, he laughed long and heartily. I watched him, half prepared to feel offended, until he had satisfied his mirth; and then, 'You must have no pity on these animals,' said he; and, plucking a switch out of a thicket, he began to lace Modestine about the stern-works, uttering a cry. The rogue pricked up her ears and broke into a good round pace, which she kept up without flagging, and without exhibiting the least symptom of distress, as long as the peasant kept beside us. Her former panting and shaking had been, I regret to say, a piece of comedy.

My deus ex machinâ, before he left me, supplied some excellent, if inhumane, advice; presented me with the switch, which he declared she would feel more tenderly than my cane; and finally taught me the true cry or masonic word of donkey-drivers, 'Proot!' All the time, he regarded me with a comical, incredulous air, which was embarrassing to confront; and smiled over my donkey-driving, as I might have smiled over his orthography, or his green tail-coat. But it was not my turn for the moment.

I was proud of my new lore, and thought I had learned the art to perfection. And certainly Modestine did wonders for the rest of the fore-noon, and I had a breathing space to look about me. It was Sabbath; the mountain-fields were all vacant in the sunshine; and as we came down through St. Martin de Frugères, the church was crowded to the door, there were people kneeling without upon the steps, and the sound of the priest's chanting came forth out of the dim interior. It gave me a home feeling on the spot; for I am a countryman of the Sabbath, so to speak, and all Sabbath observances, like a Scottish accent, strike in me mixed feelings, grateful and the reverse. It is only a traveller, hurrying by like a person from another planet, who can rightly enjoy the peace and beauty of the great ascetic feast. The sight of the resting country does his spirit good. There is something better than music in the wide unusual silence; and it disposes him to amiable thoughts, like the sound of a little river or the warmth of sunlight.

In this pleasant humour I came down the hill to where Goudet stands in a green end of a valley, with Château Beaufort opposite upon a rocky steep, and the stream, as clear as crystal, lying in a deep pool between them. Above and below, you may hear it wimpling over the stones, an amiable stripling of a river, which it seems absurd to call the Loire. On all sides, Goudet is shut in by mountains; rocky footpaths, practicable at best for donkeys, join it to the outer world of France; and the men and women drink and swear, in their green corner, or look up at the snow-clad peaks in winter from the threshold of their homes, in an isolation, you would think, like that of Homer's Cyclops. But it is not so; the postman reaches Goudet with the letter-bag; the aspiring youth of Goudet are within a day's walk of the railway at Le Puy; and here in the inn you may find an engraved portrait of the host's nephew, Régis Senac, 'Professor of Fencing and Champion of the two Americas,' a distinction gained by him, along with the sum of five hundred dollars, at Tammany Hall, New York, on the 10th April 1876.

I hurried over my midday meal, and was early forth again. But, alas, as we climbed the interminable hill upon the other side, 'Proot!' seemed to have lost its virtue. I prooted like a lion, I prooted mellifluously like a sucking-dove; but Modestine would be neither softened nor intimidated. She held doggedly to her pace; nothing but a blow would move her, and that only for a second. I must follow at her heels, incessantly belabouring. A moment's pause in this ignoble toil, and she relapsed into her own private gait. I think I never heard of any one in as mean a situation. I must reach the lake of Bouchet, where I meant to camp, before sundown, and, to have even a hope of this, I must instantly maltreat this uncomplaining animal. The sound of my own blows sickened me. Once, when I looked at her, she had a faint resemblance to a lady of my acquaintance who formerly loaded me with kindness; and this increased my horror of my cruelty.

To make matters worse, we encountered another donkey, ranging at will upon the roadside; and this other donkey chanced to be a gentleman. He and Modestine met nickering for joy, and I had to separate the pair and beat down their young romance with a renewed and feverish bastinado. If the other donkey had had the heart of a male under his hide, he would have fallen upon me tooth and hoof; and this was a kind of consolation—he was plainly unworthy of Modestine's affection. But the incident saddened me, as did everything that spoke of my donkey's sex.

It was blazing hot up the valley, windless, with vehement sun upon my shoulders; and I had to labour so consistently with my stick that the sweat ran into my eyes. Every five minutes, too, the pack, the basket, and the pilot-coat would take an ugly slew to one side or the other; and I had to stop Modestine, just when I had got her to a tolerable pace of about two miles an hour, to tug, push, shoulder, and readjust the load. And at last, in the village of Ussel, saddle and all, the whole hypothec turned round and grovelled in the dust below the donkey's belly. She, none better pleased, incontinently drew up and seemed to smile; and a party of one man, two women, and two children came up, and, standing round me in a half-circle, encouraged her by their example.

I had the devil's own trouble to get the thing righted; and the instant I had done so, without hesitation, it toppled and fell down upon the other side. Judge if I was hot! And yet not a hand was offered to assist me. The man, indeed, told me I ought to have a package of a different shape. I suggested, if he knew nothing better to the point in my predicament, he might hold his tongue. And the good-natured dog agreed with me smilingly. It was the most despicable fix. I must plainly content myself with the pack for Modestine, and take the following items for my own share of the portage: a cane, a quart-flask, a pilot-jacket heavily weighted in the pockets, two pounds of black bread, and an open basket full of meats and bottles. I believe I may say I am not devoid of greatness of soul; for I did not recoil from this infamous burden. I disposed it, Heaven knows how, so as to be mildly portable, and then proceeded to steer Modestine through the village. She tried, as was indeed her invariable habit, to enter every house and every courtyard in the whole length; and, encumbered as I was, without a hand to help myself, no words can render an idea of my difficulties. A priest, with six or seven others, was examining a church in process of repair, and he and his acolytes laughed loudly as they saw my plight.

I remembered having laughed myself when I had seen good men struggling with adversity in the person of a jackass, and the recollection filled me with penitence. That was in my old light days, before this trouble came upon me. God knows at least that I shall never laugh again, thought I. But oh, what a cruel thing is a farce to those engaged in it!

A little out of the village, Modestine, filled with the demon, set her heart upon a by-road, and positively refused to leave it. I dropped all my bundles, and, I am ashamed to say, struck the poor sinner twice across the face. It was pitiful to see her lift her head with shut eyes, as if waiting for another blow. I came very near crying; but I did a wiser thing than that, and sat squarely down by the roadside to consider my situation under the cheerful influence of tobacco and a nip of brandy. Modestine, in the meanwhile, munched some black bread with a contrite hypocritical air. It was plain that I must make a sacrifice to the gods of shipwreck. I threw away the empty bottle destined to carry milk; I threw away my own white bread, and, disdaining to act by general average, kept the black bread for Modestine; lastly, I threw away the cold leg of mutton and the egg-whisk, although this last was dear to my heart. Thus I found room for everything in the basket, and even stowed the boating-coat on the top. By means of an end of cord I slung it under one arm; and although the cord cut my shoulder, and the jacket hung almost to the ground, it was with a heart greatly lightened that I set forth again.

I had now an arm free to thrash Modestine, and cruelly I chastised her. If I were to reach the lakeside before dark, she must bestir her little shanks to some tune. Already the sun had gone down into a windy-looking mist; and although there were still a few streaks of gold far off to the east on the hills and the black fir-woods, all was cold and grey about our onward path. An infinity of little country by-roads led hither and thither among the fields. It was the most pointless labyrinth. I could see my destination overhead, or rather the peak that dominates it; but choose as I pleased, the roads always ended by turning away from it, and sneaking back towards the valley, or northward along the margin of the hills. The failing light, the waning colour, the naked, unhomely, stony country through which I was travelling, threw me into some despondency. I promise you, the stick was not idle; I think every decent step that Modestine took must have cost me at least two emphatic blows. There was not another sound in the neighbourhood but that of my unwearying bastinado.

Suddenly, in the midst of my toils, the load once more bit the dust, and, as by enchantment, all the cords were simultaneously loosened, and the road scattered with my dear possessions. The packing was to begin again from the beginning; and as I had to invent a new and better system, I do not doubt but I lost half an hour. It began to be dusk in earnest as I reached a wilderness of turf and stones. It had the air of being a road which should lead everywhere at the same time; and I was falling into something not unlike despair when I saw two figures stalking towards me over the stones. They walked one behind the other like tramps, but their pace was remarkable. The son led the way, a tall, ill-made, sombre, Scottish-looking man; the mother followed, all in her Sunday's best, with an elegantly embroidered ribbon to her cap, and a new felt hat atop, and proffering, as she strode along with kilted petticoats, a string of obscene and blasphemous oaths.

I hailed the son, and asked him my direction. He pointed loosely west and north-west, muttered an inaudible comment, and, without slackening his pace for an instant, stalked on, as he was going, right athwart my path. The mother followed without so much as raising her head. I shouted and shouted after them, but they continued to scale the hillside, and turned a deaf ear to my outcries. At last, leaving Modestine by herself, I was constrained to run after them, hailing the while. They stopped as I drew near, the mother still cursing; and I could see she was a handsome, motherly, respectable-looking woman. The son once more answered me roughly and inaudibly, and was for setting out again. But this time I simply collared the mother, who was nearest me, and, apologising for my violence, declared that I could not let them go until they had put me on my road. They were neither of them offended—rather mollified than otherwise; told me I had only to follow them; and then the mother asked me what I wanted by the lake at such an hour. I replied, in the Scottish manner, by inquiring if she had far to go herself. She told me, with another oath, that she had an hour and a half's road before her. And then, without salutation, the pair strode forward again up the hillside in the gathering dusk.

I returned for Modestine, pushed her briskly forward, and, after a sharp ascent of twenty minutes, reached the edge of a plateau. The view, looking back on my day's journey, was both wild and sad. Mount Mézenc and the peaks beyond St. Julien stood out in trenchant gloom against a cold glitter in the east; and the intervening field of hills had fallen together into one broad wash of shadow, except here and there the outline of a wooded sugar-loaf in black, here and there a white irregular patch to represent a cultivated farm, and here and there a blot where the Loire, the Gazeille, or the Laussonne wandered in a gorge.

Soon we were on a high-road, and surprise seized on my mind as I beheld a village of some magnitude close at hand; for I had been told that the neighbourhood of the lake was uninhabited except by trout. The road smoked in the twilight with children driving home cattle from the fields; and a pair of mounted stride-legged women, hat and cap and all, dashed past me at a hammering trot from the canton where they had been to church and market. I asked one of the children where I was. At Bouchet St. Nicolas, he told me. Thither, about a mile south of my destination, and on the other side of a respectable summit, had these confused roads and treacherous peasantry conducted me. My shoulder was cut, so that it hurt sharply; my arm ached like toothache from perpetual beating; I gave up the lake and my design to camp, and asked for the auberge.

I HAVE A GOAD

The auberge of Bouchet St. Nicolas was among the least pretentious I have ever visited; but I saw many more of the like upon my journey. Indeed, it was typical of these French highlands. Imagine a cottage of two stories, with a bench before the door; the stable and kitchen in a suite, so that Modestine and I could hear each other dining; furniture of the plainest, earthern floors, a single bedchamber for travellers, and that without any convenience but beds. In the kitchen cooking and eating go forward side by side, and the family sleep at night. Any one who has a fancy to wash must do so in public at the common table. The food is sometimes spare; hard fish and omelette have been my portion more than once; the wine is of the smallest, the brandy abominable to man; and the visit of a fat sow, grouting under the table and rubbing against your legs, is no impossible accompaniment to dinner.

But the people of the inn, in nine cases out of ten, show themselves friendly and considerate. As soon as you cross the doors you cease to be a stranger; and although these peasantry are rude and forbidding on the highway, they show a tincture of kind breeding when you share their hearth. At Bouchet, for instance, I uncorked my bottle of Beaujolais, and asked the host to join me. He would take but little.

'I am an amateur of such wine, do you see?' he said, 'and I am capable of leaving you not enough.'

In these hedge-inns the traveller is expected to eat with his own knife;

unless he ask, no other will be supplied: with a glass, a whang of bread, and an iron fork, the table is completely laid. My knife was cordially admired by the landlord of Bouchet, and the spring filled him with wonder.

'I should never have guessed that,' he said. 'I would bet,' he added, weighing it in his hand, 'that this cost you not less than five francs.'

When I told him it had cost me twenty, his jaw dropped.

He was a mild, handsome, sensible, friendly old man, astonishingly ignorant. His wife, who was not so pleasant in her manners, knew how to read, although I do not suppose she ever did so. She had a share of brains and spoke with a cutting emphasis, like one who ruled the roast.

'My man knows nothing,' she said, with an angry nod; 'he is like the beasts.'

And the old gentleman signified acquiescence with his head. There was no contempt on her part, and no shame on his; the facts were accepted loyally, and no more about the matter.

I was tightly cross-examined about my journey; and the lady understood in a moment, and sketched out what I should put into my book when I got home. 'Whether people harvest or not in such or such a place; if there were forests; studies of manners; what, for example, I and the master of the house say to you; the beauties of Nature, and all that.' And she interrogated me with a look.

'It is just that,' said I.

'You see,' she added to her husband, 'I understood that.'

They were both much interested by the story of my misadventures.

'In the morning,' said the husband, 'I will make you something better than your cane. Such a beast as that feels nothing; it is in the proverb—dur comme un âne; you might beat her insensible with a cudgel, and yet you would arrive nowhere.'

Something better! I little knew what he was offering.

The sleeping-room was furnished with two beds. I had one; and I will own I was a little abashed to find a young man and his wife and child in the act of mounting into the other. This was my first experience of the sort; and if I am always to feel equally silly and extraneous, I pray God it be my last as well. I kept my eyes to myself, and know nothing of the woman except that she had beautiful arms, and seemed no whit embarrassed by my appearance. As a matter of fact, the situation was more trying to me than to the pair. A pair keep each other in countenance; it is the single gentleman who has to blush. But I could not help attributing my sentiments to the husband, and sought to conciliate his tolerance with a cup of brandy from my flask. He told me that he was a cooper of Alais travelling to St. Etienne in search of work, and that in his spare moments he followed the fatal calling of a maker of matches. Me he readily enough divined to be a brandy merchant.

I was up first in the morning (Monday, September 23rd), and hastened my toilette guiltily, so as to leave a clear field for madam, the cooper's wife. I drank a bowl of milk, and set off to explore the neighbourhood of Bouchet. It was perishing cold, a grey, windy, wintry morning; misty clouds flew fast and low; the wind piped over the naked platform; and the only speck of colour was away behind Mount Mézenc and the eastern hills, where the sky still wore the orange of the dawn.

It was five in the morning, and four thousand feet above the sea; and I had to bury my hands in my pockets and trot. People were trooping out to the labours of the field by twos and threes, and all turned round to stare upon the stranger. I had seen them coming back last night, I saw them going afield again; and there was the life of Bouchet in a nutshell.

When I came back to the inn for a bit of breakfast, the landlady was in the kitchen combing out her daughter's hair; and I made her my compliments upon its beauty.

'Oh no,' said the mother; 'it is not so beautiful as it ought to be. Look, it is too fine.'

Thus does a wise peasantry console itself under adverse physical circumstances, and, by a startling democratic process, the defects of the majority decide the type of beauty.

'And where,' said I, 'is monsieur?'

'The master of the house is upstairs,' she answered, 'making you a goad.'

Blessed be the man who invented goads! Blessed the innkeeper of Bouchet St. Nicolas, who introduced me to their use! This plain wand, with an eighth of an inch of pin, was indeed a sceptre when he put it in my hands. Thenceforward Modestine was my slave. A prick, and she passed the most inviting stable door. A prick, and she broke forth into a gallant little trotlet that devoured the miles. It was not a remarkable speed, when all was said; and we took four hours to cover ten miles at the best of it. But what a heavenly change since yesterday! No more wielding of the ugly cudgel; no more flailing with an aching arm; no more broadsword exercise, but a discreet and gentlemanly fence. And what although now and then a drop of blood should appear on Modestine's mouse-coloured wedge-like rump? I should have preferred it otherwise, indeed; but yesterday's exploits had purged my heart of all humanity. The perverse little devil, since she would not be taken with kindness, must even go with pricking.

It was bleak and bitter cold, and, except a cavalcade of stride-legged ladies and a pair of post-runners, the road was dead solitary all the way to Pradelles. I scarce remember an incident but one. A handsome foal with a bell about his neck came charging up to us upon a stretch of common, sniffed the air martially as one about to do great deeds, and suddenly thinking otherwise in his green young heart, put about and galloped off as he had come, the bell tinkling in the wind. For a long while afterwards I saw his noble attitude as he drew up, and heard the note of his bell; and when I struck the high-road, the song of the telegraph-wires seemed to continue the same music.

Pradelles stands on a hillside, high above the Allier, surrounded by rich meadows. They were cutting aftermath on all sides, which gave the neighbourhood, this gusty autumn morning, an untimely smell of hay. On the opposite bank of the Allier the land kept mounting for miles to the horizon: a tanned and sallow autumn landscape, with black blots of fir-wood and white roads wandering through the hills. Over all this the clouds shed a uniform and purplish shadow, sad and somewhat menacing, exaggerating height and distance, and throwing into still higher relief the twisted ribbons of the highway. It was a cheerless prospect, but one stimulating to a traveller. For I was now upon the limit of Velay, and all that I beheld lay in another county—wild Gévaudan, mountainous, uncultivated, and but recently disforested from terror of the wolves.

Wolves, alas, like bandits, seem to flee the traveller's advance; and you may trudge through all our comfortable Europe, and not meet with an adventure worth the name. But here, if anywhere, a man was on the frontiers of hope. For this was the land of the ever-memorable BEAST, the Napoleon Bonaparte of wolves. What a career was his! He lived ten months at free quarters in Gévaudan and Vivarais; he ate women and children and 'shepherdesses celebrated for their beauty'; he pursued armed horsemen; he has been seen at broad noonday chasing a post-chaise and outrider along the king's high-road, and chaise and outrider fleeing before him at the gallop. He was placarded like a political offender, and ten thousand francs were offered for his head. And yet, when he was shot and sent to Versailles, behold! a common wolf, and even small for that. 'Though I could reach from pole to pole,' sang Alexander Pope; the Little Corporal shook Europe; and if all wolves had been as this wolf, they would have changed the history of man. M. Élie Berthet has made him the hero of a novel, which I have read, and do not wish to read again.

I hurried over my lunch, and was proof against the landlady's desire that I should visit our Lady of Pradelles, 'who performed many miracles, although she was of wood'; and before three-quarters of an hour I was goading Modestine down the steep descent that leads to Langogne on the Allier. On both sides of the road, in big dusty fields, farmers were preparing for next spring. Every fifty yards a yoke of great-necked stolid oxen were patiently haling at the plough. I saw one of these mild formidable servants of the glebe, who took a sudden interest in Modestine and me. The furrow down which he was journeying lay at an angle to the road, and his head was solidly fixed to the yoke like those of caryatides below a ponderous cornice; but he screwed round his big honest eyes and followed us with a ruminating look, until his master bade him turn the plough and proceed to reascend the field. From all these furrowing ploughshares, from the feet of oxen, from a labourer here and there who was breaking the dry clods with a hoe, the wind carried away a thin dust like so much smoke. It was a fine, busy, breathing, rustic landscape; and as I continued to descend, the highlands of Gévaudan kept mounting in front of me against the sky.

I had crossed the Loire the day before; now I was to cross the Allier; so near are these two confluents in their youth. Just at the bridge of Langogne, as the long-promised rain was beginning to fall, a lassie of some seven or eight addressed me in the sacramental phrase, 'D'où'st-ce-que vous venez?' She did it with so high an air that she set me laughing; and this cut her to the quick. She was evidently one who reckoned on respect, and stood looking after me in silent dudgeon, as I crossed the bridge and entered the county of Gévaudan.

UPPER GÉVAUDAN

The way also here was very wearisome through dirt and slabbiness; nor was there on all this ground so much as one inn or victualling-house wherein to refresh the feebler sort.

PILGRIM'S PROGRESS.

<u>A CAMP IN THE DARK</u>

The next day (Tuesday, September 24th), it was two o'clock in the afternoon before I got my journal written up and my knapsack repaired, for I was determined to carry my knapsack in the future and have no more ado with baskets; and half an hour afterwards I set out for Le Cheylard l'Évêque, a place on the borders of the forest of Mercoire. A man, I was told, should walk there in an hour and a half; and I thought it scarce too ambitious to suppose that a man encumbered with a donkey might cover the same distance in four hours.

All the way up the long hill from Langogne it rained and hailed alternately; the wind kept freshening steadily, although slowly; plentiful hurrying clouds—some dragging veils of straight rain-shower, others massed and luminous as though promising snow—careered out of the north and followed me along my way. I was soon out of the cultivated basin of the Allier, and away from the ploughing oxen, and such-like sights of the country. Moor, heathery marsh, tracts of rock and pines, woods of birch all jewelled with the autumn yellow, here and there a few naked cottages and bleak fields,—these were the characters of the country. Hill and valley followed valley and hill; the little green and stony cattle-tracks wandered in and out of one another, split into three or four, died away in marshy hollows, and began again sporadically on hillsides or at the borders of a wood.

There was no direct road to Cheylard, and it was no easy affair to make a passage in this uneven country and through this intermittent labyrinth of tracks. It must have been about four when I struck Sagnerousse, and went on my way rejoicing in a sure point of departure. Two hours afterwards, the dusk rapidly falling, in a lull of the wind, I issued from a fir-wood where I had long been wandering, and found, not the looked-for village, but another marish bottom among rough-and-tumble hills. For some time past I had heard the ringing of cattle-bells ahead; and now, as I came out of the skirts of the wood, I saw near upon a dozen cows and perhaps as many more black figures, which I conjectured to be children, although the mist had almost unrecognisably exaggerated their forms. These were all silently following each other round and round in a circle, now taking hands, now breaking up with chains and reverences. A dance of children appeals to very innocent and lively thoughts; but, at nightfall on the marshes, the thing was eerie and fantastic to behold. Even I, who am well enough read in Herbert Spencer, felt a sort of silence fall for an instant on my mind. The next, I was pricking Modestine forward, and guiding her like an unruly ship through the open. In a path, she went doggedly ahead of her own accord, as before a fair wind; but once on the turf or among heather, and the brute became demented. The tendency of lost travellers to go round in a circle was developed in her to the degree of passion, and it took all the steering I had in me to keep even a decently straight course through a single field.

While I was thus desperately tacking through the bog, children and cattle began to disperse, until only a pair of girls remained behind. From these I sought direction on my path. The peasantry in general were but little disposed to counsel a wayfarer. One old devil simply retired into his house, and barricaded the door on my approach; and I might beat and shout myself hoarse, he turned a deaf ear. Another, having given me a direction which, as I found afterwards, I had misunderstood, complacently watched me going wrong without adding a sign. He did not care a stalk of parsley if I wandered all night upon the hills! As for these two girls, they were a pair of impudent sly sluts, with not a thought but mischief. One put out her tongue at me, the other bade me follow the cows; and they both giggled and jogged each other's elbows. The Beast of Gévaudan ate about a hundred children of this district; I began to think of him with sympathy.

Leaving the girls, I pushed on through the bog, and got into another wood and upon a well-marked road. It grew darker and darker. Modestine, suddenly beginning to smell mischief, bettered the pace of her own accord, and from that time forward gave me no trouble. It was the first sign of intelligence I had occasion to remark in her. At the same time, the wind freshened into half a gale, and another heavy discharge of rain came flying up out of the north. At the other side of the wood I sighted some red windows in the dusk. This was the hamlet of Fouzilhic; three houses on a hillside, near a wood of birches. Here I found a delightful old man, who came a little way with me in the rain to put me safely on the road for Cheylard. He would hear of no reward; but shook his hands above his head almost as if in menace, and refused volubly and shrilly, in unmitigated patois.

All seemed right at last. My thoughts began to turn upon dinner and a fireside, and my heart was agreeably softened in my bosom. Alas, and I was on the brink of new and greater miseries! Suddenly, at a single swoop, the night fell. I have been abroad in many a black night, but never in a blacker. A glimmer of rocks, a glimmer of the track where it was well beaten, a certain fleecy density, or night within night, for a tree,—this was all that I could discriminate. The sky was simply darkness overhead; even the flying clouds pursued their way invisibly to human eyesight. I could not distinguish my hand at arm's-length from the track, nor my goad, at the same distance, from the meadows or the sky.

Soon the road that I was following split, after the fashion of the country, into three or four in a piece of rocky meadow. Since Modestine had shown such a fancy for beaten roads, I tried her instinct in this predicament. But the instinct of an ass is what might be expected from the name; in half a minute she was clambering round and round among some boulders, as lost a donkey as you would wish to see. I should have camped long before had I been properly provided; but as this was to be so short a stage, I had brought no wine, no bread for myself, and little over a pound for my lady friend. Add to this, that I and Modestine were both handsomely wetted by the showers. But now, if I could have found some water, I should have camped at once in spite of all. Water, however, being entirely absent, except in the form of rain, I determined to return to Fouzilhic, and ask a guide a little farther on my way—'a little farther lend thy guiding hand.'

The thing was easy to decide, hard to accomplish. In this sensible roaring blackness I was sure of nothing but the direction of the wind. To this I set my face; the road had disappeared, and I went across country, now in marshy opens, now baffled by walls unscalable to Modestine, until I came once more in sight of some red windows. This time they were differently disposed. It was not Fouzilhic, but Fouzilhac, a hamlet little distant from the other in space, but worlds away in the spirit of its inhabitants. I tied Modestine to a gate, and groped forward, stumbling among rocks, plunging mid-leg in bog, until I gained the entrance of the village. In the first lighted house there was a woman who would not open to me. She could do nothing, she cried to me through the door, being alone and lame; but if I would apply at the next house, there was a man who could help me if he had a mind.

They came to the next door in force, a man, two women, and a girl, and brought a pair of lanterns to examine the wayfarer. The man was not ill-looking, but had a shifty smile. He leaned against the doorpost, and heard me state my case. All I asked was a guide as far as Cheylard.

'C'est que, voyez-vous, il fait noir,' said he.

I told him that was just my reason for requiring help.

'I understand that,' said he, looking uncomfortable; 'mais—c'est—de la peine.'

I was willing to pay, I said. He shook his head. I rose as high as ten francs; but he continued to shake his head. 'Name your own price, then,' said I.

'Ce n'est pas ça,' he said at length, and with evident difficulty; 'but I am not going to cross the door—mais je ne sortirai pas de la porte.'

I grew a little warm, and asked him what he proposed that I should do.

'Where are you going beyond Cheylard?' he asked by way of answer.

'That is no affair of yours,' I returned, for I was not going to indulge his bestial curiosity; 'it changes nothing in my present predicament.'

'C'est vrai, ça,' he acknowledged, with a laugh; 'oui, c'est vrai. Et d'où venez-vous?'

A better man than I might have felt nettled.

'Oh,' said I, 'I am not going to answer any of your questions, so you may spare yourself the trouble of putting them. I am late enough already; I want help. If you will not guide me yourself, at least help me to find some one else who will.'

'Hold on,' he cried suddenly. 'Was it not you who passed in the meadow while it was still day?'

'Yes, yes,' said the girl, whom I had not hitherto recognised; 'it was monsieur; I told him to follow the cow.'

'As for you, mademoiselle,' said I, 'you are a farceuse.'

'And,' added the man, 'what the devil have you done to be still here?'

What the devil, indeed! But there I was.

'The great thing,' said I, 'is to make an end of it'; and once more proposed that he should help me to find a guide.

'C'est que,' he said again, 'c'est que—il fait noir.'

'Very well,' said I; 'take one of your lanterns.'

'No,' he cried, drawing a thought backward, and again intrenching himself behind one of his former phrases; 'I will not cross the door.'

I looked at him. I saw unaffected terror struggling on his face with unaffected shame; he was smiling pitifully and wetting his lip with his tongue, like a detected schoolboy. I drew a brief picture of my state, and asked him what I was to do.

'I don't know,' he said; 'I will not cross the door.'

Here was the Beast of Gévaudan, and no mistake.

'Sir,' said I, with my most commanding manners, 'you are a coward.'

And with that I turned my back upon the family party, who hastened to retire within their fortifications; and the famous door was closed again, but not till I had overheard the sound of laughter. Filia barbara pater barbarior. Let me say it in the plural: the Beasts of Gévaudan.

The lanterns had somewhat dazzled me, and I ploughed distressfully among stones and rubbish-heaps. All the other houses in the village were both dark and silent; and though I knocked at here and there a door, my knocking was unanswered. It was a bad business; I gave up Fouzilhac with my curses. The rain had stopped, and the wind, which still kept rising, began to dry my coat and trousers. 'Very well,' thought I, 'water or no water, I must camp.' But the first thing was to return to Modestine. I am pretty sure I was twenty minutes groping for my lady in the dark; and if it had not been for the unkindly services of the bog, into which I once more stumbled, I might have still been groping for her at the dawn. My next business was to gain the shelter of a wood, for the wind was cold as well as boisterous. How, in this well-wooded district, I should have been so long in finding one, is another of the insoluble mysteries of this day's adventures; but I will take my oath that I put near an hour to the discovery.

At last black trees began to show upon my left, and, suddenly crossing the road, made a cave of unmitigated blackness right in front. I call it a cave without exaggeration; to pass below that arch of leaves was like entering a dungeon. I felt about until my hand encountered a stout branch, and to this I tied Modestine, a haggard, drenched, desponding donkey. Then I lowered my pack, laid it along the wall on the margin of the road, and unbuckled the straps. I knew well enough where the lantern was; but where were the candles? I groped and groped among the tumbled articles, and, while I was thus groping, suddenly I touched the spirit-lamp. Salvation! This would serve my turn as well. The wind roared unwearyingly among the trees; I could hear the boughs tossing and the leaves churning through half a mile of forest; yet the scene of my encampment was not only as black as the pit, but admirably sheltered. At the second match the wick caught flame. The light was both livid and shifting; but it cut me off from the universe, and doubled the darkness of the surrounding night.

I tied Modestine more conveniently for herself, and broke up half the black bread for her supper, reserving the other half against the morning. Then I gathered what I should want within reach, took off my wet boots and gaiters, which I wrapped in my waterproof, arranged my knapsack for a pillow under the flap of my sleeping-bag, insinuated my limbs into the interior, and buckled myself in like a bambino. I opened a tin of Bologna sausage and broke a cake of chocolate, and that was all I had to eat. It may sound offensive, but I ate them together, bite by bite, by way of bread and meat. All I had to wash down this revolting mixture was neat brandy: a revolting beverage in itself. But I was rare and hungry; ate well, and smoked one of the best cigarettes in my experience. Then I put a stone in my straw hat, pulled the flap of my fur cap over my neck and eyes, put my revolver ready to my hand, and snuggled well down among the sheepskins.

I questioned at first if I were sleepy, for I felt my heart beating faster than usual, as if with an agreeable excitement to which my mind remained a stranger. But as soon as my eyelids touched, that subtle glue leaped between them, and they would no more come separate. The wind among the trees was my lullaby. Sometimes it sounded for minutes together with a steady, even rush, not rising nor abating; and again it would swell and burst like a great crashing breaker, and the trees would patter me all over with big drops from the rain of the afternoon. Night after night, in my own bedroom in the country, I have given ear to this perturbing concert of the wind among the woods; but whether it was a difference in the trees, or the lie of the ground, or because I was myself outside and in the midst of it, the fact remains that the wind sang to a different tune among these woods of Gévaudan. I hearkened and hearkened; and meanwhile sleep took gradual possession of my body and subdued my thoughts and senses; but still my last waking effort was to listen and distinguish, and my last conscious state was one of wonder at the foreign clamour in my ears.

Twice in the course of the dark hours—once when a stone galled me underneath the sack, and again when the poor patient Modestine, growing angry, pawed and stamped upon the road—I was recalled for a brief while to consciousness, and saw a star or two overhead, and the lace-like edge of the foliage against the sky. When I awoke for the third time (Wednesday, September 25th), the world was flooded with a blue light, the mother of the dawn. I saw the leaves labouring in the wind and the ribbon of the road; and, on turning my head, there was Modestine tied to a beech, and standing half across the path in an attitude of inimitable patience. I closed my eyes again, and set to thinking over the experience of the night. I was surprised to find how easy and pleasant it had been, even in this tempestuous weather. The stone which annoyed me would not have been there, had I not been forced to camp blindfold in the opaque night; and I had felt no other inconvenience, except when my feet encountered the lantern or the second volume of Peyrat's Pastors of the Desert among the mixed contents of my sleeping-bag; nay, more, I had felt not a touch of cold, and awakened with unusually lightsome and clear sensations.

With that, I shook myself, got once more into my boots and gaiters, and, breaking up the rest of the bread for Modestine, strolled about to see in what part of the world I had awakened. Ulysses, left on Ithaca, and with a mind unsettled by the goddess, was not more pleasantly astray. I have been after an adventure all my life, a pure dispassionate adventure, such as befell early and heroic voyagers; and thus to be found by morning in a random woodside nook in Gévaudan—not knowing north from south, as strange to my surroundings as the first man upon the earth, an inland castaway—was to find a fraction of my day-dreams realised. I was on the skirts of a little wood of birch, sprinkled with a few beeches; behind, it adjoined another wood of fir; and in front, it broke up and went down in open order into a shallow and meadowy dale. All around there were bare hilltops, some near, some far away, as the perspective closed or opened, but none apparently much higher than the rest. The wind huddled the trees. The golden specks of autumn in the birches tossed shiveringly. Overhead the sky was full of strings and shreds of vapour, flying, vanishing, reappearing, and turning about an axis like tumblers, as the wind hounded them through heaven. It was wild weather and famishing cold. I ate some chocolate, swallowed a mouthful of brandy, and smoked a cigarette before the cold should have time to disable my fingers. And by the time I had got all this done, and had made my pack and bound it on the pack-saddle, the day was tiptoe on the threshold of the east. We had not gone many steps along the lane, before the sun, still invisible to me, sent a glow of gold over some cloud mountains that lay ranged along the eastern sky.

The wind had us on the stern, and hurried us bitingly forward. I buttoned myself into my coat, and walked on in a pleasant frame of mind with all men, when suddenly, at a corner, there was Fouzilhic once more in front of me. Nor only that, but there was the old gentleman who had escorted me so far the night before, running out of his house at sight of me, with hands upraised in horror.

'My poor boy!' he cried, 'what does this mean?'

I told him what had happened. He beat his old hands like clappers in a mill, to think how lightly he had let me go; but when he heard of the man of Fouzilhac, anger and depression seized upon his mind.

'This time, at least,' said he, 'there shall be no mistake.'

And he limped along, for he was very rheumatic, for about half a mile, and until I was almost within sight of Cheylard, the destination I had hunted for so long.

CHEYLARD AND LUC

Candidly, it seemed little worthy of all this searching. A few broken ends of village, with no particular street, but a succession of open places heaped with logs and fagots; a couple of tilted crosses, a shrine to Our Lady of all Graces on the summit of a little hill; and all this, upon a rattling highland river, in the corner of a naked valley. What went ye out for to see? thought I to myself. But the place had a life of its own. I found a board, commemorating the liberalities of Cheylard for the past year, hung up, like a banner, in the diminutive and tottering church. In 1877, it appeared, the inhabitants subscribed forty-eight francs ten centimes for the 'Work of the Propagation of the Faith.' Some of this, I could not help hoping, would be applied to my native land. Cheylard scrapes together halfpence for the darkened souls in Edinburgh; while Balquhidder and Dunrossness bemoan the ignorance of Rome. Thus, to the high entertainment of the angels, do we pelt each other with evangelists, like schoolboys bickering in the snow.

The inn was again singularly unpretentious. The whole furniture of a not ill-to-do family was in the kitchen: the beds, the cradle, the clothes, the plate-rack, the meal-chest, and the photograph of the parish priest. There were five children, one of whom was set to its morning prayers at the stair-foot soon after my arrival, and a sixth would ere long be forthcoming. I was kindly received by these good folk. They were much interested in my misadventure. The wood in which I had slept belonged to them; the man of Fouzilhac they thought a monster of iniquity, and counselled me warmly to summon him at law—'because I might have died.' The good wife was horror-stricken to see me drink over a pint of uncreamed milk.

'You will do yourself an evil,' she said. 'Permit me to boil it for you.'

After I had begun the morning on this delightful liquor, she having an infinity of things to arrange, I was permitted, nay requested, to make a bowl of chocolate for myself. My boots and gaiters were hung up to dry, and, seeing me trying to write my journal on my knee, the eldest daughter let down a hinged table in the chimney-corner for my convenience. Here I wrote, drank my chocolate, and finally ate an omelette before I left. The table was thick with dust; for, as they explained, it was not used except in winter weather. I had a clear look up the vent, through brown agglomerations of soot and blue vapour, to the sky; and whenever a handful of twigs was thrown on to the fire, my legs were scorched by the blaze.

The husband had begun life as a muleteer, and when I came to charge Modestine showed himself full of the prudence of his art. 'You will have to change this package,' said he; 'it ought to be in two parts, and then you might have double the weight.'

I explained that I wanted no more weight; and for no donkey hitherto created would I cut my sleeping-bag in two.

'It fatigues her, however,' said the innkeeper; 'it fatigues her greatly on the march. Look.'

Alas, there were her two forelegs no better than raw beef on the inside, and blood was running from under her tail. They told me when I started, and I was ready to believe it, that before a few days I should come to love Modestine like a dog. Three days had passed, we had shared some misadventures, and my heart was still as cold as a potato towards my beast of burden. She was pretty enough to look at; but then she had given proof of dead stupidity, redeemed indeed by patience, but aggravated by flashes of sorry and ill-judged light-heartedness. And I own this new discovery seemed another point against her. What the devil was the good of a she-ass if she could not carry a sleeping-bag and a few necessaries? I saw the end of the fable rapidly approaching, when I should have to carry Modestine. Æsop was the man to know the world! I assure you I set out with heavy thoughts upon my short day's march.

It was not only heavy thoughts about Modestine that weighted me upon the way; it was a leaden business altogether. For first, the wind blew so rudely that I had to hold on the pack with one hand from Cheylard to Luc; and second, my road lay through one of the most beggarly countries in the world. It was like the worst of the Scottish Highlands, only worse; cold, naked, and ignoble, scant of wood, scant of heather, scant of life. A road and some fences broke the unvarying waste, and the line of the road was marked by upright pillars, to serve in time of snow.

Why any one should desire to visit either Luc or Cheylard is more than my much-inventing spirit can suppose. For my part, I travel not to go anywhere, but to go. I travel for travel's sake. The great affair is to move; to feel the needs and hitches of our life more nearly; to come down off this feather-bed of civilisation, and find the globe granite underfoot and strewn with cutting flints. Alas, as we get up in life, and are more preoccupied with our affairs, even a holiday is a thing that must be worked for. To hold a pack upon a pack-saddle against a gale out of the freezing north is no high industry, but it is one that serves to occupy and compose the mind. And when the present is so exacting, who can annoy himself about the future?

I came out at length above the Allier. A more unsightly prospect at this season of the year it would be hard to fancy. Shelving hills rose round it on all sides, here dabbled with wood and fields, there rising to peaks alternately naked and hairy with pines. The colour throughout was black or ashen, and came to a point in the ruins of the castle of Luc, which pricked up impudently from below my feet, carrying on a pinnacle a tall white statue of Our Lady, which, I heard with interest, weighed fifty quintals, and was to be dedicated on the 6th of October. Through this sorry landscape trickled the Allier and a tributary of nearly equal size, which came down to join it through a broad nude valley in Vivarais. The weather had somewhat lightened, and the clouds massed in squadron; but the fierce wind still hunted them through heaven, and cast great ungainly splashes of shadow and sunlight over the scene.

Luc itself was a straggling double file of houses wedged between hill and river. It had no beauty, nor was there any notable feature, save the old castle overhead with its fifty quintals of brand-new Madonna. But the inn was clean and large. The kitchen, with its two box-beds hung with clean check curtains, with its wide stone chimney, its chimney-shelf four yards long and garnished with lanterns and religious statuettes, its array of chests and pair of ticking clocks, was the very model of what a kitchen ought to be; a melodrama kitchen, suitable for bandits or noblemen in disguise. Nor was the scene disgraced by the landlady, a handsome, silent, dark old woman, clothed and hooded in black like a nun. Even the public bedroom had a character of its own, with the long deal tables and benches, where fifty might have dined, set out as for a harvest-home, and the three box-beds along the wall. In one of these, lying on straw and covered with a pair of table-napkins, did I do penance all night long in goose-flesh and chattering teeth, and sigh, from time to time as I awakened, for my sheepskin sack and the lee of some great wood.

OUR LADY OF THE SNOWS

'I behold

The House, the Brotherhood austere—

And what am I, that I am here?'

MATTHEW ARNOLD.

FATHER APOLLINARIS

Next morning (Thursday, 26th September) I took the road in a new order. The sack was no longer doubled, but hung at full length across the saddle, a green sausage six feet long with a tuft of blue wool hanging out of either end. It was more picturesque, it spared the donkey, and, as I began to see, it would ensure stability, blow high, blow low. But it was not without a pang that I had so decided. For although I had purchased a new cord, and made all as fast as I was able, I was yet jealously uneasy lest the flaps should tumble out and scatter my effects along the line of march.

My way lay up the bald valley of the river, along the march of Vivarais and Gévaudan. The hills of Gévaudan on the right were a little more naked, if anything, than those of Vivarais upon the left, and the former had a monopoly of a low dotty underwood that grew thickly in the gorges and died out in solitary burrs upon the shoulders and the summits. Black bricks of fir-wood were plastered here and there upon both sides, and here and there were cultivated fields. A railway ran beside the river; the only bit of railway in Gévaudan, although there are many proposals afoot and surveys being made, and even, as they tell me, a station standing ready built in Mende. A year or two hence and this may be another world. The desert is beleaguered. Now may some Languedocian Wordsworth turn the sonnet into patois: 'Mountains and vales and floods, heard YE that whistle?'

At a place called La Bastide I was directed to leave the river, and follow a road that mounted on the left among the hills of Vivarais, the modern

Ardèche; for I was now come within a little way of my strange destination, the Trappist monastery of Our Lady of the Snows. The sun came out as I left the shelter of a pine-wood, and I beheld suddenly a fine wild landscape to the south. High rocky hills, as blue as sapphire, closed the view, and between these lay ridge upon ridge, heathery, craggy, the sun glittering on veins of rock, the underwood clambering in the hollows, as rude as God made them at the first. There was not a sign of man's hand in all the prospect; and indeed not a trace of his passage, save where generation after generation had walked in twisted footpaths, in and out among the beeches, and up and down upon the channelled slopes. The mists, which had hitherto beset me, were now broken into clouds, and fled swiftly and shone brightly in the sun. I drew a long breath. It was grateful to come, after so long, upon a scene of some attraction for the human heart. I own I like definite form in what my eyes are to rest upon; and if landscapes were sold, like the sheets of characters of my boyhood, one penny plain and twopence coloured, I should go the length of twopence every day of my life.

But if things had grown better to the south, it was still desolate and inclement near at hand. A spidery cross on every hill-top marked the neighbourhood of a religious house; and a quarter of a mile beyond, the outlook southward opening out and growing bolder with every step, a white statue of the Virgin at the corner of a young plantation directed the traveller to Our Lady of the Snows. Here, then, I struck leftward, and pursued my way, driving my secular donkey before me, and creaking in my secular boots and gaiters, towards the asylum of silence.

I had not gone very far ere the wind brought to me the clanging of a bell, and somehow, I can scarce tell why, my heart sank within me at the sound. I have rarely approached anything with more unaffected terror than the monastery of Our Lady of the Snows. This it is to have had a Protestant education. And suddenly, on turning a corner, fear took hold on me from head to foot—slavish, superstitious fear; and though I did not stop in my advance, yet I went on slowly, like a man who should have passed a bourne unnoticed, and strayed into the country of the dead. For there, upon the narrow new-made road, between the stripling pines, was a mediaeval friar,

271

fighting with a barrowful of turfs. Every Sunday of my childhood I used to study the Hermits of Marco Sadeler—enchanting prints, full of wood and field and mediaeval landscapes, as large as a county, for the imagination to go a-travelling in; and here, sure enough, was one of Marco Sadeler's heroes. He was robed in white like any spectre, and the hood falling back, in the instancy of his contention with the barrow, disclosed a pate as bald and yellow as a skull. He might have been buried any time these thousand years, and all the lively parts of him resolved into earth and broken up with the farmer's harrow.

I was troubled besides in my mind as to etiquette. Durst I address a person who was under a vow of silence? Clearly not. But drawing near, I doffed my cap to him with a far-away superstitious reverence. He nodded back, and cheerfully addressed me. Was I going to the monastery? Who was I? An Englishman? Ah, an Irishman, then?

'No,' I said, 'a Scotsman.'

A Scotsman? Ah, he had never seen a Scotsman before. And he looked me all over, his good, honest, brawny countenance shining with interest, as a boy might look upon a lion or an alligator. From him I learned with disgust that I could not be received at Our Lady of the Snows; I might get a meal, perhaps, but that was all. And then, as our talk ran on, and it turned out that I was not a pedlar, but a literary man, who drew landscapes and was going to write a book, he changed his manner of thinking as to my reception (for I fear they respect persons even in a Trappist monastery), and told me I must be sure to ask for the Father Prior, and state my case to him in full. On second thoughts he determined to go down with me himself; he thought he could manage for me better. Might he say that I was a geographer?

No; I thought, in the interests of truth, he positively might not.

'Very well, then' (with disappointment), 'an author.'

It appeared he had been in a seminary with six young Irishmen, all priests long since, who had received newspapers and kept him informed of the state of ecclesiastical affairs in England. And he asked me eagerly after Dr. Pusey, for whose conversion the good man had continued ever since to pray night and morning.

'I thought he was very near the truth,' he said; 'and he will reach it yet; there is so much virtue in prayer.'

He must be a stiff, ungodly Protestant who can take anything but pleasure in this kind and hopeful story. While he was thus near the subject, the good father asked me if I were a Christian; and when he found I was not, or not after his way, he glossed it over with great good-will.

The road which we were following, and which this stalwart father had made with his own two hands within the space of a year, came to a corner, and showed us some white buildings a little farther on beyond the wood. At the same time, the bell once more sounded abroad. We were hard upon the monastery. Father Apollinaris (for that was my companion's name) stopped me.

'I must not speak to you down there,' he said. 'Ask for the Brother Porter, and all will be well. But try to see me as you go out again through the wood, where I may speak to you. I am charmed to have made your acquaintance.'

And then suddenly raising his arms, flapping his fingers, and crying out twice, 'I must not speak, I must not speak!' he ran away in front of me, and disappeared into the monastery door.

I own this somewhat ghastly eccentricity went a good way to revive my terrors. But where one was so good and simple, why should not all be alike? I took heart of grace, and went forward to the gate as fast as Modestine, who seemed to have a disaffection for monasteries, would permit. It was the first door, in my acquaintance of her, which she had not shown an indecent haste to enter. I summoned the place in form, though with a quaking heart. Father Michael, the Father Hospitaller, and a pair of brown-robed brothers came to the gate and spoke with me a while. I think my sack was the great attraction; it had already beguiled the heart of poor Apollinaris, who had charged me on my life to show it to the Father Prior. But whether it was my address, or the sack, or the idea speedily published among that part of the brotherhood who attend on strangers that I was not a pedlar after all, I found no difficulty as to my reception. Modestine was led away by a layman to the stables, and I and my pack were received into Our Lady of the Snows.

THE MONKS

Father Michael, a pleasant, fresh-faced, smiling man, perhaps of thirty-five, took me to the pantry, and gave me a glass of liqueur to stay me until dinner. We had some talk, or rather I should say he listened to my prattle indulgently enough, but with an abstracted air, like a spirit with a thing of clay. And truly, when I remember that I descanted principally on my appetite, and that it must have been by that time more than eighteen hours since Father Michael had so much as broken bread, I can well understand that he would find an earthly savour in my conversation. But his manner, though superior, was exquisitely gracious; and I find I have a lurking curiosity as to Father Michael's past.

The whet administered, I was left alone for a little in the monastery garden. This is no more than the main court, laid out in sandy paths and beds of parti-coloured dahlias, and with a fountain and a black statue of the Virgin in the centre. The buildings stand around it four-square, bleak, as yet unseasoned by the years and weather, and with no other features than a belfry and a pair of slated gables. Brothers in white, brothers in brown, passed silently along the sanded alleys; and when I first came out, three hooded monks were kneeling on the terrace at their prayers. A naked hill commands the monastery upon one side, and the wood commands it on the other. It lies exposed to wind; the snow falls off and on from October to May, and sometimes lies six weeks on end; but if they stood in Eden, with a climate like heaven's, the buildings themselves would offer the same wintry and cheerless aspect; and for my part, on this wild September day, before I was called to dinner, I felt chilly in and out.

When I had eaten well and heartily, Brother Ambrose, a hearty conversible Frenchman (for all those who wait on strangers have the liberty to speak), led me to a little room in that part of the building which is set apart for MM. les retraitants. It was clean and whitewashed, and furnished with strict necessaries, a crucifix, a bust of the late Pope, the Imitation in French, a book of religious meditations, and the Life of Elizabeth Seton, evangelist, it would appear, of North America and of New England in particular. As far as my experience goes, there is a fair field for some more evangelisation in these quarters; but think of Cotton Mather! I should like to give him a reading of this little work in heaven, where I hope he dwells; but perhaps he knows all that already, and much more; and perhaps he and Mrs. Seton are the dearest friends, and gladly unite their voices in the everlasting psalm. Over the table, to conclude the inventory of the room, hung a set of regulations for MM. les retraitants: what services they should attend, when they were to tell their beads or meditate, and when they were to rise and go to rest. At the foot was a notable N.B.: 'Le temps libre est employé à l'examen de conscience, à la confession, à faire de bonnes résolutions, etc.' To make good resolutions, indeed! You might talk as fruitfully of making the hair grow on your head.

I had scarce explored my niche when Brother Ambrose returned. An English boarder, it appeared, would like to speak with me. I professed my willingness, and the friar ushered in a fresh, young, little Irishman of fifty, a deacon of the Church, arrayed in strict canonicals, and wearing on his head what, in default of knowledge, I can only call the ecclesiastical shako. He had lived seven years in retreat at a convent of nuns in Belgium, and now five at Our Lady of the Snows; he never saw an English newspaper; he spoke French imperfectly, and had he spoken it like a native, there was not much chance of conversation where he dwelt. With this, he was a man eminently sociable, greedy of news, and simple-minded like a child. If I was pleased to have a guide about the monastery, he was no less delighted to see an English face and hear an English tongue.

He showed me his own room, where he passed his time among breviaries, Hebrew Bibles, and the Waverley Novels. Thence he led me to the cloisters, into the chapter-house, through the vestry, where the brothers' gowns and broad straw hats were hanging up, each with his religious name upon a board—names full of legendary suavity and interest, such as Basil, Hilarion, Raphael, or Pacifique; into the library, where were all the works of Veuillot and Chateaubriand, and the Odes et Ballades, if you please, and even Molière, to say nothing of innumerable fathers and a great variety of local and general historians. Thence my good Irishman took me round the workshops, where brothers bake bread, and make cartwheels, and take photographs; where one superintends a collection of curiosities, and another a gallery of rabbits. For in a Trappist monastery each monk has an occupation of his own choice, apart from his religious duties and the general labours of the house. Each must sing in the choir, if he has a voice and ear, and join in the haymaking if he has a hand to stir; but in his private hours, although he must be occupied, he may be occupied on what he likes. Thus I was told that one brother was engaged with literature; while Father Apollinaris busies himself in making roads, and the Abbot employs himself in binding books. It is not so long since this Abbot was consecrated, by the way; and on that occasion, by a special grace, his mother was permitted to enter the chapel and witness the ceremony of consecration. A proud day for her to have a son a mitred abbot; it makes you glad to think they let her in.

In all these journeyings to and fro, many silent fathers and brethren fell in our way. Usually they paid no more regard to our passage than if we had been a cloud; but sometimes the good deacon had a permission to ask of them, and it was granted by a peculiar movement of the hands, almost like that of a dog's paws in swimming, or refused by the usual negative signs, and in either case with lowered eyelids and a certain air of contrition, as of a man who was steering very close to evil.

The monks, by special grace of their Abbot, were still taking two meals a day; but it was already time for their grand fast, which begins somewhere in September and lasts till Easter, and during which they eat but once in the twenty-four hours, and that at two in the afternoon, twelve hours after they have begun the toil and vigil of the day. Their meals are scanty, but even of these they eat sparingly; and though each is allowed a small carafe of wine, many refrain from this indulgence. Without doubt, the most of mankind grossly overeat themselves; our meals serve not only for support, but as a hearty and natural diversion from the labour of life. Yet, though excess may be hurtful, I should have thought this Trappist regimen defective. And I am astonished, as I look back, at the freshness of face and cheerfulness of manner of all whom I beheld. A happier nor a healthier company I should scarce suppose that I have ever seen. As a matter of fact, on this bleak upland, and with the incessant occupation of the monks, life is of an uncertain tenure, and death no infrequent visitor, at Our Lady of the Snows. This, at least, was what was told me. But if they die easily, they must live healthily in the meantime, for they seemed all firm of flesh and high in colour; and the only morbid sign that I could observe, an unusual brilliancy of eye, was one that served rather to increase the general impression of vivacity and strength.

Those with whom I spoke were singularly sweet-tempered, with what I can only call a holy cheerfulness in air and conversation. There is a note, in the direction to visitors, telling them not to be offended at the curt speech of those who wait upon them, since it is proper to monks to speak little. The note might have been spared; to a man the hospitallers were all brimming with innocent talk, and, in my experience of the monastery, it was easier to begin than to break off a conversation. With the exception of Father Michael, who was a man of the world, they showed themselves full of kind and healthy interest in all sorts of subjects—in politics, in voyages, in my sleeping-sack— and not without a certain pleasure in the sound of their own voices.

As for those who are restricted to silence, I can only wonder how they bear their solemn and cheerless isolation. And yet, apart from any view of mortification, I can see a certain policy, not only in the exclusion of women, but in this vow of silence. I have had some experience of lay phalansteries, of an artistic, not to say a bacchanalian character; and seen more than one association easily formed and yet more easily dispersed. With a Cistercian rule, perhaps they might have lasted longer. In the neighbourhood of women it is but a touch-and-go association that can be formed among defenceless men; the stronger electricity is sure to triumph; the dreams of boyhood, the schemes of youth, are abandoned after an interview of ten minutes, and the arts and sciences, and professional male jollity, deserted at once for two sweet eyes and a caressing accent. And next after this, the tongue is the great divider.

I am almost ashamed to pursue this worldly criticism of a religious rule; but there is yet another point in which the Trappist order appeals to me as a model of wisdom. By two in the morning the clapper goes upon the bell, and so on, hour by hour, and sometimes quarter by quarter, till eight, the hour of rest; so infinitesimally is the day divided among different occupations. The man who keeps rabbits, for example, hurries from his hutches to the chapel, the chapter-room, or the refectory, all day long: every hour he has an office to sing, a duty to perform; from two, when he rises in the dark, till eight, when he returns to receive the comfortable gift of sleep, he is upon his feet and occupied with manifold and changing business. I know many persons, worth several thousands in the year, who are not so fortunate in the disposal of their lives. Into how many houses would not the note of the monastery bell, dividing the day into manageable portions, bring peace of mind and healthful activity of body! We speak of hardships, but the true hardship is to be a dull fool, and permitted to mismanage life in our own dull and foolish manner.

From this point of view, we may perhaps better understand the monk's existence. A long novitiate and every proof of constancy of mind and strength of body is required before admission to the order; but I could not find that many were discouraged. In the photographer's studio, which figures so strangely among the outbuildings, my eye was attracted by the portrait of a young fellow in the uniform of a private of foot. This was one of the novices, who came of the age for service, and marched and drilled and mounted guard for the proper time among the garrison of Algiers. Here was a man who had surely seen both sides of life before deciding; yet as soon as he was set free from service he returned to finish his novitiate.

This austere rule entitles a man to heaven as by right. When the Trappist sickens, he quits not his habit; he lies in the bed of death as he has prayed and laboured in his frugal and silent existence; and when the Liberator comes, at the very moment, even before they have carried him in his robe to lie his little last in the chapel among continual chantings, joy-bells break forth, as if for a marriage, from the slated belfry, and proclaim throughout the neighbourhood that another soul has gone to God.

At night, under the conduct of my kind Irishman, I took my place in the gallery to hear compline and Salve Regina, with which the Cistercians bring every day to a conclusion. There were none of those circumstances which strike the Protestant as childish or as tawdry in the public offices of Rome. A stern simplicity, heightened by the romance of the surroundings, spoke

278

directly to the heart. I recall the whitewashed chapel, the hooded figures in the choir, the lights alternately occluded and revealed, the strong manly singing, the silence that ensued, the sight of cowled heads bowed in prayer, and then the clear trenchant beating of the bell, breaking in to show that the last office was over and the hour of sleep had come; and when I remember, I am not surprised that I made my escape into the court with somewhat whirling fancies, and stood like a man bewildered in the windy starry night.

But I was weary; and when I had quieted my spirits with Elizabeth Seton's memoirs—a dull work—the cold and the raving of the wind among the pines (for my room was on that side of the monastery which adjoins the woods) disposed me readily to slumber. I was wakened at black midnight, as it seemed, though it was really two in the morning, by the first stroke upon the bell. All the brothers were then hurrying to the chapel; the dead in life, at this untimely hour, were already beginning the uncomforted labours of their day. The dead in life—there was a chill reflection. And the words of a French song came back into my memory, telling of the best of our mixed existence:

'Que t'as de belles filles,

Giroflé!

Girofla!

Que t'as de belles filles,

L'Amour let comptera!'

And I blessed God that I was free to wander, free to hope, and free to love.

THE BOARDERS

But there was another side to my residence at Our Lady of the Snows. At this late season there were not many boarders; and yet I was not alone in the public part of the monastery. This itself is hard by the gate, with a small dining-room on the ground-floor and a whole corridor of cells similar to mine upstairs. I have stupidly forgotten the board for a regular retraitant; but it was somewhere between three and five francs a day, and I think most probably the first. Chance visitors like myself might give what they chose as a free-will offering, but nothing was demanded. I may mention that when I was going away, Father Michael refused twenty francs as excessive. I explained the reasoning which led me to offer him so much; but even then, from a curious point of honour, he would not accept it with his own hand. 'I have no right to refuse for the monastery,' he explained, 'but I should prefer if you would give it to one of the brothers.'

I had dined alone, because I arrived late; but at supper I found two other guests. One was a country parish priest, who had walked over that morning from the seat of his cure near Mende to enjoy four days of solitude and prayer. He was a grenadier in person, with the hale colour and circular wrinkles of a peasant; and as he complained much of how he had been impeded by his skirts upon the march, I have a vivid fancy portrait of him, striding along, upright, big-boned, with kilted cassock, through the bleak hills of Gévaudan. The other was a short, grizzling, thick-set man, from forty-five to fifty, dressed in tweed with a knitted spencer, and the red ribbon of a decoration in his button-hole. This last was a hard person to classify. He was an old soldier, who had seen service and risen to the rank of commandant; and he retained some of the brisk decisive manners of the camp. On the other hand, as soon as his resignation was accepted, he had come to Our Lady of the Snows as a boarder, and, after a brief experience of its ways, had decided to remain as a novice. Already the new life was beginning to modify his appearance; already he had acquired somewhat of the quiet and smiling air of the brethren; and he was as yet neither an officer nor a Trappist, but partook of the character of each. And certainly here was a man in an interesting nick of life. Out of the noise of cannon and trumpets, he was in the act of passing into this still country bordering on the grave, where men sleep nightly in their grave-clothes, and, like phantoms, communicate by signs.

At supper we talked politics. I make it my business, when I am in France, to preach political good-will and moderation, and to dwell on the example of Poland, much as some alarmists in England dwell on the example of Carthage. The priest and the commandant assured me of their sympathy with all I said, and made a heavy sighing over the bitterness of contemporary feeling.

'Why, you cannot say anything to a man with which he does not absolutely agree,' said I, 'but he flies up at you in a temper.'

They both declared that such a state of things was antichristian.

While we were thus agreeing, what should my tongue stumble upon but a word in praise of Gambetta's moderation. The old soldier's countenance was instantly suffused with blood; with the palms of his hands he beat the table like a naughty child.

'Comment, monsieur?' he shouted. 'Comment? Gambetta moderate? Will you dare to justify these words?'

But the priest had not forgotten the tenor of our talk. And suddenly, in the height of his fury, the old soldier found a warning look directed on his face; the absurdity of his behaviour was brought home to him in a flash; and the storm came to an abrupt end, without another word.

It was only in the morning, over our coffee (Friday, September 27th), that this couple found out I was a heretic. I suppose I had misled them by some admiring expressions as to the monastic life around us; and it was only by a point-blank question that the truth came out. I had been tolerantly used both by simple Father Apollinaris and astute Father Michael; and the good Irish deacon, when he heard of my religious weakness, had only patted me upon the shoulder and said, 'You must be a Catholic and come to heaven.' But I was now among a different sect of orthodox. These two men were bitter and upright and narrow, like the worst of Scotsmen, and indeed, upon my heart, I fancy they were worse. The priest snorted aloud like a battle-horse.

'Et vous prétendez mourir dans cette espèce de croyance?' he demanded; and there is no type used by mortal printers large enough to qualify his accent.

I humbly indicated that I had no design of changing.

But he could not away with such a monstrous attitude. 'No, no,' he cried; 'you must change. You have come here, God has led you here, and you must embrace the opportunity.'

I made a slip in policy; I appealed to the family affections, though I was speaking to a priest and a soldier, two classes of men circumstantially divorced from the kind and homely ties of life.

'Your father and mother?' cried the priest. 'Very well; you will convert them in their turn when you go home.'

I think I see my father's face! I would rather tackle the Gaetulian lion in his den than embark on such an enterprise against the family theologian.

But now the hunt was up; priest and soldier were in full cry for my conversion; and the Work of the Propagation of the Faith, for which the people of Cheylard subscribed forty-eight francs ten centimes during 1877, was being gallantly pursued against myself. It was an odd but most effective proselytising. They never sought to convince me in argument, where I might have attempted some defence; but took it for granted that I was both ashamed and terrified at my position, and urged me solely on the point of time. Now, they said, when God had led me to Our Lady of the Snows, now was the appointed hour.

'Do not be withheld by false shame,' observed the priest, for my encouragement.

For one who feels very similarly to all sects of religion, and who has never been able, even for a moment, to weigh seriously the merit of this or that creed on the eternal side of things, however much he may see to praise or blame upon the secular and temporal side, the situation thus created was both unfair and painful. I committed my second fault in tact, and tried to plead that it was all the same thing in the end, and we were all drawing near by different sides to the same kind and undiscriminating Friend and Father. That, as it seems to lay spirits, would be the only gospel worthy of the name. But different men think differently; and this revolutionary aspiration brought down the priest with all the terrors of the law. He launched into harrowing details of hell. The damned, he said—on the authority of a little book which he had read not a week before, and which, to add conviction to conviction, he had fully intended to bring along with him in his pocket—were to occupy the same attitude through all eternity in the midst of dismal tortures. And as he thus expatiated, he grew in nobility of aspect with his enthusiasm.

As a result the pair concluded that I should seek out the Prior, since the Abbot was from home, and lay my case immediately before him.

'C'est mon conseil comme ancien militaire,' observed the commandant; 'et celui de monsieur comme prêtre.'

'Oui,' added the curé, sententiously nodding; 'comme ancien militaire—et comme prêtre.'

At this moment, whilst I was somewhat embarrassed how to answer, in came one of the monks, a little brown fellow, as lively as a grig, and with an Italian accent, who threw himself at once into the contention, but in a milder and more persuasive vein, as befitted one of these pleasant brethren. Look at him, he said. The rule was very hard; he would have dearly liked to stay in his own country, Italy—it was well known how beautiful it was, the beautiful Italy; but then there were no Trappists in Italy; and he had a soul to save; and here he was.

I am afraid I must be at bottom, what a cheerful Indian critic has dubbed me, 'a faddling hedonist,' for this description of the brother's motives gave me somewhat of a shock. I should have preferred to think he had chosen the life for its own sake, and not for ulterior purposes; and this shows how profoundly I was out of sympathy with these good Trappists, even when I was doing my best to sympathise. But to the curé the argument seemed decisive.

'Hear that!' he cried. 'And I have seen a marquis here, a marquis, a marquis'—he repeated the holy word three times over—'and other persons high in society; and generals. And here, at your side, is this gentleman, who has been so many years in armies—decorated, an old warrior. And here he is, ready to dedicate himself to God.'

I was by this time so thoroughly embarrassed that I pled cold feet, and made my escape from the apartment. It was a furious windy morning, with a sky much cleared, and long and potent intervals of sunshine; and I wandered until dinner in the wild country towards the east, sorely staggered and beaten upon by the gale, but rewarded with some striking views.

At dinner the Work of the Propagation of the Faith was recommenced, and on this occasion still more distastefully to me. The priest asked me many questions as to the contemptible faith of my fathers, and received my replies with a kind of ecclesiastical titter.

'Your sect,' he said once; 'for I think you will admit it would be doing it too much honour to call it a religion.'

'As you please, monsieur,' said I. 'La parole est à vous.'

At length I grew annoyed beyond endurance; and although he was on his own ground and, what is more to the purpose, an old man, and so holding a claim upon my toleration, I could not avoid a protest against this uncivil usage. He was sadly discountenanced.

'I assure you,' he said, 'I have no inclination to laugh in my heart. I have no other feeling but interest in your soul.'

And there ended my conversion. Honest man! he was no dangerous deceiver; but a country parson, full of zeal and faith. Long may he tread Gévaudan with his kilted skirts—a man strong to walk and strong to comfort his parishioners in death! I daresay he would beat bravely through a snowstorm where his duty called him; and it is not always the most faithful believer who makes the cunningest apostle.

UPPER GÉVAUDAN (continued)

The bed was made, the room was fit,

By punctual eve the stars were lit;

The air was still, the water ran;

No need there was for maid or man,

When we put up, my ass and I,

At God's green caravanserai.

OLD PLAY.

ACROSS THE GOULET

The wind fell during dinner, and the sky remained clear; so it was under better auspices that I loaded Modestine before the monastery gate. My Irish friend accompanied me so far on the way. As we came through the wood, there was Père Apollinaire hauling his barrow; and he too quitted his labours to go with me for perhaps a hundred yards, holding my hand between both of his in front of him. I parted first from one and then from the other with unfeigned regret, but yet with the glee of the traveller who shakes off the dust of one stage before hurrying forth upon another. Then Modestine and I mounted the course of the Allier, which here led us back into Gévaudan towards its sources in the forest of Mercoire. It was but an inconsiderable burn before we left its guidance. Thence, over a hill, our way lay through a naked plateau, until we reached Chasseradès at sundown.

The company in the inn kitchen that night were all men employed in survey for one of the projected railways. They were intelligent and conversible, and we decided the future of France over hot wine, until the state of the clock frightened us to rest. There were four beds in the little upstairs room; and we slept six. But I had a bed to myself, and persuaded them to leave the window open.

'Hé, bourgeois; il est cinq heures!' was the cry that wakened me in the morning (Saturday, September 28th). The room was full of a transparent darkness, which dimly showed me the other three beds and the five different nightcaps on the pillows. But out of the window the dawn was growing ruddy in a long belt over the hill-tops, and day was about to flood the plateau. The hour was inspiriting; and there seemed a promise of calm weather, which was perfectly fulfilled. I was soon under way with Modestine. The road lay for a while over the plateau, and then descended through a precipitous village into the valley of the Chassezac. This stream ran among green meadows, well hidden from the world by its steep banks; the broom was in flower, and here and there was a hamlet sending up its smoke.

At last the path crossed the Chassezac upon a bridge, and, forsaking this deep hollow, set itself to cross the mountain of La Goulet. It wound up

285

through Lestampes by upland fields and woods of beech and birch, and with every corner brought me into an acquaintance with some new interest. Even in the gully of the Chassezac my ear had been struck by a noise like that of a great bass bell ringing at the distance of many miles; but this, as I continued to mount and draw nearer to it, seemed to change in character, and I found at length that it came from some one leading flocks afield to the note of a rural horn. The narrow street of Lestampes stood full of sheep, from wall to wall—black sheep and white, bleating with one accord like the birds in spring, and each one accompanying himself upon the sheep-bell round his neck. It made a pathetic concert, all in treble. A little higher, and I passed a pair of men in a tree with pruning-hooks, and one of them was singing the music of a bourrée. Still further, and when I was already threading the birches, the crowing of cocks came cheerfully up to my ears, and along with that the voice of a flute discoursing a deliberate and plaintive air from one of the upland villages. I pictured to myself some grizzled, apple-cheeked, country schoolmaster fluting in his bit of a garden in the clear autumn sunshine. All these beautiful and interesting sounds filled my heart with an unwonted expectation; and it appeared to me that, once past this range which I was mounting, I should descend into the garden of the world. Nor was I deceived, for I was now done with rains and winds and a bleak country. The first part of my journey ended here; and this was like an induction of sweet sounds into the other and more beautiful.

There are other degrees of feyness, as of punishment, besides the capital; and I was now led by my good spirits into an adventure which I relate in the interest of future donkey-drivers. The road zigzagged so widely on the hillside, that I chose a short cut by map and compass, and struck through the dwarf woods to catch the road again upon a higher level. It was my one serious conflict with Modestine. She would none of my short cut; she turned in my face; she backed, she reared; she, whom I had hitherto imagined to be dumb, actually brayed with a loud hoarse flourish, like a cock crowing for the dawn. I plied the goad with one hand; with the other, so steep was the ascent, I had to hold on the pack-saddle. Half-a-dozen times she was nearly over backwards on the top of me; half-a-dozen times, from sheer weariness of spirit, I was nearly giving it up, and leading her down again to follow the road. But I took the thing as a wager, and fought it through. I was surprised, as I went on my way again, by what appeared to be chill rain-drops falling on my hand, and more than once looked up in wonder at the cloudless sky. But it was only sweat which came dropping from my brow.

Over the summit of the Goulet there was no marked road—only upright stones posted from space to space to guide the drovers. The turf underfoot was springy and well scented. I had no company but a lark or two, and met but one bullock-cart between Lestampes and Bleymard. In front of me I saw a shallow valley, and beyond that the range of the Lozère, sparsely wooded and well enough modelled in the flanks, but straight and dull in outline. There was scarce a sign of culture; only about Bleymard, the white high-road from Villefort to Mende traversed a range of meadows, set with spiry poplars, and sounding from side to side with the bells of flocks and herds.

A NIGHT AMONG THE PINES

From Bleymard after dinner, although it was already late, I set out to scale a portion of the Lozère. An ill-marked stony drove-road guided me forward; and I met nearly half-a-dozen bullock-carts descending from the woods, each laden with a whole pine-tree for the winter's firing. At the top of the woods, which do not climb very high upon this cold ridge, I struck leftward by a path among the pines, until I hit on a dell of green turf, where a streamlet made a little spout over some stones to serve me for a water-tap. 'In a more sacred or sequestered bower . . . nor nymph nor faunus haunted.' The trees were not old, but they grew thickly round the glade: there was no outlook, except north-eastward upon distant hill-tops, or straight upward to the sky; and the encampment felt secure and private like a room. By the time I had made my arrangements and fed Modestine, the day was already beginning to decline. I buckled myself to the knees into my sack and made a hearty meal; and as soon as the sun went down, I pulled my cap over my eyes and fell asleep.

Night is a dead monotonous period under a roof; but in the open world it passes lightly, with its stars and dews and perfumes, and the hours are marked by changes in the face of Nature. What seems a kind of temporal death to people choked between walls and curtains, is only a light and living slumber to the man who sleeps afield. All night long he can hear Nature breathing deeply and freely; even as she takes her rest, she turns and smiles; and there is one stirring hour unknown to those who dwell in houses, when a wakeful influence goes abroad over the sleeping hemisphere, and all the outdoor world are on their feet. It is then that the cock first crows, not this time to announce the dawn, but like a cheerful watchman speeding the course of night. Cattle awake on the meadows; sheep break their fast on dewy hillsides, and change to a new lair among the ferns; and houseless men, who have lain down with the fowls, open their dim eyes and behold the beauty of the night.

At what inaudible summons, at what gentle touch of Nature, are all these sleepers thus recalled in the same hour to life? Do the stars rain down an influence, or do we share some thrill of mother earth below our resting bodies? Even shepherds and old country-folk, who are the deepest read in these arcana, have not a guess as to the means or purpose of this nightly resurrection. Towards two in the morning they declare the thing takes place; and neither know nor inquire further. And at least it is a pleasant incident. We are disturbed in our slumber only, like the luxurious Montaigne, 'that we may the better and more sensibly relish it.' We have a moment to look upon the stars. And there is a special pleasure for some minds in the reflection that we share the impulse with all outdoor creatures in our neighbourhood, that we have escaped out of the Bastille of civilisation, and are become, for the time being, a mere kindly animal and a sheep of Nature's flock.

When that hour came to me among the pines, I wakened thirsty. My tin was standing by me half full of water. I emptied it at a draught; and feeling broad awake after this internal cold aspersion, sat upright to make a cigarette. The stars were clear, coloured, and jewel-like, but not frosty. A faint silvery vapour stood for the Milky Way. All around me the black fir-points stood upright and stock-still. By the whiteness of the pack-saddle, I could see Modestine walking round and round at the length of her tether; I could hear her steadily munching at the sward; but there was not another sound, save the indescribable quiet talk of the runnel over the stones. I lay lazily smoking and studying the colour of the sky, as we call the void of space, from where it showed a reddish grey behind the pines to where it showed a glossy blue-black between the stars. As if to be more like a pedlar, I wear a silver ring. This I could see faintly shining as I raised or lowered the cigarette; and at each whiff the inside of my hand was illuminated, and became for a second the highest light in the landscape.

A faint wind, more like a moving coolness than a stream of air, passed down the glade from time to time; so that even in my great chamber the air was being renewed all night long. I thought with horror of the inn at Chasseradès and the congregated nightcaps; with horror of the nocturnal prowesses of clerks and students, of hot theatres and pass-keys and close rooms. I have not often enjoyed a more serene possession of myself, nor felt more independent of material aids. The outer world, from which we cower into our houses, seemed after all a gentle habitable place; and night after night a man's bed, it seemed, was laid and waiting for him in the fields, where God keeps an open house. I thought I had rediscovered one of those truths which are revealed to savages and hid from political economists: at the least, I had discovered a new pleasure for myself. And yet even while I was exulting in my solitude I became aware of a strange lack. I wished a companion to lie near me in the starlight, silent and not moving, but ever within touch. For there is a fellowship more quiet even than solitude, and which, rightly understood, is solitude made perfect. And to live out of doors with the woman a man loves is of all lives the most complete and free.

As I thus lay, between content and longing, a faint noise stole towards me through the pines. I thought, at first, it was the crowing of cocks or the barking of dogs at some very distant farm; but steadily and gradually it took articulate shape in my ears, until I became aware that a passenger was going by upon the high-road in the valley, and singing loudly as he went. There was more of good-will than grace in his performance; but he trolled with ample lungs; and the sound of his voice took hold upon the hillside and set the air shaking in the leafy glens. I have heard people passing by night in sleeping cities; some of them sang; one, I remember, played loudly on the bagpipes. I have heard the rattle of a cart or carriage spring up suddenly after hours of stillness, and pass, for some minutes, within the range of my hearing as

I lay abed. There is a romance about all who are abroad in the black hours, and with something of a thrill we try to guess their business. But here the romance was double: first, this glad passenger, lit internally with wine, who sent up his voice in music through the night; and then I, on the other hand, buckled into my sack, and smoking alone in the pine-woods between four and five thousand feet towards the stars.

When I awoke again (Sunday, 29th September), many of the stars had disappeared; only the stronger companions of the night still burned visibly overhead; and away towards the east I saw a faint haze of light upon the horizon, such as had been the Milky Way when I was last awake. Day was at hand. I lit my lantern, and by its glow-worm light put on my boots and gaiters; then I broke up some bread for Modestine, filled my can at the water-tap, and lit my spirit-lamp to boil myself some chocolate. The blue darkness lay long in the glade where I had so sweetly slumbered; but soon there was a broad streak of orange melting into gold along the mountain-tops of Vivarais. A solemn glee possessed my mind at this gradual and lovely coming in of day. I heard the runnel with delight; I looked round me for something beautiful and unexpected; but the still black pine-trees, the hollow glade, the munching ass, remained unchanged in figure. Nothing had altered but the light, and that, indeed, shed over all a spirit of life and of breathing peace, and moved me to a strange exhilaration.

I drank my water-chocolate, which was hot if it was not rich, and strolled here and there, and up and down about the glade. While I was thus delaying, a gush of steady wind, as long as a heavy sigh, poured direct out of the quarter of the morning. It was cold, and set me sneezing. The trees near at hand tossed their black plumes in its passage; and I could see the thin distant spires of pine along the edge of the hill rock slightly to and fro against the golden east. Ten minutes after, the sunlight spread at a gallop along the hillside, scattering shadows and sparkles, and the day had come completely.

I hastened to prepare my pack, and tackle the steep ascent that lay before me; but I had something on my mind. It was only a fancy; yet a fancy will sometimes be importunate. I had been most hospitably received and punctually served in my green caravanserai. The room was airy, the water excellent, and the dawn had called me to a moment. I say nothing of the tapestries or the inimitable ceiling, nor yet of the view which I commanded from the windows; but I felt I was in some one's debt for all this liberal entertainment. And so it pleased me, in a half-laughing way, to leave pieces of money on the turf as I went along, until I had left enough for my night's lodging. I trust they did not fall to some rich and churlish drover.

THE COUNTRY OF THE CAMISARDS

We travelled in the print of olden wars;

Yet all the land was green;

And love we found, and peace,

Where fire and war had been.

They pass and smile, the children of the sword—

No more the sword they wield;

And O, how deep the corn

Along the battlefield!

W. P. BANNATYNE.

ACROSS THE LOZÈRE

The track that I had followed in the evening soon died out, and I continued to follow over a bald turf ascent a row of stone pillars, such as had conducted me across the Goulet. It was already warm. I tied my jacket on the pack, and walked in my knitted waistcoat. Modestine herself was in high spirits, and broke of her own accord, for the first time in my experience, into a jolting trot that set the oats swashing in the pocket of my coat. The view, back upon the northern Gévaudan, extended with every step; scarce a tree, scarce a house, appeared upon the fields of wild hill that ran north, east, and west, all blue and gold in the haze and sunlight of the morning. A multitude of little birds kept sweeping and twittering about my path; they perched on the stone pillars, they pecked and strutted on the turf, and I saw them circle in volleys in the blue air, and show, from time to time, translucent flickering wings between the sun and me.

Almost from the first moment of my march, a faint large noise, like a distant surf, had filled my ears. Sometimes I was tempted to think it the voice of a neighbouring waterfall, and sometimes a subjective result of the utter stillness of the hill. But as I continued to advance, the noise increased, and became like the hissing of an enormous tea-urn, and at the same time breaths of cool air began to reach me from the direction of the summit. At length I understood. It was blowing stiffly from the south upon the other slope of the Lozère, and every step that I took I was drawing nearer to the wind.

Although it had been long desired, it was quite unexpectedly at last that my eyes rose above the summit. A step that seemed no way more decisive than many other steps that had preceded it—and, 'like stout Cortez when, with eagle eyes, he stared on the Pacific,' I took possession, in my own name, of a new quarter of the world. For behold, instead of the gross turf rampart I had been mounting for so long, a view into the hazy air of heaven, and a land of intricate blue hills below my feet.

The Lozère lies nearly east and west, cutting Gévaudan into two unequal parts; its highest point, this Pic de Finiels, on which I was then standing, rises upwards of five thousand six hundred feet above the sea, and in clear weather commands a view over all lower Languedoc to the Mediterranean Sea. I have spoken with people who either pretended or believed that they had seen, from the Pic de Finiels, white ships sailing by Montpellier and Cette. Behind was the upland northern country through which my way had lain, peopled by a dull race, without wood, without much grandeur of hill-form, and famous in the past for little beside wolves. But in front of me, half veiled in sunny haze, lay a new Gévaudan, rich, picturesque, illustrious for stirring events. Speaking largely, I was in the Cevennes at Monastier, and during all my journey; but there is a strict and local sense in which only this confused and shaggy country at my feet has any title to the name, and in this sense the peasantry employ the word. These are the Cevennes with an emphasis: the Cevennes of the Cevennes. In that undecipherable labyrinth of hills, a war of bandits, a war of wild beasts, raged for two years between the Grand Monarch with all his troops and marshals on the one hand, and a few thousand Protestant mountaineers upon the other. A hundred and eighty years ago, the Camisards held a station even on the Lozère, where I stood; they had an organisation, arsenals, a military and religious hierarchy; their affairs were 'the discourse of every coffee-house' in London; England sent fleets in their support; their leaders prophesied and murdered; with colours and drums, and the singing of old French psalms, their bands sometimes affronted daylight, marched before walled cities, and dispersed the generals of the king; and sometimes at night, or in masquerade, possessed themselves of strong castles, and avenged treachery upon their allies and cruelty upon their foes. There, a hundred and eighty years ago, was the chivalrous Roland, 'Count and Lord Roland, generalissimo of the Protestants in France,' grave, silent, imperious, pock-marked ex-dragoon, whom a lady followed in his wanderings out of love. There was Cavalier, a baker's apprentice with a genius for war, elected brigadier of Camisards at seventeen, to die at fifty-five the English governor of Jersey. There again was Castanet, a partisan leader in a voluminous peruke and with a taste for controversial divinity. Strange generals, who moved apart to take counsel with the God of Hosts, and fled or offered battle, set sentinels or slept in an unguarded camp, as the Spirit whispered to their hearts! And there, to follow these and other leaders, was the rank and file of prophets and disciples, bold, patient, indefatigable, hardy to run upon the mountains, cheering their rough life with psalms, eager to fight, eager to pray, listening devoutly to the oracles of brain-sick children, and mystically putting a grain of wheat among the pewter balls with which they charged their muskets.

I had travelled hitherto through a dull district, and in the track of nothing more notable than the child-eating beast of Gévaudan, the Napoleon Bonaparte of wolves. But now I was to go down into the scene of a romantic chapter—or, better, a romantic footnote in the history of the world. What was left of all this bygone dust and heroism? I was told that Protestantism still survived in this head seat of Protestant resistance; so much the priest himself had told me in the monastery parlour. But I had yet to learn if it were a bare survival, or a lively and generous tradition. Again, if in the northern Cevennes the people are narrow in religious judgments, and more filled with zeal than charity, what was I to look for in this land of persecution and reprisal—in a land where the tyranny of the Church produced the Camisard rebellion, and the terror of the Camisards threw the Catholic peasantry into legalised revolt upon the other side, so that Camisard and Florentin skulked for each other's lives among the mountains?

Just on the brow of the hill, where I paused to look before me, the series of stone pillars came abruptly to an end; and only a little below, a sort of track appeared and began to go down a break-neck slope, turning like a corkscrew as it went. It led into a valley between falling hills, stubbly with rocks like a reaped field of corn, and floored farther down with green meadows. I followed the track with precipitation; the steepness of the slope, the continual agile turning of the line of the descent, and the old unwearied hope of finding something new in a new country, all conspired to lend me wings. Yet a little lower and a stream began, collecting itself together out of many fountains, and soon making a glad noise among the hills. Sometimes it would cross the track in a bit of waterfall, with a pool, in which Modestine refreshed her feet.

The whole descent is like a dream to me, so rapidly was it accomplished. I had scarcely left the summit ere the valley had closed round my path, and the sun beat upon me, walking in a stagnant lowland atmosphere. The track became a road, and went up and down in easy undulations. I passed cabin after cabin, but all seemed deserted; and I saw not a human creature, nor heard any sound except that of the stream. I was, however, in a different country from the day before. The stony skeleton of the world was here vigorously displayed to sun and air. The slopes were steep and changeful. Oak-trees clung along the hills, well grown, wealthy in leaf, and touched by the autumn with strong and luminous colours. Here and there another stream would fall in from the right or the left, down a gorge of snow-white and tumultuary boulders. The river in the bottom (for it was rapidly growing a river, collecting on all hands as it trotted on its way) here foamed a while in desperate rapids, and there lay in pools of the most enchanting sea-green shot with watery browns. As far as I have gone, I have never seen a river of so changeful and delicate a hue; crystal was not more clear, the meadows were not by half so green; and at every pool I saw I felt a thrill of longing to be out of these hot, dusty, and material garments, and bathe my naked body in the mountain air and water. All the time as I went on I never forgot it was the Sabbath; the stillness was a perpetual reminder; and I heard in spirit the church-bells clamouring all over Europe, and the psalms of a thousand churches.

At length a human sound struck upon my ear—a cry strangely

295

modulated between pathos and derision; and looking across the valley, I saw a little urchin sitting in a meadow, with his hands about his knees, and dwarfed to almost comical smallness by the distance. But the rogue had picked me out as I went down the road, from oak wood on to oak wood, driving Modestine; and he made me the compliments of the new country in this tremulous high-pitched salutation. And as all noises are lovely and natural at a sufficient distance, this also, coming through so much clean hill air and crossing all the green valley, sounded pleasant to my ear, and seemed a thing rustic, like the oaks or the river.

A little after, the stream that I was following fell into the Tarn at Pont de Montvert of bloody memory.

PONT DE MONTVERT

One of the first things I encountered in Pont de Montvert was, if I remember rightly, the Protestant temple; but this was but the type of other novelties. A subtle atmosphere distinguishes a town in England from a town in France, or even in Scotland. At Carlisle you can see you are in the one country; at Dumfries, thirty miles away, you are as sure that you are in the other. I should find it difficult to tell in what particulars Pont de Montvert differed from Monastier or Langogne, or even Bleymard; but the difference existed, and spoke eloquently to the eyes. The place, with its houses, its lanes, its glaring river-bed, wore an indescribable air of the South.

All was Sunday bustle in the streets and in the public-house, as all had been Sabbath peace among the mountains. There must have been near a score of us at dinner by eleven before noon; and after I had eaten and drunken, and sat writing up my journal, I suppose as many more came dropping in one after another, or by twos and threes. In crossing the Lozère I had not only come among new natural features, but moved into the territory of a different race. These people, as they hurriedly despatched their viands in an intricate sword-play of knives, questioned and answered me with a degree of intelligence which excelled all that I had met, except among the railway folk at Chasseradès. They had open telling faces, and were lively both in speech and manner. They not only entered thoroughly into the spirit of my little trip, but more than one declared, if he were rich enough, he would like to set forth on such another.

Even physically there was a pleasant change. I had not seen a pretty woman since I left Monastier, and there but one. Now of the three who sat down with me to dinner, one was certainly not beautiful—a poor timid thing of forty, quite troubled at this roaring table d'hôte, whom I squired and helped to wine, and pledged and tried generally to encourage, with quite a contrary effect; but the other two, both married, were both more handsome than the average of women. And Clarisse? What shall I say of Clarisse? She waited the table with a heavy placable nonchalance, like a performing cow; her great grey eyes were steeped in amorous languor; her features, although fleshy, were of an original and accurate design; her mouth had a curl; her nostril spoke of dainty pride; her cheek fell into strange and interesting lines. It was a face capable of strong emotion, and, with training, it offered the promise of delicate sentiment. It seemed pitiful to see so good a model left to country admirers and a country way of thought. Beauty should at least have touched society; then, in a moment, it throws off a weight that lay upon it, it becomes conscious of itself, it puts on an elegance, learns a gait and a carriage of the head, and, in a moment, patet dea. Before I left I assured Clarisse of my hearty admiration. She took it like milk, without embarrassment or wonder, merely looking at me steadily with her great eyes; and I own the result upon myself was some confusion. If Clarisse could read English, I should not dare to add that her figure was unworthy of her face. Hers was a case for stays; but that may perhaps grow better as she gets up in years.

Pont de Montvert, or Greenhill Bridge, as we might say at home, is a place memorable in the story of the Camisards. It was here that the war broke out; here that those southern Covenanters slew their Archbishop Sharp. The persecution on the one hand, the febrile enthusiasm on the other, are almost equally difficult to understand in these quiet modern days, and with our easy modern beliefs and disbeliefs. The Protestants were one and all beside their right minds with zeal and sorrow. They were all prophets and prophetesses. Children at the breast would exhort their parents to good works. 'A child of fifteen months at Quissac spoke from its mother's arms, agitated and sobbing, distinctly and with a loud voice.' Marshal Villars has seen a town where all the women 'seemed possessed by the devil,' and had trembling fits, and uttered prophecies publicly upon the streets. A prophetess of Vivarais was hanged at Montpellier because blood flowed from her eyes and nose, and she declared that she was weeping tears of blood for the misfortunes of the Protestants. And it was not only women and children. Stalwart dangerous fellows, used to swing the sickle or to wield the forest axe, were likewise shaken with strange paroxysms, and spoke oracles with sobs and streaming tears. A persecution unsurpassed in violence had lasted near a score of years, and this was the result upon the persecuted; hanging, burning, breaking on the wheel, had been in vain; the dragoons had left their hoof-marks over all the countryside; there were men rowing in the galleys, and women pining in the prisons of the Church; and not a thought was changed in the heart of any upright Protestant.

Now the head and forefront of the persecution—after Lamoignon de Bâvile—François de Langlade du Chayla (pronounce Chéïla), Archpriest of the Cevennes and Inspector of Missions in the same country, had a house in which he sometimes dwelt in the town of Pont de Montvert. He was a conscientious person, who seems to have been intended by nature for a pirate, and now fifty-five, an age by which a man has learned all the moderation of which he is capable. A missionary in his youth in China, he there suffered martyrdom, was left for dead, and only succoured and brought back to life by the charity of a pariah. We must suppose the pariah devoid of second-sight, and not purposely malicious in this act. Such an experience, it might be thought, would have cured a man of the desire to persecute; but the human spirit is a thing strangely put together; and, having been a Christian martyr, Du Chayla became a Christian persecutor. The Work of the Propagation of the Faith went roundly forward in his hands. His house in Pont de Montvert served him as a prison. There he closed the hands of his prisoners upon live coal, and plucked out the hairs of their beards, to convince them that they were deceived in their opinions. And yet had not he himself tried and proved the inefficacy of these carnal arguments among the Buddhists in China?

Not only was life made intolerable in Languedoc, but flight was rigidly forbidden. One Massip, a muleteer, and well acquainted with the mountain-paths, had already guided several troops of fugitives in safety to Geneva; and on him, with another convoy, consisting mostly of women dressed as men, Du Chayla, in an evil hour for himself, laid his hands. The Sunday following, there was a conventicle of Protestants in the woods of Altefage upon Mount Bougès; where there stood up one Séguier—Spirit Séguier, as his companions called him—a wool-carder, tall, black-faced, and toothless, but a man full of prophecy. He declared, in the name of God, that the time for submission had gone by, and they must betake themselves to arms for the deliverance of their brethren and the destruction of the priests.

The next night, 24th July 1702, a sound disturbed the Inspector of Missions as he sat in his prison-house at Pont de Montvert: the voices of many men upraised in psalmody drew nearer and nearer through the town. It was ten at night; he had his court about him, priests, soldiers, and servants, to the number of twelve or fifteen; and now dreading the insolence of a conventicle below his very windows, he ordered forth his soldiers to report. But the psalm-singers were already at his door, fifty strong, led by the inspired Séguier, and breathing death. To their summons, the archpriest made answer like a stout old persecutor, and bade his garrison fire upon the mob. One Camisard (for, according to some, it was in this night's work that they came by the name) fell at this discharge: his comrades burst in the door with hatchets and a beam of wood, overran the lower story of the house, set free the prisoners, and finding one of them in the vine, a sort of Scavenger's Daughter of the place and period, redoubled in fury against Du Chayla, and sought by repeated assaults to carry the upper floors. But he, on his side, had given absolution to his men, and they bravely held the staircase.

'Children of God,' cried the prophet, 'hold your hands. Let us burn the house, with the priest and the satellites of Baal.'

The fire caught readily. Out of an upper window Du Chayla and his men lowered themselves into the garden by means of knotted sheets; some escaped across the river under the bullets of the insurgents; but the archpriest himself fell, broke his thigh, and could only crawl into the hedge. What were his reflections as this second martyrdom drew near? A poor, brave, besotted, hateful man, who had done his duty resolutely according to his light both in the Cevennes and China. He found at least one telling word to say in his defence; for when the roof fell in and the upbursting flames discovered his retreat, and they came and dragged him to the public place of the town, raging and calling him damned—'If I be damned,' said he, 'why should you also damn yourselves?'

Here was a good reason for the last; but in the course of his inspectorship he had given many stronger which all told in a contrary direction; and these he was now to hear. One by one, Séguier first, the Camisards drew near and stabbed him. 'This,' they said, 'is for my father broken on the wheel. This for my brother in the galleys. That for my mother or my sister imprisoned in your cursed convents.' Each gave his blow and his reason; and then all kneeled and sang psalms around the body till the dawn. With the dawn, still singing, they defiled away towards Frugères, farther up the Tarn, to pursue the work of vengeance, leaving Du Chayla's prison-house in ruins, and his body pierced with two-and-fifty wounds upon the public place.

'Tis a wild night's work, with its accompaniment of psalms; and it seems as if a psalm must always have a sound of threatening in that town upon the Tarn. But the story does not end, even so far as concerns Pont de Montvert, with the departure of the Camisards. The career of Séguier was brief and bloody. Two more priests and a whole family at Ladevèze, from the father to the servants, fell by his hand or by his orders; and yet he was but a day or two at large, and restrained all the time by the presence of the soldiery. Taken at length by a famous soldier of fortune, Captain Poul, he appeared unmoved before his judges.

'Your name?' they asked.

'Pierre Séguier.'

'Why are you called Spirit?'

'Because the Spirit of the Lord is with me.'

'Your domicile?'

'Lately in the desert, and soon in heaven.'

300

'Have you no remorse for your crimes?'

'I have committed none. My soul is like a garden full of shelter and of fountains.'

At Pont de Montvert, on the 12th of August, he had his right hand stricken from his body, and was burned alive. And his soul was like a garden? So perhaps was the soul of Du Chayla, the Christian martyr. And perhaps if you could read in my soul, or I could read in yours, our own composure might seem little less surprising.

Du Chayla's house still stands, with a new roof, beside one of the bridges of the town; and if you are curious you may see the terrace-garden into which he dropped.

IN THE VALLEY OF THE TARN

A new road leads from Pont de Montvert to Florac by the valley of the Tarn; a smooth sandy ledge, it runs about half-way between the summit of the cliffs and the river in the bottom of the valley; and I went in and out, as I followed it, from bays of shadow into promontories of afternoon sun. This was a pass like that of Killiecrankie; a deep turning gully in the hills, with the Tarn making a wonderful hoarse uproar far below, and craggy summits standing in the sunshine high above. A thin fringe of ash-trees ran about the hill-tops, like ivy on a ruin; but on the lower slopes, and far up every glen, the Spanish chestnut-trees stood each four-square to heaven under its tented foliage. Some were planted, each on its own terrace no larger than a bed; some, trusting in their roots, found strength to grow and prosper and be straight and large upon the rapid slopes of the valley; others, where there was a margin to the river, stood marshalled in a line and mighty like cedars of Lebanon. Yet even where they grew most thickly they were not to be thought of as a wood, but as a herd of stalwart individuals; and the dome of each tree stood forth separate and large, and as it were a little hill, from among the domes of its companions. They gave forth a faint sweet perfume which pervaded the air of the afternoon; autumn had put tints of gold and tarnish in the green; and the sun so shone through and kindled the broad foliage, that each chestnut was relieved against another, not in shadow, but in light.

A humble sketcher here laid down his pencil in despair.

I wish I could convey a notion of the growth of these noble trees; of how they strike out boughs like the oak, and trail sprays of drooping foliage like the willow; of how they stand on upright fluted columns like the pillars of a church; or like the olive, from the most shattered bole can put out smooth and youthful shoots, and begin a new life upon the ruins of the old. Thus they partake of the nature of many different trees; and even their prickly top-knots, seen near at hand against the sky, have a certain palm-like air that impresses the imagination. But their individuality, although compounded of so many elements, is but the richer and the more original. And to look down upon a level filled with these knolls of foliage, or to see a clan of old unconquerable chestnuts cluster 'like herded elephants' upon the spur of a mountain, is to rise to higher thoughts of the powers that are in Nature.

Between Modestine's laggard humour and the beauty of the scene, we made little progress all that afternoon; and at last finding the sun, although still far from setting, was already beginning to desert the narrow valley of the Tarn, I began to cast about for a place to camp in. This was not easy to find; the terraces were too narrow, and the ground, where it was unterraced, was usually too steep for a man to lie upon. I should have slipped all night, and awakened towards morning with my feet or my head in the river.

After perhaps a mile, I saw, some sixty feet above the road, a little plateau large enough to hold my sack, and securely parapeted by the trunk of an aged and enormous chestnut. Thither, with infinite trouble, I goaded and kicked the reluctant Modestine, and there I hastened to unload her. There was only room for myself upon the plateau, and I had to go nearly as high again before I found so much as standing-room for the ass. It was on a heap of rolling stones, on an artificial terrace, certainly not five feet square in all. Here I tied her to a chestnut, and having given her corn and bread and made a pile of chestnut-leaves, of which I found her greedy, I descended once more to my own encampment.

The position was unpleasantly exposed. One or two carts went by upon the road; and as long as daylight lasted I concealed myself, for all the world

302

like a hunted Camisard, behind my fortification of vast chestnut trunk; for I was passionately afraid of discovery and the visit of jocular persons in the night. Moreover, I saw that I must be early awake; for these chestnut gardens had been the scene of industry no further gone than on the day before. The slope was strewn with lopped branches, and here and there a great package of leaves was propped against a trunk; for even the leaves are serviceable, and the peasants use them in winter by way of fodder for their animals. I picked a meal in fear and trembling, half lying down to hide myself from the road; and I daresay I was as much concerned as if I had been a scout from Joani's band above upon the Lozère, or from Salomon's across the Tarn, in the old times of psalm-singing and blood. Or, indeed, perhaps more; for the Camisards had a remarkable confidence in God; and a tale comes back into my memory of how the Count of Gévaudan, riding with a party of dragoons and a notary at his saddlebow to enforce the oath of fidelity in all the country hamlets, entered a valley in the woods, and found Cavalier and his men at dinner, gaily seated on the grass, and their hats crowned with box-tree garlands, while fifteen women washed their linen in the stream. Such was a field festival in 1703; at that date Antony Watteau would be painting similar subjects.

This was a very different camp from that of the night before in the cool and silent pine-woods. It was warm and even stifling in the valley. The shrill song of frogs, like the tremolo note of a whistle with a pea in it, rang up from the river-side before the sun was down. In the growing dusk, faint rustlings began to run to and fro among the fallen leaves; from time to time a faint chirping or cheeping noise would fall upon my ear; and from time to time I thought I could see the movement of something swift and indistinct between the chestnuts. A profusion of large ants swarmed upon the ground; bats whisked by, and mosquitoes droned overhead. The long boughs with their bunches of leaves hung against the sky like garlands; and those immediately above and around me had somewhat the air of a trellis which should have been wrecked and half overthrown in a gale of wind.

Sleep for a long time fled my eyelids; and just as I was beginning to feel quiet stealing over my limbs, and settling densely on my mind, a noise at my head startled me broad awake again, and, I will frankly confess it, brought my heart into my mouth.

It was such a noise as a person would make scratching loudly with a finger-nail; it came from under the knapsack which served me for a pillow, and it was thrice repeated before I had time to sit up and turn about. Nothing was to be seen, nothing more was to be heard, but a few of these mysterious rustlings far and near, and the ceaseless accompaniment of the river and the frogs. I learned next day that the chestnut gardens are infested by rats; rustling, chirping, and scraping were probably all due to these; but the puzzle, for the moment, was insoluble, and I had to compose myself for sleep, as best I could, in wondering uncertainty about my neighbours.

I was wakened in the grey of the morning (Monday, 30th September) by the sound of foot-steps not far off upon the stones, and opening my eyes, I beheld a peasant going by among the chestnuts by a footpath that I had not hitherto observed. He turned his head neither to the right nor to the left, and disappeared in a few strides among the foliage. Here was an escape! But it was plainly more than time to be moving. The peasantry were abroad; scarce less terrible to me in my nondescript position than the soldiers of Captain Poul to an undaunted Camisard. I fed Modestine with what haste I could; but as I was returning to my sack, I saw a man and a boy come down the hillside in a direction crossing mine. They unintelligibly hailed me, and I replied with inarticulate but cheerful sounds, and hurried forward to get into my gaiters.

The pair, who seemed to be father and son, came slowly up to the plateau, and stood close beside me for some time in silence. The bed was open, and I saw with regret my revolver lying patently disclosed on the blue wool. At last, after they had looked me all over, and the silence had grown laughably embarrassing, the man demanded in what seemed unfriendly tones:

'You have slept here?'

'Yes,' said I. 'As you see.'

'Why?' he asked.

'My faith,' I answered lightly, 'I was tired.'

He next inquired where I was going and what I had had for dinner; and then, without the least transition, 'C'est bien,' he added, 'come along.' And he and his son, without another word, turned off to the next chestnut-tree but one, which they set to pruning. The thing had passed of more simply than I hoped. He was a grave, respectable man; and his unfriendly voice did not imply that he thought he was speaking to a criminal, but merely to an inferior.

I was soon on the road, nibbling a cake of chocolate and seriously occupied with a case of conscience. Was I to pay for my night's lodging? I had slept ill, the bed was full of fleas in the shape of ants, there was no water in the room, the very dawn had neglected to call me in the morning. I might have missed a train, had there been any in the neighbourhood to catch. Clearly, I was dissatisfied with my entertainment; and I decided I should not pay unless I met a beggar.

The valley looked even lovelier by morning; and soon the road descended to the level of the river. Here, in a place where many straight and prosperous chestnuts stood together, making an aisle upon a swarded terrace, I made my morning toilette in the water of the Tarn. It was marvellously clear, thrillingly cool; the soap-suds disappeared as if by magic in the swift current, and the white boulders gave one a model for cleanliness. To wash in one of God's rivers in the open air seems to me a sort of cheerful solemnity or semi-pagan act of worship. To dabble among dishes in a bedroom may perhaps make clean the body; but the imagination takes no share in such a cleansing. I went on with a light and peaceful heart, and sang psalms to the spiritual ear as I advanced.

Suddenly up came an old woman, who point-blank demanded alms.

'Good,' thought I; 'here comes the waiter with the bill.'

And I paid for my night's lodging on the spot. Take it how you please, but this was the first and the last beggar that I met with during all my tour.

A step or two farther I was overtaken by an old man in a brown nightcap, clear-eyed, weather-beaten, with a faint excited smile. A little girl followed him, driving two sheep and a goat; but she kept in our wake, while the old man walked beside me and talked about the morning and the valley. It was not much past six; and for healthy people who have slept enough, that is an hour of expansion and of open and trustful talk.

'Connaissez-vous le Seigneur?' he said at length.

I asked him what Seigneur he meant; but he only repeated the question with more emphasis and a look in his eyes denoting hope and interest.

'Ah,' said I, pointing upwards, 'I understand you now. Yes, I know Him; He is the best of acquaintances.'

The old man said he was delighted. 'Hold,' he added, striking his bosom; 'it makes me happy here.' There were a few who knew the Lord in these valleys, he went on to tell me; not many, but a few. 'Many are called,' he quoted, 'and few chosen.'

'My father,' said I, 'it is not easy to say who know the Lord; and it is none of our business. Protestants and Catholics, and even those who worship stones, may know Him and be known by Him; for He has made all.'

I did not know I was so good a preacher.

The old man assured me he thought as I did, and repeated his expressions of pleasure at meeting me. 'We are so few,' he said. 'They call us Moravians here; but down in the Department of Gard, where there are also a good number, they are called Derbists, after an English pastor.'

I began to understand that I was figuring, in questionable taste, as a member of some sect to me unknown; but I was more pleased with the pleasure of my companion than embarrassed by my own equivocal position. Indeed, I can see no dishonesty in not avowing a difference; and especially in these high matters, where we have all a sufficient assurance that, whoever may be in the wrong, we ourselves are not completely in the right. The truth is much talked about; but this old man in a brown nightcap showed himself so simple, sweet, and friendly, that I am not unwilling to profess myself his convert. He was, as a matter of fact, a Plymouth Brother. Of what that involves in the way of doctrine I have no idea nor the time to inform myself; but I know right well that we are all embarked upon a troublesome world, the children of one Father, striving in many essential points to do and to become the same. And although it was somewhat in a mistake that he shook hands with me so often and showed himself so ready to receive my words, that was a mistake of the truth-finding sort. For charity begins blindfold; and only through a series of similar misapprehensions rises at length into a settled principle of love and patience, and a firm belief in all our fellow-men. If I deceived this good old man, in the like manner I would willingly go on to deceive others. And if ever at length, out of our separate and sad ways, we should all come together into one common house, I have a hope, to which I cling dearly, that my mountain Plymouth Brother will hasten to shake hands with me again.

Thus, talking like Christian and Faithful by the way, he and I came down upon a hamlet by the Tarn. It was but a humble place, called La Vernède, with less than a dozen houses, and a Protestant chapel on a knoll. Here he dwelt; and here, at the inn, I ordered my breakfast. The inn was kept by an agreeable young man, a stone-breaker on the road, and his sister, a pretty and engaging girl. The village schoolmaster dropped in to speak with the stranger. And these were all Protestants—a fact which pleased me more than I should have expected; and, what pleased me still more, they seemed all upright and simple people. The Plymouth Brother hung round me with a sort of yearning interest, and returned at least thrice to make sure I was enjoying my meal. His behaviour touched me deeply at the time, and even now moves me in recollection. He feared to intrude, but he would not willingly forego one moment of my society; and he seemed never weary of shaking me by the hand.

When all the rest had drifted off to their day's work, I sat for near half an hour with the young mistress of the house, who talked pleasantly over her seam of the chestnut harvest, and the beauties of the Tarn, and old family affections, broken up when young folk go from home, yet still subsisting. Hers, I am sure, was a sweet nature, with a country plainness and much delicacy underneath; and he who takes her to his heart will doubtless be a fortunate young man.

The valley below La Vernède pleased me more and more as I went forward. Now the hills approached from either hand, naked and crumbling, and walled in the river between cliffs; and now the valley widened and became green. The road led me past the old castle of Miral on a steep; past a battlemented monastery, long since broken up and turned into a church and parsonage; and past a cluster of black roofs, the village of Cocurès, sitting among vineyards, and meadows, and orchards thick with red apples, and where, along the highway, they were knocking down walnuts from the roadside trees, and gathering them in sacks and baskets. The hills, however much the vale might open, were still tall and bare, with cliffy battlements and here and there a pointed summit; and the Tarn still rattled through the stones with a mountain noise. I had been led, by bagmen of a picturesque turn of mind, to expect a horrific country after the heart of Byron; but to my Scottish eyes it seemed smiling and plentiful, as the weather still gave an impression of high summer to my Scottish body; although the chestnuts were already picked out by the autumn, and the poplars, that here began to mingle with them, had turned into pale gold against the approach of winter.

There was something in this landscape, smiling although wild, that explained to me the spirit of the Southern Covenanters. Those who took to the hills for conscience' sake in Scotland had all gloomy and bedevilled thoughts; for once that they received God's comfort they would be twice engaged with Satan; but the Camisards had only bright and supporting visions. They dealt much more in blood, both given and taken; yet I find no obsession of the Evil One in their records. With a light conscience, they pursued their life in these rough times and circumstances. The soul of Séguier, let us not forget, was like a garden. They knew they were on God's side, with a knowledge that has no parallel among the Scots; for the Scots, although they might be certain of the cause, could never rest confident of the person.

'We flew,' says one old Camisard, 'when we heard the sound of psalm-singing, we flew as if with wings. We felt within us an animating ardour, a transporting desire. The feeling cannot be expressed in words. It is a thing that must have been experienced to be understood. However weary we might be, we thought no more of our weariness, and grew light so soon as the psalms fell upon our ears.'

The valley of the Tarn and the people whom I met at La Vernède not only explain to me this passage, but the twenty years of suffering which those, who were so stiff and so bloody when once they betook themselves to war, endured with the meekness of children and the constancy of saints and peasants.

<u>FLORAC</u>

On a branch of the Tarn stands Florac, the seat of a sub-prefecture, with an old castle, an alley of planes, many quaint street-corners, and a live fountain welling from the hill. It is notable, besides, for handsome women, and as one of the two capitals, Alais being the other, of the country of the Camisards.

The landlord of the inn took me, after I had eaten, to an adjoining café, where I, or rather my journey, became the topic of the afternoon. Every one had some suggestion for my guidance; and the sub-prefectorial map was fetched from the sub-prefecture itself, and much thumbed among coffee-cups and glasses of liqueur. Most of these kind advisers were Protestant, though I observed that Protestant and Catholic intermingled in a very easy manner; and it surprised me to see what a lively memory still subsisted of the religious war. Among the hills of the south-west, by Mauchline, Cumnock, or Carsphairn, in isolated farms or in the manse, serious Presbyterian people still recall the days of the great persecution, and the graves of local martyrs are still piously regarded. But in towns and among the so-called better classes, I fear that these old doings have become an idle tale. If you met a mixed company in the King's Arms at Wigton, it is not likely that the talk would run on Covenanters. Nay, at Muirkirk of Glenluce, I found the beadle's wife had not so much as heard of Prophet Peden. But these Cévenols were proud of their ancestors in quite another sense; the war was their chosen topic; its exploits were their own patent of nobility; and where a man or a race has had but one adventure, and that heroic, we must expect and pardon some prolixity of reference. They told me the country was still full of legends hitherto uncollected; I heard from them about Cavalier's descendants—not direct descendants, be it understood, but only cousins or nephews—who were still prosperous people in the scene of the boy-general's exploits; and one farmer had seen the bones of old combatants dug up into the air of an afternoon in the nineteenth century, in a field where the ancestors had fought, and the great-grandchildren were peaceably ditching.

Later in the day one of the Protestant pastors was so good as to visit me: a young man, intelligent and polite, with whom I passed an hour or two in talk. Florac, he told me, is part Protestant, part Catholic; and the difference in religion is usually doubled by a difference in politics. You may judge of my surprise, coming as I did from such a babbling purgatorial Poland of a place as Monastier, when I learned that the population lived together on very quiet terms; and there was even an exchange of hospitalities between households thus doubly separated. Black Camisard and White Camisard, militiaman and Miquelet and dragoon, Protestant prophet and Catholic cadet of the White Cross, they had all been sabring and shooting, burning, pillaging, and murdering, their hearts hot with indignant passion; and here, after a hundred and seventy years, Protestant is still Protestant, Catholic still Catholic, in mutual toleration and mild amity of life. But the race of man, like that indomitable nature whence it sprang, has medicating virtues of its own; the years and seasons bring various harvests; the sun returns after the rain; and mankind outlives secular animosities, as a single man awakens from the passions of a day. We judge our ancestors from a more divine position; and the dust being a little laid with several centuries, we can see both sides adorned with human virtues and fighting with a show of right.

I have never thought it easy to be just, and find it daily even harder than I thought. I own I met these Protestants with a delight and a sense of coming home. I was accustomed to speak their language, in another and deeper sense of the word than that which distinguishes between French and English; for the true Babel is a divergence upon morals. And hence I could hold more free communication with the Protestants, and judge them more justly, than the Catholics. Father Apollinaris may pair off with my mountain Plymouth Brother as two guileless and devout old men; yet I ask myself if I had as ready a feeling for the virtues of the Trappist; or, had I been a Catholic, if I should have felt so warmly to the dissenter of La Vernède. With the first

I was on terms of mere forbearance; but with the other, although only on a misunderstanding and by keeping on selected points, it was still possible to hold converse and exchange some honest thoughts. In this world of imperfection we gladly welcome even partial intimacies. And if we find but one to whom we can speak out of our heart freely, with whom we can walk in love and simplicity without dissimulation, we have no ground of quarrel with the world or God.

IN THE VALLEY OF THE MIMENTE

On Tuesday, 1st October, we left Florac late in the afternoon, a tired donkey and tired donkey-driver. A little way up the Tarnon, a covered bridge of wood introduced us into the valley of the Mimente. Steep rocky red mountains overhung the stream; great oaks and chestnuts grew upon the slopes or in stony terraces; here and there was a red field of millet or a few apple-trees studded with red apples; and the road passed hard by two black hamlets, one with an old castle atop to please the heart of the tourist.

It was difficult here again to find a spot fit for my encampment. Even under the oaks and chestnuts the ground had not only a very rapid slope, but was heaped with loose stones; and where there was no timber the hills descended to the stream in a red precipice tufted with heather. The sun had left the highest peak in front of me, and the valley was full of the lowing sound of herdsmen's horns as they recalled the flocks into the stable, when I spied a bight of meadow some way below the roadway in an angle of the river. Thither I descended, and, tying Modestine provisionally to a tree, proceeded to investigate the neighbourhood. A grey pearly evening shadow filled the glen; objects at a little distance grew indistinct and melted bafflingly into each other; and the darkness was rising steadily like an exhalation. I approached a great oak which grew in the meadow, hard by the river's brink; when to my disgust the voices of children fell upon my ear, and I beheld a house round the angle on the other bank. I had half a mind to pack and be gone again, but the growing darkness moved me to remain. I had only to make no noise until the night was fairly come, and trust to the dawn to call me early in the morning. But it was hard to be annoyed by neighbours in such a great hotel.

A hollow underneath the oak was my bed. Before I had fed Modestine and arranged my sack, three stars were already brightly shining, and the others were beginning dimly to appear. I slipped down to the river, which looked very black among its rocks, to fill my can; and dined with a good appetite in the dark, for I scrupled to light a lantern while so near a house. The moon, which I had seen a pallid crescent all afternoon, faintly illuminated the summit of the hills, but not a ray fell into the bottom of the glen where I was lying. The oak rose before me like a pillar of darkness; and overhead the heartsome stars were set in the face of the night. No one knows the stars who has not slept, as the French happily put it, à la belle étoile. He may know all their names and distances and magnitudes, and yet be ignorant of what alone concerns mankind,—their serene and gladsome influence on the mind. The greater part of poetry is about the stars; and very justly, for they are themselves the most classical of poets. These same far-away worlds, sprinkled like tapers or shaken together like a diamond dust upon the sky, had looked not otherwise to Roland or Cavalier, when, in the words of the latter, they had 'no other tent but the sky, and no other bed than my mother earth.'

All night a strong wind blew up the valley, and the acorns fell pattering over me from the oak. Yet, on this first night of October, the air was as mild as May, and I slept with the fur thrown back.

I was much disturbed by the barking of a dog, an animal that I fear more than any wolf. A dog is vastly braver, and is besides supported by the sense of duty. If you kill a wolf, you meet with encouragement and praise; but if you kill a dog, the sacred rights of property and the domestic affections come clamouring round you for redress. At the end of a fagging day, the sharp cruel note of a dog's bark is in itself a keen annoyance; and to a tramp like myself, he represents the sedentary and respectable world in its most hostile form. There is something of the clergyman or the lawyer about this engaging animal; and if he were not amenable to stones, the boldest man would shrink from travelling afoot. I respect dogs much in the domestic circle; but on the highway, or sleeping afield, I both detest and fear them.

I was wakened next morning (Wednesday, October 2nd) by the same dog—for I knew his bark—making a charge down the bank, and then, seeing me sit up, retreating again with great alacrity. The stars were not yet quite extinguished. The heaven was of that enchanting mild grey-blue of the early morn. A still clear light began to fall, and the trees on the hillside were outlined sharply against the sky. The wind had veered more to the north, and no longer reached me in the glen; but as I was going on with my preparations, it drove a white cloud very swiftly over the hill-top; and looking up, I was surprised to see the cloud dyed with gold. In these high regions of the air, the sun was already shining as at noon. If only the clouds travelled high enough, we should see the same thing all night long. For it is always daylight in the fields of space.

As I began to go up the valley, a draught of wind came down it out of the seat of the sunrise, although the clouds continued to run overhead in an almost contrary direction. A few steps farther, and I saw a whole hillside gilded with the sun; and still a little beyond, between two peaks, a centre of dazzling brilliancy appeared floating in the sky, and I was once more face to face with the big bonfire that occupies the kernel of our system.

I met but one human being that forenoon, a dark military-looking wayfarer, who carried a game-bag on a baldric; but he made a remark that seems worthy of record. For when I asked him if he were Protestant or Catholic—

'Oh,' said he, 'I make no shame of my religion. I am a Catholic.'

He made no shame of it! The phrase is a piece of natural statistics; for it is the language of one in a minority. I thought with a smile of Bavile and his dragoons, and how you may ride rough-shod over a religion for a century, and leave it only the more lively for the friction. Ireland is still Catholic; the Cevennes still Protestant. It is not a basketful of law-papers, nor the hoofs and pistol-butts of a regiment of horse, that can change one tittle of a ploughman's thoughts. Outdoor rustic people have not many ideas, but such as they have are hardy plants, and thrive flourishingly in persecution. One who has grown a long while in the sweat of laborious noons, and under the stars at night, a frequenter of hills and forests, an old honest countryman, has, in the end, a sense of communion with the powers of the universe, and amicable relations towards his God. Like my mountain Plymouth Brother, he knows the Lord. His religion does not repose upon a choice of logic; it is the poetry of the man's experience, the philosophy of the history of his life. God, like a great power, like a great shining sun, has appeared to this simple fellow in the course of years, and become the ground and essence of his least reflections; and you may change creeds and dogmas by authority, or proclaim a new religion with the sound of trumpets, if you will; but here is a man who has his own thoughts, and will stubbornly adhere to them in good and evil. He is a Catholic, a Protestant, or a Plymouth Brother, in the same indefeasible sense that a man is not a woman, or a woman not a man. For he could not vary from his faith, unless he could eradicate all memory of the past, and, in a strict and not a conventional meaning, change his mind.

THE HEART OF THE COUNTRY

I was now drawing near to Cassagnas, a cluster of black roofs upon the hillside, in this wild valley, among chestnut gardens, and looked upon in the clear air by many rocky peaks. The road along the Mimente is yet new, nor have the mountaineers recovered their surprise when the first cart arrived at Cassagnas. But although it lay thus apart from the current of men's business, this hamlet had already made a figure in the history of France. Hard by, in caverns of the mountain, was one of the five arsenals of the Camisards; where they laid up clothes and corn and arms against necessity, forged bayonets and sabres, and made themselves gunpowder with willow charcoal and saltpetre boiled in kettles. To the same caves, amid this multifarious industry, the sick and wounded were brought up to heal; and there they were visited by the two surgeons, Chabrier and Tavan, and secretly nursed by women of the neighbourhood.

Of the five legions into which the Camisards were divided, it was the oldest and the most obscure that had its magazines by Cassagnas. This was the band of Spirit Séguier; men who had joined their voices with his in the 68th Psalm as they marched down by night on the archpriest of the Cevennes. Séguier, promoted to heaven, was succeeded by Salomon Couderc, whom Cavalier treats in his memoirs as chaplain-general to the whole army of the Camisards. He was a prophet; a great reader of the heart, who admitted people to the sacrament or refused them, by 'intensively viewing every man' between the eyes; and had the most of the Scriptures off by rote. And this was surely happy; since in a surprise in August 1703, he lost his mule, his portfolios, and his Bible. It is only strange that they were not surprised more often and more effectually; for this legion of Cassagnas was truly patriarchal in its theory of war, and camped without sentries, leaving that duty to the angels of the God for whom they fought. This is a token, not only of their faith, but of the trackless country where they harboured. M. de Caladon, taking a stroll one fine day, walked without warning into their midst, as he might have walked into 'a flock of sheep in a plain,' and found some asleep and some awake and psalm-singing. A traitor had need of no recommendation to insinuate himself among their ranks, beyond 'his faculty of singing psalms'; and even the prophet Salomon 'took him into a particular friendship.' Thus, among their intricate hills, the rustic troop subsisted; and history can attribute few exploits to them but sacraments and ecstasies.

People of this tough and simple stock will not, as I have just been saying, prove variable in religion; nor will they get nearer to apostasy than a mere external conformity like that of Naaman in the house of Rimmon. When Louis XVI., in the words of the edict, 'convinced by the uselessness of a century of persecutions, and rather from necessity than sympathy,' granted at last a royal grace of toleration, Cassagnas was still Protestant; and to a man, it is so to this day. There is, indeed, one family that is not Protestant, but neither is it Catholic. It is that of a Catholic curé in revolt, who has taken to his bosom a schoolmistress. And his conduct, it is worth noting, is disapproved by the Protestant villagers.

'It is a bad idea for a man,' said one, 'to go back from his engagements.'

The villagers whom I saw seemed intelligent after a countrified fashion, and were all plain and dignified in manner. As a Protestant myself, I was well looked upon, and my acquaintance with history gained me further respect. For we had something not unlike a religious controversy at table, a gendarme and a merchant with whom I dined being both strangers to the place, and Catholics. The young men of the house stood round and supported me; and the whole discussion was tolerantly conducted, and surprised a man brought up among the infinitesimal and contentious differences of Scotland. The merchant, indeed, grew a little warm, and was far less pleased than some others with my historical acquirements. But the gendarme was mighty easy over it all.

'It's a bad idea for a man to change,' said he; and the remark was generally applauded.

That was not the opinion of the priest and soldier at Our Lady of the Snows. But this is a different race; and perhaps the same great-heartedness that upheld them to resist, now enables them to differ in a kind spirit. For courage respects courage; but where a faith has been trodden out, we may look for a mean and narrow population. The true work of Bruce and Wallace was the union of the nations; not that they should stand apart a while longer, skirmishing upon their borders; but that, when the time came, they might unite with self-respect.

The merchant was much interested in my journey, and thought it dangerous to sleep afield.

'There are the wolves,' said he; 'and then it is known you are an Englishman. The English have always long purses, and it might very well enter into some one's head to deal you an ill blow some night.'

I told him I was not much afraid of such accidents; and at any rate judged it unwise to dwell upon alarms or consider small perils in the arrangement of life. Life itself, I submitted, was a far too risky business as a whole to make each additional particular of danger worth regard. 'Something,' said I, 'might burst in your inside any day of the week, and there would be an end of you, if you were locked into your room with three turns of the key.'

'Cependant,' said he, 'coucher dehors!'

'God,' said I, 'is everywhere.'

'Cependant, coucher dehors!' he repeated, and his voice was eloquent of terror.

He was the only person, in all my voyage, who saw anything hardy in so simple a proceeding; although many considered it superfluous. Only one, on the other hand, professed much delight in the idea; and that was my Plymouth Brother, who cried out, when I told him I sometimes preferred sleeping under the stars to a close and noisy ale-house, 'Now I see that you know the Lord!'

The merchant asked me for one of my cards as I was leaving, for he said I should be something to talk of in the future, and desired me to make a note of his request and reason; a desire with which I have thus complied.

A little after two I struck across the Mimente, and took a rugged path southward up a hillside covered with loose stones and tufts of heather. At the top, as is the habit of the country, the path disappeared; and I left my she-ass munching heather, and went forward alone to seek a road.

I was now on the separation of two vast water-sheds; behind me all the streams were bound for the Garonne and the Western Ocean; before me was the basin of the Rhone. Hence, as from the Lozère, you can see in clear weather the shining of the Gulf of Lyons; and perhaps from here the soldiers of Salomon may have watched for the topsails of Sir Cloudesley Shovel, and the long-promised aid from England. You may take this ridge as lying in the heart of the country of the Camisards; four of the five legions camped all round it and almost within view—Salomon and Joani to the north, Castanet and Roland to the south; and when Julien had finished his famous work, the devastation of the High Cevennes, which lasted all through October and November 1703, and during which four hundred and sixty villages and hamlets were, with fire and pickaxe, utterly subverted, a man standing on this eminence would have looked forth upon a silent, smokeless, and dispeopled land. Time and man's activity have now repaired these ruins; Cassagnas is once more roofed and sending up domestic smoke; and in the chestnut gardens, in low and leafy corners, many a prosperous farmer returns, when the day's work is done, to his children and bright hearth. And still it was perhaps the wildest view of all my journey. Peak upon peak, chain upon chain of hills ran surging southward, channelled and sculptured by the winter streams, feathered from head to foot with chestnuts, and here and there breaking out into a coronal of cliffs. The sun, which was still far from setting, sent a drift of misty gold across the hill-tops, but the valleys were already plunged in a profound and quiet shadow.

A very old shepherd, hobbling on a pair of sticks, and wearing a black cap of liberty, as if in honour of his nearness to the grave, directed me to the road for St. Germain de Calberte. There was something solemn in the isolation of this infirm and ancient creature. Where he dwelt, how he got upon this high ridge, or how he proposed to get down again, were more than I could fancy. Not far off upon my right was the famous Plan de Font Morte, where Poul with his Armenian sabre slashed down the Camisards of Séguier. This, methought, might be some Rip van Winkle of the war, who had lost his comrades, fleeing before Poul, and wandered ever since upon the mountains. It might be news to him that Cavalier had surrendered, or Roland had fallen fighting with his back against an olive. And while I was thus working on my fancy, I heard him hailing in broken tones, and saw him waving me to come back with one of his two sticks. I had already got some way past him; but, leaving Modestine once more, retraced my steps.

Alas, it was a very commonplace affair. The old gentleman had forgot to ask the pedlar what he sold, and wished to remedy this neglect.

I told him sternly, 'Nothing.'

'Nothing?' cried he.

I repeated 'Nothing,' and made off.

It's odd to think of, but perhaps I thus became as inexplicable to the old man as he had been to me.

The road lay under chestnuts, and though I saw a hamlet or two below me in the vale, and many lone houses of the chestnut farmers, it was a very solitary march all afternoon; and the evening began early underneath the trees. But I heard the voice of a woman singing some sad, old, endless ballad not far off. It seemed to be about love and a bel amoureux, her handsome sweetheart; and I wished I could have taken up the strain and answered her, as I went on upon my invisible woodland way, weaving, like Pippa in the poem, my own thoughts with hers. What could I have told her? Little enough; and yet all the heart requires. How the world gives and takes away, and brings sweethearts near only to separate them again into distant and strange lands; but to love is the great amulet which makes the world a garden; and 'hope, which comes to all,' outwears the accidents of life, and reaches with tremulous hand beyond the grave and death. Easy to say: yea, but also, by God's mercy, both easy and grateful to believe!

We struck at last into a wide white high-road carpeted with noiseless dust. The night had come; the moon had been shining for a long while upon the opposite mountain; when on turning a corner my donkey and I issued ourselves into her light. I had emptied out my brandy at Florac, for I could bear the stuff no longer, and replaced it with some generous and scented Volnay; and now I drank to the moon's sacred majesty upon the road. It was but a couple of mouthfuls; yet I became thenceforth unconscious of my limbs, and my blood flowed with luxury. Even Modestine was inspired by this purified nocturnal sunshine, and bestirred her little hoofs as to a livelier measure. The road wound and descended swiftly among masses of chestnuts. Hot dust rose from our feet and flowed away. Our two shadows—mine deformed with the knapsack, hers comically bestridden by the pack—now lay before us clearly outlined on the road, and now, as we turned a corner, went off into the ghostly distance, and sailed along the mountain like clouds. From time to time a warm wind rustled down the valley, and set all the chestnuts dangling their bunches of foliage and fruit; the ear was filled with whispering music, and the shadows danced in tune. And next moment the breeze had gone by, and in all the valley nothing moved except our travelling feet. On the opposite slope, the monstrous ribs and gullies of the mountain were faintly designed in the moonshine; and high overhead, in some lone house, there burned one lighted window, one square spark of red in the huge field of sad nocturnal colouring.

At a certain point, as I went downward, turning many acute angles, the moon disappeared behind the hill; and I pursued my way in great darkness, until another turning shot me without preparation into St. Germain de Calberte. The place was asleep and silent, and buried in opaque night. Only from a single open door, some lamplight escaped upon the road to show me that I was come among men's habitations. The two last gossips of the evening, still talking by a garden wall, directed me to the inn. The landlady was getting her chicks to bed; the fire was already out, and had, not without grumbling, to be rekindled; half an hour later, and I must have gone supperless to roost.

THE LAST DAY

When I awoke (Thursday, 2nd October), and, hearing a great flourishing of cocks and chuckling of contented hens, betook me to the window of the clean and comfortable room where I had slept the night, I looked forth on a sunshiny morning in a deep vale of chestnut gardens. It was still early, and the cockcrows, and the slanting lights, and the long shadows encouraged me to be out and look round me.

St. Germain de Calberte is a great parish nine leagues round about. At the period of the wars, and immediately before the devastation, it was inhabited by two hundred and seventy-five families, of which only nine were Catholic; and it took the curé seventeen September days to go from house to house on horseback for a census. But the place itself, although capital of a canton, is scarce larger than a hamlet. It lies terraced across a steep slope in the midst of mighty chestnuts. The Protestant chapel stands below upon a shoulder; in the midst of the town is the quaint old Catholic church.

It was here that poor Du Chayla, the Christian martyr, kept his library and held a court of missionaries; here he had built his tomb, thinking to lie among a grateful population whom he had redeemed from error; and hither on the morrow of his death they brought the body, pierced with two-and-fifty wounds, to be interred. Clad in his priestly robes, he was laid out in state in the church. The curé, taking his text from Second Samuel, twentieth chapter and twelfth verse, 'And Amasa wallowed in his blood in the highway,' preached a rousing sermon, and exhorted his brethren to die each at his post, like their unhappy and illustrious superior. In the midst of this eloquence there came a breeze that Spirit Séguier was near at hand; and behold! all the assembly took to their horses' heels, some east, some west, and the curé himself as far as Alais.

Strange was the position of this little Catholic metropolis, a thimbleful of Rome, in such a wild and contrary neighbourhood. On the one hand, the legion of Salomon overlooked it from Cassagnas; on the other, it was cut off from assistance by the legion of Roland at Mialet. The curé, Louvrelenil, although he took a panic at the arch-priest's funeral, and so hurriedly decamped to Alais, stood well by his isolated pulpit, and thence uttered fulminations against the crimes of the Protestants. Salomon besieged the village for an hour and a half, but was beaten back. The militiamen, on guard before the curé's door, could be heard, in the black hours, singing Protestant psalms and holding friendly talk with the insurgents. And in the morning, although not a shot had been fired, there would not be a round of powder in their flasks. Where was it gone? All handed over to the Camisards for a consideration. Untrusty guardians for an isolated priest!

That these continual stirs were once busy in St. Germain de Calberte, the imagination with difficulty receives; all is now so quiet, the pulse of human life now beats so low and still in this hamlet of the mountains. Boys followed me a great way off, like a timid sort of lion-hunters; and people turned round to have a second look, or came out of their houses, as I went by. My passage was the first event, you would have fancied, since the Camisards. There was nothing rude or forward in this observation; it was but a pleased and wondering scrutiny, like that of oxen or the human infant; yet it wearied my spirits, and soon drove me from the street.

I took refuge on the terraces, which are here greenly carpeted with sward, and tried to imitate with a pencil the inimitable attitudes of the chestnuts as they bear up their canopy of leaves. Ever and again a little wind went by, and the nuts dropped all around me, with a light and dull sound, upon the sward. The noise was as of a thin fall of great hailstones; but there went with it a cheerful human sentiment of an approaching harvest and farmers rejoicing in their gains. Looking up, I could see the brown nut peering through the husk, which was already gaping; and between the stems the eye embraced an amphitheatre of hill, sunlit and green with leaves.

I have not often enjoyed a place more deeply. I moved in an atmosphere of pleasure, and felt light and quiet and content. But perhaps it was not the place alone that so disposed my spirit. Perhaps some one was thinking of me in another country; or perhaps some thought of my own had come and gone unnoticed, and yet done me good. For some thoughts, which sure would be the most beautiful, vanish before we can rightly scan their features; as though a god, travelling by our green highways, should but ope the door, give one smiling look into the house, and go again for ever. Was it Apollo, or Mercury, or Love with folded wings? Who shall say? But we go the lighter about our business, and feel peace and pleasure in our hearts.

I dined with a pair of Catholics. They agreed in the condemnation of a young man, a Catholic, who had married a Protestant girl and gone over to the religion of his wife. A Protestant born they could understand and respect; indeed, they seemed to be of the mind of an old Catholic woman, who told me that same day there was no difference between the two sects, save that 'wrong was more wrong for the Catholic,' who had more light and guidance; but this of a man's desertion filled them with contempt.

'It is a bad idea for a man to change,' said one.

It may have been accidental, but you see how this phrase pursued me; and for myself, I believe it is the current philosophy in these parts. I have some difficulty in imagining a better. It's not only a great flight of confidence for a man to change his creed and go out of his family for heaven's sake; but the odds are—nay, and the hope is—that, with all this great transition in the eyes of man, he has not changed himself a hairbreadth to the eyes of God. Honour to those who do so, for the wrench is sore. But it argues something narrow, whether of strength or weakness, whether of the prophet or the fool, in those who can take a sufficient interest in such infinitesimal and human operations, or who can quit a friendship for a doubtful process of the mind. And I think I should not leave my old creed for another, changing only words for other words; but by some brave reading, embrace it in spirit and truth, and find wrong as wrong for me as for the best of other communions.

The phylloxera was in the neighbourhood; and instead of wine we drank at dinner a more economical juice of the grape—La Parisienne, they call it. It is made by putting the fruit whole into a cask with water; one by one the berries ferment and burst; what is drunk during the day is supplied at night in water: so, with ever another pitcher from the well, and ever another grape exploding and giving out its strength, one cask of Parisienne may last a family till spring. It is, as the reader will anticipate, a feeble beverage, but very pleasant to the taste.

What with dinner and coffee, it was long past three before I left St. Germain de Calberte. I went down beside the Gardon of Mialet, a great glaring watercourse devoid of water, and through St. Etienne de Vallée Française, or Val Francesque, as they used to call it; and towards evening began to ascend the hill of St. Pierre. It was a long and steep ascent. Behind me an empty carriage returning to St. Jean du Gard kept hard upon my tracks, and near the summit overtook me. The driver, like the rest of the world, was sure I was a pedlar; but, unlike others, he was sure of what I had to sell. He had noticed the blue wool which hung out of my pack at either end; and from this he had decided, beyond my power to alter his decision, that I dealt in blue-wool collars, such as decorate the neck of the French draught-horse.

I had hurried to the topmost powers of Modestine, for I dearly desired to see the view upon the other side before the day had faded. But it was night when I reached the summit; the moon was riding high and clear; and only a few grey streaks of twilight lingered in the west. A yawning valley, gulfed in blackness, lay like a hole in created nature at my feet; but the outline of the hills was sharp against the sky. There was Mount Aigoal, the stronghold of Castanet. And Castanet, not only as an active undertaking leader, deserves some mention among Camisards; for there is a spray of rose among his laurel; and he showed how, even in a public tragedy, love will have its way. In the high tide of war he married, in his mountain citadel, a young and pretty lass called Mariette. There were great rejoicings; and the bridegroom released five-and-twenty prisoners in honour of the glad event. Seven months afterwards, Mariette, the Princess of the Cevennes, as they called her in derision, fell into the hands of the authorities, where it was like to have gone hard with her. But Castanet was a man of execution, and loved his wife. He fell on Valleraugue, and got a lady there for a hostage; and for the first and last time in that war there was an exchange of prisoners. Their daughter, pledge of some starry night upon Mount Aigoal, has left descendants to this day.

Modestine and I—it was our last meal together—had a snack upon the top of St. Pierre, I on a heap of stones, she standing by me in the moonlight and decorously eating bread out of my hand. The poor brute would eat more heartily in this manner; for she had a sort of affection for me, which I was soon to betray.

It was a long descent upon St. Jean du Gard, and we met no one but a carter, visible afar off by the glint of the moon on his extinguished lantern.

Before ten o'clock we had got in and were at supper; fifteen miles and a stiff hill in little beyond six hours!

FAREWELL, MODESTINE!

On examination, on the morning of October 3rd, Modestine was pronounced unfit for travel. She would need at least two days' repose, according to the ostler; but I was now eager to reach Alais for my letters; and, being in a civilised country of stage-coaches, I determined to sell my lady friend and be off by the diligence that afternoon. Our yesterday's march, with the testimony of the driver who had pursued us up the long hill of St. Pierre, spread a favourable notion of my donkey's capabilities. Intending purchasers were aware of an unrivalled opportunity. Before ten I had an offer of twenty-five francs; and before noon, after a desperate engagement, I sold her, saddle and all, for five-and-thirty. The pecuniary gain is not obvious, but I had bought freedom into the bargain.

St Jean du Gard is a large place, and largely Protestant. The maire, a Protestant, asked me to help him in a small matter which is itself characteristic of the country. The young women of the Cevennes profit by the common religion and the difference of the language to go largely as governesses into England; and here was one, a native of Mialet, struggling with English circulars from two different agencies in London. I gave what help I could; and volunteered some advice, which struck me as being excellent.

One thing more I note. The phylloxera has ravaged the vineyards in this neighbourhood; and in the early morning, under some chestnuts by the river, I found a party of men working with a cider-press. I could not at first make out what they were after, and asked one fellow to explain.

'Making cider,' he said. 'Oui, c'est comme ça. Comme dans le nord!'

There was a ring of sarcasm in his voice: the country was going to the devil.

It was not until I was fairly seated by the driver, and rattling through a rocky valley with dwarf olives, that I became aware of my bereavement. I had lost Modestine. Up to that moment I had thought I hated her; but now she was gone,

        'And oh!

        The difference to me!'

For twelve days we had been fast companions; we had travelled upwards of a hundred and twenty miles, crossed several respectable ridges, and jogged along with our six legs by many a rocky and many a boggy by-road. After the first day, although sometimes I was hurt and distant in manner, I still kept my patience; and as for her, poor soul! she had come to regard me as a god. She loved to eat out of my hand. She was patient, elegant in form, the colour of an ideal mouse, and inimitably small. Her faults were those of her race and sex; her virtues were her own. Farewell, and if for ever—

Father Adam wept when he sold her to me; after I had sold her in my turn, I was tempted to follow his example; and being alone with a stage-driver and four or five agreeable young men, I did not hesitate to yield to my emotion.

About Author

Childhood and youth

Stevenson was born at 8 Howard Place, Edinburgh, Scotland on 13 November 1850 to Thomas Stevenson (1818–87), a leading lighthouse engineer, and his wife Margaret Isabella (born Balfour, 1829–97). He was christened Robert Lewis Balfour Stevenson. At about age 18, he changed the spelling of "Lewis" to "Louis", and he dropped "Balfour" in 1873.

Lighthouse design was the family's profession; Thomas's father (Robert's grandfather) was civil engineer Robert Stevenson, and Thomas's brothers (Robert's uncles) Alan and David were in the same field. Thomas's maternal grandfather Thomas Smith had been in the same profession. However, Robert's mother's family were gentry, tracing their lineage back to Alexander Balfour who had held the lands of Inchyra in Fife in the fifteenth century. His mother's father Lewis Balfour (1777–1860) was a minister of the Church of Scotland at nearby Colinton, and her siblings included physician George William Balfour and marine engineer James Balfour. Stevenson spent the greater part of his boyhood holidays in his maternal grandfather's house. "Now I often wonder what I inherited from this old minister," Stevenson wrote. "I must suppose, indeed, that he was fond of preaching sermons, and so am I, though I never heard it maintained that either of us loved to hear them."

Lewis Balfour and his daughter both had weak chests, so they often needed to stay in warmer climates for their health. Stevenson inherited a tendency to coughs and fevers, exacerbated when the family moved to a damp, chilly house at 1 Inverleith Terrace in 1851. The family moved again to the sunnier 17 Heriot Row when Stevenson was six years old, but the tendency to extreme sickness in winter remained with him until he was 11. Illness was a recurrent feature of his adult life and left him extraordinarily thin. Contemporaneous views were that he had tuberculosis, but more recent views are that it was bronchiectasis or even sarcoidosis.

Stevenson's parents were both devout Presbyterians, but the household was not strict in its adherence to Calvinist principles. His nurse Alison Cunningham (known as Cummy) was more fervently religious. Her mix of Calvinism and folk beliefs were an early source of nightmares for the child, and he showed a precocious concern for religion. But she also cared for him tenderly in illness, reading to him from John Bunyan and the Bible as he lay sick in bed and telling tales of the Covenanters. Stevenson recalled this time of sickness in "The Land of Counterpane" in A Child's Garden of Verses (1885), dedicating the book to his nurse.

Stevenson was an only child, both strange-looking and eccentric, and he found it hard to fit in when he was sent to a nearby school at age 6, a problem repeated at age 11 when he went on to the Edinburgh Academy; but he mixed well in lively games with his cousins in summer holidays at Colinton. His frequent illnesses often kept him away from his first school, so he was taught for long stretches by private tutors. He was a late reader, learning at age 7 or 8, but even before this he dictated stories to his mother and nurse, and he compulsively wrote stories throughout his childhood. His father was proud of this interest; he had also written stories in his spare time until his own father found them and told him to "give up such nonsense and mind your business." He paid for the printing of Robert's first publication at 16, entitled The Pentland Rising: A Page of History, 1666. It was an account of the Covenanters' rebellion which was published in 1866, the 200th anniversary of the event.

Education

In September 1857, Stevenson went to Mr Henderson's School in India Street, Edinburgh, but because of poor health stayed only a few weeks and did not return until October 1859. During his many absences he was taught by private tutors. In October 1861, he went to Edinburgh Academy, an independent school for boys, and stayed there sporadically for about fifteen months. In the autumn of 1863, he spent one term at an English boarding school at Spring Grove in Isleworth in Middlesex (now an urban area of West London). In October 1864, following an improvement to his health, he was sent to Robert Thomson's private school in Frederick Street, Edinburgh, where he remained until he went to university. In November 1867, Stevenson entered the University of Edinburgh to study engineering. He showed from the start no enthusiasm for his studies and devoted much energy to avoiding lectures. This time was more important for the friendships he made with other students in the Speculative Society (an exclusive debating club), particularly with Charles Baxter, who would become Stevenson's financial agent, and with a professor, Fleeming Jenkin, whose house staged amateur drama in which Stevenson took part, and whose biography he would later write. Perhaps most important at this point in his life was a cousin, Robert Alan Mowbray Stevenson (known as "Bob"), a lively and light-hearted young man who, instead of the family profession, had chosen to study art. Each year during vacations, Stevenson travelled to inspect the family's engineering works—to Anstruther and Wick in 1868, with his father on his official tour of Orkney and Shetland islands lighthouses in 1869, and for three weeks to the island of Erraid in 1870. He enjoyed the travels more for the material they gave for his writing than for any engineering interest. The voyage with his father pleased him because a similar journey of Walter Scott with Robert Stevenson had provided the inspiration for Scott's 1822 novel The Pirate. In April 1871, Stevenson notified his father of his decision to pursue a life of letters. Though the elder Stevenson was naturally disappointed, the surprise cannot have been great, and Stevenson's mother reported that he was "wonderfully resigned" to his son's choice. To provide some security, it was agreed that Stevenson should read Law (again at Edinburgh University) and be called to the Scottish bar. In his 1887 poetry collection Underwoods, Stevenson muses on his having turned from the family profession:

> *Say not of me that weakly I declined*
>
> *The labours of my sires, and fled the sea,*
>
> *The towers we founded and the lamps we lit,*
>
> *To play at home with paper like a child.*
>
> *But rather say: In the afternoon of time*

A strenuous family dusted from its hands

The sand of granite, and beholding far

Along the sounding coast its pyramids

And tall memorials catch the dying sun,

Smiled well content, and to this childish task

Around the fire addressed its evening hours.

In other respects too, Stevenson was moving away from his upbringing. His dress became more Bohemian; he already wore his hair long, but he now took to wearing a velveteen jacket and rarely attended parties in conventional evening dress. Within the limits of a strict allowance, he visited cheap pubs and brothels. More importantly, he had come to reject Christianity and declared himself an atheist. In January 1873, his father came across the constitution of the LJR (Liberty, Justice, Reverence) Club, of which Stevenson and his cousin Bob were members, which began: "Disregard everything our parents have taught us". Questioning his son about his beliefs, he discovered the truth, leading to a long period of dissension with both parents:

What a damned curse I am to my parents! As my father said "You have rendered my whole life a failure". As my mother said "This is the heaviest affliction that has ever befallen me". O Lord, what a pleasant thing it is to have damned the happiness of (probably) the only two people who care a damn about you in the world.

Early writing and travels

Stevenson was visiting a cousin in England in late 1873 when he met two people who became very important to him: Sidney Colvin and Fanny (Frances Jane) Sitwell. Sitwell was a 34-year-old woman with a son, who was separated from her husband. She attracted the devotion of many who met her, including Colvin, who married her in 1901. Stevenson was also drawn to her, and they kept up a warm correspondence over several years in which he wavered between the role of a suitor and a son (he addressed her as "Madonna"). Colvin became Stevenson's literary adviser and was the first editor of his letters after his death. He placed Stevenson's first paid contribution in The Portfolio, an essay entitled "Roads".

Stevenson was soon active in London literary life, becoming acquainted with many of the writers of the time, including Andrew Lang, Edmund Gosse, and Leslie Stephen, the editor of the Cornhill Magazine who took an interest in Stevenson's work. Stephen took Stevenson to visit a patient at the Edinburgh Infirmary named William Ernest Henley, an energetic and talkative man with a wooden leg. Henley became a close friend and occasional literary collaborator, until a quarrel broke up the friendship in 1888, and he is often considered to be the model for Long John Silver in Treasure Island.

Stevenson was sent to Menton on the French Riviera in November 1873 to recuperate after his health failed. He returned in better health in April 1874 and settled down to his studies, but he returned to France several times after that. He made long and frequent trips to the neighborhood of the Forest of Fontainebleau, staying at Barbizon, Grez-sur-Loing, and Nemours and becoming a member of the artists' colonies there. He also traveled to Paris to visit galleries and the theatres. He qualified for the Scottish bar in July 1875, and his father added a brass plate to the Heriot Row house reading "R.L. Stevenson, Advocate". His law studies did influence his books, but he never practised law; all his energies were spent in travel and writing. One of his journeys was a canoe voyage in Belgium and France with Sir Walter Simpson, a friend from the Speculative Society, a frequent travel companion, and the author of The Art of Golf (1887). This trip was the basis of his first travel book An Inland Voyage (1878).

Marriage

The canoe voyage with Simpson brought Stevenson to Grez in September 1876 where he met Fanny Van de Grift Osbourne (1840–1914), born in Indianapolis. She had married at age 17 and moved to Nevada to rejoin husband Samuel after his participation in the American Civil War. Their children were Isobel (or "Belle"), Lloyd, and Hervey (who died in 1875). But anger over her husband's infidelities led to a number of separations. In 1875, she had taken her children to France where she and Isobel studied art.

Stevenson returned to Britain shortly after this first meeting, but Fanny apparently remained in his thoughts, and he wrote the essay "On falling in love" for the Cornhill Magazine. They met again early in 1877 and became lovers. Stevenson spent much of the following year with her and her children in France. In August 1878, she returned to San Francisco and Stevenson remained in Europe, making the walking trip that formed the basis for Travels with a Donkey in the Cévennes (1879). But he set off to join her in August 1879, against the advice of his friends and without notifying his parents. He took second-class passage on the steamship Devonia, in part to save money but also to learn how others traveled and to increase the adventure of the journey. He then traveled overland by train from New York City to California. He later wrote about the experience in The Amateur Emigrant. It was good experience for his writing, but it broke his health.

He was near death when he arrived in Monterey, California, where some local ranchers nursed him back to health. He stayed for a time at the French Hotel located at 530 Houston Street, now a museum dedicated to his memory called the "Stevenson House". While there, he often dined "on the cuff," as he said, at a nearby restaurant run by Frenchman Jules Simoneau which stood at what is now Simoneau Plaza; several years later, he sent Simoneau an inscribed copy of his novel Strange Case of Dr Jekyll and Mr Hyde (1886), writing that it would be a stranger case still if Robert Louis Stevenson ever forgot Jules Simoneau. While in Monterey, he wrote an evocative article about "the Old Pacific Capital" of Monterey.

By December 1879, Stevenson had recovered his health enough to continue to San Francisco where he struggled "all alone on forty-five cents a day, and sometimes less, with quantities of hard work and many heavy thoughts," in an effort to support himself through his writing. But by the end of the winter, his health was broken again and he found himself at death's door. Fanny was now divorced and recovered from her own illness, and she came to his bedside and nursed him to recovery. "After a while," he wrote, "my spirit got up again in a divine frenzy, and has since kicked and spurred my vile body forward with great emphasis and success." When his father heard of his condition, he cabled him money to help him through this period.

Fanny and Robert were married in May 1880, although he said that he was "a mere complication of cough and bones, much fitter for an emblem of mortality than a bridegroom." He travelled with his new wife and her son Lloyd north of San Francisco to Napa Valley and spent a summer honeymoon at an abandoned mining camp on Mount Saint Helena. He wrote about this experience in The Silverado Squatters. He met Charles Warren Stoddard, co-editor of the Overland Monthly and author of South Sea Idylls, who urged Stevenson to travel to the South Pacific, an idea which returned to him many years later. In August 1880, he sailed with Fanny and Lloyd from New York to Britain and found his parents and his friend Sidney Colvin on the wharf at Liverpool, happy to see him return home. Gradually, his wife was able to patch up differences between father and son and make herself a part of the family through her charm and wit.

Attempted settlement in Europe and the US

Stevenson searched in vain between 1880 and 1887 for a residence suitable to his health. He spent his summers at various places in Scotland and England, including Westbourne, Dorset, a residential area in Bournemouth. It was during his time in Bournemouth that he wrote the story Strange Case of Dr Jekyll and Mr Hyde, naming the character Mr. Poole after the town of Poole which is situated next to Bournemouth. In Westbourne, he named his house Skerryvore after the tallest lighthouse in Scotland, which his uncle Alan had built (1838–44). In the wintertime, Stevenson travelled to France and lived at Davos Platz and the Chalet de Solitude at Hyères, where he was very happy for a time. "I have so many things to make life sweet for me," he wrote, "it seems a pity I cannot have that other one thing—health. But though you will be angry to hear it, I believe, for myself at least, what is is best." In spite of his ill health, he produced the bulk of his best-known work during these years. Treasure Island was published under the pseudonym "Captain George North" and became his first widely popular book; he wrote it during this time, along with Kidnapped, Strange Case of Dr Jekyll and Mr Hyde (which established his wider reputation), The Black Arrow: A Tale of the Two Roses, A Child's Garden of Verses, and Underwoods. He gave a copy of Kidnapped to his friend and frequent Skerryvore visitor Henry James.

His father died in 1887 and Stevenson felt free to follow the advice of his physician to try a complete change of climate, so he headed for Colorado with his mother and family. But after landing in New York, they decided to spend the winter in the Adirondacks at a cure cottage now known as Stevenson Cottage at Saranac Lake, New York. During the intensely cold winter, Stevenson wrote some of his best essays, including Pulvis et Umbra. He also began The Master of Ballantrae and lightheartedly planned a cruise to the southern Pacific Ocean for the following summer.

Politics

Stevenson believed in Conservatism for most of his life. His cousin and biographer Sir Graham Balfour said that "he probably throughout life would, if compelled to vote, have always supported the Conservative candidate." In 1866, Stevenson voted for Benjamin Disraeli, future Conservative Prime Minister of the United Kingdom, over Thomas Carlyle for the Lord Rectorship of the University of Edinburgh. During his college years, he briefly identified himself as a "red-hot socialist". He wrote at age 26: "I look back to the time when I was a Socialist with something like regret…. Now I know that in thus turning Conservative with years, I am going through the normal cycle of change and travelling in the common orbit of men's opinions."

Journey to the Pacific

In June 1888, Stevenson chartered the yacht Casco and set sail with his family from San Francisco. The vessel "plowed her path of snow across the empty deep, far from all track of commerce, far from any hand of help." The sea air and thrill of adventure for a time restored his health, and for nearly three years he wandered the eastern and central Pacific, stopping for extended stays at the Hawaiian Islands where he became a good friend of King Kalākaua. He befriended the king's niece Princess Victoria Kaiulani, who also had Scottish heritage. He spent time at the Gilbert Islands, Tahiti, New Zealand, and the Samoan Islands. During this period, he completed The Master of Ballantrae, composed two ballads based on the legends of the islanders, and wrote The Bottle Imp. He preserved the experience of these years in his various letters and in his In the South Seas (which was published posthumously). He made a voyage in 1889 with Lloyd on the trading schooner Equator, visiting Butaritari, Mariki, Apaiang, and Abemama in the Gilbert Islands. They spent several months on Abemama with tyrant-chief Tem Binoka, whom Stevenson described in In the South Seas.

Stevenson left Sydney on the Janet Nicoll in April 1890 for his third and final voyage among the South Seas islands. He intended to produce another book of travel writing to follow his earlier book In the South Seas, but it was his wife who eventually published her journal of their third voyage. (Fanny misnames the ship in her account The Cruise of the Janet Nichol.) A fellow passenger was Jack Buckland, whose stories of life as an island trader became the inspiration for the character of Tommy Hadden in The Wrecker (1892), which Stevenson and Lloyd Osbourne wrote together. Buckland visited the Stevensons at Vailima in 1894.

Last years

In 1890, Stevenson purchased a tract of about 400 acres (1.6 km²) in Upolu, an island in Samoa where he established himself on his estate in the village of Vailima after two aborted attempts to visit Scotland. He took the native name Tusitala (Samoan for "Teller of Tales"). His influence spread among the Samoans, who consulted him for advice, and he soon became involved in local politics. He was convinced that the European officials who had been appointed to rule the Samoans were incompetent, and he published A Footnote to History after many futile attempts to resolve the matter. This was such a stinging protest against existing conditions that it resulted in the recall of two officials, and Stevenson feared for a time that it would result in his own deportation. He wrote to Colvin, "I used to think meanly of the plumber; but how he shines beside the politician!"

He also found time to work at his writing, although he felt that "there was never any man had so many irons in the fire". He wrote The Beach of Falesa, Catriona (titled David Balfour in the US), The Ebb-Tide, and the Vailima Letters during this period.

Stevenson grew depressed and wondered if he had exhausted his creative vein, as he had been "overworked bitterly" and that the best he could write was "ditch-water". He even feared that he might again become a helpless invalid. He rebelled against this idea: "I wish to die in my boots; no more Land of Counterpane for me. To be drowned, to be shot, to be thrown from a horse — ay, to be hanged, rather than pass again through that slow dissolution." He then suddenly had a return of energy and he began work on Weir of Hermiston. "It's so good that it frightens me," he is reported to have exclaimed. He felt that this was the best work he had done.

On 3 December 1894, Stevenson was talking to his wife and straining to open a bottle of wine when he suddenly exclaimed, "What's that?", asked his wife "does my face look strange?", and collapsed. He died within a few hours, probably of a cerebral haemorrhage. He was 44 years old. The Samoans insisted on surrounding his body with a watch-guard during the night and on bearing him on their shoulders to nearby Mount Vaea, where they buried him on a spot overlooking the sea on land donated by British Acting Vice Consul Thomas Trood. Stevenson had always wanted his Requiem inscribed on his tomb:

Under the wide and starry sky,

Dig the grave and let me lie.

Glad did I live and gladly die,

And I laid me down with a will.

This be the verse you grave for me:

Here he lies where he longed to be;

Home is the sailor, home from sea,

And the hunter home from the hill.

Stevenson was loved by the Samoans, and his tombstone epigraph was translated to a Samoan song of grief. (Source: Wikipedia)